# CELTIC

## THE OFFICIAL HISTORY

## BRIAN WILSON

This edition first published in 2017 by

Arena Sport
An Imprint of Birlinn Limited
West Newington House
10 Newington Road
Edinburgh
EH9 1QS
www.arenasportbooks.co.uk

First published in 2013 by
Celtic FC Limited
www.celticfc.net

ISBN: 9781909715370
eBook ISBN: 9780857909312

British Library Cataloguing-in-Publication Data
A catalogue record for this book is available from the British Library

Typeset by Polaris Publishing, Edinburgh

Printed in Great Britain by Clays, St Ives

*For all who have Celtic in their hearts and hopes*

# CONTENTS

# FOREWORD

THE SEASON 2016-17 will long be remembered by Celtic supporters everywhere. It was truly historic – and well justifies the updating of this Official Celtic History to include the early achievements of Brendan Rodgers, his backroom team and the excellent squad of players.

Celtic must always be judged by three measures – success on the field of play, responsible stewardship, and respect for our charitable origins. In all these respects, we are in good shape and the crescendo to last season, coinciding with the Lisbon Lions commemoration, brought all three together in perfect harmony.

When my illustrious predecessor, Jack McGinn, whose company I regularly enjoy at Celtic Park , provided the foreword to the original centenary edition, he wrote that Brian Wilson 'has quite brilliantly encapsulated the Celtic story into a most readable and interesting book'. These words stand today, so please read, enjoy and take pride in the great history of Celtic Football Club.

*Ian Bankier*
*Chairman of Celtic*

# ACKNOWLEDGEMENTS

ALL PREVIOUS ACKNOWLEDGEMENTS of advice and assistance apply. Particular mention to Frank Hannaway for statistical section and fact-checking. Thanks to Ronan Wilson for help on this edition. And I pay tribute to an old friend and much missed observer of Scottish football, Glenn Gibbons, whose input to original and first update were invaluable and who passed away in October 2014.

*Brian Wilson*

# INTRODUCTION

IN THE ANNALS of Celtic Football Club, season 2016-17 will long be linked with the name and fame of The Invincibles, the team who went through the entire domestic programme without losing a game while securing only the fourth treble in the 71 years since the advent of the Scottish League Cup made that feat possible. Equally, this memorable season will be recalled as the one in which Brendan Rodgers arrived as manager and promptly transformed both expectations and delivery.

The making of history is an ongoing process and these landmark accomplishments – very recent to us – will be admired by future generations, just as we now look back with pride on the triumphs of our great teams in the past. Tom Rogic's goal which brought it all together in stoppage time at the Scottish Cup Final will be spoken of in decades to come, wherever Celtic supporters reminisce and compare.

Brendan Rodgers came to Celtic with not only an impressive record but also a passion for the club. This helped create an immediate bond with the supporters but it was what transpired on the pitch that clinched the deal. Brendan applies to himself and those around him a simple but constantly challenging demand to 'be the best you can be'. He sets high standards and abides by them – rigorous, accessible, respectful and extremely competent. Dermot Desmond pays tribute: 'What he has achieved is exceptional – in developing the team technically, improving the quality of football, raising fitness standards . . .' On top of all that, he signed a four year contract!

Nobody has responded more positively to the Rodgers reign or contributed more to Celtic's success than Scott Brown who has been with the club for a full decade, very rare in modern football. He said: 'For me to come here, to love the club, to enjoy coming in for training day in, day out; to be a treble winner and an Invincible . . . you can't write that any better.' He recalled meeting Gordon Strachan in London to discuss a possible move to Celtic: 'I was young and naïve. For him to start talking about building a team around me and a couple of others was so exciting.' Ten years on, Scott has made an immense contribution as player and, for seven seasons, as captain and true leader.

Knowing the history is always important to Celtic supporters but rarely have the past and present of the club overlapped more perfectly than in May 2017. This was the season in which everyone with Celtic in their hearts honoured the greatest single feat in the club's history – winning the European Cup. Magnificent celebrations to mark the 50th anniversary of that stunning success – including an unforgettable night of entertainment and emotion at Glasgow's Hydro Arena with Sir Rod Stewart topping the bill – fell in the week which also delivered the triumphant climax to Brendan Rodgers' first season at Celtic Park. The choreography of events could hardly have been improved upon.

Time has taken its toll and, on March 2 2017, Tommy Gemmell passed away, as Bobby Murdoch, Ronnie Simpson and Jimmy Johnstone had before him. There was also sadness because that noblest of leaders, Billy McNeill, is now afflicted with cruel and debilitating illness. A statue recognising Billy's contribution as player, captain and manager was unveiled at the foot of the Celtic Way on December 19 2015. It is an image which will continue to evoke memories and command respect for generations to come.

The core of this book was written to mark the club's centenary in 1988. Since then, the whole football environment has been transformed. Huge television royalties have increasingly tipped the balance in favour of major European leagues and the small number of clubs who dominate them. Freedom of movement, ushered in by the Bosman ruling in 1995, revolutionised the transfer market and made it essential for all but the wealthiest clubs to create value through player development and judicious trading. A prerequisite for Celtic's current success is that they have become extremely adept at both, the academy set-up producing players such as James Forrest, Callum McGregor and Kieran Tierney with plenty more to come.

Celtic is a highly respected European club with a massive following. Playing in a small league means operating on a tiny budget by comparison with those we come up against at the highest levels. The club is constantly looking for a route out of that enigma but none has yet presented itself. Celtic will continue to be vigilant in exploring any credible option while focusing on the task in hand, which is to maintain a club run to the highest standards, dominant in Scotland and competing effectively in Europe.

The overwhelming majority of supporters recognise these constraints and respect the stewardship which is exercised. In recent years, they have not had far to look for salutary lessons. The liquidation of Rangers in 2012 is referred to in this book. Subsequent events have confirmed that the methods used to avoid taxation were both widespread and illegal. Across Scottish football, many feel that these facts have been insufficiently recognised by the Scottish football authorities. In August 2017, following the Supreme Court ruling, Celtic called for a 'comprehensive and transparent' independent review of all the circumstances including the role of the governing bodies. The least to be expected is surely that lessons must be learned for the future.

Peter Lawwell summed up the Celtic ethos in the modern era: 'The Club was founded for the best of reasons – rooted in the Irish community but open to all; a source of pride for those who identify with it; supportive of charity, family, humility, diversity. I would like to think that all these values are as present in Celtic today as they ever have been. We are built around three pillars – football, commerce and community, each reinforcing the others and all of equal importance.' In line with these values, the work of the Celtic Foundation – founded in 1995 by Fergus McCann to reinforce the club's charitable role – goes from strength to strength. Its objectives were, for example, closely tied into the Lisbon Lions celebrations and the Foundation benefited by more than £2 million as a result. Its good work, within the Glasgow East End community and far beyond, is deserving of a book on it own.

As I write, I am just back from Trondheim in Norway where Celtic defeated Rosenberg in a Champions League qualifier. Two figures associated with Celtic came to the game. Looking back on his time as manager, Ronny Deila reflected: 'It was six months after I left the club that I really began to understand how big the job had been. Nothing had prepared me for it but I would never regret doing it.' Harald Brattback – a man assured of his own place in Celtic folklore – laughed about the charity match he played in, the day after the Scottish Cup was won. 'What other club in the world could have 60,000 people in the ground, to watch middle-aged men running around to raise money for charity?' Put these two together and they create a hint of what Celtic must always be – a big club, a successful club and a special club which retains lifelong friendships with those who have served it well.

The phrase 'if you know their history' is sung wherever Celtic supporters gather. That history must never die and I hope this book will help current and future generations to understand where we came from, who we are and why it matters.

Hail, Hail!

*Brian Wilson*
*Mangersta, Isle of Lewis*
*August 2017*

# ONE

## ORIGINS:
## THE IRISH CONNECTION

THE CELTIC FOOTBALL and Athletic Club was instituted for reasons closely related to Irish identity and Catholic charity. It emerged out of the poverty that prevailed in Glasgow's East End of the 1880s. This was an age of dreadful housing conditions, high infant mortality and little formal education. It was an age when Irish emigrants retained a passionate concern for the fate of their native land. But it was also an age of innovation and enterprise, when the willingness tow accept daunting challenges was more commonplace than in any subsequent period. The men who founded Celtic would probably not, in any other context, have wished to be regarded as classic Victorians. But the spirit in which they set about their task, and the level at which their ambitions were pitched, were characteristic of that thrillingly productive and creative period.

Numerous attempts to found a distinctively Irish football club in the East End, to play at the highest level, had come and gone. Dozens of teams had been formed by the Catholic parishes, but none of these had a strong-enough organisational basis on which to build a 'senior' club. The inspiration for thoughts about a first-rate Irish club in the west of Scotland came in part from Edinburgh, where the Hibernians club had been prospering since 1875. It had been initiated by Canon Edward Hannan, and was run along exclusivist Catholic Irish and temperance lines, based on the Young Men's Catholic Society in St Andrew's parish. By the mid 1880s it had become one of the leading teams in Britain, and when Hibs won the Scottish Cup in 1887 it was a triumph in which all of Scotland's Catholic Irish shared. Before they could return to Edinburgh with the cup, the Hibs had to join in the rejoicing of the West of Scotland Irish, as later recalled by Tom Maley in the *Glasgow Observer*: 'They were fêted by their Glasgow supporters, who drove them to St Mary's Hall, East Rose Street, and gave them a dinner and later presented them with mementoes of their first great deed.'

The Hibs' secretary, John McFadden, addressed the assembly and, having recounted the club's history, urged his audience 'to go and do likewise'. The listeners included several of those who were soon to found Celtic. They observed the way in which Hibs' victory inspired community identity, pride and confidence, and that the banners carried by the Hibs supporters were often emblazoned with the words 'God Save Ireland'. There were those in that St Mary's audience who recognised that an Irish team in the west, operating at the highest level, would increase the self-confidence and strengthen the sense of identity of the Irish Catholic community as a whole.

The East End was, at this time, the only area of Glasgow which did not support a senior football team. Meetings were held among representatives of the parishes – St Andrew's, St Mary's and St Alphonsus. Willie Maley, who was to play a key role in the club's history, recorded his own version of subsequent events:

*'There emanated a desire to put the matter to the test, and several meetings were held to decide what course of action should be taken to put the proposed club right on the way. As in all things Irish at the time, jealousies arose and various good men drew out rather than submit to being shoved aside by the more*

*pushing sort always to be found. St Mary's representatives, with the greatest enthusiasm, eventually forced matters to an issue, and at a big meeting held in St Mary's Hall it was decided to proceed with the formation of the club to look for the necessary ground. The St Andrew's representatives felt themselves side-tracked and withdrew from the project, although several of their best folks stuck to their guns and helped the project along.'*

Yet a remarkable point was that, while the idea of forming a football club was accepted, there were other aspects of the Edinburgh formula that were not – including the Hibernians' name, the temperance emphasis, and the direct association with the Young Men's Catholic Society.

The initial discussions about the formation of a club involved priests and leading laymen of the East End and beyond. In particular, the headmasters of the Sacred Heart and St Mary's schools, Brother Walfrid and Brother Dorotheus respectively, enthused over the prospect of a football team. They had been fighting the effects of poverty, ignorance and alcoholism among the Eastenders for decades, and were acutely aware that many of the children in their care were hopelessly under-nourished and prone to disease. Brother Walfrid especially had become adept at inspiring others to voluntary effort on behalf of the many charities upon which the East End parishes relied. Local politicians took a leading role in the discussions. John Glass, John O'Hara and Thomas Flood led the local Catholic Union committees (the Catholic Union was the body set up to contest school board elections). Dr Conway, a much-loved GP, J.M. Nelis and Joseph Shaughnessy – all of them founder members of the St Aloysius' Association in 1887 – represented Glasgow's small Catholic professional class, while James Quillan and William McKillop were leading figures in the Irish National League in Glasgow. Such a breadth of involvement indicates that, from the start, this was a co-ordinated drive involving all sections of the Catholic community in the Glasgow area.

The landmark meeting at which the decision was taken to form the Celtic Football and Athletic Club was held in St Mary's Hall on November 6, 1887, with John Glass presiding. Glass was in business as a joiner, a member of St Mary's and a leading figure in Glasgow Irish political circles. His commitment and imaginative approach to the Celtic concept were to prove vital in bringing it to fruition and in sustaining it through the early years. He was later to be described by Willie Maley as the man 'to whom the club owes its existence' and by J.H McLaughlin as 'the originator and motivator' of Celtic.

From the very earliest days, there were differing shades of opinion about what the precise nature and purpose of the new club should be. These centered largely on the extent to which the example of Edinburgh Hibernians should be emulated. But enough was resolved by the time of that November meeting for a committee to be formed and a constitution adopted. The name of Celtic was also agreed upon (with the strong support of Brother Walfrid), as opposed to the widely-canvassed alternative of Glasgow Hibernians. Within a week of the St Mary's Hall meeting, six acres of vacant ground had been leased adjacent to Janefield Cemetery, and voluntary work was soon under way on constructing a new stadium. Meanwhile, fund-raising efforts were in hand and the following circular was issued in January 1888. It did not, it must be said, make any concession to ecumenism, and it cannot be accepted as the definitive statement of Celtic's aims.

**CELTIC FOOTBALL AND ATHLETIC CLUB**
**Celtic Park, Parkhead**
**(Corner of Dalmarnock and Janefield Streets)**
Patrons
His Grace the Archbishop of Glasgow and the Clergy of St

Mary's, Sacred Heart and St Michael's Missions, and the principal Catholic laymen of the East End.

*'The above Club was formed in November 1887, by a number of the Catholics of the East End of the city.*

*'The main object is to supply the East End conferences of the St Vincent de Paul Society with funds for the maintenance of the 'Dinner Tables' of our needy children in the Missions of St Mary's, Sacred Heart and St Michael's. Many cases of sheer poverty are left unaided through lack of means. It is therefore with this principle object that we have set afloat the 'Celtic' and we invite you as one of our ever-ready friends to assist in putting our new Park in proper working order for the coming football season.*

*'We have already several of the leading Catholic football players of the West of Scotland on our membership list. They have most thoughtfully offered to assist in the good work.*

*'We are fully aware that the 'elite' of football players belong to this City and suburbs, and we know that from there we can select a team which will be able to do credit to the Catholics of the West of Scotland as the Hibernians have been doing in the East. Again there is also the desire to have a large recreation ground where our Catholic young men will be able to enjoy the various sports which will build them up physically, and we feel sure we will have many supporters with us in this laudable object.'*

The good and great of Catholic Glasgow headed the subscription list, with Archbishop Eyre's name at the top. The Archbishop of Glasgow 'knew nothing of football but was always prepared to support any scheme that had for its object the welfare of the poor of his flock'. In less than six months from the date of the St Mary's Hall meeting, a level pitch had been formed, surrounded by a cycle track. A rudimentary open-air stand, to accommodate 1,000 spectators, was erected with dressing rooms and committee rooms underneath. The committee met weekly and the opening date for the new Celtic Park was fixed for May 8, 1888, with Hibs and Cowlairs as the attraction. Earlier that day, Queen Victoria was to be in Glasgow for the opening of the great Glasgow International Exhibition of Industry, Science and Art at Kelvingrove, described by its promoters as a 'vast encyclopedia of innovation and manufacture'. In the East End of the city, however, enthusiasm was centred on the opening of Celtic Park rather than on the Royal occasion. The event was advertised in the *Glasgow Observer*, and the paper commented:

> *'The courage of the committee in venturing such a grand undertaking at the commencement is the surprise of many. Some idea may be formed of it when we state that it is the opinion of competent judges that the Celtic Park is second to none in the country, and that is saying a great deal… It is with unqualified pleasure we offer our Celtic friends our congratulations on the great success that has crowned their labours so far and we with them a long and prosperous career.'*
>
> *'The following week, the* Observer *reported: 'On Tuesday evening the weather was all that could be desired; a trifle chilly perhaps, but bright and pleasant notwithstanding. In and around the pavilion were clusters of clergy and people… Prompt to the advertised time, Dr Conway and Mr Shaughnessy emerged from the pavilion and entered the field, heading the procession of players. The Doctor placed the ball amid the cheers of the spectators, who numbered fully 5,000.'*

After a goal-less draw had been played out, the players and officials adjourned to the Royal Hotel, George Square. Dr Conway, who was the club's first chairman and honorary president, presided and proposed a toast to 'The Hibernians'. In response, Mr McFadden of Hibs declared that 'it would be a sorry day indeed for the Irish in Scotland when residents of one city should act in an unfriendly way towards those of another'. Mr Thomas E. Maley then gave a reciprocal toast to 'The Celtic'.

On Monday, May 28, Celtic played their own first game in front of 2,000 spectators. Rangers provided the opposition and Celtic, who won 5-2, wore white shirts with green collars and a Celtic cross in red and green on the left breast. The first Celtic team was: M. Dolan (Drumpellier), E. Pearson (Carfin Shamrock) and J. McLaughlin (Govan Whitfield); W. Maley (Cathcart), J. Kelly (Renton), and P. Murray (Cambuslang Hibs); N. McCallum (Renton) and T. Maley (Cathcart); J. Madden (Dumbarton), M. Dunbar (Edinburgh Hibs) and C. Gorevin (Govan Whitfield). After the game, St Mary's Hall was once again the venue for supper and with much toasting and music, 'proceedings were of the happiest character'. Celtic were in business. They now applied to join the Glasgow and Scottish Football Associations, and further games were quickly arranged.

The early history of Celtic, and the personnel involved, continued to be of unusual relevance because of the remarkable continuity which persisted thoughout the first century of the club's existence. The man who dominated the first five of these decades, Willie Maley, played at right-half in that inaugural side, although he had come to be involved, by his own account, more by accident than design. Within a few weeks of the St Mary's Hall meeting, three of Celtic's founding fathers – John Glass, Brother Walfrid and Pat 'Tailor' Welsh – visited the Maley home in Cathcart, with a view of securing the services of Tom Maley, a schoolmaster, who had played with Partick Thistle, Third Lanark and Edinburgh Hibernians. It was a shrewd move by the emissaries, who must have known that, apart from offering his own considerable ability, Tom Maley was also the man whom others would follow westwards from Hibernians. Willie Maley recalled:

*'Tom was not at home, and I arranged to get him to meet the party in Glasgow to hear the proposals. Brother Walfrid said, 'Why don't you come with him?' I replied that I was only a second-rater and had almost decided to give up the game for cross-country running. He persuaded me to come in with Tom, and when Tom decided to join up my name went down too, and so I was at once initiated into the wonderful scheme of things that this committee of men, with no football knowledge at all, had built up, and which their tremendous enthusiasm brought to fruition.'*

Willie Maley joined Celtic as a player, but quickly became a committee man. He then took on the duties of match secretary, and this post was later converted into the managership, which he retained until 1940. John Glass was the architect of such recruiting efforts, and he shrewdly concentrated his attentions on one of the finest players in Scotland at that time, James Kelly. This was another signing, before Celtic had kicked a ball, which had enormous implications for the club's subsequent history. The son of Irish parents who had immigrated to Scotland in 1842, Kelly was born in 1865 in the village of Renton, on the banks of the Leven. His story is representative of those who would soon establish Celtic as one of Britain's leading football club. During Kelly's childhood, the new sport of football was developing rapidly in the Dumbarton area; the spacious flat land along the Leven, and a tradition of team games such as shinty in the area, helped to ensure that football developed more rapidly there than anywhere else in Scotland. James Kelly started playing for Renton when he was eighteen. Throughout his youth, he was involved in the local Young Ireland Association and the Irish National League. No doubt he was present when Michael Davitt – the founder of the Irish National League – addressed a rally in Dumbarton in 1887. His father, David, was a hammer-man in the local forge, and the extreme poverty of his family pushed him towards professional football, which did exist in practice, if not in theory, at the time.

By the time he signed for Celtic in the summer of 1888, James Kelly had been in a Scottish Cup-winning side, and had also starred in Renton's celebrated 'world club championship' victory over West Bromwich Albion just ten days before Celtic's first game. It had seemed likely that he would be attracted to the Edinburgh Hibernians, for whom he had played on several occasions, but was wooed to the fledging Glasgow club by the persuasive Irish tongue of John Glass. The signing of Kelly represented a huge success, which ensured that other high-quality players would follow. He quickly became very much involved in the running of the club, was one of the first directors in 1897, and initiated a Kelly dynasty within Celtic which survived into the club's second century. If John Glass had set his sights a little lower than Tom Maley and James Kelly, the subsequent history of Celtic would have been very different.

The second fixture at Celtic Park was against Dundee Harp, who went down 1-0 to the infant club in front of 6,000 spectators. By the end of June, Celtic had drawn 3-3 with Mossend Swifts and lost 4-3 to Clyde. The life-span of new clubs tended to be brief in those days – a point illustrated by the company in which Celtic found themselves when being admitted to membership of the Scottish Football Association on August 21, 1888. The other successful applicants that day were Champfleurie and Adventurers from Edinburgh, Leith Harp, Balaclava Rangers from Oban, Temperance Athletic of Glasgow, Whifflet Shamrock and Britannia of Auchinleck! None survived to tell the tale.

Although the Scottish League did not yet exist, it was possible to put together a very full programme of fixtures during Celtic's first full season, 1888/89. Of fifty-six matches played, forty-two were won and three were drawn. Celtic lost the major tournament, the Scottish Cup, to Third Lanark only in a replayed final at Hampden, after accounting for Shettleston, Cowlairs, Albion Rovers, St Bernard's, Clyde, East Stirling and Dumbarton. The major power in the land was still Queen's Park, who deprived Celtic of the Glasgow Cup, while Renton gave them a quick knock-out from the Charity Cup. Cowlairs eliminated Celtic from the Exhibition Cup – held to celebrate the great imperial event which Glasgow was hosting – but they won their first ever trophy by defeating the same club in the less prestigious North Eastern Cup at Barrowfield.

Celtic travelled remarkably far from home in that first season. There were games in Newcastle, Burnley, Bolton, London and Belfast. Their guests at Celtic Park included the mighty Corinthians, whom they beat 6-2 in front of a crowd of over 16,000 on January 3, 1889, although losing 3-1 when they went to London for a return challenge. Within their first year of existence, Celtic even acquired their first 'brake club' (a brake was a type of vehicle hired by a club's supporters to transport them to wherever their team was playing). Appropriately, it hailed from the parish of St Mary's, and the banner gave pride of place to the features of Tom Maley. Others quickly followed, usually under the auspices of a parish's League of the Cross, a temperance organisation. Each brake held twenty-five people. Soon they would start to assemble at Carlton Place and proceed to the appointed venue of the day.

By the time the club held its annual meeting in June 1889 there was already much to celebrate, and when Tom Maley responded to the vote of thanks, 'the meeting rose en masse and sang out lustily, '*He's a Jolly Good Fellow*'. Prior to the election of officers, Mr Shaughnessy moved that Michael Davitt should be made honorary patron of the club, and 'this was received with acclamation'. Davitt had confirmed his popularity among the Glasgow Irish with a memorable St Patrick's Day address in the City Hall when he condemned Irish landlordism as a system which 'breeds Irish poverty, nourishes Irish crime, feeds Irish discontent, disturbs Irish peace, paralyses Irish industry and enterprise, checks material and social progress and arrests in the work of development and expansion the genius of a nation. (Loud cheers) Home Rule or no Home Rule, Irish landlordism has got to go'. These were sentiments close to the hearts of those people who had founded, as well as those who supported, Celtic. Most, perhaps all, of the inaugural committee were deeply committed to the politics of Ireland, and they included several who were to become at least as well known through their activities in that arena as through the Celtic connection. Once again, this strain in the club's tradition has remained relevant to an understanding of its nature and character.

Reports of the annual meeting in 1889 indicate that there were already 'malcontents' among the membership, none of whom was elected to the committee – 'for which the Celtic Football Club have every reason to be thankful', snorted Scottish Sport. The cause of the unrest concerned the development of the club's nature and priorities. It had been clear from the start that Celtic would generate substantial sums of money and great community influence for those who controlled the club. The malcontents remained adamant that it should be Catholic, amateur and charitable. In particular, they disliked the connection which had developed with the licensed trade. For many in the Irish immigrant community, drink was undoubtedly a curse. For some, however, it was the only business opportunity apart from pawnbroking available to them. Inevitably, therefore, the input of Glasgow's Catholic businessmen into Celtic came largely from publicans and restaurant owners, including the McKillops, J. H. McLaughlin and James Quillan. Equally inevitably, some of the players ended up with jobs, either nominal or real, in the licensed premises.

In spite of the great start Celtic had enjoyed, some of the

malcontents sought to encourage Hibernians to move west as a rival club. The goodwill towards the new Glasgow organisation exuded by Mr McFadden of Hibs in the early days had dissipated rapidly as several leading players had been lured to Celtic Park, particularly in the wake of James Kelly's decision to go there rather than to Hibs. When Celtic played them in Edinburgh in October 1888, there had been a hostile reception from the crowd – scarcely eased by the fact that Celtic won 3-0. However, negotiations with Hibs fell through and the malcontents made their own short-lived effort to establish a club called Glasgow Hibernians. The choice of name was significant, for here, indeed, was an attempt to establish an alternative club along the lines that Celtic had deliberately chosen not to follow. The rival school of thought about Celtic's proper nature and purpose would linger on. But it is important to note that the debate was there from the start and that it was consistently won by those who saw Celtic's charitable function as the by-product of creating a successful, well-organised and inclusive club.

Within the space of nineteen months which separated these two St Mary's Hall meetings, Celtic had not only been brought into existence but had also established themselves as a major power in Scottish football. They had won respect from further afield, both for their playing prowess and for the efficiency of their management. They had equipped themselves with a fine stadium and proved their crowd-pulling power. Never had a club enjoyed such an auspicious start and, for good measure, they were able to donate £421 19s 6d to charity, in addition to raising several hundred pounds by playing invitation games and distributing match tickets for sale by the local conferences of the St Vincent de Paul Society. That section of Scottish society which did not much fancy the idea of a football club that was largely Irish in identity and successful on the playing field would, for the rest of time, have to learn to live with that reality.

# TWO

## SOCIAL BACKGROUND:
## RELIGION AND POLITICS

GLASGOW IN 1888 was dominated by the hallmarks, both good and ill, of the Industrial Revolution. The credit side of the picture was amply illustrated in the Great Exhibition – the largest ever held outside London – opened by Queen Victoria on the same day as the inauguration of the first Celtic Park. The Exhibition was a testimony to the second city of the Empire's primary place as a hotbed of industrial innovation, manufacture and trade. Glasgow was at the height of its powers as a workshop of the world, with the greatest concentrations of engineering works and factories in the city's East End. To the west, along the Clyde, shipbuilding was in its heyday and 234 ships were launched on the river in 1888. The volume of the Corporation-published Statistics of Glasgow for that year reported: 'In every department of the city's well-being – municipal, commercial, educational, artistic and philanthropic – evidences of conspicuous advance present themselves.'

And so they did, so long as one did not look much beneath the surface. For instance, the City Chambers in George Square were completed in 1888 (the foundation stone having been laid five year earlier by Sir John Ure, Lord Provost, 'with full Masonic rites'). The citizenry watched the building's progress 'with ever-growing interest as it rose from the ground course by course and storey by storey, the interest intensifying as it effloresced into domes and towers'. When the Shah of Persia visited a few months later, the new chambers were described as 'an edifice which combines the solid purpose of a Western business city with Oriental ideas of splendor'. But for reasons that were political and cultural as well as social and economic, the grandeur of George Square was far more remote from the great majority of people in Glasgow's impoverished East End than mere geography suggested. It would, for example, be another decade before the first Catholic councillor was elected in the City.

In 1888, there were 11,675 registered deaths in Glasgow of which 4,750 were of infants under five. Another 1,192 failed to reach the age of twenty, and fewer than 2,000 had made it to sixty. Among the children, the principal plagues were measles, whooping cough and scarlet fever – diseases associated with poverty and overcrowding. In the jerry-built slums of the East End, the world into which Celtic arrived, conditions were at their most miserable. The Irish immigrant population was heavily represented in this area of the city, particularly since the great influx of refugees after the potato famine in Ireland in the 1840s. Catholic marriages in Glasgow between 1885 and 1888 accounted for almost one in six of the total – an indication of how the Irish had become a substantial minority within the city. Nineteenth-century Glasgow had, among British cities, been second only to Liverpool as a magnet for Irish immigrants.

The Irish had been driven to Scotland and other lands by the inability of the rack-rented, colonised country to sustain them. The political complexities of the situation, and the reinforced sense of grievance felt by the Irish people, were of little interest to most people in Presbyterian Scotland, who viewed the Irish influx with varying degrees of apprehension and hostility. Yet governments did nothing to stop it, because of the flow of cheap labour it provided. The keeper at Glasgow's statistical records probably spoke for much of Presbyterian Scotland at this time, when he felt bold enough to offer the unscientific opinion: 'The sufferings of Ireland have not been the offspring of Saxon tyranny but of racial fertility beyond the capabilities of soil.' He recommended immigration to North America rather than the slums of Glasgow where, he noted, 'the practice amongst the poor of two families living together is on the increase'. The reality was a scene very different from the revelry that accompanied the Great Exhibition.

Scotland in the latter half of the nineteenth century was fired by fierce religious controversy, to which the Roman Catholic minority was peripheral. The ranks of Presbyterians had been split into deeply opposed churches by various schisms, notably the disruption of 1843 which created the Free Church of Scotland. Indigenous Scottish Catholicism had been marginalised by the Reformation, and had survived principally in the remote areas of the Highlands and Islands. This meant, therefore, that Catholicism and Irishness became largely interchangeable terms in lowland Scotland as the immigration influx increased during the century. The feuding Presbyterians found unity in their hostility towards the Catholic Irish incursion. In 1867 Bishop Gray, who led the Catholic mission in Scotland, advised an English visitor: 'The Scottish are animated by a strong hereditary hatred of Catholicity, nor is the feeling of the country favourable to Irish settlers… The religion, the history, the character and habits of the two peoples show many elements not of difference but of antagonism'.

By and large, the Irish immigrants in Glasgow filled the more menial jobs, being untrained for those aspects of industrialisation which required skills. Along with the displaced Highlanders they acquired the reputation of being prepared to undercut their fellows in terms of wages and conditions in order to obtain jobs at any price. This secular source of resentment went hand-in-hand with the anti-Catholic propaganda which was maintained by the Presbyterian churches. Signs of Catholic progress, such as the restoration of the Scottish hierarchy in 1878, were meat and drink for those whose vested interest was in warning against the Catholic-Irish 'threat'.

While never resting easily alongside mainstream Scottish Presbyterianism, the Orange Order was another ingredient in the mix which ensured that Glasgow's Irish population would create its own social structures and defence mechanisms. The Order had its origins in supporting Protestant landholding in Armagh in the late eighteenth century. Glasgow did not have its first Orange Lodge until 1860, by which time the organisation was established as an all-purpose vehicle for anti-Irish Catholic sentiment as well as for political Conservatism. The substantial number of Ulster Protestant immigrants to Scotland formed the basis of Orange strength.

The religious distinctiveness of the Irish community was matched by its political preoccupations. It was the politics of Ireland which held the attention of the expatriates, and it was along Irish lines that they had organised themselves politically. Irish Home Rule was the prime demand, with land reform not far behind it. Their interest in British politics had been measured largely in terms of the relevance to Ireland. Thus the Liberalism to which most of Glasgow still subscribed in the 1880s was shared by the Irish only in so far as Gladstone was seen to be delivering on Home Rule. Lowland Scottish suspicion of that cause (and the Catholicism which went with it) was regularly fuelled by Fenian outrages – the attempted bombings in 1883 of Tradeston Gas Works, Buchanan Street Goods Station and

Ruchill Canal Bridge certainly helped to condition Glasgow attitudes in the latter part of the same decade. From 1881, Michael Davitt, a former Fenian prisoner and the most radical of the Irish political leaders, was an extremely popular visitor to the Irish in Glasgow. The City's Catholic Irish press reflected the political interests of the readership. The same issue of the *Glasgow Observer* which announced the opening of Celtic Park carried much more prominent headlines concerning such matters as: 'Double Execution in the Tralee'; 'Shocking Eviction' in Co. Carlow; and Pope Leo XIII's condemnation of the tactic known as boycotting in Ireland. The contrast with the news carried in the mainstream Scottish press was total.

The decision to form Celtic Football Club is rightly identified with the needs of Catholic charity in the East End of Glasgow. But the early nature of the club, and the direction it pursued, owe at least as much to the influence exercised by the political organisation which spoke for the vast majority of the Irish in Scotland in the 1880s, the Irish National League, and specifically one of its branches in Glasgow, known as the Home Government Branch. Among those involved in setting up Celtic, John Glass, James Quillan, the McKillops and the Murphys were heavily involved in the Home Government Branch. Glass was its treasurer, Quillan, Celtic's first vice-president, was also vice-president of the branch. Hugh Murphy was president of the Home Government Branch and also a member of Celtic, while his brother Arthur would serve on Celtic's committee for its first decade. Later, Thomas White would also preside over the Home Government Branch.

The Home Government Branch of the Irish National League in Glasgow was founded in 1871 by John Ferguson, a Belfast Protestant described by Michael Davitt as the 'father of the Irish movement in Scotland'. It was the start of an organisation which would grow to 600 branches throughout Britain by the mid 1880s. The Home Government Branch dominated Irish politics in Scotland and had the closest of links with the Irish parliamentary party, in its struggle for Home Rule. It raised large amounts of money for the parliamentary party and its own weekly meetings were known as 'the parliament of the Irish people in Glasgow'. Each year, it was the Home Government Branch which organised the St Patrick's Day celebrations in Glasgow and made sure that all the leading figures of the Irish movement visited the city, including Isaac Butt, Parnell and Davitt. The influence which the leading figures in the Home Government Branch exercised in the founding of Celtic ensured that the primary aim would be to create a club that was outward-looking, proudly Irish and excellent, rather than a 'Glasgow Hibernians' founded on the Catholic parishes.

The Irish National League was a non-sectarian organisation, and the Home Government Branch was in the forefront of practicing this doctrine, reinforced by the role of Ferguson, whose leadership had already been challenged unsuccessfully on the grounds that he was not a Catholic. That matter had come to a head in 1875 over a commemoration rally for the Irish national hero Daniel O'Connell. The rally had physically split into two groups – those, under Church influence, who wanted to recall only O'Connell's role in achieving Catholic emancipation, and those – under Ferguson's leadership – who saw it as a more political occasion. Ferguson had emerged all the stronger from this dispute, and he remained the dominant figure in Home Rule politics in Glasgow until after the turn of the century. It is unthinkable that people who were his closest allies in the Home Government Branch in the following decade would have had any interest in forming a football club which retreated into Catholic exclusivism.

The choice of Celtic as the club's name can also be traced to the strategy of the Irish National League in Scotland at the time. By placing emphasis upon the struggle against Irish landlordism, of which the campaign for Home Rule was only part, they were building bridges with the Scottish Highland community, both at home and in Glasgow. The impoverished state of the Highland and Islands was the dominant political issue in Scotland at that time and it was reasonable belief that identifying a common cause with predominantly Presbyterian Highlanders would help to break down the suspicions within Ulster that the Home Rule movement would lead them into 'Rome Rule'. The Home Government Branch of the INL was most enthusiastic about applying this strategy – hence the repeated visits of Davitt to Glasgow and, indeed, the Highlands and Islands which he toured under the branch's auspices in 1887. The proceeds of the St Patrick's Day rally that year were given to the crofters' movement. Wherever he went, Davitt emphasised the common Celtic background of the Scots and Irish. The main Catholic paper, the *Glasgow Observer*, accorded huge deadlines to his visit: 'Davitt in Highlands – the Tribune of the Celtic Race'. When he met with John Murdoch, a leading figure in the crofters' movement, 'so loud and hearty was the cheering that the mountains as well as the buildings echoed in celebrations of a meeting of Celt with Celt'.

A few months later, the name 'Celtic' was adopted for the new football club, with Brother Walfrid prominent in advocating it. This was consistent with the fact that he previously organised teams under the name 'Columba', which evoked the common religious inheritance of Scotland and Ireland. The Catholic Irish had been naming teams for the previous fifteen or twenty years, and Celtic never appears to have arisen as a suggestion – Hibernians, Harp, Erin, Shamrock and Emerald were the popular choices. Even as late as August 1887, an Irish select team played Partick Thistle at Whiteinch under the name of Western Hibernians. The side included James Kelly, Wille

Groves and John Coleman, all soon to be Celtic regulars. But over the next few months, the argument in favour of 'Celtic' was won. For those who wished to build bridges between the Scots and the Irish, it was perfect. So unfamiliar were the Glasgow Irish with the name that they immediately mispronounced it with a soft 'C'. To his dying day, Brother Walfrid maintained the proper pronunciation.

The divisions over how Catholic and charitable Celtic should be, and the Home Government Branch's crucial role in determining the outcome, were paralleled at exactly the same time, and involving many of the same people, by the vital debate over the political direction of the Irish community. Also in May 1888 the Home Government Branch endorsed Keir Hardie, the first Labour candidate in Britain, in the Mid Lanark by-election. John Ferguson became a founding vice-president of the Scottish Labour Party at its inception. Had the Home Government Branch supported instead the formation of an Irish Party in Scotland – as was being mooted in some Catholic circles at the time – then the subsequent political development of the country might have been very different.

By 1880 there were still only eighteen Catholic churches in Glasgow. One of the largest was St Mary's in Abercromby Street, founded in 1842, which served a population of 10,000 in the surrounding East End districts. A school had been attached to the church since 1850, and it was run by the Marist Brothers from 1863. The 1872 Education Act had made the provision of schooling the responsibility of the state, but the Catholic Church continued to run its own 'voluntary' schools, in order to ensure the maintenance of Catholic education. They were entitled to state support only through parliamentary grant and not from the rates, which the newly-created school boards could levy. In 1874 another school, attached to the Sacred Heart church, was opened and Brother Walfrid moved from

St Mary's School to this new charge. He continued to work closely with Brother Dorotheus, head of St Mary's School, in the common cause of fund-raising to sustain the schools, allow for expansion and provide assistance to those pupils who required it. The 'penny dinner' scheme was initiated by Walfrid in Sacred Heart and taken up by Dorotheus in St Mary's. As a centenary history of the latter school recalled:

> 'For some lads it was not indifference but the lack of means that made the absentees. Even in the cruellest days of winter then a barefooted boy was no uncommon sight and raggedness and an ill-filled belly were the daily lot of many an urchin… The penny was charged only when no great hardship was involved, to preserve the self-respect of the beneficiaries. Many parents whose children needed the meal would have baulked at the idea of receiving charity but were reconciled by the face-saving device of token payment.'

The scheme was off the ground by December 1885, and a few months later a football match was organised between Edinburgh Hibernians and St Peter's, Partick, to raise money for its funding, proceeds going to Sacred Heart, St Mary's and St Michael's in the Gallowgate. Organised football had by this time been around for some twenty years. Its attractiveness as a team game, capable of arousing mass enthusiasm, had grown steadily as Saturday afternoons off work became the norm. Queen's Park, founded in 1867, were deeply involved in codifying the rules of the game – the prerequisite for its popularity as a spectator sport. The extent to which the game had caught on in a big way among Glasgow's youth can be gauged from these recollections in the history of St Mary's School.

> 'The use of footballs to kick in the yard before school was

*one of the schemes in St Mary's to encourage good time-keeping; and football matches for the perfect attenders with prizes for the winning teams helped in the good work. As the government grant to the managers of the Catholic schools varied with roll and attendance, teachers tried all kinds of schemes to ensure the highest possible daily attendance.'*

*The same account notes, incidentally: 'The attractions that lured the fickle attender from his duty, thought not so many as in modern times, were just as potent as today. Among other seductions, the St Mary's logbook lists at various intervals the Paisley Races, the Wild Beast Show at Vinegar Hill, Buffalo Bill's Wild West Show – though staging it in Duke Street was surely demanding superhuman restraint from any St Mary's boy – and the Glasgow Exhibition of 1888.'*

Such were the temptations in the 1880s against which football in the playground was weighed! When placed in the context of history, and given the nature of Scottish society and attitudes in the 1880s, Celtic's emergence as a club with a strong Irish identity is wholly understandable. Brother Walfrid's discovery of football – a game of which the cleric from Ballymote, County Sligo had little prior knowledge – as a splendid fund-raiser made the origination of a substantial club from within the East End parishes a very natural extension of this principle. The wonder is that the Edinburgh example had not been followed, and such a club successfully established, long before 1888.

The rapid flourishing of the St Mary's Hall enterprise was due entirely to the fact that several quite outstanding individuals invested their enthusiasm in it. Disparaging references to the 'bunch of publicans' who founded Celtic or carried the club through its inevitable transition to the status of limited company, can be based only on ignorance, for the truth is that Celtic's pioneers included several men of real interest and character, whose public activities extended well beyond football. The careers of Glass, Shaughnessy, Kelly, the McKillops, White (who entered the scene a little later) and others who were to the fore in these early years would all be worthy of study in their own right, and in each case the Celtic involvement would represent just one strand of the story to be told.

Just as the reasons for Celtic's emergence can be readily understood, so too it can be seen as inevitable that the club would attract hostility, with its roots in issues which had little or nothing to do with footballing prowess. It took time for this antagonism to develop into a clearly defined counterforce. But from the day of Celtic's birth, there must have been a sizeable proportion of Scottish public opinion which resented the club's very existence, as a manifestation of the Irish presence in Scotland.

That was the nature of the world into which Celtic were born and, as in so many other respects, the world has not entirely mended its ways in the course of the past one hundred and thirty years. Celtic have not sought to appease the unappeasable by denying their origins and identity. But success on the field of play, dignity in their affairs and adherence to the founding principles have transcended all prejudices other than those which exist in the minds of their harshest detractors.

# THREE

## THE EARLY DAYS:
## PIONEERING AND PROFESSIONALISM

WITHIN A FEW months of Celtic taking to the field, sports writers were claiming to discern a distinctive style in their play. In November 1888, *Scottish Sport* commented upon 'the clever dribbling and short accurate passing which is characteristic of their play'. When they met Dumbarton in the third round of the Scottish Cup, the *Scottish Referee* observed:

> *'The Celts' style is modelled on that of Preston North End, and whilst it demands speed, strength and all the essentials which go to make up the stock-in-trade of the football player, the one thing needful is head. The cool, calculating, easy-going manner in which the Celts wrought the ball must have been a revelation to the Dumbarton people…'*

Celtic's progress to the final of the Scottish Cup in their inaugural season stands out as their first great playing achievement, which immediately commanded respect – however grudging – in Scottish football circles. Their progress was, however, accompanied by the kind of controversies that marked these pioneering days of the organised game. In the fifth round, Willie Maley as match secretary lodged a protest after Clyde had won 1-0 at Celtic Park, on the grounds that the last ten minutes had been played in darkness due to Clyde's late readiness for the game. The protest was upheld by one vote, and Clyde were so incensed by this outcome that at the replay they refused to change in the Celtic pavilion, arriving at the ground ready for action. They lost 9-2.

The final itself was scheduled for February 2, 1889, and though Third Lanark won this game 3-0, a replay was again required. The match became known as the 'Snow Final'. As the large crowd assembled, a blizzard swept Hampden Park. Under the guidance of a solicitor who was present, the two clubs drew up a joint 'protest' against the game being played in such conditions. Dr James Handley, author of *The Celtic Story* (published in 1960), wrote: 'The agreement was a quiet one. Only a rope separated spectators and players in those days and the playing pitch would probably have been the rallying ground for a demonstration on the part of an incensed crowd, who had paid to see a final and were being fobbed off with a friendly, particularly as the admission price had been raised for the occasion from the usual sixpence to a shilling...' The final proper took place on the following Saturday, and Third Lanark won 2-1.

Celtic's second season was less auspicious than the first, losing the Glasgow Cup final to still-mighty Queen's Park and going out of the Scottish Cup in the first round to the same club. But in 1890/91 they won the Glasgow Cup – a feat which, at that time, required victories in four rounds prior to the final. This was Celtic's first major trophy, but the event of far greater significance in the 1890/91 season was the inauguration of the Scottish League, with ten clubs involved at the outset in the First Division. These were Abercorn, Cambuslang, Celtic, Cowlairs, Dumbarton, Heart of Midlothian, Rangers, St Mirren, Third Lanark and Vale of Leven. Celtic's representative at the SFA,

J.H. McLaughlin, had been very much involved in advocating the establishment of a league, which brought a much-needed edge of competition to the Scottish game at a crucial time. In the first League season, Celtic had four points deducted for fielding ineligible players and finished in third place behind the joint winners, Rangers and Dumbarton. In all, Celtic played forty-nine games in 1890/91, winning thirty-four of them and losing only eight. A reserve team had been formed and it won the Scottish Second XI Cup.

The early disagreements about the club's nature and purpose continued to fester, and came to the fore again at the annual meeting of members in 1891. The press apparently went to some trouble to be present on such occasions, and the correspondent of the *Scottish Referee* reported breathlessly that this particular meeting attracted 'a respectable but excited audience, who were so taken up with discussion amongst themselves that they did not observe me sliding under the table at the entrance and seating myself at the side of the platform to watch and hear'.

There was plenty to observe, for this turned into a showdown meeting between the rival camps, with each faction issuing 'slates' of candidates to vote for. Dr Conway, the man who had kicked the first ball on Celtic Park, led the attack on the officials of the club and, in particular, opposed the decision to pay Willie Maley a fee. Seconded by J. H. McLaughlin, he moved against this and declared that while there were plenty of men willing to work for the club for nothing, nobody should be paid for it. Clearly, Dr Conway's argument applied to players as well as to officials. He was challenging Celtic's whole approach, but this motion was lost by 102 votes to 74.

In the elections which followed, the malcontents were trounced by similar margins. Dr Conway lost his position as honorary president to Joseph Shaughnessy. He then stood against Glass for the position of president (effectively chairman), and lost again. A leading member of the Irish National League, Arthur Murphy, was added to the committee. Willie Maley was confirmed as match secretary. 'The anti-officialites, as the opposition in the Celtic committee have been called, have been cleared out', stated *Scottish Sport*. (The reported role of McLaughlin as seconder of Dr Conway's motion remains puzzling. Far from being 'cleared out', he was appointed club secretary at this meeting, and was already at that time a leading advocate of 'honest professionalism' in football. Perhaps the covert reporter got it wrong!)

The early months of the following season brought potentially crippling news for Celtic – as Willie Maley described it, 'an old affliction to Irishmen – the Landlord.' John McLaughlin went into detail at the club's half-yearly meeting in December 1891.

*'Being an Irish club, it was but natural that they should have a greedy landlord, and they had one who was working to take a place high among rack-renters in Ireland. In the old country these gentlemen were satisfied with doubling or at the worst trebling it, but the bright genius who boasted the possession of Celtic Park wanted nine times the previous rent for a new lease. Instead of £50 per year, he wished to increase the annual rent to £450.'*

With the lease due to expire at Martinmas 1892 (November), consideration was given to moving out of the East End to Possilpark or Springburn, but as the Cowlairs club had 'sort of official rights to the northern district', the idea was abandoned. In the end, Celtic did not have to look far for their alternative. An expanse of waste ground – or 'quarry hole' according to Maley – situated between the old ground and London Road was leased from the estate of Lord Hozier, initially for ten years. It seemed an unpromising, waterlogged site and 10,000 cartloads of infill were required to level it. But the work, much of it accomplished with voluntary labour, was completed in astonishingly quick time, and on Saturday, March 20, 1892 the link between Michael Davitt and Celtic was reinforced when he laid a centre sod, fresh from Donegal that morning with a clump of shamrocks growing in it. What better man, the committee must have reasoned, to celebrate this triumph over a landlord's excessive demands? John Ferguson was another who was to the fore at the ceremony which, it was noted, was a much more secular occasion than the first ground opening.

To commemorate the occasion, an understandably anonymous poem appeared in one of the Catholic papers of the day.

*On alien soil like yourself I am here;*
*I'll take root and flourish of that never fear,*
*And though I'll be crossed sore and oft by the foes*
*You'll find me as hardy as Thistle and Rose.*
*If model is needed on your own pitch you will have it,*
*Let your play honour me and my friend Michael Davitt.*

When the centre sod was promptly stolen by a nineteenth-century vandal, the poet returned to the fray:

*The curse of Cromwell blast the hand that stole the sod that Michael cut;*
*May all his praties turn to sand – the crawling, thieving scut.*
*That precious site of Irish soil with verdant shamrocks overgrown*
*Was token of glorious soil more fitting far than fretted stone.*
*Again I say, may Heaven blight that envious soulless knave*
*May all his sunshine be like night and the sod rest heavy on his grave.*

Almost fifty years later, Willie Maley recalled with pride how 'a seemingly impossible site… was converted into a palatial enclosure, and it looked, as one smart chap said, 'like leaving the graveyard to enter Paradise'. That title, seized on by a pressman, clung to the present ground for many years.' The new stadium was recognised as the best in Britain at that time. There were tracks for running and cycling, a grandstand for 3,500 spectators and a two-storeyed pavilion.

In 1891/92, Celtic won their first Scottish Cup, beating Queen's Park 5-1 in a replayed final at Ibrox. Once again, there had been an agreement in the first match – at half-time on this occasion – to make the game a friendly, this time because the very large crowd of 40,000 was occasionally spilling over on to the park. The gates had been closed, but thousands climbed over the barricades and, with no real protection against the press of the throng, there was frequent encroachment upon the area of play. There was an attendance of just 15,000 at Ibrox for the second game, scarcely justifying the presence of two hundred police.

The Scottish football press was not inclined to be generous towards Celtic in their hour of triumph. The *Scottish Referee* reported grudgingly: 'There are circumstances which tone down the triumph considerably, and make it pretty much a Pyrrhic victory. The Queen's had but a skeleton team…' *Scottish Sport* concurred that Queen's Park team difficulties and ultimate line-up had been more significant in bringing about the 5-1 scoreline 'than any inherent ability displayed by the Celtic team'. The first Celtic side to with the Scottish Cup was: Cullen, Reynolds, and Doyle; W. Maley, Kelly and Gallacher; McCallum and Brady; Dowds, McMahon and Campbell. Celtic also won the Glasgow Cup and Glasgow Charity Cup in this season to give them their first 'treble'.

A mere handful of years into their existence, season 1892/93 proved to be of landmark importance to Celtic. This was the season of their first Scottish League title. But the wider significance of the season was summed up by Willie Maley: 'It was a happy augury for the future, as it marked the opening of the new ground, and with the legalisation of professionalism, football seemed in a fair way to becoming a more honest and better organised sport.'

The principle advocate of professionalism in Scottish football was John H. McLaughlin, one of Celtic's founders, who became the club's leading figure on the legislative side of the game. Of Donegal stock, he had been the organist in St Mary's and had, like most of the Celtic founders, minimal knowledge of football prior to the Celtic initiative. According to Maley, indeed, his previous sporting interest was in cricket. When the club was founded, he was barely twenty-five years of age, but on his death in 1909, Tom Maley wrote of him: 'The late legislator entered into football at a time most dangerous. Dangerous, because an older school of leaders – conservative as a tramcar – were at the head of affairs, and progress was slow, so very slow. The establishment of the Scottish Football League as well as the legalisation of professionalism, epochs in football, are monumental to his labours.'

From the outset, Celtic had been prepared to spend money in order to build a team of merit. In theory, Scottish football was an amateur game, but only Queen's Park adhered to this principle with any sense of commitment. Football was capable of creating substantial income through the gates, and there was no obvious reason why the players who drew the crowds should not share in this wealth – then, as to some extent now, football offered one of the few legitimate devices by which young working-class men could rapidly improve their economic lot. Apart from anything else, professionalism had been recognised in England since 1875, so players were bound to drain away from Scotland as long as amateurism remained the reality there.

Celtic had from the start paid their players thirty shillings a week, and this rose to £2 in 1890 as other players went on strike for equality with those brought from England, this at a time when all were supposed to be amateurs! It was the signature of Dan Doyle from Everton that sparked off the revolt, and also caused some very reasonable questions to be asked in the sporting press. The *Scottish Referee* wondered:

> *'How can an amateur club like Celtic outbid a very wealthy professional team in Everton? It is far easier to comprehend the weaving of one of Mr Gladstone's speeches than the exact process by which the Celtic can induce a Scot, well paid in England, to return to his native land and yet keep within the rules of the Scottish Association. That Doyle now proposes to cross the border to play for an amateur club like the Celtic imposes too great a strain on the credulity.'*

The tale of the 1890 strike was told by Willie Maley almost fifty years later in *The Story of the Celtic*. It did not last long, 'as the committee had to face the increases brought about by the return of Doyle and Co'. The 'paid amateur' state of affairs was, Maley agreed, 'farcical', and it was to Celtic's credit that they were more open about their practices than others and also in the vanguard of campaigning for change. It was largely through John McLaughlin's advocacy within the SFA that the legalisation of professionalism was approved almost unanimously in 1893, after his motion to the same effect had failed narrowly the previous year. 'To the Celtic lies the credit of bringing about this honest avowal of what had existed long before their inception, aye and in clubs too that had the audacity to pose as purists on the amateur question', said the Celtic handbook.

By the time of the half-yearly meeting in December 1892, Celtic were Scottish Cup-holders and on their way to their first League title. It was time for satisfaction to be taken from these achievements, and Thomas Flood, who proposed the adoption of the secretary's report on that occasion, undoubtedly summed up the prevailing mood when he declared that the club's success 'not only reflects credit on the members of the team and their Glasgow followers, but will be welcomed by their countrymen all over Great Britain, who take a deep interest in the working of the Celtic club'. Warming to this theme, Flood elaborated upon the significance of this footballing achievement.

*'Irishmen in Scotland, in the past years, have been made little of, because they have few of their number in business or in positions of responsibility. But they have lately demonstrated that not only in commercial life can they be successful, but they have proved the possession on their part of an amount of pluck and perseverance by the manner in which they have risen to the top of the ladder in the football world. The Celtic team is the pride of the Irish race in England, Ireland and Scotland…'*

His seconder saw Celtic's achievements as 'proof of the ability of Irishmen to manage any concern on which they took interest…'

Celtic were indeed at the forefront of progressive innovation. In December 1892, the honorary president, Joseph Shaughnessy, 'gave an explanation of the negotiations of the committee with regard to the erection of electric light in the park with a view to evening matches, and explanations respecting the preservation of the field from frost'. Lighting was actually introduced at Celtic Park late in the following year, and the first game the club played under artificial light was a friendly against Clyde on Christmas night, 1893. James Handley's account of the Heath Robinson structure makes amusing reading.

*'The experiment was not a success and after a few weeks' trial was abandoned. The wires, fixed to a dozen huge wooden posts 50 feet high, were stretched across the field, with lamps attached, and along the covered enclosure additional illumination was provided by a hundred gas-jets. Apart from the unsightly mass of wires and lamps, which detracted from the appearance of the ground, the structure was apt to sag and impede the flight of the ball. St Bernard's, beaten 8-1 by Celtic in the quarter-finals of the Scottish Cup in January 1894, were moved to lodge a protest with the SFA – later withdrawn – on the account. The ball had struck the wires only twice during the course of the game, but the club claimed that its objection was based on principle. After their great centre-forward, the rigging went by the name of 'Madden's Shipyard' among the Celtic supporters.'*

# FOUR

## TOWARDS THE TWENTIETH CENTURY: BUSINESS & BATTLES

BEFORE THE TURN of the century, Celtic won the Scottish League Championship again in seasons 1893/94, '95/96 and '97/98. The Scottish Cup proved more elusive, and they did not recapture it after 1892 until 1899, when they beat Rangers 2-0 at Hampden. By the end of the 1893/94 season, only James Kelly remained of the original team. Names such as Johnny Divers, Jimmy Blessington and Barney Battles began to appear on the team-sheet. By winning the League title three times in the competition's first six years of existence, the paramount position of Celtic in Scottish football was clearly established, and this status was recognised when J. H McLaughlin stepped up from the vice-presidency to become the second president of the Scottish League in 1896.

Celtic had quickly developed the largest following in Britain, and was probably the wealthiest club, in Scotland at least, within a few years of its inception – a conclusion supported by the manner in which the ambitious undertaking of a new stadium was embarked upon. This, in turn, became the source of further revenue and was, for a few years, recognised as Scotland's international ground. Scotland's four home games with England between 1894 and 1900 were played there, with 57,000 crowding in for the 1896 encounter. There was also a flair for showmanship at Celtic Park, with Willie Maley – himself a Scottish champion sprinter – an enthusiastic advocate of athletics, boxing and cycling events as ancillary activities to the club's major business. From 1890, the Celtic Sports became an important two-day fixture on the athletics calendar each August.

The conflict of convictions which had been around since the club was first mooted had carried over to a new issue, following the defeat of the 'anti-officialites' in 1891. Most leading members of the club believed that, if it was to survive, it had to be organised on a more commercial, business-like footing, and as a limited company. A majority of the rank-and-file were determined that it should remain as a club in which all members were equal. Feelings ran high on both sides of the argument, and some of those who had rejected the purist approach of Dr Conway were, nonetheless, unhappy about the proposed transition to a limited liability company (which eventually occurred in 1897). The spirit of the debate, and the legends to which it gave rise, are reflected in the fact that the centenary history of St Mary's parish school, published in 1963, recalled the affair in starkly unequivocal terms.

*'The Penny Dinner tables lost the financial aid of the Celtic Football Club. Brother Walfrid, who had founded Celtic as a charitable trust, was changed by his superiors to London in August 1892 and the committee, freed from his restraining hand, ignored the end for which the club had been founded. The last contribution to the Poor Children's Dinner Table was made at the AGM of session 1891/92. The committee, after a bitter struggle against the honest element among the team's supporters, got their way at last and turned the club into a business with themselves as directors and shareholders.'*

James Handley, himself a Marist brother (Brother Clare), in *The Celtic Story*, scarcely took a more understanding view and referred to 'this betrayal of a charitable trust'. When this book appeared in 1960, the Celtic chairman, Robert Kelly, had his thoughts minuted at the annual general meeting of shareholders, demonstrating just how sensitive an issue it continued to be.

*'It has been brought out (by Handley) that the club was founded in the cause of charity, primarily to provide free dinners for the poor people of the East End of Glasgow. The club was eventually transformed into a limited company, and it has been expressed that the club has in consequence not done as much as it should for the charitable purposes for which it was formed. The original members had undoubtedly built a very fine stadium in those days for the club, and it is questionable whether the club could have survived had this not been done. Indeed, we must come to the conclusion that the club in its present form had over the years done more in the field of charity that it could have done had it remained in its original state.'*

In his foreword to Handley's book – and probably with the same controversy in mind – Kelly observed saltily: 'It was a great handicap to him that many vital records and books were lost in the fire which razed the old pavilion. Dr Handley had to rely on newspaper reports for much of his material, and as we well know writers then, as now, could be something less than neutral.'

That, in summary, was the case for the defence, and the general caution which Kelly offered should be respected. The arguments in favour of creating a limited liability company were not necessarily based on personal avarice, and the problems inherent in running a large organisation on strictly club lines were bound to increase as time went on. Willie Maley, writing in 1939, recalled the controversy in quite straightforward terms:

*'Various schemes were tried to put the club on a sound business footing, but each year saw the best efforts of the real managers of the club thwarted by the change of new men, who had neither the knowledge nor the time to keep the club up to standard, being elected to the committee.... The matter came to a head when at a special meeting called in 1896 to consider the club's financial position, the 'Heads' stated distinctly that the club must be put on a sound footing or else close down... Thereafter the men who actually made our club proceeded to put it on a real business footing. They felt the club must expand and the only way to do so was by making it a limited company, and so Celtic became such with a capital of £10,000. The old members had all the liabilities wiped out and each received £1 Founders share, which has since been added to by another share with 10s paid on same out of profits.'*

Put that way, it all sounded business-like and reasonable, a far cry from talk of 'a bitter struggle against the honest element among the team's supporters'. The two interpretations of events are as far apart today as they were in the 1890s, but there can surely be no doubt that Celtic would not have continued indefinitely both as highly successful competitors on the football field and as an organisation run by committee. There is certainly no other example of such a combination having flourished.

The change to full professionalism and the expenditure on the new ground had put Celtic into debt, and this required guarantors. The first motion to form a limited liability company was put forward in 1893. It was in the name of the committee which had voted 11-4 in favour of it, but the membership threw it out by 86 votes to 31. The motion was proposed by Joseph Shaughnessy and seconded by J. H McLaughlin. The main speaker against was Arthur Murphy – 'the Keir Hardie of the Celtic' as one newspaper described him, and a leading figure in Home Rule politics – evidence that the 'club v. company' dispute cut across previous alliances.

In the months that followed, the bickering intensified. Some of the committee's critics deplored the absence of charitable donations and, at the 1894 annual meeting, put forward a motion 'that no member of the committee, either ordinary or ex officio, shall, on and after this meeting, do any work for the Celtic club, directly or indirectly, receive payment for such work'. This move was defeated, but it reflected both the suspicions that existed and the gulf that separated the rival interpretations of the club's purposes. The *Glasgow Observer* – strongly pro-temperance and still distinctly agnostic towards Celtic – complained in August 1894:

> *The thing is a mere business, in the hands of publicans and others. Catholic charities get nothing out of the thousands of pounds passing through the treasurer's hands. Can we not get a club that will carry out the original idea of Brother Walfrid? The income of the Celtic club is drawn largely from our own people.'*

The row flared again when changes in the club constitution were put forward by McLaughlin. One of these would have made members liable for sums determined by the committee, to meet the club's debts. This was widely interpreted as a move towards shedding the club's less well-off members, and was heavily defeated.McLaughlin wrote: 'Not a single argument worthy of the name was brought to bear against the proposition... I had the misfortune to be sponsor for the rules as a whole, and this one in particular, and had to bear the brunt of the flapdoodle it provoked... and just to put a fitting climax on the absurdity, another commenced to talk of charity. Imagine a club with £1,500 of debt on its head asked to consider what it is going to give to charity.'

The limited company issue remained prominent, and the committee again recommended the change at the half-yearly meeting in December 1895. Tom Maley objected to such an issue being raised at a half-yearly meeting, and suggested an extraordinary meeting to debate it. This obstruction further irritated the leading lights on the committee, and was overruled. Shaughnessy said that the question of limited liability must be considered because of the club's financial responsibilities. McLaughlin threw in the information that there was a sum of £500 hanging on the settlement of the question – the Scottish Cyclists' Union had offered this amount for the use of Celtic Park for three days in 1897, subject to the cycle track being brought up to international standards. The committee had taken the view that this investment could not be carried through without the safeguard of limited liability. But scepticism among the membership again triumphed, and the suggestion that a committee should be set up to examine the pros and cons of limited liability was again thrown out by a large majority. Most members of the committee were determined, however, to press ahead with improvements to the ground – and that fact alone guaranteed that the question of limited liability would remain firmly on the agenda.

When it had been established that it would cost £900 to make the alterations necessary to the track and banking, to meet the requirements of the Scottish Cyclists' Union event, the committee summoned a special general meeting to discuss the club's future constitutional status. On February 25, 1897, about a hundred members of the club attended a meeting in St Mary's Hall, presided over by John Glass. They were told that the committee was not prepared to incur further personal liability to meet the balance of the outlay. Faced with the ultimatum that the track improvements would not go ahead on the basis of the club's existing status, this meeting finally agreed to the formation of a committee to draw up a plan for submission to a special general meeting. This was done with remarkable rapidity, and – at the same venue which had played such a significant part in the club's inception – approval was given on March 4 to the formation of a limited company. Each club member would have a fully paid-up share, carrying a vote, but otherwise only each block of ten shares would carry a vote. The seventh article of association – dismissed by Handley as 'a sop to the simple' – decreed that 'after paying a five per cent annual dividend, the directors shall have power to give for such charities as they may select such sum or sums as they may think proper'.

The first directors of the new company were Michael Dunbar, John Glass, James Grant, James Kelly, John McKillop, John H. McLaughlin and John O'Hara. To an extraordinary extent, their election – based almost wholly on their willingness and ability to subscribe to the first share allocation – determined the future pattern of control over the club for almost a century thereafter. The immediate effect of the changed commercial status was dynamic. Before the end of 1897, when the ten-year lease was half completed, the club bought the freehold of the ground from the landlord, Sir William Hozier. To support this enterprise, the issued share capital was increased by £5,000, exclusively among existing shareholders, and the ground capacity was increased to around 70,000 in the hope of attracting further international matches.

One of the directors, James Grant, was permitted in 1898 to erect football's first double-decker stand as a private enterprise. Advertised as providing 'comfortable chair accommodation with entire freedom from all atmospheric inconveniences being covered and protected on all sides by windows', it proved unpopular due to the long climb and the fact that the windows tended to steam up during games. Grant eventually sold it to the club for a small sum, having lost all his initial investment. Willie Maley later reflected:

*'From the changeover to limited liability position in 1898 (sic), the club gradually settled into a real business state, and much good work was done in making Celtic Park one of the best grounds in the country. It was a beautiful sight when on a big match or sports day, a huge crowd filled up what was then the last word in terracings. The coloured cement cycling track set off the whole field and the huge Grant Stand added to the 'tout ensemble'. Celtic at that time had a great opportunity of crowding out all opposition, if they had had the foresight to see what the game was coming to. They had then the chance of taking in all the ground right down to London Road, where the big school is now, and if that had been done the present ground could have run north to south, with room for terracings equal to Hampden of today.'*

With three League titles in 1893/94, '95/96 and '97/98, the team's playing record remained impressive throughout this troubled period, though the Scottish Cup, still the most prestigious honour, proved elusive. Celtic's worst result in their early history was probably the 4-2 defeat at the hands of lowly Arthurlie at Barrhead in the first round of the 1896/97 competition. The loss of the League title that season was attributed by Willie Maley to the second strike in the club's short history. This resulted from the sensitivity of some players in the face of adverse press comment.

*'Three of our players, Battles, Meehan and Divers, as a protest against the unfair, even brutal, criticism of a certain section of the press, refused to turn out against Hibernian at Parkhead unless the representatives of the offending paper were ejected from the press box. To this the management could not contest, although they had considerable sympathy with the malcontents, and promised to make representation in the proper quarters. The players, however, were adamant in their decision and after some delay, although I had given up the game, I turned out along with Barney Crossan, while a message was hurriedly dispatched to Hampden Park for Tommy Dunbar who was playing there for the second eleven, and he arrived long after the game had started.'*

Maley continued his account of this episode with that air of certainty which characterised his explanations for every adversity encountered by Celtic: *'The result was a draw, and those of the remaining matches were not in keeping with our previous returns – the affair costing us the Championship, as the players were naturally suspended and the playing strength suffered in consequence.'*

After three seasons in which Celtic's Scottish Cup run had not extended to more than two rounds, the 1898/99 competition took the Cup back to Celtic Park after an unaccustomed lapse of seven years. The quarter-final tie with Queen's Park was abandoned due to fading light with Celtic leading 4-2, but the replay was won 2-1. They went on to win a 4-2 semi-final victory over Port Glasgow, which took them through to a final with Rangers. The players, who won 2-0 at Hampden and thus qualified for a handsome £20 bonus, were: McArthur,

Welford and Storrier; Battles, Marshall and King; Hodge and Campbell; Divers, McMahon and Bell. McMahon and Hodge scored the winning goals. The *Glasgow Herald* published a highly complimentary report of the match.

> *'The feature of the game was the grand play of the Celtic half-backs and the utter incapacity of the Rangers forwards. It was the best-behaved and most orderly concourse of spectators of recent times. There were 25,000 and even at that number there was not the slightest indication of overcrowding at any part of the enclosure. When the increased rate of admission is considered, the attendance is a high testimonial to the drawing powers of the clubs engaged.'*

As the bells chimed in the year 1900, Celtic could look back on an extraordinarily progressive first twelve years. They had won the Scottish Cup twice (and were on their way to a third success). The club had been instrumental in forming the Scottish League, which it had then won four times in nine seasons. In days when the Glasgow cup competitions were of some standing, they had won these four and six times respectively. They had a stadium second to none, the largest support in Britain and a far-flung reputation to match. The attacking style of play, which has stayed with them throughout their history, was already a Celtic hallmark.

Another great Celtic tradition, that of rearing the club's own talent, was in the making. This, wrote Maley, was in preference to the first decade's tendency towards 'gathering in men from all over the country and from England, many of whom had been in the game for a considerable time'. As in future periods of team-building, 'it was not to be expected that success would immediately follow, as it took several years to blend the youngsters satisfactorily'.

Any other club would have bowed out of the century gracefully, satisfied with its accomplishments. Characteristically, however, Celtic were in the middle of a thoroughgoing Irish row in the last days of 1899. The villain of the piece, in the eyes of many Celtic followers, was the club's chairman, J. H. McLaughlin, a brusque man who was almost unique among its leading figures in having no apparent involvement in Irish politics. As one letter-writer to the *Glasgow Examiner* put it: 'He has been conspicuous by his absence, personally, spiritually and otherwise, from the contaminating effects of membership of any Irish national organisation having for its objects the attainment of the national aspirations of the people of Ireland.' His footballing interest had developed in the direction of how the game was administered, and the sensibilities of his own club's supporters were not among the foremost of his concerns.

When the subject of the Boer War came up at a meeting of the SFA, of which he was president, McLaughlin went out of his way to speak in support of a hundred-guinea donation to a 'patriotic fund' for the families of those fighting in South Africa. He denounced opposition to the war as being the prerogative of 'demented Irish politicians who do not represent five per cent of the population of Ireland'. All hell broke loose in the columns of Glasgow's Irish and Catholic press. In the midst of the uproar, the Scottish League presented McLaughlin with a 'magnificent diamond ring' for services rendered, and the president congratulated him on having 'spoken like a true British citizen'.

This sealed McLaughlin's fate in the court of public opinion. For most Irishmen, the Boer War was being fought against British imperialism – the curse that also afflicted Ireland. In the same week that the newspapers reported McLaughlin's outburst, John Glass was seconding the vote of thanks to an Irish MP who declared that 'the hearts of the people of Ireland go out to the people of the two South African republics who

44

are fighting for their independence, and whom England has forced into war in order to destroy their liberties, just as they did in Ireland in 1798.'

There were widespread calls for McLaughlin's removal from the Celtic chairmanship. Scottish branches of the Home Rule organisations passed resolutions of condemnation, as did the United Celtic Brake Clubs, who resolved that McLaughlin would never be given a place of honour in the association. The mood was summed up by a letter to the *Glasgow Observer* of December 30, 1899, asking if the 'silence on the part of the Celtic Ltd means approval of the denunciation of Messrs John Dillon and Michael Davitt, which would have come more fittingly from a member of any Orange Lodge than from a director of a club which lives on the money of its Irish supporters'. The writer continued: 'With such a politician at the head of its affairs, it is a small wonder that there had been a mournful slump in the Celtic enthusiasm and a corresponding ebb in Celtic gates.' Not for the first or last time, there was excited talk of forming a rival Celtic club.

Personal feelings must have been intense within the club itself, since men such as Glass, John McKillop, and, indeed, James Kelly had a very public identification with precisely those 'demented Irish politicians' referred to by McLaughlin. But the calls for his removal were to no effect, and he remained the chairman until the time of his death in 1909. Willie Maley, forty years later wrote that McLaughlin 'never held power such as did John Glass, and never was the aid to the club the cheery East End joiner was all his days'. When McLaughlin – a publican in Lanarkshire – died, there were none of the normal glowing obituaries in the Catholic press, though fastidious Tom Maley did pay tribute to his legislative contribution.

By the turn of the century, the legendary rivalry between Rangers and Celtic was well-established. Rangers had been around a lot longer – since 1872, in fact – but it was with their move to a permanent home in Govan in 1887 that the way was clear for them to build mass support. With the advent of Celtic on the other side of the city, with very distinctive origins and a natural support base, the formula for rivalry clearly existed. The clubs could meet as often as ten or twelve times in a season during the 1890s, and there were invariably good gates. Rivalry was strong, but relationships cordial, as epitomised by the fact that when a benefit match was played for the early Celtic great, Sandy McMahon, in September 1899, Rangers provided the opposition. 'In the directors' room, Mr J. McIntyre, Rangers, eulogised the worthy Celt to such an extent that there was nothing for it but to reply…'

But the seeds of future problems were being sown at the same time in Belfast, which had also acquired a 'Celtic' football club in 1896. Also in September 1899, readers of the *Glasgow Examiner* learned of 'outrageous attacks' on Catholics following a Belfast Celtic-Cliftonville game. 'The rowdies sang snatches of Orange party songs, interspersed with staves of *Rule Britannia*.' Sadly, football's potential as a vehicle for sectarian hooliganism had already begun to be realised, and was soon to be imported to Glasgow.

# FIVE

## A TASTE OF SUCCESS:
## THE SIX-IN-A-ROW SIDE

AMONG THE CROWDS who gathered at Glasgow Cross to welcome the year 1900, 'the almost universal topic of discussion was the war in South Africa, although the disputed problem as to the beginning of the new century also formed the subject of conversation'. From Celtic's point of view, it is convenient to regard January 1, 1900 as the first day of the twentieth century, since on that basis a most auspicious start was made to it, with a 3-2 victory over Rangers. The team that day was: McArthur, Davidson and Turnbull; Russell, Marshall and Orr; Bell, Somers; Divers, McMahon and Campbell. It was the age of the steamship, and the advertising columns offered an exotic array of destinations, at relatively modest cost, from the great port of Glasgow. Of more immediate interest to Celtic supporters than the option of sailing to Shanghai or the River Plate, however, might have been the advent of 'the magnificent new steamer, the Duke of Rothesay' on the Glasgow-Dublin service.

The *Glasgow Irish* newspapers continued to chronicle the progress towards constitutional change in Ireland and, as the Labour movement gathered strength, to reflect the historic debate about the compatibility of Catholicism and socialism.

More prosaically, their advertising columns reflected the fact that those members of the Irish community who went into business normally looked to the licensed trade. It was no off-chance that six of the seven founding Celtic directors had gravitated in that direction.

The early years of the century's first decade were trying ones for the Celtic supporters. In 1900, the Scottish Cup was won for the second successive season, with a 4-3 victory over Queen's Park in the final. This was to be the amateur club's last appearance at that stage of the competition. Celtic then contested six finals – two in each of the Scottish, Glasgow and Glasgow Charity Cups – before returning to their winning ways with the Charity Cup in 1903. The most noteworthy of these unsuccessful ventures was the 1901/02 Glasgow Cup final against Rangers, which was played at Ibrox and finished in a draw. Celtic held that the replay should be at Celtic Park, and when the Glasgow Association ruled against them, withdrew from the replay.

This was only one of a number of episodes around this time which laid the foundations for frosty relationships between the two clubs. Rangers, who had followed Celtic in becoming a limited company, had invested heavily in developing Ibrox and in 1902 the SFA preferred that ground to Celtic Park as venue for the international match against England. Tragically, this led to disaster when part of the terracing collapsed and twenty-six spectators were killed. That year's Charity Cup competition was subsequently opened up to Edinburgh teams, to boost the Ibrox Disaster Fund, and Hibs beat Celtic in the final.

In another fund-raising event, which came to be regarded as the British Championship, Rangers offered for competition the Exhibition Cup which they had won in the previous year. Celtic defeated Sunderland, thus qualifying to meet Rangers, who had overcome Everton. In the final at Cathkin on June 17, 1902, the teams drew 1-1. They met again two evenings later and, in the final minute of extra time, Celtic scored to make the trophy their own. It is, to this day, one of the finest exhibits in the trophy room.

In the normal competitions, success did not come immediately, but Willie Maley was building one of the greatest Celtic teams of all time, as the imported players of the 1890s phased out. Jimmy Quinn – destined to become one of Celtic's 'immortals' – was signed from Smithston Albion in 1901. Rutherglen Glencairn supplied Jimmy McMenemy, whose connection with the club was to span forty years, and Alec Bennett. Davy Adams, a junior international goalkeeper, came to Celtic Park from Dunipace. The juniors had become Celtic's main breeding ground, while from senior ranks 'Sunny Jim' Young, who had experience with Bristol Rovers, was signed from Kilmarnock, and Peter Somers returned from Blackburn Rovers – both modest acquisitions. It was at this time that the Celtic tradition of not seeking to buy success was inaugurated. However, in the 1902/03 season, the club suffered its worst record since its inception – nineteen games won, twenty-two lost and fourteen drawn. This was the slump before the storm.

For the 1903/04 season, Celtic adopted a new strip of green and white hoops in place of the previous vertical stripes. The major honours drought was ended in 1904, when Celtic beat Rangers 3-2 in the Scottish Cup final at the new Hampden Park before 65,000 spectators. The team that day was Adams, MacLeod, Orr, Young, Loney, Hay, Muir, McMenemy, Quinn, Somers and Hamilton. Two goals down at half-time, Celtic won through a hat-trick from Jimmy Quinn. By this time, Maley was able to conclude that 'the team is now a splendid blend of youth and experience'. In the final League match of the season, against Kilmarnock a week later, Quinn scored five of Celtic's six goals. Alec Bennett had not been available for the Scottish Cup final but replaced Muir on the right wing for the Charity Cup final on May 6, 1904, also against Rangers. Arguably the most famous Celtic team of the club's first half-century, therefore, lined up for the first time on that occasion: Adams, MacLeod and Orr; Young, Loney and Hay; Bennett, McMenemy, Quinn, Somers and Hamilton. Quinn was injured early on, and Celtic's ten men lost 3-2. But the way was now well paved for Celtic's 'six-in-a-row'. Maley considered that Young, Loney and Hay 'will go down to history as one of the most perfect half-back lines of all time, both for vigour and science'. The attack 'was a treat to watch in their sinuous movements and deadly attacks'.

On the evening of May 9, 1904, the 3,500-seater north stand at Celtic Park was destroyed by fire. The *Glasgow Observer* reported: 'After a brief but savagely furious conflagration, the splendid stand and the palatial pavilion were reduced to cinders.' The cost of the damage was put at £6,000, and Celtic were under-insured. But such was the security of the club's financial position by this time that no great hardship was suffered. The incident caused the club to purchase the Grant Stand, which had previously been owned privately by a director. Before the start of the new season, Willie Maley had secured the signature of Alex McNair from Stenhousemuir, who for the next twenty years was to give sterling service to Celtic, mainly as a full-back. The intensity of rivalry between Celtic and Rangers was, by this time, reaching the point of unhealthiness. The cynics noted that this was good for business, and even the *Glasgow Observer*'s 'Man in the Know' gave the impression of slight weariness with the frequency of meetings. 'In Glasgow, the rivalry of the Celtic and Rangers is responsible for a vast amount of interest, and if these teams met every day in the week for months it is not quite certain that the public would totally ignore any one of the games.'

The semi-final of the Scottish Cup, when the sides met yet again, provided one of the incidents which were to enter folklore where they could serve only to reinforce prejudice and encourage paranoia. Celtic were already down to ten men when Jimmy Quinn, one of the Celtic players most revered by the supporters, was ordered off for allegedly kicking Alex Craig of Rangers. A section of the Celtic support invaded the pitch, and the game was abandoned, with J. H. McLaughlin of Celtic promptly renouncing any right to a replay. But the matter did not end there. Several newspapers made savage criticism of Quinn and Celtic. The *Glasgow Observer* hit back at 'the ruffianly shrieking of a bigoted section of the anti-Irish press' and complained that 'as Quinn retired' one of his opponents had observed: 'Serves you right, you Papish...' Quinn denied that any kick had been involved, and Craig confirmed this. The affair ended up in court, with Quinn suing a newspaper which had reported him as having 'savagely kicked' Craig in the face. Quinn won the somewhat Pyrrhic victory of a shilling in damages – the sheriff found that he had stamped on Craig but not kicked him deliberately. It was a minor sensation in its day, but it was the kind of episode which poisoned relations between supporters of the clubs, rather than the clubs themselves – Craig and his mother both gave evidence for Quinn. More than sixty years later, Robert Kelly devoted a whole chapter of his book to the affair.

A more poignant example of how mass interest in football and footballers had developed was given in February 1905, when Barney Battles died at the age of thirty-two. By then a Kilmarnock player, Battles had been an heroic defender for Celtic and was one of the players involved in the strike over hostile press comment. It was reported that 40,000 people lined the route to Dalbeth Cemetery in Glasgow's East End, to pay tribute to him.

Celtic won the League in 1904/05 by the narrowest of margins. They finished level on points with Rangers after twenty-six games and, fortunately, neither goal average nor goal difference applied in those days. A play-off was held at Hampden, and Celtic won 2-1 – the first of six successive League titles. Their league record over these seasons was as shown in the table.

| Season | P | W | D | L | F | A | Pts |
|--------|-----|-----|-----|-----|-----|-----|-----|
| 1904/05 | 26 | 18 | 5 | 3 | 68 | 31 | 41 |
| 1905/06 | 30 | 24 | 1 | 5 | 76 | 19 | 49 |
| 1906/07 | 34 | 23 | 9 | 2 | 80 | 30 | 55 |
| 1907/08 | 34 | 24 | 7 | 3 | 86 | 27 | 55 |
| 1908/09 | 34 | 23 | 5 | 6 | 71 | 24 | 51 |
| 1909/10 | 34 | 24 | 6 | 4 | 63 | 22 | 54 |
| **Totals** | **192** | **136** | **33** | **23** | **444** | **153** | **305** |

In the course of this remarkable title-winning run, which the Scottish League marked by striking a special shield bearing the names of all the players who had participated in the Championship successes, Celtic also won the Scottish Cup in 1906/07 and 1907/08, the Glasgow Cup in five of the six seasons, and the Glasgow Charity Cup in two. The team which brought this great run of honours to Celtic Park had cost less than £200 to assemble, Willie Maley proudly affirmed. He wrote of these six great League-winning seasons:

> *'Only once during that period did we fail to gain an additional honour – in 1908/09 – when after a drawn battle with Rangers in the final, the Cup was withheld following the regrettable Hampden riot. I mention this in order to show that our players not only proved their consistency in the League competition but in others also, and it will ever stand as a memento to the judgment and foresight of the management that the number of*

*players included in the teams of that wonderful six seasons was comparatively small.'*

The 1909 Cup final riot resulted from the old, vexed question of whether finals and replays should be pursued to a conclusion rather than strain the pockets of the paying public. Celtic and Rangers drew 2-2 in the first game and then 1-1 in the replay. The SFA rules said that there should be no extra-time, and that a decision should be left to a third game. However, there had been some press speculation about the clubs agreeing to go into extra-time in the event of the second replay finishing level. The rules did not permit this, but expectations had been aroused. Even some of the players seemed to expect extra-time. When it became clear that this was not to be, hundreds of people spilled on to the park, lit a bonfire, fought with police and generally created the worst scenes so far experienced by the Scottish game. The *Glasgow Herald* thundered: 'Never in the memory of even the oldest inhabitant of the football world have scenes like Saturday's been witnessed. There have been outbreaks from time to time, but for downright malevolent, cowardly and brutal conduct, Saturday's display, one is glad to think, has no parallel.'

The directors of Celtic and Rangers met promptly and issued a joint statement: 'Although it was mooted during the week that extra time might be played in the event of a draw, it was found that the Cup competition rules prevented this. On account of the regrettable occurrences of Saturday, both clubs agree to petition the Association that the final tie be abandoned.'

The SFA council accepted this course of action by a vote of 15 to 11. The motion passed was: 'That to mark the Association's disapproval of the riotous conduct of a section of the spectators at Hampden Park, and to avoid a repetition, the Cup competition for this season be finished and the cup and medals be withheld'. Maley described it as 'the most unsatisfactory competition in the history of the Scottish Cup'.

The break-up of the great Celtic side began in 1908 with the transfer of Alec Bennett to Rangers. Ironically, his place was taken initially by Willie Kivlichan, who had earlier been transferred by the Ibrox club to Celtic. Kivlichan, a native of Galashiels, was one of the handful of Catholics to be ever signed by Rangers. He later became a police surgeon in Glasgow and, for a time, Celtic club doctor. Several careers then began to tail off simultaneously, and by the 1910/11 season the whole transition process was under way. Peter Somers moved to Hamilton after thirteen seasons at Celtic Park. Jimmy Hay was transferred to Newcastle. Orr retired, and the great Jimmy Quinn's best days were behind him. In his lyrical account of the six-in-a-row side's qualities, Willie Maley chose to concentrate on two of his charges from this great Celtic era. He described 'Sunny Jim' Young as:

*'...the greatest clubman of them all. Jamie would play night or day, in sunshine or rain, and never spared himself. He was a source of inspiration to the rest of the team and never ceased to urge them on to greater effort. He was a man and a half in any team, and his place has never been filled since that fatal day he twisted his knee at Paisley and had to give up the game, to die tragically through a motor-cycle accident a few years later at Hurlford.'*

Maley was equally lyrical on the subject of Jimmy Quinn, the quiet pipe-smoking miner from Croy.

*'The picture of Quinn set for goal with his sturdy well-knit frame in the perfect condition he always kept himself in, and striving all the way to keep the ball in control as he charged*

*off attacking defenders, was a sight never to be forgotten, and when to crown all, the finishing effort of a cannon-ball shot came from him, he would be a very cold-blooded enthusiast who could refrain from cheering the sturdy collier laddie whom I signed for £2 a week in the row where he was reared.'*

Celtic did not at that time operate a reserve side, but the rebuilding process was carried out with a speed and efficiency which once again reflected favourably upon Maley's skills. He recalled: 'Towards the end of our record run Joe Dodds, Peter Johnstone, Andy McAtee, John Brown, Tom McGregor and John Mulrooney had been discovered and were by this time able to take their place in the team. And, in November 1911, a slip of a lad, who was afterwards to carve a niche in the history of the game, was signed, and forced his way almost immediately into the League side. I refer to 'Patsy' Gallacher.'

For many of the generation which watched him, Patsy Gallacher was the greatest player of them all. Signed from Clydebank Juniors, this frail lad soon revealed himself as an inspired inside-forward – fast and skilful on the ball, he could also pass superbly and score extraordinary goals.

'Gallacher is a marvel,' wrote one observer. 'He has no stamina to make a song about, but he takes risks that many a bigger and heavier man would not think of, and the marvel is that he comes out of it scatheless.' James Handley recalled him as 'a shrimp of a man, whose frolics on the field were the wonder of the football world'. Around him the team could be rebuilt, and in the period prior to the outbreak of the First World War this was accomplished with near-complete success. They won the Scottish Cup in three seasons out of four from 1910/11 until the outbreak of war. In 1913/14 they achieved the League and Cup double for the first time since 1907/08.

But the tragedy of war and the slaughter of a young generation now intervened.

To mark Willie Maley's silver jubilee with the club – as player, secretary and manager – Celtic gifted him three hundred guineas at a celebration in June 1913. With Celtic on the crest of a wave, the tributes to Maley's twenty-five-year reign were ecstatic. One admirer wrote in the *Glasgow Observer*: 'What price Mr William Maley of the Celtic FC as our greatest living Scotsman?' The scribe explained: 'Mr Maley seems somehow to possess the knack of 'roping in' players rich in those vital qualities of ardour, aggressiveness and resolution. He catches them young and breathes into them the old traditional Celtic fire, of which he himself appears to be the very living fountain and source... Yes, a great man is William Maley, Prince of Team Managers and Discoverer of Quinn, McMenemy, Hay, McNair, Gallacher and all the other 'gems of purest ray serene' – not forgetting the one and only 'Sunny Jim', the truest Celt of the lot.' The season 1913/14 was a marvellous one for Celtic and their supporters. Patsy Gallacher was the sensation of Scottish football and, in an age when poetry and football went hand-in-hand, amateur bards vied with one another to pay adequate tribute to Peerless Patsy. This was one of the better efforts:

*You're a funny little nipper, oft I've watched you wriggling through, Even Sunny Jim, our skipper, never caused a laugh like you. Though in size you're not imposing, it's miraculous what you do. So, dear Patrick, just in closing, here's my heart and hand to you.*

The New Year's Day game against Rangers was won 4-0. The football writers praised Celtic's 'iron-clad defence' as they put together a run of twenty-three games without defeat, during which fifty-two goals were scored and only two conceded. After a goalless draw with Hibs, the Scottish Cup was won 4-1 at Ibrox in the replay. The team was: Shaw, McNair and Dodds; Young, Johnstone and McMaster; McAtee and Gallacher; McColl, McMenemy and Browning.

The League title was also won in that season, after a three-year break, and Celtic set off on a European tour in the finest of fettles, little knowing that the dark days of war would soon be upon the continent. For good measure, the major political aspiration of many Celtic supporters appeared to be on the verge of fulfilment, through Asquith's Home Rule Bill. With Belfast Celtic due to play a friendly match in Glasgow in March 1914, the Glasgow Observer was concerned that the football crowd should pay due attention to the performance of the Rory Oge Pipe Band.

> *'Apart from the interest taken in the rival Celtic clubs, the pipers are well worth seeing and now that Home Rule is practically certain, sympathisers with the old country should take the opportunity of seeing the national dress and listening to the music of Ireland as a nation, for what our dear isle once was, it will become again.'*

Along with much else, this prediction was promptly overtaken by war. The 1914 annual general meeting of shareholders was a happy occasion. One observer wrote: 'I never remember such an enthusiastic meeting of the club, and the harmony was in marked contrast to the brave days of old . . .' Fourteen Celtic players, accompanied by directors Kelly, Dunbar and McKillop, 'with Mr Maley as guide, philosopher and friend', set off on the adventurous journey into Central Europe. The *Glasgow Observer*'s 'Man in the Know' accompanied the party, and was able to report that, after the stately twenty-seven-hour journey across mainland Europe, the first sight-seeing call in Budapest was to 'the great church of St Stephen's dating from the 12th century... of the 48,000,000 people [in Austro-Hungary], fully 80 per cent are Catholic and proud of it'. Celtic won their first game against local opposition, allowing 25,000 spectators to see 'the real football, for once'.

By the following week, even 'Man in the Know' had forgotten twelfth-century cathedrals and reassuring statistics on the state of Austro-Hungarian Catholicism. 'Wild Scenes – Players at Loggerheads' was the headline on his report of a game against Burnley in Budapest, to raise money for the unemployed, which ended in an undignified draw. Celtic travelled home early in June, via Vienna, Berlin and Leipzig. 'Man in the Know' assured the faithful at home: 'Of course, the players enjoyed themselves to the full during their three weeks out, but always in a rational manner, and it was a case of early to bed when a game was due next day.'

# SIX

## THE GREAT WAR:
## HOSTILITIES AT HOME AND AWAY

YEARS OF WAR cannot be accepted as normal periods in the organisation of football, or of anything else. The call to arms takes young men away from their homes and careers. Diversions and entertainments must carry on, but are inevitably relegated in significance and acquire a makeshift quality. An air of unreality develops, as reports of incidents on the football field jostle for newspaper space with accounts of battles which cost tens of thousands of lives. The First World War, it was fondly believed by British public opinion, would all be over by Christmas. The irrepressible 'Man in the Know' reflected a mood of detached interest in this minor skirmish when he wrote: 'None will follow the fortunes of the present war with greater keenness than the Celtic players and officials, for few saw more of the various combatants than those who made the last two trips to Austro-Hungary and Germany.' At Mass in Prague, 'the German soldiers struck us as well set-up, well-behaved young fellows, many of them showing by their manners that they have come from good families'.

Most Celtic supporters were, in these early days of war, at least as interested in the news that was coming out of Ireland, where Sir Edward Carson was engaged in playing 'the Orange card' against the prospect of Home Rule. Life went on quite normally at first, and Celtic held their two-day sports event as usual – though for the first time there were no cycling events, as the cycle track had been removed in order to increase spectator accommodation. Willie Maley nostalgically recalled the era which had brought the World Championships to Celtic Park: 'The public went simply mad on the sport around the end of the last century and the beginning of the present... we old timers cannot help sighing as we recall the days when Celtic sports, with a galaxy of champions – track, field and cycling – were events anticipated and enjoyed as the greatest of the year.'

Military recruitment at football grounds, including Celtic Park, became a regular feature, prompting the 'Man in the Know' to comment: 'There will come very little out of this football ground recruiting. The only fellows likely to fall in there are those who are disgusted at their club's non-success. Instead of going home and beating their wives because their team lost, they will now set about beating the Germans for spite.'

Half-time announcements urging potential recruits to 'join up before the fun's over' were broadcast at Celtic Park, and there were recruiting events at the ground. This was symptomatic of the fact that the Irish community, under guidance from the Scottish hierarchy, adopted a much more 'British' attitude towards the First World War than had ever previously been the case. British reaction to the Easter Rising of 1916, and the impact of the unanticipated slaughter in the war itself, would however, soon cause many loyalties to be reconsidered.

Celtic opened the 1914/15 season by beating Burnley 2-1 in the return match following the angry encounter in Budapest. But there was by then considerable public debate about whether or not football and other public entertainments should continue at all for the duration of what, it was beginning to be recognised, would be a long and bloody war.

The argument against carrying on was that the incentive for young men to sign up for the trenches would be enhanced if there were no counter- attractions at home. Indeed, in the first year of the war, the Scottish and English FA agreed to abandon international matches, and the Scottish Cup was also scrapped after consultation with the Government.

But the more general argument against the continuation of professional football did not prevail. Players' wages were cut to ensure that they took their places in the factories. League matches were confined to Saturdays and holidays. When the team had to travel, no early release was available for players from workplaces. Willie Maley's account of the period states:

*'With all our regulars and a few new recruits to bring along, our prospects for 1914/15 were bright indeed, but as the season was on the point of beginning, the drums of war resounded throughout the land. A number of the lads answered the call immediately, although no one realised that it was going to last so long, and as time went on our ranks were depleted gradually. Still, the game went on – it was the expressed wish of the authorities – but those who remained at home did their bit in the factories and workshops that were so necessary for the service of the country. The other clubs were similarly affected, so that the competition was just as keen as before . . .'*

Celtic retained the League title in 1914/15, finishing six points ahead of Rangers and using only sixteen players in the course of the campaign. The normal team that season was: Shaw, McNair and Dodds; Young, Johnstone and McMaster; McAtee and Gallacher; McColl, McMenemy and Browning. Jimmy Quinn, now concluding his playing career after fourteen seasons of the highest distinction, turned out six times in the course of 1914/15 and young men came to gaze upon the near-legendary figure. The Glasgow writer Colm Brogan recalled the character of Quinn many years later:

*'Quinn was a quiet, rather shy man who played football because he loved it, and wanted to be left to live his private life alone. The partisan passions of his most devoted supporters did not please him at all, and he was strongly opposed to that excess of passion which interpreted a Celtic-Rangers match in terms of civil war. No man gave heavier punishment on the field and no man had heavier retaliation... The power of his spectacular attack sometimes blinded both friend and foe to the fact that nobody could challenge a whole team as he did without suffering. But he took his wounds, if not meekly, then without rancour. In the only true sense of an abused word, he was an amateur. He played the game because he loved it, he gave his whole heart to it and, if he had had another source of living, I fancy he would have played for nothing. But he was a miner (who had to return to the pits in his later days) and he never made more than a very modest living from a prowess that was unique, and a fame that was without parallel.'*

Off the field, James Kelly handed over the chairmanship during the first wartime season to Tom White, the lawyer who had joined the board in 1906 on the death of John Glass. There was speculation about backroom disputes, but Kelly insisted that he merely wanted to devote more time to his duties as parish councillor and school board member, as well as his business interests. White would now preside over the club's destinies for a record period of thirty-three years. On the death of director James Grant in Toomebridge in 1914, it was recorded: 'He never pretended to know much about the playing abilities of the boys, and took no great interest in the selection of the team, knowing that Messrs Kelly, Dunbar and Maley were able to deal with that sort of thing.' He had, however, bequeathed the Grandstand to the club and had superintended steady improvements to the ground over his years of service.

The annual report submitted to shareholders by Willie Maley on June 1, 1915 provides an interesting glimpse both of Celtic nostalgia and of attitudes in these troubled times. First, Maley reflected on the deaths which had occurred over the past year. Brother Walfrid had been 'the last of the leading founders of the Celtic club... He must have spent a considerable period near the Blarney Stone in his young days, as his persuasive powers once experienced could never be forgotten.' His work for Celtic had been 'a labour of love' and, until the time of his death, 'he remained as keen as ever to hear how his 'boys', as he termed the team, were doing'. James Grant and John McKillop, said Maley, had been 'of the old school' and had triumphed over 'the hardships of an Irishman's struggles for existence in this city forty years ago'.

Three hundred footballs had been sent out by Celtic to 'the men whom we all hope will bring us the victory in this awful war'. Director John Shaughnessy, with the rank of Lieutenant Colonel, 'has been honoured by the City of Glasgow with the command of the 18th Battalion Highland Light Infantry, and out of his command of 1,600 men you will be glad to know there are 500 of our Faith under his command'. Maley continued: 'Most of our players are working in Government employment, and three of the young ones in Cassidy, Gilhooly and O'Kane have joined the colours... The cruel war is still with us and God alone knows where it will all end.'

Once again, Celtic won the wartime League Championship in 1915/16, but Maley's recollection of this season indicates just how ad hoc the competition was.

*'Although we were often in sore straits to field a team, the*

*players, sometimes almost complete strangers to our regulars*
*but proud to wear our colours, with traditional enthusiasm,*
*upheld our reputation so well that another title was won,*
*with the loss of only eight points in 38 games.'*

The season ended with a rush of games, and a unique curiosity in the club's history arose on April 15, 1916 when they were forced to play two League games on the same day. With games limited to Saturdays and holidays, Celtic ran out of match days when snow forced a cancellation at Motherwell as late as March 25. Three weeks later they undertook the Saturday double. The team which lined up against Raith Rovers at Celtic Park at 3.15pm was: Shaw, McNair and McGregor; Young, Dodds and McMaster; McAtee, Gallacher, O'Kane, McMenemy and Browning. They polished off this task with ease, Patsy Gallacher scoring a hat-trick in the course of a 6-0 victory. The team then motored to Motherwell, where the game kicked off at 6pm. Trooper Joe Cassidy, home on leave, replaced the injured O'Kane and Celtic won this game 3-1. For good measure, in the course of the evening Celtic beat the record for the number of League goals in a season. Quite a day!

The only Celtic regular to miss that day's play was McColl, who was injured, but the *Glasgow Observer* reported that he was 'the happiest man in the Bank Restaurant where the boys met for a snack and a chat on Saturday night' – an indication that Willie Maley's establishment had, by that time, become a regular Celtic retreat. Celtic had by 1916 won the League title thirteen times – as often as all other clubs put together. Rangers had been successful on seven occasions, as well as tying with Dumbarton in the inaugural competition. Hearts had been champions twice, and Dumbarton, Third Lanark and Hibs once each.

Recruitment for war service continued to eat into Celtic's playing reserves, and the club had some difficulty in assembling a team for the following season. But they recruited several players from other clubs who were working in the Glasgow area. A fourth successive title was duly won, but a clean sweep of wartime flags was denied the next season when Rangers pipped them by a single point, beating Clyde on the last day of the season while Celtic could manage only a home draw with Motherwell. The Ibrox club had assembled an all-star line-up on wartime 'temporary transfers' from all over Britain – a policy which incensed their detractors. 'League Flag for Ibrox – Title Without Honour' opined the Glasgow Observer, going on to expand upon this theme: 'When the Scottish League clubs have to be fine-combed, English and Irish clubs asked for drafts to furnish an eleven that will hold its own with Celtic, that is the right way of showing the dread some people have of our fellows.'

There was consolation for Celtic in the shape of the War Fund Shield, yet another acquisition for the trophy room, which was secured with a victory over Morton at Hampden after the Greenock club had ousted Rangers in the semi-final. The state of relationships between the two major Glasgow clubs had declined sharply by this time, and a substantial number of Rangers supporters went along to cheer on Morton. 'Man in the Know's' reflections on this behaviour provide an interesting insight into how Celtic supporters – a category into which the *Glasgow Observer*'s correspondent most certainly fell – viewed the development of Scottish football rivalries at that stage. He wrote:

*'The present war is said to mean much regarding the future. The press is never tired telling us that we shall have to look upon things in a different light, that such things as wages, politics, social and economic life in general will have to undergo many changes . . . But after what we saw and heard at Hampden on Saturday, we may count one feature as to*

remain unchanged. Blind and unreasoning hostility to the Celtic team will continue; the anti-Celts will carry on pretty much as they have done for the last 30 years. New generations will arise; the old spirit will remain.

'I can remember when Rangers occupied a minor position in Scottish football; when the gates at Kinning Park and old Ibrox were very moderate. Queen's Park, Clyde, Thistle, Cowlairs, Northern, Partick, Pilgrims, Battlefield and Pollokshields Athletic all ranked higher in public esteem; the majority of them had better support than Rangers. Things are very different today. Rangers are the most popular team in the city, in the country – I might say in the world as far as Glasgow enthusiasts are concerned. The fact is undeniable, the explanation very simple.

'When the Celtic club began business in 1888, it immediately proceeded to make history – and enemies. For a time, Queen's Park, Third Lanark and Cowlairs managed to hold their own with the new club, and the two city clubs scored heavily in national and local cup ties. But gradually the Celts drew ahead, and took a clear lead in league and club football. None of the others had a look in, and after a time people began to get disgusted at seeing the Irish club getting the better of every opponent.

'Then Rangers got a good eleven together, won the league championship four times in succession and became first favourites. Those who had got tired of waiting to see Queen's Park, Cowlairs, Third Lanark and other clubs take it out on Celtic flocked down to Govan to cheer on the long-awaited and anxiously-expected conquerors of the Irishmen, and from that day to this Ibrox has become the Mecca of the anti-Celt.'

In the view of the *Glasgow Observer*'s correspondent – who must be regarded as the best available source of the official Celtic view from this era – the 'anti-Celt' category extended into the ranks of officials responsible for army recruitment, in these latter stages of the war. The inconsistent nature of the call-up selection process was the source of controversy and anger in the wider community, and the uneven impact on Scottish football clubs was a minor manifestation of this debate.

The feelings of 'Man in the Know' on this emotive subject spilled over when, during the summer of 1918, Jimmy McMenemy – one of whose brothers had been killed in the war, with another maimed – was notified of impending call-up for the trenches. 'There are several good reasons why a well-conducted chap like the Parkhead favourite should be left at home, at least until the streets and public works are cleared of the fit, the undesirables and unwilling currently masquerading as munition experts.' Players of other clubs who were on military service were 'to be seen in the city at the weekend, never having smelt powder or poison gas – and we have Peter Johnstone dead, John McMaster wounded, Dodds sent over after 11 weeks training, an entire Celtic eleven on the unsafe side of the Channel. I fear that kissing is not the only thing that goes by favour.' (Johnstone, the centre-half, had been killed in France in 1917.) In fact, the armistice came on November 11, without McMenemy having departed for the field of battle, though 'for a long time to come, Dodds and McAtee might do all their football on a barrack square somewhere in Germany, and both are badly wanted on the home front'.

Though many players were still in uniform, something approaching normality returned in the 1918/19 season and Celtic took their fifteenth Scottish League title. This time the single-point difference between them and Rangers was to Celtic's advantage, and the neck-and-neck position at this time exacerbated a rivalry that had already grown too bitter. Of the condition of the Celtic side at this time, Willie Maley wrote: 'It was only to be expected that following the conclusion of war a process of rebuilding would require to be faced, as those who had carried the flag during these four awful years could not fail to show the strain.' Once again, Celtic set about signing young players, and Tommy McInally, from St Anthony's, was one of future 'greats' who was recruited at this time.

In 1919 Jimmy McMenemy, a veteran of the six-in-a-row side from before the war, was finally transferred to Partick Thistle for the autumn of his career (where he promptly helped them to win the Scottish Cup against Rangers). James Handley wrote of the man known to a generation of Celtic supporters as 'Napoleon': 'McMenemy was a master of the deceptive movement. His facility for shaking off a cloud of opponents by one simple unexpected turn was unequalled. Nobody excelled him in the art of making an adversary look foolish. It was quite impossible to anticipate his moves...'

The last of the pre-war personalities to leave the club was the full-back McNair. We stay with James Handley for an assessment of that Celtic giant: 'He would have been the perfect subject for a 'time-and-motion' study if they had troubled about such things in those days. No footballer was his peer in the science of achieving the maximum result with the minimum of effort. The most dashing forward seemed to be mesmerised by his presence...'

Celtic had come through the war era, and were once more embarked on a youth policy which would take several years to come to fruition. But they left the appalling First World War years behind with their reputation as Scotland's leading club intact, while Maley's managership, particularly in the crucial matter of developing young talent, was recognised as the best in the land. With all the waste of human life at home, the war years had also given Celtic further opportunity to maintain their charitable traditions. It was recorded in the *Glasgow Observer* of May 26, 1917:

> 'As everyone knows, the Celtic club was founded for charity's sake, and that object has never been lost sight of. But everyone does not know that the Celts are always giving, that never a week passes without an appeal coming before the directors from some of our local orphanages or other deserving institutions. The club, founded 30 years ago to provide dinners for hungry little ones, still keeps up the good work; Smyllum, Nazareth House, St Joseph's Home have reason to know this. Broken men and jaded women know also that a Celtic 'line' has enabled them to get over a bad accident or long illness, and secure a new lease of life in one or other of our convalescent homes.'

In the pre-welfare state age, such generosity mattered much. As the First World War drew to a close, the attention of the Scottish Catholic community was diverted to the passage of the 1918 Education Act, which enshrined the position of Catholic schools within the state system. Section 18 of the Act allowed for the transfer of Catholic schools to the local education authorities, to be financed from the public purse. It was a vital development in determining the future identity and status of Scotland's Catholic minority. Inevitably, it was attacked by Protestant extremists as 'Rome on the Rates' and provided them with a convenient peg on which to hang their anti-Catholicism. But the rights won by the Catholic community in 1918 have been jealously safeguarded ever since.

A by-product of the schooling settlement was to ensure a reservoir of footballing talent upon which Celtic has had first call, while always also looking to other sources. It might be that the links between the Catholic Irish community and the club to which it gave birth would, in any case, have remained strong.

But the existence of denominational schools undoubtedly minimised the dilution in identity which might otherwise have occurred in the days when the vast majority of players came from within Scotland itself. The wider implications of the 1918 Act continue to be debated passionately. But it is worth remembering that the legislation was introduced as a response to Catholic fears, based on hard experience, of seeing their religious rights trampled underfoot by an unsympathetic majority. It was not responsible for creating the attitudes which had given rise to these fears.

# SEVEN

## THE TWENTIES:
## TAKING A BACK SEAT

THE 1920s ARE generally regarded as having been a period of rather modest achievement by Celtic, during which supremacy in Scottish football passed decisively, for the time being at least, to Rangers. That acknowledged, there were still three Scottish Cup triumphs to celebrate in 1923, 1925 and 1927. The League title was won in 1921/22 and 1925/26, but a gap of ten years was then to occur before the flag was again hoisted over Celtic Park. Clearly, the inter-war years did not match the almost continuous success which had characterised the club's development pre-1914. Perhaps this was inevitable, as the financial stakes had become higher and the competition accordingly fiercer.

There had been a change in regime at Ibrox, where the death by drowning of the manager, William Wilton, had led to the emergence of William Struth as his successor in 1920. Here was the iron disciplinarian who turned Rangers into a much more consistently effective playing force than they had previously been. Sadly, he also came to personify that club's adherence to the policies of religious sectarianism which have done so much to divide Scottish football and Scottish society. Rangers came to be regarded as a hard-nosed business concern, willing to invest in order to achieve success. Celtic preferred financial caution. Under Struth, Rangers also acquired the reputation which stayed with them for physical play. In October 1920, the *Glasgow Observer* complained:

> *'As kickers the Rangers' rearguard could vie with the most competent of Army mules; as tacticians they could give the Black-and-Tans a long start and a whacking. If there were to be any extension of the liberty taken by the Blue defence on Saturday, the Rangers might as well arm their men with hatchets.'*

In the seasons 1919/20 and 1920/21, Rangers won the League title, while Celtic had to make do with the modest consolation of carrying off the two Glasgow trophies in each season. However, things looked up in the 1921/22 season when Celtic won their sixteenth League title with the recognised team of: Shaw, McNair and Dodds; Gilchrist, Cringan and McMaster; McAtee, Gallacher, McInally, Cassidy and McLean. They played twenty-three successive League games without losing a goal, and dropped only two points at home. The title was won on the last day of the season, in dramatic fashion. With 23,000 packed into Cappielow Park and thousands more outside, Celtic secured the draw which they needed to win the title with only eight minutes remaining, McAtee being the scorer. But that team did not stay together. Joe Dodds, recognised as one of the finest left-backs in the club's history, dropped out of League football. The quixotic Tommy McInally was sent packing to Third Lanark early in the 1922/23 season, after the Celtic board had held his wage demands to be unreasonable.

There were serious long-term implications in the winding-up of the reserve team, also in 1922. On the credit side, youngsters were being signed who would take their places in time among the greatest players to wear the Celtic colours. Alec

Thomson was recruited from the Fife junior side Glencraig Celtic, and Jimmy McGrory, signed from St Roch's, made his Celtic first-team debut, as stand-in for Patsy Gallacher, against Third Lanark at Cathkin on January 20, 1923. McGrory, the great centre-forward from Garngad, who was to have over fifty years' involvement with Celtic, signed in the St Roch's chapel house after Bury had had him on trial – and rejected him.

That season Celtic finished third in the League, but won only nineteen of their thirty-eight games. They did, however, make amends by beating Hibernian in the final of the Scottish Cup. According to contemporary accounts, the forty-year-old McNair stood head and shoulders above the rest of the players. James Handley wrote lyrically:

> 'Like the veteran actor who summons to his aid all the dramatic skill and experience of a lifetime to give the greatest performance of his career on the eve of his retirement, Alec, realising probably that this was his last appearance in a Scottish Cup final, proceeded to illustrate, in the effortless way that was characteristic of his play, what perfect defensive work could look like.'

This was Celtic's tenth Scottish Cup success, equalling Queen's Park's record, but as far as the League title was concerned, Rangers were reigning supreme. They took the Championship three times in a row from 1922/23. Peter Wilson, from Barrmill in Ayrshire, was among those signed by Maley in time for the following season, which yielded only the Glasgow Charity Cup as the young, new-look team took time to settle. Small wonder, when one considers the following extraordinary story, as attributed to Wilson, who signed for Celtic when he was just seventeen:

> 'All I knew about Celtic was what I had read in the

newspapers. I had never seen them play. Indeed, I had never been out of Ayrshire in my life. After a match for Beith Amateurs a man with a raincoat over his arm asked me if I would like to play for Celtic. I grinned and said "Yes". He then produced a form, which I signed, and handed me £20. The money I took home to my mother. She wouldn't believe that anybody would give me such a big amount of cash for playing football, and put it in a vase on the mantelpiece, saying she would keep it there until somebody or other came along and claimed it. I wondered if she thought I had stolen the money.

'Anyway, several months went past until one day I received a postcard instructing me to report to the Bank Restaurant, Glasgow. That restaurant was run by Mr William Maley, manager of Celtic. I had never been in Glasgow before, and when I arrived at St Enoch Station I enquired of a policeman the way to the Bank Restaurant. He looked at the wee country laddie, and led me by the hand to the howff. I wasn't even wearing long trousers, but a suit of schoolboy knickerbockers.

'At the restaurant, I asked for Mr Maley, and met him for the first time. He eyed me up and down, and led me into a private room. "Better have some lunch", he said, and brusquely introduced me to the others at the table. I was meeting famous players whom I faintly recognised from their photos in the press. They made me welcome, and I tackled a bowl of soup.

'Half an hour later, I was on a bus. I didn't know where I was going. I was too shy to ask. The bus stopped at a football ground. I got out with the others and passed through the official entrance. While the rest of the players went into the dressing-room, I hung about the corridors. There I met a middle-aged man. "Where am I?" I queried. He looked at *me in a strange sort of way, concluded that I wasn't cheekily attempting to pull his leg, and answered "Fir Park". I was in Motherwell. I knew Celtic were to play Motherwell that day. A few minutes later, Mr Maley came along. "Come on, sonny," he said. "It's time you stripped", and led me to the dressing-room.*

*'I had brought my own boots with me. Nothing else, and was thrown pants, socks and jersey by the hamper-man. The jersey was several sizes too big for me, and the sleeves had to be sewn to make them nearer my arms' length. I felt like a laddie wearing a fully-grown man's suit.*

*'Mr Maley reappeared. "You're playing at right half, sonny," he intimated.*

*'"Motherwell have an outside-left called Ferrier. He has a good left foot. Possibly you've heard of him." Heard of Bob Ferrier! He was one of Scotland's star players, and I was opposed to him.'*

However, the following season brought the Scottish Cup back to Celtic Park, after a campaign of great character and incident, culminating in 'Patsy Gallacher's Final'. In the 5-1 defeat of Third Lanark at Cathkin in the first round of the cup, McGrory – by now revered by the fans as at last a man worthy to take on the mantle of Quinn – scored a hat-trick and 'Gallacher gave a brilliant performance in swerving, feinting, side-slipping and distribution'. Alloa Athletic and Solway Star were disposed of before Celtic faced St Mirren in the fourth round. After two drawn games, the sides met at Ibrox. James Handley takes up the story.

*'McGrory scored a goal and the game had almost run its course when Gillies of St Mirren, darting towards Shevlin, was tackled by McStay and fell on the penalty line. The*

*referee, Mr Craigmyle, knelt down dramatically to examine the spot closely and awarded a free kick against Celtic. St Mirren would have none of it. A penalty was their demand, and they refused to touch the ball, which the referee had placed for the free kick. The teams faced each other, immobile and silent. The seconds ticked off without anyone stirring. Then the expiry of the game solved the dilemma and Mr Craigmyle whistled for the game to finish.'*

There were persistent suggestions throughout the early 1920s that disputes over the club's alleged parsimony towards the players were rife at Celtic Park, and had contributed to several unwelcome departures. In September 1923, the *Glasgow Observer*'s 'Man in the Know' complained of 'the seeming mercenary spirit of the players, who were expected to respect the proud traditional and exalted spirit of the green-and-white brigade and wear the famous colours more for love than money'. This was after the directors had turned down the idea of bonuses to the players, who were on £8 per week, for wins and draws. Chairman Tom White regarded it as 'an impossible request', since there was no guarantee that wins and draws would secure the League Championship, for which the club had traditionally paid substantial bonuses. Celtic's attitude throughout this period was apparently to accept a few seasons of little achievement while waiting for the promise of youth to bloom. It is a phlegmatic approach which has recurred from time to time in the course of the club's history.

There was a crowd of 100,000 at Hampden for the semi-final with Rangers, who had not won the Scottish Cup for twenty-two years. This turned out to be one of the great Celtic performances against the Ibrox club. The team which provided a memorable 5-0 victory was: Shevlin, W. McStay and Hilley; Wilson, J. McStay and McFarlane; Connolly and Gallacher;

McGrory, Thomson and McLean. McGrory and McLean both scored twice, with Thomson getting the other. And so on to a final with Dundee, which might have proved an anti-climax had it not been for the contribution of 'Peerless Patsy'. Over to Handley:

> 'Dundee opened the scoring and with seven minutes to go they were leading by one goal to nil. Great excitement and pleasurable anticipation prevailed among the Dundee supporters in the park and at home, where the game was being relayed movement by movement. In the final few minutes Peter Wilson passed to Gallacher and Patsy, with that peculiar dragging motion of his, meandered past man after man until the Dundee left-back made a desperate effort to stop him. Gallacher fell to a roar of 'Penalty!' from the Celtic supporters, but in falling the crafty Gallacher had kept the ball gripped between his feet and somersaulted with it right over the goal-line and into the back of the net, from the cords of which his team-mates had to extricate him before they could shake his hand. It was a wonderful bit of individualism.'

According to Willie Maley: 'It was one of those incidents which has to be seen to be appreciated, and it was with difficulty, so I was told after the game, that the Dundee players refrained from joining in the tribute to that wonderful little player.' This was indeed the stuff of which legends are made, especially since a Jimmy McGrory header gave Celtic victory in the closing minutes. For McGrory it was his first Scottish Cup final, and for Gallacher his last.

After three seasons in exile, Celtic brought Tommy McInally back from Third Lanark in time for the 1925/26 season. Providing grand service to Adam McLean on the left wing, he made a considerable contribution to the club's quite unexpected success in bringing the League title to Celtic Park after a gap of three campaigns. Rangers had emerged triumphant on each of these occasions, and this break in their run proved to be a very temporary success for Celtic supporters to savour. The League flag would not be hoisted over Celtic Park for another ten years, while Rangers would capture eight out of the nine intervening titles.

This was indeed the Ibrox club's golden age. It was a time of great poverty and unemployment, culminating in the General Strike of 1926 as the response to an attempt to cut miners' wages. Many could not afford the charges of admission to football grounds, in spite of Celtic's practice of operating a special cheap gate for the unemployed, and the *Glasgow Observer* commented in December 1925:

> *'How often you and I have seen and pitied the forlorn groups hanging around outside Celtic Park gazing longingly and enviously at lucky fellows able to plank down their shillings at the turnstiles... the "great excluded" shivering in the rain outside the barricade and trying to figure out what was happening within, reading a meaning into the crowd's cheers, yells and groans, and visualising Gallacher, McLean, McGrory or McFarlane shining like demi-gods in the unseen fray.'*

For Celtic supporters both inside and outside the ground, the news for that season at least was an uplift at a time of deprivation. With Rangers languishing in sixth place, Celtic took the title by eight clear points from Airdrie – but it was very definitely a case of one 'off-season' for the dominant Ibrox club.

In that season Celtic had high hopes of achieving the fourth League/ Scottish Cup double in their history, but these were thwarted by St Mirren, who unexpectedly beat them 2-0 in front of a 98,620 crowd in the final at Hampden. For a time it appeared as if Celtic could maintain their League supremacy in the 1926/27 season, with Jimmy McGrory scoring so freely. Three times that season he scored five goals in a game, and on three other occasions he made a personal contribution of four goals in the course of setting a new Scottish League record of forty-nine goals in a season. An injury which kept him out of the season's last few games prevented the tally from becoming even more unbeatable. On February 12, 1927, Willie Maley introduced an eighteen-year-old goalkeeper into the side for a League game at Dens Park, Dundee. This was the debut of John Thomson, signed from Wellesley Juniors in his native Fife, and Celtic won the match 2-1. However, they allowed the prospect of retaining the League title to slip away from them as Rangers came through strongly.

Securing the Scottish Cup for the third time since the competition had been revived after the war was a significant consolation, giving Thomson and John McMenemy – son of 'Napoleon' – winners' medals in their first season. In the final, Second Division side East Fife provided the opposition, and after taking an early lead, the underdogs went down 3-1. With McGrory missing, McInally returned to his old position as centre-forward and clowned his way through the game. The Celtic team was: J. Thomson, W. McStay and Hilley; Wilson, J. McStay and McFarlane; Connolly, A. Thomson, McInally, McMenemy and McLean. The fine defender Hugh Hilley subsequently retired from the game, and Peter McGonagle took over as left-back for the new season.

It opened brightly, with Celtic retaining the Glasgow Cup when they beat Rangers 2-1 in front of 90,000 spectators. Progress was maintained into the New Year and, on January 14, 1928, the incredible Jimmy McGrory set a new world record (or so it was believed) when he scored EIGHT goals in a game against Dunfermline, but Celtic again faded in the

Championship race and finished behind Rangers. Twice in the course of the season McInally was suspended for indiscipline. Willie Maley was away from Celtic Park through illness for much of the season and, one way and another, the auguries were not good when the team returned to Hampden for the Scottish Cup final against Rangers. The Celtic team which lined up in front of a record crowd of 118,115 was: J. Thomson. W. McStay and Donoghue; Wilson, J. McStay and McFarlane; Connolly, A. Thomson, McGrory, McInally and McLean. A scoreline of 4-0 in the Ibrox club's favour brought them their first Scottish Cup in twenty-five years – an extraordinary contrast with their League record. The famous Rangers attack which broke Celtic hearts that day comprised Archibald, Cunningham, Fleming, McPhail and Morton. Maley wrote:

> *'It was truly a meeting of giants in which tactics, strategy and craft were ever in evidence; and while Rangers eventually triumphed as they merited, they were indebted to many 'breaks' which, I willingly agree, had been denied them during their quarter of a century's failure to win the national trophy.'*

It was a characteristically grudging analysis of a result which emphasised the gap which existed between the sides at that time. Inevitably, the crushing defeat accelerated the pace of change at Celtic Park.

The wayward genius of Tommy McInally was transferred for a second time – to Sunderland at a fee of £2,500. An inside-forward of legendary skills who had replaced Patsy Gallacher in the affections of the Celtic supporters, he had never found it easy to live with the disciplines of Celtic Park. It was ironic that, though he was a great personality and humorist, he took a very dim view of practical jokes which were played upon him. One of the flare-ups which led to his second estrangement from

Celtic occurred at Seamill, when a fellow player, egged on by colleagues, phoned up Mclnally at his hotel, posing as a press man. Mclnally duly parted with some indiscreet information about team injuries, to the great amusement of the Celtic players crowded round the other end of the phone. When he found that he had been tricked, albeit with no malicious intent, Mclnally walked out of training in a sulk on the eve of a cup-tie against Motherwell, and caught the train from Ardrossan back to Glasgow. He was suspended indefinitely and, though he returned briefly to the team, he was transferred at the end of the season, soon to be followed to Roker Park by his left-wing partner, Adam McLean.

One unlikely side-effect of Mclnally's departure was that it upset the close-season holiday plans in which he had been involved. This story captures curious aspects of a Celtic age long gone. It had been planned that Mclnally, the boxer Tommy Milligan, Jimmy McGrory and Willie Maley would go off together for a pilgrimage to Lourdes. Mclnally and Milligan dropped out of these plans, leaving the manager and the goal-scorer to travel together. At this time Celtic were engaged in all-out efforts to sell McGrory to Arsenal – a remarkably shortsighted course of action, which was thwarted only because of the player's absolute reluctance to leave Celtic Park, unless for a very large sum of money (£2,000 was the figure McGrory mentioned, against the legal maximum signing-on fee of £650). The free-spending Arsenal manager, Herbert Chapman, came to Glasgow and the Celtic directors set up a meeting between him and McGrory. 'If a way had been found out of the impasse to grant my terms – my word, I'd have been a sorry man', wrote McGrory later. A record fee – around £10,000 – was being offered by Arsenal, and Celtic wanted to do business. But McGrory turned down the move, and two weeks later set off to Lourdes with his manager.

They first caught the train to London and, to McGrory's astonishment (though presumably not to any great surprise of his fellow pilgrim), Chapman and two Arsenal directors were waiting there to greet them. The party went off to a West End restaurant and then Chapman, Maley and McGrory headed for Drury Lane to see Paul Robeson in *Showboat*. They parted company without a transfer being mentioned. However, after five days in Lourdes, Maley and McGrory returned to Victoria Station to be met again by Chapman. After a private chat between the two managers, Chapman got to work on McGrory once more. But the player remained adamant that he would move only on terms which he knew to be impossible. Chapman gave up, and McGrory subsequently wrote: 'I came home next day with a light heart. I'd be carrying on for Celtic' Whether the supporters would have been quite so light-hearted at the time if they had known of the club's efforts to sell the star player is another matter.

Maley's own position was called into question, after forty-one years at the helm, and the decade ended with Rangers winning the League and Kilmarnock – conquerors of Celtic in the semi-finals – the Scottish Cup in the 1928/29 season. In part, Celtic's willingness to sell players was connected to the need to raise money for ground improvements. The Grant Stand had become unsafe and was in the process of being demolished when, on March 28, 1929, fire also destroyed the old pavilion. Most of Celtic's early official records were lost in this fire – an immense loss to subsequent chroniclers of the club's history. The remainder of the season's home games had to be played at Shawfield.

At the end of this disappointing campaign, which yielded only the Glasgow Cup, the clear-out of players continued with the departure of veterans Willie McStay and 'Jean' McFarlane. The following season started with the opening of a fine grandstand which was to serve the club well until 1971. But success on the field of play remained elusive, and Celtic finished 1929/30 with their first 'bare cupboard' since 1901 – usually, even in lean years, either the Glasgow Cup or Glasgow Charity Cup competition could be relied upon to provide a piece of silverware. This time, Rangers had won all four major competitions.

The 1920s, that decade of poverty and depression, had been an increasingly unsatisfactory period in the club's history, far from comparable, as James Handley put it, 'in brilliance with the decade that had immediately preceded the war'. As in so many other walks of life, adjustment to post-war conditions had been difficult for a football club which carried so many of a poor community's hopes. But by the turn of the decade, and notwithstanding that season without honours, it did look as though another outstanding Celtic team was on the verge of making its appearance. The fine young players who had been drawn to Celtic Park were maturing, and the scene seemed set for a return to dominance of Scottish football when Celtic triumphed in the Scottish Cup final of April 11, 1931.

Motherwell provided the opposition for a long-remembered match. The names of the Celtic players that day would trip off the tongues of generations yet unborn: J. Thomson, Cook and McGonagle; Wilson, McStay and Geatons; R. Thomson, A. Thomson, McGrory, Scarff and Napier. At half-time the score was 2-0 to Motherwell, and it was still the same with eight minutes left for play. Then Jimmy McGrory scored, and this was followed, in the closing seconds, by an own goal from a luckless Motherwell defender, Alan Craig. It was 'one of the most exciting finishes one could hope to see', wrote Maley, and Celtic won the replay 4-2 with two goals each from Jimmy McGrory and Bert Thomson. The League title was lost only in a tight three-way finish with Rangers – who again prevailed – and Motherwell.

From the early years of the century, Celtic had been contemplating a tour of the United States of America – a land where they were bound to receive a huge reception from the population of Irish descent, which had been further boosted by emigrations from Scotland during the 1920s. Finally, on May 13, 1931, a party of about two dozen boarded the Anchor Line's Caledonia at Yorkhill Quay, with 'crowds occupying every point of vantage from Yorkhill to Greenock to cheer their heroes on their journey to the far west'. There were four directors – Tom Colgan, James Kelly, James McKillop and Tom White – in the party, while the seventeen players comprised the Cup-winning side plus Morrison, Whitelaw, Currie, Hughes, McGhee and Smith. Nine days later (for transatlantic travel was a civilised business by this time) they landed in New York to a rapturous reception, at the start of a tour which will always hold memories of special poignancy for the club, for nobody could have foreseen the tragedy that was soon to ensue.

Expatriates, even in the United States of the Depression, travelled hundreds of miles to see a game and catch a glimpse of the Scottish Cup, which Celtic had taken with them. The *Glasgow Observer* stated: 'The Celts have countless thousands of followers in the States but they are all Irish and will expect to see their favourites in an Irish atmosphere.' Sure enough, it transpired that some of the local organisers either did not understand, or did not want to understand, the fact that Celtic were at least one step removed from the old country. In Chicago, for instance, they were billed as 'Irish Holders of the World's Championship'.

The non-stop round of receptions, allied to the unaccustomed heat, made it a gruelling experience for the Celtic party. Thirteen games were played, all against American opposition, and Celtic won nine, with one drawn and three lost. They beat the New York Giants in front of a 40,000 crowd. When Fall River beat them 1-0, the hero was a young American goalkeeper by the name of Joe Kennaway. Against the New York Jewish team of Hakoah, Jimmy McGrory had his jaw fractured, while Napier and Scarff were sent off with two of the opposition. Football in the United States was a rough, tough affair. Back home in Glasgow, 'Man in the Know' protested: 'The Yankee game as exploited by most of the clubs savours more of the menagerie or the bull-ring than of the sports field.' Exhausted by their American endeavours, the party sailed back from New York on the liner Transylvania – stopping at Moville, Co. Donegal, where Jimmy McGrory disembarked for his wedding!

Since the end of the season, one of the main talking points in the Scottish sporting press had been the possibility of John Thomson pressing his apparent desire for a transfer from Celtic. The tragedy that was soon to follow was to call into question the whole tradition of hostility between Glasgow's two rival clubs.

# EIGHT

## JOHN THOMSON:
## THE LEGEND LIVES ON

THE GRAVESTONE IN the cemetery at Cardenden bears the epitaph: 'They never die who live in the hearts they leave behind.' John Thomson was only twenty-two, and at the height of his powers, when he died from injuries sustained during a League game at Ibrox Park on September 5, 1931. Desmond White, the former Celtic chairman, spoke for the collective Celtic consciousness of that era when he said of John Thomson: 'He was certainly the best goalkeeper I have ever seen. He was not a tall man, but he had the ability of a ballet dancer to jump much higher than other people. There was a great deal of magic about what he was doing, and this came across to those who watched him.'

Magic for the masses who followed Celtic in an age of depression was rare enough, and they had taken this complete football hero to their hearts. Thomson was the quiet teetotal lad from the Fife pits who, when he took the field, became a tiger full of courage and grace. Sir Robert Kelly, who saw him play his first game for Celtic in 1927, as well as his last, wrote of him:

*'It was the natural athletic gracefulness of Thomson that*

*appealed to everyone. He was not tall as goalkeepers go, but at 5ft 9½ in. and 11st. he was perfectly built. He had the sure clutching hands and fingers of a world-class fielder in cricket and he had ability remarkable in one of his tender years to read opponents' moves before they tried to complete them. Many a time he gave the impression of being off his mark in a leap or dive to save before the opponent had made the effort. But if young John made up his mind to go in a particular way he was right 19 times out of 20.'*

That fateful Saturday the *Glasgow Herald* reported: 'Many people will learn with regret that Sam English, the Ibrox centre-forward, is unfit to play.' But the unfortunate English did play on a wet and miserable Saturday afternoon, and the die was cast for an episode of poignant tragedy. The teams lined up:

**Rangers:** *Dawson, Gray, McAulay; Meiklejohn, Simpson, Brown; Fleming, Marshall, English, McPhail, Morton.*

**Celtic:** *J. Thomson, Cook, McGonagle; Wilson, McStay, Geatons; R. Thomson, A. Thomson, McGrory, Scarff, Napier.*

The same newspaper reported on the Monday morning: *'Shortly after the interval, Rangers centre-forward English worked past the Celtic backs and, in a desperate and daring effort to save his goal from imminent downfall, John Thomson, the brilliant young Celtic goalkeeper, threw himself at the forward's feet as the latter delivered his shot, and received the impact of the kick as both players fell to the ground.'*

The *Daily Express* said: *'The accident which cost Thomson his life occurred five minutes after the start of the second half. The ball was sent forward towards Celtic's goal and*

*English, the Rangers' centre-forward, and Thomson ran to gain possession. English arrived first. A goal seemed certain. Thomson threw himself at the centre-forward's feet. His head crashed against English's knee. The centre-forward fell, and rose limping. Thomson lay unconscious, his head bleeding.*

*'The players shouted for a doctor and the ambulance men. The trainers of both teams rushed to Thomson's assistance, and Mr Struth, the Rangers' manager, and Mr Maley, the Celtic manager, also ran to the prostrate player. Dr Kivlichan, a former Rangers and Celtic player, examined Thomson, bandaged him hurriedly, and ordered his removal to the Victoria Infirmary. Eighty-thousand spectators remained silent and sympathetic as Thomson was carried to the pavilion on a stretcher. A discordant note was struck during the tragic occurrence by the cheering of hundreds of Rangers spectators when they saw Thomson fall to the ground. They did not realise the seriousness of the accident. Meiklejohn, the Rangers half-back, went to the touchline and quietened the cheering section. A young woman rushed to the pavilion where Thomson lay unconscious. Tears rushed down her cheeks, and a cry came from her lips as she saw him on the stretcher. She was Miss Margaret Finlay, of Bedlormie, West Lothian, Thomson's fiancee, who accompanied him to many of the games in which he played.'*

Many years later, John Thomson's brother Jim recalled the sense of dreadful foreboding that engulfed him as he watched the incident from the Ibrox stand. 'I knew at once it was serious from the way his hand fell slowly. I left my seat and went straight to the dressing room. I went into the ambulance with him and one ambulance man said to the other, 'That's the end of him.' I was angry. I knew it myself, but I didn't want it confirmed.'

He telegraphed to the Post Office in Cardenden, and his

parents were informed by a policeman as they sat down to their evening meal. They rushed to Kirkcaldy to catch a train and arrived just a few minutes before John died at 9pm without regaining consciousness. He had a depressed fracture of the skull. 'Nobody in the family ever questioned that it was a complete accident,' said Jim Thomson. 'They were both going for the ball. I felt very, very sorry for Sam English.' A fatal accident enquiry subsequently confirmed this conclusion. 'John had been injured a few times before, because he always went straight for the ball,' Jim recalled. 'I had asked him the previous time he was injured if he wasn't going to stop going in like that. He said he should, but it was the ball he was after. He didn't see anyone else or anything else.'

Though there was certainly no specific blame to be apportioned for the fatal incident, the death of John Thomson in the charged Ibrox atmosphere, and particularly the immediate response from a section of the 80,000 crowd, led to an angry debate in the press about the whole Rangers-Celtic syndrome. One commentator wrote: 'They tell me it is a tradition. I was brought up to believe that too, but I am now satisfied that it is not traditional at all, but a menace to Scottish football.' Old Firm games, he suggested, were 'events to satisfy the emotions of the partisan and bigot'. For a few brief days, however, the fires of pseudo-religious hostility were doused by common humanity and a sense of national loss. In a shop window at Bridgeton Cross, a wreath from the local Rangers Supporters' Club was filed past by thousands.

John Thomson, like many of Celtic's greatest players, was not a Catholic. His family had belonged to a sect without ministers called the Church of Christ and it was in Trinity Congregational Church, Glasgow, that a memorial service was held the following Tuesday. Five thousand people crammed into the church and surrounding streets. Even at this distance in time the words of the minister, the Reverend MacLelland, are worth recalling, for their relevance is undimmed:

*'There is one way in which his death might bring a great gain. Those thoughtless crowds who call themselves Celtic or Rangers followers, whom both teams disown, who gather behind the goals of their respective favourites and cheer themselves hoarse when a member of the opposing team lies writhing in pain, if they can be brought to realise by this tragic happening the brutal cruelty of their action, John Thomson will not have given his young life in vain. Do they realise that their shameless jeering was the last sound that ever reached John Thomson's dying brain?'*

The emotional scenes at the memorial service were surpassed the following day, when John Thomson was buried at Bowhill Cemetery in his native Cardenden. Unemployed men had walked the fifty-five miles from Glasgow. Grown men wept openly on a day of unbridled emotion, at the end of which Mr Tom White, the Celtic chairman, thanked the huge assembly 'for this spontaneous demonstration of your love'. This moving account, from the *Daily Express*, stands the test of time:

## 30,000 PEOPLE AT A FUNERAL – JOHN THOMSON, LAST GREAT TRIBUTE

*John Thomson has had a funeral worthy of such a Prince of Sportsmen. Amid banks of wonderful wreaths and through dense lanes of 30,000 people, the Celtic players carried him from his home in Balgreggie Road to Bowhill Cemetery, almost half-a-mile away. The only sound which disturbed the slow tramping of thousands was the mournful tunes of* the pipe band heading the procession. On his oak coffin there was a wreath shaped in the fashion of goalposts and crossbar, the gift of the Bowhill Football Club, and immediately behind another wreath of lilies and heather on the top of which proudly lay one of his international caps.

'From the early morning, people have poured into this village from all over Scotland. Most of them were the humble folk of football. The miners of Fife, among whom Thomson worked as a boy of fourteen, were there in their hundreds squatting, as miners do, by the roadside talking in subdued tones and now and then proudly picking out famous footballers as they walked past to the Thomson home. Hundreds of them climbed the high crags which overlook the Thomson home, and there from the road they looked like sentinels of sorrow silhouetted against the sky line.

'The funeral service was due to start at three o'clock, but an hour before that the narrow streets of Cardenden were a seething mass of sympathisers. Many of the younger men climbed the roofs of the houses or on to the high walls and hedge rows which lined the road. People converged on Cardenden from every point of the compass. When I came up from Dunfermline, seven miles away, the road was black with silent mourners walking to the scene. Then when three special trains came in from Glasgow and motor-cars by the score unloaded their passengers there was hardly room to move. The surrounding pits were idle for the day. Neighbouring villages were deserted. Every man, woman, and child for miles around came to Cardenden to pay their simple tribute.

'The scene at the Thomson home was magnificent in its simple grandeur. They had brought the oak casket out to the little garden in front of the house. There it rested, with a background of rambling roses waving in the sunshine, as if bidding sad farewell to their young master. There were gorgeous wreaths everywhere. They lined the tops of the privet hedges, lay along the garden paths, peeped out of every little corner, while dozens of mourners continued to arrive carrying more floral tributes. They filled two huge motor-lorries with them and even then there were more. Celtic players preceded the coffin carrying masses of floral beauty, and half-a-mile behind the cortege were mourners bearing their tributes, patiently waiting to lay them on the grave.

'Mr Duncan Adamson, an elder of the Church of Christ, conducted the service in the garden. The players and officials of the Celtic club lined up on one side, on the other were the leading legislators of the Scottish Football Association and the Scottish Football League, while at the head of the coffin stood Mr Thomson, the father of the dead international, and his brother and sisters. The service was as simple as the homage of the village folk. Mr Adamson conducted the ceremony after the fashion of his church. He read a chapter from the Bible, and then delivered a brief address. Women sobbed, and the eyes of many men glistened in tears as he finished by saying: "Good night, dear brother, good night!"'Then when they had driven a lane through the obedient crowd the Celtic players hoisted the coffin on their shoulders and the pathetic procession moved off. High up on the crags the sentinels stood like statues looking down on an unprecedented scene.

'I joined the procession along with John McMenemy and George Stevenson, of Motherwell, and Mr William McCartney, the manager of the Hearts. All the famous players of Scotland were there. I noticed Alec McNair and Joe Dodds, the famous Celtic full backs of a decade ago, marching side by side. As the procession crawled along a man in front of me, overcome by the heat, fell to the ground in a faint. He was carried to a nearby shop for attention. Then, when the coffin passed into *the main road, an old man overcome by emotion fell on his knees crying "Oh, John Thomson, we will never see your like again." I had fallen in some twenty yards behind the bier, but as the procession had reached the cemetery I was far behind. Meanwhile the police had thought it wise to close the cemetery gates. Thousands of mourners stood outside while the service at the graveside proceeded. The Rangers players and some of the officials were among those caught in the dense crowd which jammed the roadway. Finally, however, a way was made through the crowd and, led by Mr W. Roger Simpson, the secretary, the Ibrox players pushed and squeezed their way through to the cemetery gates. Here again the Rangers were held up. One of the officers on duty doubted the identity of Alan Morton, and it was not until Morton had been vouched for by a colleague inside the gate that he and his colleagues were allowed to pass.*

*'Inside a service was conducted at the grave by Mr John Howie, another elder of the Church of Christ. The grave was just inside the boundary wall, which was lined by hundreds of villagers. Now and then a crackling of twigs at the roadside wall indicated that another impatient mourner had climbed the railings from the outside and burst through the shrubbery. On the far side of the cemetery, bank upon bank of wreaths stretched for yards and yards along the foot of the wall. John Thomson is buried in flowers. When the service had concluded people filed past the open grave and threw their floral tributes on top of the coffin.*

*'After Mr Howie had paid a long tribute to the dead international, Mr Tom White, the Celtic chairman, associated himself and his club with all that had been said by Mr Howie. Not 'til the service was over were hundreds of mourners able to enter the cemetery and look into the grave. They are still filing past as I write – people of all stations in*

*life paying their silent tributes to the greatest boy Scottish
football has ever known.'*

Thirty years later, James Handley reflected: 'It is hard for those
who did not know him to appreciate the power of the spell he
cast on all who watched him regularly in action. 'A man who
has not read Homer,' wrote Bagehot, 'is like a man who has not
seen the ocean. There is a great object of which he has no idea.'
In like manner, a generation that did not see John Thomson
has missed a touch of greatness in sport, for he was a brilliant
virtuoso, as Gigli was and Menuhin is. One artiste employs
the voice as his instrument, another the violin or cello. For
Thomson it was a handful of leather. We shall not look upon
his like again.'

At least the name of John Thomson has stayed alive among
subsequent generations of Celtic supporters, many of whom
have made the pilgrimage to that cemetery in Bowhill,
Cardenden. There are many good reasons why the name of
John Thomson has stayed alive for so long. He was the Prince
of Goalkeepers, the symbol of clean-living youth, the epitome
of great talent unfulfilled and the young man who, in death,
exposed the shallowness and futility of sectarianism in the
name of sport. In short, he was the stuff of which legends are
made.

The following Saturday there was a home game with Queen's
Park, and the Celtic supporters had their opportunity to pay a
last tribute in the stadium which Thomson had so often graced.
Before the game, pipers played *The Flowers of the Forest*, a bugler
sounded 'The Last Post', and a silver band 'in soft cadence and
with exquisite sympathy played Newton's immortal hymn,
*Lead Kindly Light.*' The *Glasgow Observer* reported:

*'With bowed heads, players and spectators heard the solemn*

*strains die slowly away. It was a sign of mourning so touching and poignant that its memory will linger with us for years to come. There was grief for the bright young life cut off in its bloom; and oh, what a gap, what an aching void has Thomson's passing left in the place where he was wont to captivate all hearts with his magical personality – the lingering light of his boyhood's grace. No wonder the players seemed heavy-hearted and leaden-footed. Johnny's tragic death was a crushing blow.'*

# NINE

## FIFTY YEARS OF CELTIC:
## THE GOLDEN JUBILEE
## AND THE EMPIRE EXHIBITION

THROUGHOUT THE INTER-WAR years, crowd trouble at Celtic-Rangers matches was commonplace, and the bitterness of emotions intense. Percy Sillitoe, who arrived in Glasgow as Chief Constable in 1933, was soon to threaten to ban the fixtures as part of his drive against violent crime in the city. The gangs which proliferated in Glasgow during the 1920s and 1930s tended to divide along sectarian lines and, for sociological, historical and political reasons which went far beyond football, quasi-religious hostility was established as an endemic feature of Scottish society. Celtic's origins and Rangers' policies ensured that football would continue to be used as a vehicle for these unhealthy emotions.

The *Glasgow Observer* occasionally carried appeals to the Celtic supporters to 'ignore the taunting challenges and silly flag-waving of the opposition' and to cut out 'chanting of childish ditties, varied – and this is the most objectionable feature – by verses of a hymn'. But such pleas fell on a significant number of deaf ears. The truth was that encounters between the two sides had, at their fringes, become thoroughly unpleasant occasions; the best which could be said for this aspect of Celtic-Rangers encounters was that they acted as safety-valves for prejudices which might otherwise have found expression outside football. On October 3, 1931, just two months after its latest admonition to supporters, the *Glasgow Observer* reported that – at the first Old Firm game since the death of John Thomson – 'not a vestige of colour was to be seen, hardly a sound heard ... no singing, no flag-waving, no provocative challenges'. But it did not last long.

'The shock [of Thomson's death] had a tremendous effect on our players,' wrote Willie Maley, 'one which we firmly believe was responsible for many failures during the next few years.' Faced with the grim task of finding a successor, Maley remembered the performance of Joe Kennaway of Fall River during the close-season American tour. He was invited over, and made his first appearance on October 31, 1931 against Motherwell. Kennaway soon proved himself equal to the challenge and became a big Celtic favourite, staying in Glasgow until the outbreak of the Second World War took him back across the Atlantic. But the melancholy of Thomson's death was to hang over the remainder of that season and beyond. The club was hard-hit by injuries, and Peter Scarff had to retire from football with an illness which soon ended his life. Celtic finished third in the League, and the only consolation lay in the preservation of a record – Motherwell took the title, thus preventing Rangers, who were in second place, from equalling the 'six in a row'.

As Celtic struggled to emerge from their slough of despond, a Scottish Cup triumph came as a surprise to even their warmest admirers. This was in the 1932/33 season, during which the new faces making their appearances included Malcolm MacDonald, signed from St Anthony's, and teenager Bobby Hogg from Royal Albert who took over at right-back when Willie Cook moved to Everton in December 1932. Both were destined to have long careers at Celtic Park. The brothers Frank and Hugh O'Donnell, from Wellesley Juniors, and Johnny Crum from Ashfield Juniors also entered upon the scene. There were clearly the makings of another very good homespun side, but consistency was lacking in League games and Celtic finished a modest fourth.

Their Cup form was more impressive. Dunfermline, Falkirk, Partick Thistle and Albion Rovers were disposed of before Hearts went down to goals from the extraordinarily prolific Jimmy McGrory and Alec Thomson in a semi-final replay, after a goal-less draw. The Celtic team for the final, in front of a 102,000 Hampden crowd, was: Kennaway, Hogg and McGonagle; Wilson, McStay and Geatons; R. Thomson, A. Thomson, McGrory, Napier and H. O'Donnell. In a game which lacked the drama of 1931, a goal from Jimmy McGrory took the cup back to Celtic Park.

But this was still a troubled period for the club in these Depression years of poverty and mass unemployment. Bert Thomson, the popular winger, was transferred to Blackpool after breaches of training discipline. There were disputes about signing terms and familiar accusations that Celtic were not prepared to spend money to acquire or retain experienced players. Season 1933/34 saw another undistinguished League campaign and a Scottish Cup exit at home to St Mirren. Willie Maley was much affected by the death from tuberculosis of Peter Scarff on December 9, 1933, at the age of twenty-five – a reminder in this more prosperous age of how that terrible plague had ravaged the population until relatively recently. Maley later wrote that, at that time, 'we seemed doomed to continual misfortune'. He summed up the mood of the period in the handbook which preceded the 1934/35 campaign:

*'In reviewing the season that has gone, I regret to have to put it down as the most disappointing one that we have ever had... Since 1931 our lot has been one of trial and disappointment.*

*We won the cup in 1933 against all the odds but we have since failed badly in the League race where our consistency used to tell its tale and where we wore down all opposition for years. That spirit seems to have been lost by our team...'*

Though the shedding of experienced players appeared carelessly over-regular, credit had to be given to Maley for the way in which – even at this time – he continued to come up with outstanding new material, almost exclusively from the junior ranks. Jimmy Delaney, a youngster from Cleland who had played just a few games with Stoneyburn Juniors, was the outstanding acquisition of 1934. He had worked for two years in the Lanarkshire pits, but was by then unemployed. Delaney recalled receiving £2 per week in wages as a 'provisional' Celtic signing, after Maley and chief scout Steve Callaghan had watched him in a trial match. John Divers, signed from Renfrew Juniors, was also ready to make his breakthrough, while Jimmy McStay's career with Celtic ended when he went to Hamilton on a free transfer. Alec Thomson and Peter Wilson were also soon to depart, and money was again a factor. The great Wilson, at Celtic Park for over a decade, was quoted as complaining: 'The boss expects you to play like a genius on Saturdays, and to think like a half-wit on pay-days.'

The bad start to the 1934/35 season proved to be a mixed blessing. Only nine points were taken from the first ten games, gates were falling and, in response, the five-man board took the unprecedented step of appointing a coach – 'Napoleon' himself, Jimmy McMenemy. This was to prove a vital appointment in generating a Celtic revival, and it immediately coincided with a dramatic improvement in form, as young players were drafted into the first team, which finished second to Rangers in the League Championship, and went out of the Scottish Cup to Aberdeen. The only consistent consolation for the Celtic supporters during these lean years was the performance of the reserve side, which dominated the honours and exuded promise for the future. But the Celtic support was, by the middle of the decade, tired of waiting.

The last Scottish League title had been won in 1925/26, and the gap which had followed was easily the longest in the club's history. The intermittent Scottish Cup successes had staved off total embarrassment, but the reality was that Rangers had been the dominant club of the 1920s and 1930s, claiming no fewer than thirteen out of eighteen League titles since the end of the First World War – including eight out of nine since Celtic's last success. Even the Glasgow honours had become rare sights on the Celtic sideboard. Since the dawn of the thirties, there had not been a solitary Charity Cup success and the Glasgow Cup had been secured only in 1930/31 – the season which had held out so much promise before the dark days set in.

The prelude to the 1935/36 season included yet another clear-out of the experienced players. Napier went to Derby County, the O'Donnells to Preston North End and McGonagle to Dunfermline Athletic, where he joined Alec Thomson. Only Chic Geatons (signed in 1928 from Lochgelly Celtic) and Jimmy McGrory (signed back in 1923 from St Roch's) now remained of the 1931 Scottish Cup-winning team, with Joe Kennaway the only other 'veteran' from the 1933 side. The transition had been extremely rapid, and there was a general feeling that Celtic had thrown away their immediate prospects of success by releasing too many of their older players within such a short space of time. But into the team, soon to become captain, came centre-half Willie Lyon from Queen's Park, and the half-back line of Geatons, Lyon and Paterson was destined to become as legendary as Young, Loney and Hay.

A 3-1 defeat by Aberdeen in the opening League game seemed to endorse the pessimistic view, but then Celtic hit the kind of successful run which had long eluded them – sixteen games with the loss of only one point. When they beat Dunfermline Athletic on September 16, Jimmy McGrory's hat-trick set a new Celtic and Scottish record of 351 goals in first-class football. The following week Rangers were beaten 2-1 at Ibrox – astonishingly, the first League victory for Celtic at the ground since 1920/21. These were portents which encouraged the long-suffering supporters to believe that there really was new hope at Celtic Park. A 4-3 defeat against Rangers on New Year's Day was one of the few setbacks as this newly-moulded side raced to its first League title in a decade, with sixty-six points from thirty-eight games. Appropriately, Jimmy McGrory scored a hat-trick on the day the title was won at Ayr – his seventh of the season – but an injury ruled him out of the final game, against Partick Thistle, when he would have had the chance to improve his fifty goals in the season and perhaps even beat the Scottish record of fifty-two, held by Motherwell's MacFadyen.

A rather ignominious Scottish Cup exit to St Johnstone could be overlooked in the light of League success, and the Celtic supporters heaved a collective sigh of relief. This was reflected in the pre-season handbook for 1936/37, which looked back on the disappointing events since 'the tragic days of 1931' and reflected on 'the gleam of hope if our lads get going properly' which had sustained the Celtic support. Three players were singled out for praise: Joe Kennaway, who, the handbook complained, was 'despised and rejected of the Scotland selectors'; Jimmy McGrory, who had confirmed his status as 'one of the great Celts this club has been blessed with'; and Willie Lyon – 'strong as the proverbial Lion, he scorns to use the strength God gave him except in the straightest and fairest manner, and he has never lost anything by doing so'. McMenemy was praised for 'his influence with the younger generation'.

For good measure in 1935/36, the club won the Charity Cup ('for which trophy we have always had a special fondness') after a ten-year break. The club handbook, in this moment of long-awaited glory, also had a lofty – and surely ill-merited – word of chastisement for the club's followers:

*'It is good to know that our support has returned to us again. Our people roll up when the team does well, but are inclined to be ready to sit back when fortune does not follow us. This is not the real Celtic spirit nor the one which has brought the club to the position it holds. Never-say-die is our motto, and the followers of the club should learn that it is only by unswerving support that any club can hope to maintain a position such as they wish us to occupy.'*

The same publication contained a tribute to Tom E. Maley, the Celtic pioneer who had died in 1935. He had gone on to be a successful manager with Manchester City, Bradford Park Avenue and Southport, but on retiring to Glasgow, 'his strong and undying affection for Celtic FC was evinced in the quiet, unobtrusive but practical interest he took in all that appertained to its good'. Season 1936/37 opened with the same team – a rare event in recent seasons. James Handley summed up their attributes thus: 'Kennaway was superbly safe in goal, Hogg and Morrison were first-rate backs, the half-back line was as good as ever, Delaney had developed into a great winger, Buchan was a player in the Wilson mould with an easy, graceful, almost lazy style, and McGrory was playing with his usual sprightliness.'

Crum and Murphy formed the equally exhilarating left-wing pairing. It was a great Celtic team, but surprisingly the League challenge fell away in the latter part of the season. However, there was steady progress towards the final of the Scottish Cup after a close shave against Stenhousemuir in the first round, when a replay was required. Albion Rovers, East Fife, Motherwell and Clyde were disposed of before Celtic lined up at Hampden against Aberdeen in front of a British record crowd for a club match (a record which survives right up to the present day) of 146,433, with an estimated 30,000 locked outside. Willie Maley pondered on that great congregation and could not help recalling 'the struggles of our early days – days when nothing but great enthusiasm and dogged determination kept the flag flying'.

The team on that historic day was one whose names would be revered by a whole generation: Kennaway, Hogg and Morrison; Geatons, Lyon and Paterson; Delaney, Buchan, Crum, McGrory and Murphy. Jimmy Delaney – who the previous week had played in front of an even bigger crowd for Scotland against England – recalled the atmosphere as 'tremendous'. Crum gave Celtic an early lead, but Armstrong soon equalised. The winning goal came twenty minutes from the end, when McGrory set up a chance for Buchan – and so another milestone became Celtic's permanent (it can now be reasonably assumed) property – victory in front of that never-to-be-exceeded British club attendance.

There were high hopes that the League flag would be regained during the club's Golden Jubilee season of 1937/38, but there was a poor start, followed by some disappointing developments for the supporters. Willie Buchan was transferred to Blackpool for the large fee of £10,000. Jimmy McGrory retired from the playing side of the game in October 1937. In his final game, against Queen's Park, he scored a goal to bring his career tally to 550, spanning fifteen seasons. Robert Kelly wrote: 'Nobody has ever excelled McGrory in the art of heading the ball; he had the extraordinary ability of diverting the strongest cross down towards the goal-line... equally well will Jimmy be remembered by older Celtic supporters as a man who time after time rallied the team with his unquenchable enthusiasm.'

For James Handley, he had been 'the greatest menace to goalkeepers in the history of the game'. At the time of his retirement from playing, prompted by persistent injuries, he was 'wearing well – not so fast as of old, but still the greatest opportunist in Scottish football when he was on the field'. The supreme tribute came shortly afterwards from Willie Maley, McGrory's mentor throughout his playing career:

> 'With all respect to the many other splendid Celts we have had and still have, I want to say this: We have never had, with one exception, a player whose prowess and o'erflowing enthusiasm have led us to so many brilliant victories. The exception is Paddy Gallacher. As a goal-getter McGrory stands supreme...'

In December 1937, McGrory retired from playing on being offered the managership of Kilmarnock, a post for which he had not applied. In an article at that time, he looked back on his long and prolific career and selected his own choice of the best goal he had ever scored. Few of the fans who had seen the incredibly low, diving header against Aberdeen at Celtic Park on December 21, 1935 would have dissented from the choice. 'Johnny Crum sent the ball over from the left, and my directors told me later that they considered it an impossible ball for heading purposes. But I made a dive, and when I was in a horizontal position headed into the net.' Celtic had co-operated fully in allowing McGrory to accept the Rugby Park job, but there was no room for sentiment when Kilmarnock promptly eliminated Celtic from the Scottish Cup in the third round – an upset which came as a bitter blow in the jubilee year and, to Maley's considerable irritation, focused attention on the possibility of McGrory soon returning to Celtic Park as manager.

With McGrory's departure, the standard Celtic forward line had been rearranged into a notably skilful combination of Delaney, MacDonald, Crum, Divers and Murphy, with Joe Carruth, a versatile signing from Petershill, and Matt Lynch from St Anthony's, who tended to come in for Delaney, as regular performers when injury struck. As the season wore on, the team's League form became steadily more impressive, but it seemed that the title might slip from their grasp when they went down 3-0 to Falkirk in the first game of April. However, there followed a 4-1 victory over Motherwell, and Dundee were overcome both home and away in the space of three days, after which on April 23, 1938, a 3-1 victory at Love Street secured the title, for the nineteenth time, in this eventful fiftieth season. The Charity Cup was also taken, and the coincidence of dates between Celtic's founding and the great Glasgow Exhibition of 1888 soon provided another memorable anniversary event to add to the celebrations of their own half-century as a club.

To mark the passing of fifty years since the original, another great exhibition was held, centred upon Bellahouston Park. This was the Empire Exhibition, which combined displays of the achievements of Scottish industry and enterprise with pavilions full of presentations from all countries of the Empire. King George attended the opening ceremony at Ibrox Park on May 3, 1938, and the event totally captured the imagination of the Glasgow people – pushing aside, at least temporarily, the grim prospect of war, which was intensifying each day as Hitler's conquests expanded and Franco edged the Spanish fascists towards power. 'In this pleasant Glasgow park,' wrote one commentator, 'a remarkable thing has been done. A microcosm of Empire, an enclave of sanity and order, has been created, in which it is possible to walk for a space almost forgetting that there are such things as crazy ambition and bomb-wrecked towns, shellfire and the clash of armies.'

A football tournament was included in the festivities, with Celtic, Rangers, Hearts and Aberdeen challenged by Sunderland, Chelsea, Everton and Brentford from the south. The competition, like the Exhibition as a whole, drew a tremendous public response and there were 54,000 at Ibrox, where all the games were played, for Celtic's opening tie against Sunderland. It ended without score, but in the following evening's replay, two goals from Divers and one from Crum took Celtic through to meet Hearts. In that game Crum scored the only goal, and so Celtic were in the final against the mighty Everton, who had previously disposed of Rangers and Aberdeen, and who had ten internationalists from the four home countries to call on.

A crowd of 82,000 witnessed a great final, in which Lawton was of especial menace to Kennaway's goal. But ninety minutes were concluded without score and, seven minutes into extra-time, John Crum shot home the goal which took the trophy – 'the replica in silver of the Tower of Empire' – to a permanent home at Celtic Park. The Empire Exhibition competition stimulated a great interest in the idea of a regular competition which would bring together the best in Scotland and England, and this might well have come into being had war not soon intervened.

Jimmy Delaney recalled the Exhibition Trophy-winning side as the best he had ever played in, and Malcolm MacDonald as 'the finest all-round player I've seen'. Delaney's recollections give an insight into life at Celtic Park in the 1930s.

*'The directors left everything about the running of the club to Maley. There was very little coaching or anything like that. Five minutes before we went out, he would put his head round the dressing-room door and say 'Good luck, boys'. That was it. If someone didn't play well, he would call him into his office on a Monday morning. He would ask if*

there was anything wrong at home; anything worrying the player – questions like that. The thinking was that if you had been signed to play for Celtic, they expected you to be a good footballer without being told how to play. It was left to you to read the game and, if you'd played against the opposition before, you knew their weaknesses. There really weren't any tactic talks. We weren't told to run here or run there. During the week, the trainer got us fit – most of the training was running round the track and short sprints. The discipline was strict. If you were five minutes late, you were told very firmly to get there in time. But the atmosphere was terrific. Kennaway and Crum were the two comedians – they kept the spirits up.

'For a young man in these days, being asked to play for Rangers or Celtic was the greatest thing that could happen to him. The biggest occasions for us were when we were playing against Rangers. We were always on a big bonus against them. Relations between the players were very good though you always had a couple of nags on the park. Off the field, if you saw a Rangers player, you would walk over and have a drink with him. I remember my first international in 1935 when we met in an hotel and the first man who came to me was Bob McPhail. He told me just to play the way I did for Celtic. That was pretty typical. The religious thing didn't really enter into it among the players – in the '30s, of course, half the Celtic team wasn't Catholic. Maley was a great man, and Celtic all his days. He and the directors were very strict on drink – they didn't like to hear of you being seen in a pub during the week. We went to Maley's Bank Restaurant before and after a game. A lot of supporters would go there for a drink, and to have a word with the players. That was where we were to report – nowhere else.'

Throughout this period, all Celtic publications carried an invitation to wine and dine at 'The Bank' in Queen Street: 'There are two places you can dine in comfort – at home and here.'

Celtic's Golden Jubilee was celebrated at a dinner on June 16, 1938, when representatives of football interests in Scotland, England and Ireland were present. On display were the Exhibition Cup of 1901, which Celtic had captured from Rangers the following year, the Exhibition Trophy won the previous week, the shield presented by the SFA in recognition of the 'six in a row', and the Glasgow Charity Cup. Tom White presided, and a cheque for 2,500 guineas – 50 guineas for each year of service – was presented to Willie Maley. The toast to the Celtic club was proposed by Sir John T. Cargill, honorary president of Rangers and of the Glasgow Merchants' Charity Cup Committee, who recalled that he had performed the same task at Rangers' jubilee dinner. Rangers and Celtic had been great rivals, said Sir John, but they were also great friends.

*'Celtic Football Club is an Irish club, and one of the great characteristics of the Irish race is not only their generosity and large-heartedness but they are the greatest sportsmen in the world. They take an interest in every sport, and played every sport magnificently as only Irishmen could.'*

Turning to the management of the club, Sir John noted that Tom White had also been president of the SFA.

*'He brought to the football world a delightfully breezy manner which made him and his club so popular... Then they had Mr Maley, who answered the description, in a way, of the strong but not silent man. He was a strong man with strong views, but one needed that to succeed as manager of a football club.'*

Sir John's tribute was certainly unstinting, and before Tom White – always in great demand as an after-dinner speaker – replied, the company sang '*The Dear Little Shamrock*'. It was an occasion to disappoint sectarians – though the more radical members of the audience must have had mixed feelings about the words of Sir John Cargill, described by Patrick Dollan in *Forward* as 'the patron saint of Tory capitalism in the West of Scotland'. In administrative circles, if not on the terraces, the Celtic and Rangers clubs co-existed quite happily and to their mutual financial benefit.

There was no indication at the jubilee dinner of events which were soon to follow, when Tom White declared that 'the triumphs of the Celtic club are the triumphs of Mr [Willie] Maley, whose life has been indissolubly allied to Celtic... The name of Maley is synonymous with the Celtic club and almost with the name of soccer.' Maley, who had just turned seventy, thanked Almighty God for his guidance and goodness. His work for Celtic, he said, had been a labour of love. He listed the club's achievements on and off the field of play, recalling in particular the crucial role of Brother Walfrid and John Glass in ensuring the club's survival when 'funds were low and the opposition of a section of the public very strong', and noting that only John Madden, who had been in Prague as a coach for thirty years, and he himself survived of the first Celtic side. When his own enthusiasm had led him into 'some indiscretions', the board knew all the time that it was 'just his old Irish heart beating too fast, and that it was all meant for the best'. Maley expressed pride in the fact that 'never has there been any club manager with such complete liberty of action or fullness of power as the Celtic management has accorded to me, and in all my years with them, I have never betrayed that faith'.

The triumphant Celtic team entered the new season with a 9-1 victory over McGrory's Kilmarnock, and the Glasgow

Cup was soon won. But injuries set in and the high hopes of continuing glory evaporated. The most serious of these injuries befell Jimmy Delaney on April 1, 1939 at Arbroath, when he was pushed to the ground as he challenged for the ball from a corner kick. He fell awkwardly and sustained an arm injury which was to keep him out of the game for two years and three months. Delaney recalled: 'The professor said the arm was just like a jigsaw puzzle. If it had been an industrial injury, they would have taken the arm off.' Celtic went out of the Scottish Cup to Motherwell and finished with forty-eight league points from thirty-eight games.

Maley characterised it as 'one of the most disappointing, if not the most disappointing, in our fifty-one years of existence'. As usual, in his annual report, Maley complained a great deal about referees, but concluded: 'With the yearly leaven of youth, we go forward to 1939/40 with that confident optimism which has carried us over the long years, and I sincerely hope that the new season will see us regain our poise and bring to Celtic Park the old form and real good football which is indelibly associated with the name of our club the world over.

He had, however, reckoned without Adolf Hitler, whose long shadow was eventually to fall over the whole of Europe.

# TEN

## AT WAR AGAIN:
## APATHY AND UNREST AT CELTIC PARK

THE 1939/40 SEASON opened as Europe drifted rapidly towards war. When Celtic met Clyde on September 2 and won by a John Divers goal, the thoughts of the Shawfield crowd were elsewhere. That weekend, the Government was putting into effect the scheme to evacuate children from the cities, and the Saturday newspapers announced the start of conscription. Parliament was sitting that afternoon; the black-out had begun, and before the weekend was out, Britain was at war with Germany. Monday's reports were of the sinking of the Athenia, most of whose crew were Glaswegians.

Once again, sport became a marginal activity as society adjusted to the rigorous demands of war. But whereas aeroplanes had been 'more of a curiosity than the deadly menace they are today' in 1914-18, the threat of aerial bombing was now a strong factor in making the Government apprehensive about allowing large crowds to gather in confined spaces. At first, this high level of expectation that the outbreak of war would quickly lead to regular air raids on our cities led to a complete ban on sport and entertainment. Scottish football administrators were very active in lobbying the Government for a relaxation of the ban, and they appear to have been influential in securing a change in attitude. Football matches – at first friendlies only – would be allowed on Saturdays and public holidays, with crowds at big grounds like Celtic Park limited to 15,000. Within a few weeks, guidelines had been drawn up for the return of competitive football. As in 1914, the Government had concluded that the game's beneficial impact on morale outweighed the arguments in favour of banning it. But there was no reason for footballers to be exempted from war duties, and the ruling which emerged was that players would be allowed to appear for whichever club was convenient, according to their location at any given time. Some English clubs simply closed down for the war years, and their Scottish players returned home. Restrictions on travel added further complications, and at first, the Scottish League decided to operate two regional divisions, East and West. As James Handley recalled:

*'The demands of wartime industry with its heavy and prolonged hours of labour, the difficulties engendered by curtailed transport and multiplied when petrol rationing was introduced served, without the necessity of official interference, to diminish the crowds at First Division football matches generally to three or four thousand; and the players themselves often arrived at the pavilion straight from work, with blackened faces and tired limbs.'*

Celtic's first game under this set-up was on October 21, 1939 against Hamilton Academicals, who had three Anglo-Scottish 'guests' in their team, while Celtic had just one, Willie Buchan, who had transferred to Blackpool in 1937. They lost 4-3, and the pattern was set for the club's miserable wartime record. Unlike other clubs, notably Rangers, Celtic did not take wartime football too seriously. They made little effort to attract big-name guests, and went into a period of lethargy from which it subsequently proved difficult to emerge.

The severe winter of 1939/40 was a particularly miserable one for those who sought to draw comfort from the diversion of supporting Celtic, and matters came to a head when the club's board took the plunge and decided to part company with Willie Maley – by then in his seventy-second year and his fifty-second of intimate involvement with the affairs of the club. The astonishing longevity of his reign, and the fact that he had only recently recovered from a long illness, did not prevent him from reacting with great bitterness when his resignation was finally sought.

Maley, largely on the strength of his football connections, had become a substantial businessman in his own right, and Celtic had dealt generously with him at the time of the jubilee. A substantial ex-gratia payment was also made on his retirement. In retrospect, the need to initiate change when a manager is over seventy years of age appears self-evident. But Maley took umbrage, an undignified row developed over who should pay the tax on his 'golden handshake', and the parting left wounds which were never really healed. The Celtic directors, particularly chairman Tom White, had simply had enough of Maley's autocratic and increasingly secretive style, and his reaction to their decision to retire him hints at the correctness of their conclusion. For an old man, steeped in football, it was nevertheless a bitter blow. A few months later Maley wrote:

*'My thoughts go back to August 1939 when we started off in what we well imagined would be another successful season and which I did not think would be my last year in football management... It has been to me the end of my football career and has robbed me of the very tang of life. Football*

*has been my thoughts morning, noon and night for all the*
*52 years I have been in it, and it has been hard to drop out*
*of my regular ways.'*

The circumstances of the parting were not conducive to handsome financial tributes, and Celtic were criticised for not acknowledging Maley's long and generally distinguished service more formally. A programme note briefly announced his departure, which 'cannot fail to cause widespread regret, and to Mr Maley probably most of all, as the club and all it stands for has been his life's work. May his leisure be long and full of happiness is the prayer of every true Celt!' For some years thereafter Maley would not enter Celtic Park, but this was remedied during the last years of his life. When Maley died in July 1958, chairman Robert Kelly – whose father had played alongside Maley in the very first Celtic team – paid tribute at a board meeting to 'that grand old man of the game' and added that he had 'visited the park up to six months prior to his death'.

Maley had been a disciplinarian, an outstanding judge of young players, and a reasonable tactician in an era when management generally had little to do with on-field tactics. He was also an assiduous worker for charity, and the leading figure in that school of thought which has always maintained that Celtic do not receive fair treatment at the hands of football officialdom, on and off the park. Robert Kelly recalled Maley's approach:

*'The best way, he said, to ensure that a referee did not affect a Celtic result was to hit so many goals into the opposing team's net that the referee could hardly knock most of them off. That was especially the case, he used to insist, if the opponents were Rangers. My father and he once decided that they would*

*congratulate our great rivals when they won the League by a minimum of five points; that was the start, they reckoned, that Rangers had over the other clubs.'*

After Maley's departure, Jimmy McStay was appointed in his place, but the suspicion persisted that the proprietor of the Bank Restaurant continued to wield considerable influence – a perception which, in turn, helped to undermine the new manager's authority. McStay, the great centre-half of the thirties, had gone on to obtain some managerial experience in Ireland and with Alloa Athletic. But his five-year tenure as Celtic manager was not a particularly happy one. It is doubtful whether McStay was aware of the fact that he was looked upon only as a stop-gap manager, but this was subsequently made clear by Robert Kelly – at that time the rising star of the Celtic board – who wrote: 'Jimmy never had the chance to become a famous manager such as Maley. In the first place, his appointment came in time of war when football was at sixes and sevens and Celtic were having a doleful period. In any case, we had already earmarked the man who we hoped would become Celtic manager. He was Jimmy McGrory.'

It was perhaps scarcely surprising, in the light of that revelation, combined with their tendency to produce unpredictable line-ups, that Celtic drifted aimlessly through the war years with only a minimal contribution to public morale, at least among their own supporters. The first wartime season was already dead for Celtic when McStay took over in February 1940, and they finished in a miserable thirteenth place in the League, having won only nine of their thirty games. But as James Handley wrote: 'No matter what the SFA might determine to give the impression of business pretty much as usual in the prevailing conditions, the man who paid his humble bob at the turnstile was not deceived. He handed over his money to see in action the team he had come to know and he was not going to be fobbed off by a weekly frolic of permutations and combinations on the part of the management.'

After one season of the unsatisfactory arrangement of the Scottish League being split into two regions, the official body gave up and left it to the clubs to organise themselves into competitions. A new Southern League was formed with sixteen clubs, and wages continued to be fixed at a £2 maximum – though the clubs which had 'guests' on their books certainly made additional payments to them. This was equally certainly a factor in persuading Celtic to rely largely on players from the junior and Boys' Guild ranks. There was a substantial public, eager for wartime football of a reasonably serious variety, and – crowd restrictions having been further relaxed – 50,000 turned out to see Celtic and Rangers contest a goal-less draw on September 7, 1940.

But decline soon set in, and Celtic finished fifth in this second season of war. As many who were looking for some relief from the privations of these days still recall, Celtic supporters were frustrated by the club's exceedingly modest ambitions during this period. The Celtic handbook complained lamely of 'how unlucky we were on the whole, due to draws and defeats by the odd-goal results, due in no small measure to the old fault of our players' poor finishing'. The only encouraging news was that, after more than two years out of the game with his arm injury, Jimmy Delaney was ready to return for the start of the 1941/42 season.

The first encounter of this season against Rangers was marred by crowd trouble at Ibrox, after both Delaney and Crum had been carried from the field on stretchers. There were five arrests, and the SFA made the extraordinary decision to close not Ibrox but Celtic Park for a month – one of the occasional episodes, scattered throughout the club's history, which have given credibility to conspiracy theorists. This time, Celtic managed third place in the League, while Rangers continued to rule the wartime roost.

Prior to the start of the 1942/43 season, the Celtic guide noted: 'The departure of Willie Corbett to the Royal Navy deprives the club of the most brilliant young centre-half discovered in Scotland since the war. His going will provide an opportunity for young John McPhail.' The eighteen-year-old McPhail, who was to become one of the outstanding Celtic personalities of the generally bleak forties and fifties, had been signed after only a few junior games with Strathclyde, having played most of his football for St Mungo's Academy. By this time, Celtic had only six players from before the war on their books – Crum, Hogg, Delaney, Malcolm MacDonald, Lynch and Murphy. The 1942/43 guide also included a poem, 'The Faithful in Arms', which provided the quite famous lines: 'And the question slips from Celtic lips/How did 'the boys' get on?' The poem continued somewhat fancifully, given the on-field reality at that time.

*Tho' seas divide they think with pride of the team that they left behind,*
*They are faithful still, through good and ill, they bear the Celts in mind;*
*So memory clings in their wanderings to lighten a trooper's load –*
*The tramp of feet down Janefield Street or a vision of London Road.*

The load of Celtic-supporting troopers must, however, have felt a good deal heavier during the ensuing season. Not only were the directors uninterested in bringing players of reputation into the side, they apparently made little effort to hang on to those who were already there. In 1942/43, Celtic fielded six players who had been in Boys' Guild sides a few months earlier, while Crum followed Divers to Morton as the outflow of experienced players continued. They finished tenth in the League, and the depths of ignominy were plumbed in the New Year's Day fixture when a team in Celtic colours lost 8-1 at Ibrox after both Malcolm MacDonald and Lynch had been sent off for arguing with the referee. Whatever the exonerating circumstances, it was by far the club's worst result in the long history of the fixture. The club policy, if it existed, was difficult to discern. The decision not to pursue big-name guests extended even to Matt Busby of Manchester City and United fame, who – having returned to his native Lanarkshire – was desperate to play for Celtic. The directors turned down McStay's request to field him and he went to Hibernian instead, doing much good work at Easter Road in the fostering of young talent.

There was considerable improvement in the 1943/44 season, with Divers returning from Morton and Delaney to something like his best form. Celtic finished second in the Southern League with forty-three points from thirty games – seven behind Rangers. The most promising portents came from John McPhail who, having switched positions, made a strong impression as partner to Jimmy Delaney, and Willie Miller, a fine goalkeeper signed from Maryhill Harp. With the course of the war turning in the Allies' favour, enthusiasm for diversions such as football increased, and the first all-ticket League game in Scotland attracted 75,000 to Celtic Park on New Year's Day 1944.

But the circumstances under which the competition was conducted continued to be extremely difficult. The Celtic handbook reported: 'On the question of transport the matter is serious. On various occasions last season the Celtic players had to travel in hopelessly overcrowded trains, even in the guard's van, with first-class tickets in their pockets.' Players found it difficult to reach the ground for evening training, 'and even to arrive in time for the kick-off on match days'. Jimmy Delaney recalls that his inside partner was, quite often, someone he had never previously met! But another youngster who was to become a Celtic 'great' was signed from St Anthony's in 1944 – Bobby Evans. He was to make his debut, as a forward, against Albion Rovers in the second game of the new season.

Celtic made an indifferent start to this season, and though they rallied with a run of seventeen undefeated games, this was not enough to catch Rangers. James Handley neatly summarised the Celtic condition as the war drew to a close:

*'At this stage the team had physique and power, but the old guile and polish were pretty much confined to Malcolm MacDonald and Delaney. MacDonald was a useful coach for the younger players. Mallan, who had come from Pollok in 1942, was a sound centre-half, and the team as a whole had at last evolved into a satisfactory combination considering the conditions of the time, but they were far from being in the old Parkhead tradition and still had the unhappy wartime knack of giving the occasional performance that played tricks with the blood pressure of their followers.'*

The Glasgow Cup in 1940/41 and the Charity Cup in 1942/43 had been Celtic's only wartime honours, but the managership of Jimmy McStay did at least conclude on a high note with the Victory-in-Europe Cup coming to Celtic Park on May 9, 1945. This trophy had been put up by the Glasgow Charity Cup committee, to raise money for war charities, with Celtic and Rangers invited to meet. Rangers declined, however, and Queen's Park provided the opposition at Hampden. In these days, corners were sometimes used to separate the teams for 'sudden-death' purposes, and Celtic had a single corner advantage when the game ended 1-1. That was enough to secure the presence of another of these magnificent 'once and for all' trophies which adorn Celtic Park. The Celtic team for the occasion was: Miller, Hogg and P. McDonald; Lynch, Mallan and McPhail; Paton and M. MacDonald; Gallacher, Evans and McLaughlin. Only Bobby Hogg and Malcolm MacDonald had been members of the Exhibition Cup-winning side of 1938. Two months later, Jimmy McStay was asked to resign in order to make way for Jimmy McGrory. He did so with considerable resentment over the way in which he had been treated – the final insult being that he learned of his impending departure from a newspaper billboard, as he returned home from a holiday in Ayr. But McStay was later to return to Celtic Park as chief scout under McGrory, in which role he played a significant part during the 1950s in building for future glory. The Celtic handbook announced, more than a little disingenuously:

*'No more acceptable appointment to the managerial chair could be made than that of Mr James McGrory, which took place during the close season. The indifferent achievements of the team last season provided the need, and the resignation of Jimmy McStay gave the opportunity, of making a change. It is 22 years since Jimmy McGrory joined the Celtic.'*

McGrory faced an uphill struggle. The few remaining players who had been alongside him in pre-war teams were sceptical about his managerial potential, because they doubted whether he was sufficiently firm or decisive for the job. Although the war in Europe was over, normality could not yet return as call-up intensified for the continuing struggle against Japan. As Celtic faced the 1945/46 season, thirteen of their players were still on active service – including Willie Lyon, a captain in the Royal Artillery, who had been awarded the Military Cross for bravery.

By this time, the Celtic Supporters' Association had been brought into existence. The initiative was taken in September 1944 when a newspaper announcement attracted just fourteen supporters to a meeting. It was nonetheless decided to hold a further meeting at the AOH Hall, Alexandra Parade, and this time large crowds turned up. By the end of the war, the Association had grown into a large network of branches, the first being founded in Coatbridge. The old 'brake clubs' tradition had been revived, and adapted to modern conditions. In his message to all Celtic supporters, contained in the first magazine produced by the Association in 1946, its president, Joe Regan, reflected: 'The war years have not brought much glory to our team. It has to be admitted that they don't get many breaks – Fate and 'other elements' seem to take a hand just when things look best... Our team has not reached the standards one associates with the name of Celtic, but now that we are back to pre-war conditions we are looking forward to the future for much better results than has been our lot in recent years.'

# ELEVEN

## TURMOIL AND TRAVEL:
## THE QUEST FOR DIVINE INSPIRATION?

IT SOON BECAME clear that Celtic's wasted war years would be paid for dearly, as the new 'A' division was formed from the clubs with greatest drawing power. Along with McGrory, Chic Geatons had been brought back to Celtic Park as coach. The supporters' hopes of changed fortunes were enhanced by the signing of Tommy Kiernan, a former Albion Rovers inside-forward who had been in the forces for five years, and Tommy Bogan from Hibs. (The latter was signed to replace Jackie Gallacher, the popular centre-forward who had been called up to the RAF.) But Malcolm MacDonald had departed for Kilmarnock, and in January 1945, Jimmy Delaney – now aged thirty-one and anxious to obtain a more secure future for himself after losing the best of his career to the war years – played his last game, against Falkirk, before joining Manchester United. This move reflected his dissatisfaction with the wages offered by Celtic at this time, and dismayed the by now long-suffering supporters, some of whom even volunteered to 'top up' his earnings. Delaney declined with thanks, believing that it was the club which should be giving him a better reward – particularly since he and other top players had been held to £2 a week during the war while knowing that guests were being more handsomely remunerated.

Celtic could do no better than finish fourth in the League, with thirty-five points from thirty games. They also failed to take the Victory Cup – one of those one-off competitions in which they had traditionally excelled – as the result of a notorious semi-final replay with Rangers. Two Celtic players, Jimmy Mallan and George Paterson, were suspended for three months after being sent off for disputing a penalty award. Another, Matt Lynch, was suspended for a month, although he had not been sent off and Duncanson, his immediate opponent in the Rangers side, testified to his innocence. Celtic were fined and censured for scathing references to the referee in the club's handbook. Jimmy McGrory, in his report on the season, wrote: 'History will surely record that indiscretions in refereeing and harshness of punishment have imposed an undeserved penalty on club and players alike.' Another writer went further, complaining that 'the referee's peculiar interpretation of the laws of football reduced the contest to a farce', and reproduced a six-year-old match report of a game between Rangers and St Mirren in which the referee was alleged to have discriminated heavily in Rangers' favour! Celtic were also ordered to post warning notices against crowd trouble. It was yet another of these episodes which soured relationships between Celtic and Scottish football officialdom.

Things went from bad to worse in the next two seasons. Starting the 1946/47 campaign without the suspended players and with John McPhail recuperating from illness, they took only four points from their first nine games, and eventually finished seventh. They failed to qualify for their League Cup section, and made an immediate exit from the Scottish Cup at the hands of Dundee. In March 1947, the *Evening Citizen* opined: 'Celtic have been going through a bad time for several years. At no other time in their illustrious history have they slipped so low.'

After the initial euphoria surrounding McGrory's return, the supporters soon started asking the questions which were never to be far away from Celtic Park throughout his twenty years as manager: Who was really in charge? Who picked the team? How much say did Jimmy McGrory have? There were demonstrations in the second post-war season which called for the resignation of chairman Tom White, who was by now an old man in failing health. Increasingly since Maley's departure, power at Celtic Park had moved towards Robert Kelly, a director since his father's death in 1931 and a stockbroker by profession. The enigmatic figure of Kelly, who became the sixth Celtic chairman upon Tom White's death on March 4, 1947, was to dominate the next quarter-century of Celtic's history.

Kelly and his family were part of the Celtic fabric. His father, James, had become a successful businessman on the strength of his football fame. He and his wife, Margaret McErlean, daughter of another Celtic founder, had had six sons (of whom Robert was the fourth) and four daughters. James Kelly – 'the finest man I have known' – was the dominant influence on Robert's life. The doctrines of the Kelly household were sportsmanship, hard work and, above all, the Celtic tradition – a term which, according to Robert Kelly's writings, encompassed a respect for the club's origins, a determination that it should remain non-sectarian, and a devotion to attacking football.

Like many successful Catholics, James Kelly had been encouraged to send his sons to be educated at St Joseph's, Dumfries, one of the new fee-paying schools which had been opened to further the development of a professional Catholic middle-class in Scotland. It was an education which ensured that Robert would have little in common, in social terms, with most of the lads who played for Celtic. His upbringing also left him an extremely devout Catholic all his days. It was Robert Kelly's great regret that he had not played for Celtic himself.

Having sustained permanent damage to his right arm in an early traffic accident, his playing days were restricted to the junior grade. But with his elevation to the board in 1932, he was able to devote a greater proportion of his time to the club he had been brought up to love.

Kelly was far more interested in the club's traditions than in its balance sheet, although it is true that the former largely ensured the health of the latter. He certainly never amassed personal wealth from the club's success, as became apparent at the time of his death. There was never any likelihood of Celtic buying their way out of trouble as long as Kelly was in control, though the signing of occasional experienced players was acceptable. He found his delight in giving youngsters the opportunity to better themselves in the Celtic colours. Normally, these were Catholic youngsters, because it was overwhelmingly footballers from that background who aspired to play for Celtic. Whilst acknowledging that reality, Kelly nonetheless dealt firmly with any suggestion of turning Celtic into a 'Catholic club'. But it was central to his philosophy that Celtic's success should be a powerful vehicle for improving the morale and status of the community from which it drew the great bulk of its support.

Kelly's background and attitudes became extremely relevant to the story of Celtic, because there is not the slightest doubt that he dominated every aspect of the club's affairs and outlook throughout the managership of Jimmy McGrory. From the late 1940s onwards, his direct involvement in team affairs seemed like a distinctly dubious blessing to the increasingly restless supporters.

Kelly's first full season as chairman took Celtic closer than ever before or since to relegation. By the time Rangers won the New Year fixture 4-0, Celtic had played seventeen games, won six, drawn three and lost eight. They continued to struggle in the League, though they reached the semi-final of the Scottish Cup before going down to Morton. Facing their last game of the season at Dundee, they had taken only twenty-three points from twenty-nine games and were thus one of four clubs who could join Queen's Park in relegation. Only by overcoming Dundee at Dens Park on April 17 could they be sure of avoiding that fate – though defeat, it must be said, would not have ensured it. The men who carried the responsibility that day were: Miller, Hogg and Mallan; Evans, Corbett and McAuley; Weir and McPhail; Lavery, Gallacher and Paton. Robert Kelly later described it as 'the greatest ordeal I experienced in watching football in well over fifty years'. He vowed that 'we would never again, whatever the circumstances, reach the depths of 1948'. Jimmy McGrory was ready to resign if Celtic lost.

In the game's early stages, John McPhail had the ball in the net twice, but both were disallowed. Jock Weir – signed earlier in the season from Blackburn Rovers in a desperate attempt to obtain a goal-scorer – scrambled the ball home, but Dundee equalised before the interval. Then, after an hour's play, Dundee took the lead and Celtic hearts sank. But Weir brought the score back to 2-2 and then, with just two minutes remaining, completed his hat-trick to save the honour of his new club. Never had a transfer fee been more handsomely repaid in the space of ninety minutes, and Jock Weir's place in Celtic mythology was ensured. There were 31,000 at Dens Park that day, and it was some consolation for Kelly that 'Celtic in adversity were tremendously well-supported'.

The directors were stung into action, and before the start of the 1948/49 season, Jimmy Hogan, the former Burnley player who had helped to develop the game in Hungary but was now nearing seventy, was appointed as coach. He had been the English FA's coach for six years and had also managed

Aston Villa. It was an imaginative appointment for the time. Celtic also set their sights on three players from Belfast Celtic, but secured only one – the legendary Charles Patrick Tully – for the fee of £8,000, in the face of stiff English competition. They also pipped Everton for the signature of Bobby Collins, an eighteen-year-old from Pollok Juniors. In spite of the SFA upholding a claim by the English club that Collins had agreed to join them, he refused to go, and Celtic gained a valuable recruit. Celtic had even signed a Polish left-winger who caused some short-lived excitement with his reserve-team performances – Konrad Kapler had been 'spotted' while playing with the Polish Army at Johnstone.

There was some promise in all of this, and in an entertainment-starved era of huge football crowds there were 55,000 at Celtic Park for the opening game of the 1948/49 season, with high hopes of something better transpiring. Charlie Tully made a disappointing debut, and the game ended in a goal-less draw. The promise soon evaporated, and Celtic finished joint seventh in the League, their solitary trophy for the season being the Glasgow Cup. 'We have the players, but it appears we haven't got a team,' said Robert Kelly, though Hogan's coaching was producing signs of a more constructive approach. Nevertheless, the attendances that the club continued to draw were truly astonishing: 43,000 at Celtic Park for a first-round Glasgow Cup tie with Partick Thistle; 87,000 for the final with Third Lanark; and 105,000 for a League Cup game at Ibrox.

If the Celtic legions could not yet be rewarded with success, the least they deserved was entertainment. Tully quickly demonstrated that he was the man to provide it. His previous career had been with exotically-named clubs such as Forth River and Ballyclare Comrades, as well as Belfast Celtic where he was 'the bane of manager Elisha Scott's life', according to a published history of Irish football. He was first spotted by

Jimmy McGrory playing in five-a-sides at the RUC sports in Belfast, a comfortable arena for what Tully described as his 'tricks' with the ball. He was persuaded to board the *Royal Ulsterman*, which he was to keep regularly entertained for some years to come, and head for the Broomielaw. It took him six games in 1948 to make an impression, but his breakthrough came against Rangers – 'the game that put Charlie Tully on the map', said the Celtic handbook – and that made it all the more welcome in the eyes of the Celtic supporters. John Rafferty later wrote: 'Celtic fans immediately canonised him. This was the prophet they had waited for through many long, barren years. He did lead them to the promised land, kept the country talking. He was good for the game.'

This season also saw the departure of Bobby Hogg, who left after being at Celtic Park since 1931 to become manager of Alloa Athletic. The handbook which appeared at the start of the 1949/50 season contained for the first time 'A Message from the Chairman', in which Kelly denied that 'the old glory has departed for ever' and expressed confidence that 'we shall soon begin to recover some of our former greatness'. The choice of language is an indication of just how depressed things had become by this time. Celtic finished fifth in the League in 1949/50, and went out of the Scottish Cup in the first round to then lowly Dundee United. The main encouragement came from the performances of Tully, Collins – a dynamic workhorse in midfield – and Bobby Evans, who had grown indispensable in the right-half position. Among the other late-1940s signings which offered some of the promise for the future on which Celtic supporters were perennially asked to rely, were those of Bertie Peacock, a nineteen-year-old amateur from Glentoran, Willie Fernie from the Fife junior club Kinglassie, and Jimmy Walsh from Bo'ness Juniors.

The grim relationship which had developed between the SFA

and Celtic was further exacerbated by the 'Tully-Cox incident' in a League Cup tie early in the 1949/50 season, when the Rangers back appeared to kick the new darling of the green-and-white battalions but went unpunished. This led to crowd trouble, and eventually to an enquiry by the SFA Referees' Committee – soon to be an even bigger tormentor of Celtic. The Committee reached the extraordinary conclusion that both clubs should post warning notices at their grounds, and that both players should be severely reprimanded – Cox for kicking, and Tully for having 'simulated any slight injury he might have received'. The SFA council upheld this wildly illogical outcome, and Celtic's appeals for a further enquiry were turned down. Once more, Celtic faith in the neutrality of the game's rulers was shaken.

Over twenty years later, Robert Kelly felt the episode important enough to devote a full chapter to it in his book of recollections. Whether or not such memories are selective and accorded an importance out of proportion to their true significance must remain a matter of judgement. But it is important to an understanding of Celtic's history that any tendency towards a persecution complex that may exist has been generously fuelled at regular intervals. Indeed, relations quickly went from bad to worse when Celtic exited from the Glasgow Cup to a controversial goal by Findlay of Rangers, with the Celtic players protesting that the ball had not been 'dead' when Willie Waddell took a free kick. This modestly important source of indignation led the Celtic board into what was probably the club's only attempt at encouraging a crowd boycott. Jimmy McGrory explained:

*'The incident, coming so soon after the Cox affair at Ibrox, caused a great deal of controversy and it was felt that some protest should be made by the club. It was difficult to know*

*just what to do, because our request to have a special enquiry into the Ibrox match had been turned down by the Scottish Football Association. It was therefore decided to ask the Scottish Football League to allow us to withdraw from the two League fixtures with Rangers. The League turned down this request and ordered us to play these matches, and our next meeting took place at Ibrox on September 24. This day will go down in history as 'boycott Saturday', as the Celtic supporters showed their approval of the directors' action by staying away from the match.'*

This proved to have been a good piece of judgement on the part of the Celtic supporters, irrespective of the high principles involved, since the team – without Tully – put on an appalling show and lost 4-0. This season of feuds between the two clubs did end on a higher note, however, with Celtic, beating Rangers 3-2 in the Glasgow Charity Cup final – a game that is remembered as the 'Danny Kaye Final', because of the American comedian's presence. This helped to swell the gate to the 81,000 who saw the old trophy secured by two goals from John McPhail and a deflection off Cox. The Celtic team was: Bonnar, Haughney and Milne; Evans, McGrory and Baillie; Collins, Fernie, McPhail, Peacock and Tully.

Jimmy Hogan's valuable two-year stint with Celtic ended after the 1949/50 season, as the supporters wondered aloud if good times were ever going to return to Celtic Park. A League Championship had not been won since 1937/38, nor the Scottish Cup – which had, of course, been in abeyance during the war years – since 1936/37. In 1950, Sean Fallon signed from Glenavon. For the Sligo man it was the start of an involvement that lasted over thirty years, yet the initial financial arrangements were inauspicious. Jimmy McGrory offered him £10 per week, falling to £8 in the close season, plus £1 towards digs money. At that time he was earning £6 with Glenavon and £8 at his trade as a confectioner. However, since learning as a boy of the role of another County Sligo man – Brother Walfrid – in the Celtic history, there was no other club he wanted to play for. 'What Mr McGrory offered me was much less than would have been expected from other clubs of the same status. But signing for Celtic was realising a boyhood dream.'

In spite of the uncertain fortunes on the field of play it was, he recalls, a fine time to be a Celtic player in terms of good comradeship and exciting experiences. As soon as the season ended in 1950 – Holy Year – the club embarked on a tour which had as its highlight a meeting with the Pope. 'Everyone was making their way to Rome that year, and our chairman was very much that way inclined,' Fallon recalls. 'Wherever we went, even in eastern Europe, the first place he would look for would be the church.'

Fourteen players, along with McGrory, Hogan and four directors (including Tom Devlin, who had joined the board) set out on May 24, 1950 for this epic tour. It got off to a flying start when Bing Crosby appeared as one of their fellow passengers on the SS Royal Albert to Brussels. 'We looked into the bar and John McPhail and Charlie Tully were already having a beer with him,' recalls Fallon. 'Trust Tully!' By the time Brussels was reached, Crosby had been prevailed upon to give his version of *I Belong to Glasgow*.

A three-day train journey, with overnight stops at Lucerne and Milan, took the party to Rome, where Monsignor Flannigan of Baillieston and the Scots College became their 'guide, philosopher and interpreter'. Bobby Evans and trainer Alex Dowdells joined the party from Paris, where they had been with the Scotland team. The idyllic nature of the trip aftered, however, when Celtic played Lazio of Rome. John

McPhail was sent off in the course of a torrid game, and the players were in fear of attack as they left the stadium.

The following day the Celtic party had a more sedate appointment when they made their way to St Peter's Basilica, 'where, through the good offices of Monsignor Flannigan, we obtained a privileged spot in this huge edifice'. The Celtic team was by no means entirely Catholic at this time, but all the players joined in the visit. Having given a general blessing, the Pope went on to greet various groups in the Basilica – including the Celtic party. 'He thought we were Irish and greeted us in Gaelic', Fallon recalled. The Celtic handbook account of the event states:

> *'Now, the Celtic Club have been the initiators in many things, and in being called out in St Peter's, they rank as the only football club to have that honour. The whole scene baffled description... We left St Peter's inspired and thrilled by this wonderful experience, and thankful that we had been privileged to be present at such an august ceremony.'*

The only other football of the tour was played against the student priests of the Scots College, and after ten days in Rome the party journeyed homewards via Dijon and Paris. It was, to put it mildly, an unusual close-season expedition for a football club to undertake, but it was very much in the Kelly mould, and would long be remembered with affection by all who took part in it.

Peacock and Fernie became regulars in the 1950/51 season. George Hunter, a nineteen-year-old signed from Neilston Juniors, succeeded Miller in goal after he transferred to Clyde, and Evans, Boden and Baillie emerged as Celtic's best half-back line in a generation. This also proved to be John McPhail's finest season. James Handley described him thus:

*'He was not cast in the mould of previous successful Celtic centre-forwards. He was not a dasher, darter, juggler, dribbler or wizard with the head. Rather, he moved through the game with the ambling ease of a great St Bernard, but he had height and weight to brush aside physical challenge with insouciance and a swerve that threw many an opponent on the wrong foot. His shot was a strong one and within range of goal his extra inches were particularly effective, for he could rise high in the air to a cross and send it into the net with a skilful flick of the head.'*

The long dearth of major honours came to an end, with the winning of the Scottish Cup. It was a famous campaign in which East Fife and Duns were disposed of in the early rounds. Hunter gave a memorable goal-keeping performance as Hearts were defeated in front of a capacity Tynecastle crowd. There were 75,000 at Celtic Park for the quarter-final tie with Aberdeen, which finished with a 3-0 scoreline. Raith Rovers fell by the odd goal in five in the semi-final, and Celtic lined up against Motherwell in the final. It was a remarkable case of history repeating itself, as Handley noted: 'Twenty years before, the teams had met in such a final and Celtic, anxious to take the Scottish Cup with them on the American tour planned for the close season, saw their wishes fulfilled. Once more they were off to the States and once more they hoped to take the Scottish Cup with them.'

In front of a 134,000 crowd, John McPhail scored a first-half goal, and Celtic hung on to this lead to take the cup. The team was: Hunter, Fallon and Rollo; Evans, Boden and Baillie; Weir, Collins, McPhail, Peacock and Tully.

The club's second expedition to America was launched with another mass send-off, this time from Central Station. Lasting seven weeks, it began with a transatlantic crossing on board the *Queen Mary*. 'The last dinner on board,' reported the Celtic handbook, 'was notable for the thoughtful gesture of the crew in giving us a wonderful cake, the decoration of which depicted Hampden Park, with the two teams lined up for the start of the final. It was a work of art and every detail was carried out in the correct colours.' Who can fail to mourn the passing of those days of civilised travel?

The tour itself proved, like its predecessor of 1931, to be an exhausting round of receptions, public dinners and sightseeing with nine games in between – three of them against Fulham, with honours ending even. The defeat by Fulham in Montreal and the draw in Toronto were the only setbacks of the tour. There were victories over New York Stars, Fulham and Eintracht in New York, Philadelphia Stars, National League in Toronto, Chicago Polish Eagles in Detroit, and Kearny Select in the New Jersey home of large Scottish and Irish communities. In Toronto there was a nostalgic reunion with Bobby Muir – outside-right in the Scottish Cup-winning team of 1904! The disappointment of losing their unbeaten record to Fulham in the last game of the tour was soon overcome as the party sailed back to Liverpool on board the RMS *Parthia*. Another highly successful tour, in ambassadorial terms, had been completed.

On their return, Celtic were soon playing in the St Mungo Cup, run by Glasgow Corporation and the SFA as part of the 'Festival of Britain' celebrations. All sixteen First Division clubs were involved, and Celtic duly qualified to meet Aberdeen in the final. The team was: Hunter, Haughney and Rollo; Evans, Mallan and Baillie; Collins, Walsh, Fallon, Peacock and Tully. After going two goals down, Celtic fought back in the second half with goals from Walsh, Fallon and Tully. Thus Celtic added yet another one-off trophy to their collection, and therein lies a story.

The salmon features in Glasgow's coat of arms, and the cup's handles took the shape of that noble fish. When one salmon came away in the hand of a Celtic official, it transpired that the cup had been made in 1894 and previously competed for in 1912 when Provan Gasworks had won it by defeating the Glasgow Police. The Corporation, it transpired, had had it spruced up and re-inscribed to serve as the St Mungo Cup! The Lord Provost turned down Celtic's request for a new trophy with a pedigree more in keeping with the dignity of the occasion – and so the 'second-hand' object took, and retains, its place in the Celtic trophy room. In this period, it might be thought, Celtic were not in much of a position to be fussy about the calibre of the trophies they collected!

After the promise of the 1950/51 season, and the euphoria of the close-season activities, the following campaign came as another disappointment. In the League, Celtic took just twenty-eight points from their thirty games, while they departed from the Scottish Cup in a first-round replay against Third Lanark – the first time in more than fifty years that they had lost in a Scottish Cup replay. Following the American tour, Celtic brought Gil Heron – a Jamaican whom they had seen in action in Detroit – to Glasgow, but the 'Black Flash', as he inevitably became known, did not prove to be a lasting success. Infinitely more significant was the arrival from Llanelli of one Jock Stein.

# TWELVE

## CONFRONTATION: FLYING THE FLAG

AN EPISODE WHICH occurred in 1952 is worthy of detailed recall, since it went to the heart of the Celtic psyche and briefly threatened the club's place in Scottish football. Celtic supporters of that generation, and those to whom they have handed it down, recall the affair in straightforward – and generally accurate – terms. The stark fact is that an attempt was made to force Celtic out of business if they would not agree to remove the Irish flag from their home ground. Celtic, in the person of Robert Kelly, stood firm and lived to tell the tale. But the fact that such an effort was made, on the basis of such an issue, reinforced the instinctive suspicion that there were many in Scottish football and wider society who would have been pleased to see the back of Celtic Football Club. (The fact that Belfast Celtic had been forced into oblivion for sectarian reasons in the late 1940s was a matter of quite recent memory.) The strong suspicion that the Scottish football hierarchy is not, in general, composed of people who have much affection for Celtic Football Club persists to the present day – perhaps to an irrational degree. But the vindictive attitudes which came to the fore in those early months of 1952 encouraged over-reaction, and long memories.

The incidents which sparked off the flag controversy arose at the Celtic-Rangers match of January 1, 1952. It was an extremely unhappy day for the home side. With thirty minutes remaining, they were trailing 2-1 when Shaw, the Rangers right-back, was carried off injured. Far from improving Celtic's prospects, this led to Rangers reorganising successfully and scoring two more goals. In frustration over this humiliation, sections of the Celtic support started to fight and throw bottles, resulting in eleven arrests. It was not a particularly serious incident, but it attracted disproportionate attention because it was the latest in a number of flare-ups involving Celtic supporters.

The first to react were the members of the Magistrates' Committee of Glasgow Corporation. In 1949 control of the city had passed to the Progressives, who had not held office for fifteen years. They were relatively inexperienced in these matters, but had a record of castigating the previous Labour administration for being soft on crowd trouble at football matches. They wanted to be seen to act, and promptly arranged a meeting with the SFA and Scottish League. The Magistrates' Committee then made four proposals, none of which at first seemed very contentious. Their call upon the two clubs to avoid displaying flags which might incite feeling among the spectators seemed fairly innocuous, and the press criticised them for not doing enough, and demanded stiffer sentences. It was only when the recommendations of the Magistrates' Committee went before the SFA Referees' Committee on February 11, 1952 that warning bells began to sound for Robert Kelly.

The Referees' Committee decided that they would recommend to the full council of the SFA that Celtic should be instructed 'to refrain from displaying in their ground on match days, any flag or emblem which has no association with this country or the game'. Such an interpretation of the original magistrates' recommendation was extremely one-sided and, as Celtic argued, punitive. If the committee's interest was in stopping crowd trouble, as a result of what had transpired at the New Year's Day game, then they could scarcely argue that lowering the tricolour of Ireland would have this effect. The flag was unlikely to incite the Celtic support to violence, but Celtic were being asked to take it down. Kelly quickly realised what was happening. The report by the magistrates was being used by a powerful combination of anti-Celtic interests to pursue greater ends. Some of these, for ideological reasons, wished to see Celtic's links with Ireland severed, and others supported this aim for their own commercial reasons.

The leading forces in this combination were Harry Swan, chairman of Hibernian Football Club and president of the SFA, and George Graham, the Association's secretary. Swan had risen to prominence in Scottish football over the previous twenty years. In 1931 he had become the first non-Catholic to hold shares in Hibs, and three years later he became the chairman. He was an ambitious, far-sighted man who was to lead Hibs to their greatest period of success. But his first set of actions as chairman had been aimed at severing the Hibs' connection with all things Irish. The harp which adorned the main entrance to Easter Road was removed, the right of priests to attend free of charge was abolished, and there was talk of changing the club's name and colours. Such activities meant that Swan was credited with anti-Catholic attitudes which, according to some who knew him well, he did not hold.

The trick which he was trying to pull off was aimed at retaining the Hibs' traditional support while opening up the club to a wider cross-section of the populace. Celtic's ability to attract support from succeeding generations who belonged to the Catholic-Irish tradition, throughout Scotland, was a source of constant irritation to him, and his frustration was at its height in the late forties and early fifties when Hibs had

had an outstanding run of success on the field of play without quite breaking into the top bracket in terms of support. When the flag issue arose, Swan was eagerly encouraged to turn it into a matter of high principle by Graham, who had enjoyed a close relationship with Willie Maley but who (perhaps as a consequence) was hostile to Celtic under Kelly. (The claim, carried in several books, that Graham was a prominent Orangeman appears to be mythological, though he was certainly an active Freemason.)

Kelly reckoned that there were only a few on the SFA council who wished to see Celtic humiliated to the point at which they would close down, but he suspected that equally few fully understood the strength of the club's feelings on the matter, the majority probably believing that Celtic would take the flag down if confronted with an SFA council decision to that effect. It was up to Kelly to convince them that Celtic weren't bluffing, and that they would accept suspension rather than have the flag removed. This assurance began to seep out through the press. The 'Waverley' column in the *Daily Record* reported on February 18:

*'I have the unhappy feeling that there are many associates and adherents of the club who would be prepared to take such drastic action rather than submit to what they consider to be a grave indignity. During conversations I have had over the weekend with men who have been ardent supporters of the club for ever so long, men of good standing and a high sense of sportsmanship, I find among them the feeling that they would support a closed door decision.'*

Realising that he would have to persuade the SFA council of the genuineness of this threat, Kelly also had to ensure that he had the opinion of the Irish-Catholic community firmly behind him. Celtic's enemies would look upon any dissension in these quarters as a green light to press their attack.

On February 22 the *Glasgow Observer* took the highly unusual step of printing a speech by Robert Kelly on its front page. Significantly, it was delivered to the Glasgow Province of the Knights of St Columba, at their annual reunion, and its subject matter went far beyond the immediate problem faced by Celtic Football Club. It was about a more general threat to the standing of the Catholic community in the West of Scotland. Kelly declared: 'It is necessary that Catholics should become more and more organised, because at present in the West of Scotland they are not making their presence sufficiently felt in proportion to their number. We are not wielding the same influence as our fathers and grandfathers did. In such societies as the Knights of St Columba, it is one of our duties to make sure that Catholic laymen, in whatever profession they have been called, exert their influence to the fullest possible extent.'

The flag had indeed become a symbol, and the message to West of Scotland Catholics was simple: 'We are under threat.' The right to fly whatever flag they pleased, in commemoration of their club's origins, was a litmus test of their ability to resist the erosion of their status.

In football circles, Kelly's efforts were having their effect – but not quickly enough. The full SFA council met on Monday, February 25, later described as 'a sorry day in Scottish football administration'. Before the debate started it was moved that the representatives of Celtic and Rangers should leave the meeting. This was defeated, but it was agreed that they should be excluded from the vote. Since Celtic were the movers and Rangers the seconders of the amendment calling for the Referees' Committee recommendation to be set aside, this was surely a unique piece of procedure! But Swan, Graham and their cohorts were in no mood to have the outcome put into doubt. In insisting on his right to put the Celtic case, Kelly quietly declared: 'It may be my swansong, but I am determined to say what I have to say.'

Mr John Robbie of Aberdeen then moved the adoption of the Referees' Committee report, accusing Celtic of not having done 'everything possible' to counter the activities of hooligans. Indeed, by organising resistance to the Referees' Committee decision, he claimed, 'Celtic gave the impression to the hooligans that they were being supported in their disgraceful behaviour'. He was supported by Mr Terris of Hibs. Robert Kelly moved that the Referees' Committee report should be accepted except for the section calling on Celtic to take down the flag. He outlined the links between Celtic and the flag of Ireland.

*'It has always had a strong association with Celtic where the game of football was concerned. No one previously has blamed the flag for causing trouble and I do not believe it is even remotely concerned with such. Surely it cannot be said that the flag causes trouble among Celtic supporters.'*

He was of the opinion (fortified by legal advice) that the SFA would be exceeding its powers by seeking to have the flag removed. Kelly pointed out that there was no rule in existence under which the flag could be barred and that 'the committee or the council cannot go beyond its own rules'. He was seconded by John F. Wilson, chairman of Rangers, who stated that his club was not in the least troubled by the flag. After Kelly and Wilson had left the SFA council chamber, the Referees' Committee recommendation was carried by 26 votes to 7.

Robert Kelly left the meeting bewildered and angry. He had shown the council that they did not have the authority to take the action they were proposing, yet they had voted to go ahead.

Kelly and his fellow board members – in common with the vast majority of Celtic supporters – were now convinced that they were dealing with something much more than a rational attempt to minimise hooliganism. Some members of the SFA council were out to humiliate Celtic, and the SFA secretary, George Graham, was widely held to be the architect of this strategy. Robert Kelly later described him as 'a more powerful man in Scottish football than he had any right to be'.

Celtic remained convinced that their legal case was unassailable, and that the majority of clubs would not press the action if they were convinced that Celtic would accept closure rather than take down the flag. Kelly continued to rally the club's traditional support behind him. In another impassioned address to the Knights of St Columba, he declared: 'We have no need to be ashamed of our fathers, nor have we any cause to be ashamed that those founders [of Celtic] came from that country that has provided protagonists for liberty wherever they have settled.'

On Sunday, March 2 the Celtic Supporters' Association called a special conference and over 500 delegates met for two hours in the St Mungo Hall, Glasgow. They were addressed by Robert Kelly, who explained what had happened at the SFA council meeting. After he had spoken, a motion was passed supporting the board in whatever action they took regarding the flying of the Irish Republic's flag at Celtic Park. The issue reached Parliament when John McGovern, the Labour MP for Shettleston, asked the Secretary of State for Scotland to intervene. The SFA's action, he suggested, was 'an insult to a friendly nation'. Was the Secretary aware that the flag was a personal gift from Eamon de Valera, at that time Prime Minister of Ireland?

The day after the supporters' rally, the SFA council met again in a highly-charged atmosphere. The message that Celtic would, like their Belfast counterparts, go out of business before bowing the knee to their detractors was beginning to penetrate some cash-conscious minds. The ring-leaders changed their ground, and sought to make Celtic's refusal to comply with an SFA ruling the primary issue. Harry Swan declared:

*'We have gone far enough. This is a question of government or anarchy. No club, no matter how powerful, can be a law unto itself. If Celtic were not happy with the council's previous demand to take down the flag, their correct course would have been to accept the decision and to debate the matter afterwards. There seems to have been a misunderstanding in the minds of Celtic that they were punished for the behaviour of a section of their supporters and that one of the penalties under Article 114 should have been applied. They were not being punished at all. These hooligans must be got before they start trouble. Celtic have challenged the authority of the Association. To submit to such would lead to chaos in the management of the sport.'*

Swan then moved that 'unless Celtic give notice of their acceptance of the Association's order to remove the cause of the controversy within three days, the club and its directors be suspended'. Mr Robbie of Aberdeen seconded. 'I am a strong upholder of democratic government, and this Association is a democratic body. When a minority defies a decision of the majority, then law and order disappear.' But when Dundee United's representative, Mr Mcintosh, moved that Celtic should be given until April 30 to comply, the Celtic chairman sensed that the united front was breaking up. Too many of the clubs depended on Celtic and knew that the three-day ultimatum could just as quickly backfire upon them. Now was not the time to step back, and Kelly, visibly moved, addressed the council.

*'My club has been in existence for sixty-four years. We have been loyal, very loyal, members of the Scottish Football Association and the Scottish League. In our long history, we have added to the fame of Scottish football, not only here but all over Europe and America. I am surprised at this motion. There have been suspensions on individuals and clubs before, but these suspensions have always been for breaking the Association rules. I hold that we have broken no rules. It has been said that this is only a trivial thing. Gentlemen, it is not a trivial thing.'*

It had been said, Kelly continued, that the ruling was not intended as a penalty, yet 'no penalty they might have imposed could have had the same repercussions that the lowering of this flag will have on my club. If you decide to suspend us, no good can be served for Scottish football.' The hush of the meeting was broken by desk-thumping and foot-stamping. It was noted that Mr Wilson of Rangers was among those who applauded most loudly. Kelly realised that victory was within his grasp.

It was clear that a majority on the council was looking for a token gesture by Celtic which would recognise the SFA's authority. The amendment giving Celtic until April 30 to take the flag down was passed by 16 votes to 15, but the menace had now gone out of the situation. Kelly knew it, and merely noted the council's decision, stating: 'I cannot accede here and now to take the flag down. A decision of this sort cannot be a personal one. I will report back to my club.' Celtic were anxious now to make it as easy as possible for the SFA to complete the retreat. They agreed to write, accepting the SFA's authority and agreeing to take the flag down at the end of the season – as would normally have happened anyway. Behind the scenes, an agreement was made that a special SFA meeting would be called before the start of the 1952/53 season at which the March decision could be rescinded.

The new season duly commenced, with the flag of Ireland (as well as those of the United Kingdom and Scotland) in its familiar place. At best, the whole affair had been a case of maladministration by the SFA. At worst, it had been a blundering display of anti-Irish, anti-Catholic sentiment. Its most profound effects were on the Celtic club and the perceptions of the community from which it drew much of its support.

Whatever complex motives or complicated circumstances had caused the flag furore, the conclusions to be drawn from it were, in the eyes of many, clear. Scotland in the 1950s was still a place which harboured hostility towards the Catholic community and its Irish connections. Despite the progress that had been made in education, political representation and employment, forces still existed which would nullify it if at all possible. The one man who had stood up to these forces, winning the endorsement of Celtic supporters and sympathisers in the process, was Robert Kelly. The expert manner in which he had led Celtic through this crisis, and stood out for the club's traditions, bestowed on him an authority and position of respect which he retained for the rest of his life. It was a fund of goodwill upon which he would have to draw heavily in the course of the next dozen years. For his own part, Kelly's devotion to the cause of Celtic and the roots from which the club had sprung was reinforced by his experiences during this short period of adversity. If ever there had been a possibility of Celtic merging into the scenery of Scottish football by attempting to shed their traditional identity, it evaporated during those early months of 1952.

The flag issue was periodically to raise its head in the years that followed, though never again accompanied by such drama. Sections of the Scottish press, occasionally finding it necessary to demonstrate 'even-handedness' by criticising

Celtic and Rangers with equal force, have found it convenient to present the flying of the flag as a social evil on a par with the Ibrox club's sectarian employment policy – a ludicrous comparison, as its originators well knew. On several occasions during the 1970s, Celtic did remove the Irish flag for their own reasons – not least for the admirable purpose of displaying the nine successive League flags which were won during that glorious period in the club's history. Needless to say, there was no reciprocal 'gesture' from Ibrox, and the supposed balancing act between the clubs, as presented in the media, was revealed for the nonsense it was.

An extract from the minutes of Celtic's annual general meeting of shareholders in 1972, with seven of these League titles safely secured, provides a postscript to those dramatic days twenty years earlier. The new enclosure to replace the 'Jungle' was in hand, and one of the shareholders wondered if the Irish flag would fly from it.

> *'Mr White replied that the flag would fly again at Celtic Park, not in the old place but among the other flags of the nations. The old place where the Eire flag now flew would be given to the flag with the large 'seven' on it. Provocation had been mentioned relative to flags, and he felt that this flag with the large seven on it would cause most displeasure in certain quarters. Mr Dempsey mentioned that it was a pity that the original flag of the yellow harp on the green background had been removed. Mr White stated that he definitely had a point, but that the flag with the yellow harp on the green background was the flag of United Ireland which, possibly, it could rightly be claimed, would cause provocation.'*

A knowledge of Irish history's subtleties has always been an asset in a Celtic chairman.

# THIRTEEN

## ENTER JOCK STEIN:
## THE PLAYING DAYS

JOCK STEIN – or John, as he was known during his youth and early career – was a miner and the son of a miner. Born on October 5, 1922, he grew up in the Burnbank district of Hamilton and, like most of his fellows, went down the pit soon after leaving school at fourteen. He played amateur and juvenile football before turning out briefly for the junior Blantyre Victoria, of which his father was a committee member. In 1942, with wartime football struggling to survive and miners exempt from military call-up, he attracted the interest of Albion Rovers. Stein played three trials in the centre-half position – the first against Celtic, who were pulled back to a 4-4 draw after holding a 3-0 lead. Two heavy defeats followed for Rovers, but nonetheless Stein was offered signing terms which – after waiting a few weeks for the better offer which did not appear – he accepted. In 1948, when Albion Rovers won promotion from the Second Division, Stein was described in a publication to mark the occasion as 'the best capture the club ever made'.

By the start of the 1950/51 season, as his twenty-eighth birthday drew near, Stein was ready for a move. He had fallen out with the Coatbridge club over the parsimony of payment. Kilmarnock showed an interest but, curiously, it was a Welsh non-League club that was able to offer more favourable terms to Stein who, for the first time, was to make his full-time livelihood out of football. Llanelli would pay him a basic £12 per week – half as much again as at Cliftonhill. He left behind his wife and young daughter in a Hamilton council house – a valuable asset in those days of great housing scarcity, of which one did not lightly let go – but the Llanelli venture must have been a fairly miserable one, aggravated by news reaching him that the house in Hamilton had twice been broken into in his absence. It must, indeed, have seemed like the hand of fate reaching out when Stein learned of Celtic's interest. He had no particular affinity for the club, but was later to say that, at that time, he would have played for anyone who offered him a release from South Wales.

Celtic's need was inspired by a spate of injuries, and the reserve-team trainer, Jimmy Gribben, is given the credit for having put forward the name of Stein as a back-up possibility. A transfer fee of £1,200 was agreed and he made his first appearance at Celtic Park on December 8, 1951, against St Mirren. At this time there were three centre-halves on the books – Jimmy Mallan, Alec Boden and John McGrory – and in those days of strict demarcation, Stein had at first been consigned to the reserve-team dressing room at training. Having gained entry to the first team, Stein held his place for a month before Boden returned. However, he made the position his own from mid-February, and played in the number five role almost continuously until injury ended his playing career four years later.

As well as losing 3-0 to Rangers in the League Cup semi-final and taking only twenty-eight points from the thirty League games in 1951/52, Celtic went out of the Scottish Cup to Third Lanark in a first-round replay. This left them short of fixtures by April, and a brief tour of Ireland was undertaken during which the Celtic party met Mr de Valera in Dublin. The club returned to Belfast the following month to play in a charity match against ex-Belfast Celtic players for the funds of the De La Salle Brothers Orphans' Home, in front of a 28,000 crowd.

The great flag controversy which dominated the early months of 1952 provided Stein with ample opportunity in the first half-year of his career with the club to become familiar with the distinctive Celtic identity, which he was subsequently to emphasise with and enhance to an extraordinary degree.

Interestingly, the Celtic handbook which preceded the season of 1952/53 did not give Stein a single mention – he had already become a steady, if perhaps unspectacular part of the green and white scenery, but he was soon to become the club captain, and to lead it to its finest hour since the war. Sean Fallon, the Iron Man from Sligo, was appointed captain at the start of the season and (as was his right in those days) nominated the mature Stein as his vice-captain. Just before Christmas, however, Fallon broke an arm in a clash (ironically) with Jimmy Delaney, who was by this time with Falkirk. (Typically, Fallon finished the game at full-back before learning that the arm was broken in two places.) Fallon was injury-prone during this season, and the full captaincy soon passed to Stein. This was undoubtedly a crucial factor in allowing his talent for reading the game to develop.

Celtic had started the season without the services of Bobby Collins, who had broken an arm during the tour of Ireland in the spring. There had also been tragedy when a twenty-two-year-old player, Jackie Millsop, had died after a short illness; signed in 1948 from Blantyre Celtic, he had been an occasional first-team performer. In November – 'always a bad month for the Celtic', wrote McGrory somewhat unconvincingly – the trail of injuries started, and the League title challenge rapidly evaporated.

The Scottish Cup campaign was characterised by one of Charlie Tully's most celebrated feats, but not much else. This occurred in a third-round tie at Brockville, against a Falkirk team which included Jimmy Delaney and which was two goals up at the interval. Two minutes after the restart, Tully took a corner kick, which curled in on goal and finished up in the back of the net without another player touching the ball. The celebrations were short-lived, as the referee instructed that the kick must be taken again – probably on the grounds that the ball had been outside the marked area. Tully promptly repeated his achievement, and the crowd went wild to such an extent that some crush barriers gave way. Willie Fernie equalised, and John McGrory scored a winner, provoking an invasion of the field by a section of the Celtic supporters. The team hustled the invaders off just in time to prevent the referee from declaring the game abandoned. Unfortunately, the following round proved something of an anti-climax, Celtic going down by 2-0 at Ibrox.

Just in time for the Glasgow Charity Cup final, Celtic signed Neil Mochan from Middlesbrough for £8,000. A centre-forward with a savage shot, who hailed originally from Falkirk, Mochan had previously played for Morton. His connection with Celtic, which would span some forty years, opened in stirring fashion when he scored two of the goals which beat Queen's Park 3-1 in the Charity final.

It was a testimony to the club's reputation and drawing power, rather than to their League standing at the time, that they were included in the Coronation Cup competition of 1953 along with the top clubs in Scotland and England. Even then, Celtic came close to not participating, because of a dressing-room rebellion over money when it became known that Rangers players were looking for £100 a man to win the competition – not the kind of reward that Celtic were in the business of contemplating. Chairman Kelly called a meeting of players, and only four held out for better terms. When Kelly said that he would field a side anyway, the rebellion collapsed. Then Celtic quite unexpectedly beat mighty Arsenal 1-0 in the first round and, just as remarkably, Manchester United – who had disposed of Rangers – 2-1 in the semi-final. Hibs had overcome Newcastle United 4-0, and so it was an all-Scottish final in front of 117,000 on May 30. Fernie took over from the injured Tully on the left wing, but otherwise the team was as in the two previous games: Bonnar, Haughney and Rollo; Evans, Stein and McPhail; Collins, Walsh, Mochan, Peacock and Fernie.

The final provided a fast and thrilling game worthy of the occasion. A characteristic thirty-yard shot from Neil Mochan, from Fernie's pass, gave Celtic the lead after twenty-eight minutes. Hibs dominated most of the remaining play, but Johnny Bonnar played the game of his life, Stein marshalled his defence against an onslaught led by Johnstone, Reilly and Turnbull, and Evans – dominant in midfield and capable of defence-splitting passes – enjoyed one of his finest hours. It was appropriate that, three minutes from the end, it was an interception and pass by Evans which triggered the move from which Walsh scored Celtic's second goal. McGrory described it in the Celtic handbook as 'one of the best finals seen at Hampden for many years', and observed hopefully that the future would be 'very bright' if the Coronation Cup form was maintained.

The Celtic board was by now reduced to three men through the death of Colonel John Shaughnessy after forty-one years as a director. For many years, he had taken a particular interest in the reserves, and served for a long period on the council of the Scottish Football Association. The Shaughnessy connection went back to the club's earliest days, but no member of his family was to succeed him on the board – which would now be made up of only Kelly, White and Devlin for more than a decade. Sean Fallon recalled:

*'Bob Kelly was the boss. He was always responsible for picking*

*the team. There were no great tactics then, though players*
*worked out their own moves. I built up an understanding*
*with Bertie Peacock, my wing-half.*

*Anything coming down our right defensive side, I would*
*come in behind the centre-half and Peacock would drop back*
*to cover the square ball. If Charlie [Tully] said before the*
*game, 'I was out last night', we knew we were in trouble.'*

It really was as simple as that, but more sophisticated methods
were gradually developing elsewhere in the football world.
Stein was becoming an increasingly interested learner, and
Kelly's policy of taking the Celtic party south to see games
of significance proved to be far-sighted. This was particularly
true of the Hungarian national team's visit to Wembley in
1953, when they trounced England 6-3, introduced to an
astonished public the concept of the deep-lying centre-
forward, and really set Stein thinking in a new way about the
tactics of football.

The season of 1953/54 saw Celtic start slowly but then
race to their first League and Cup double since 1913/14. The
hero of the season was Neil Mochan, now playing on the left
wing, and possessed of one of the fiercest whip-crack shots in
football. He scored twenty-six goals in total as Celtic eventually
eased their way to a five-point superiority over Hearts in the
title race, with forty-three points from thirty games. In the
Scottish Cup, Celtic won away ties against Falkirk, Stirling and
Hamilton before facing Motherwell in the semi-final. There
was a 102,000 crowd at Hampden to witness a 2-2 draw, but
Celtic won the replay 3-1 in front of over 90,000 spectators.
Aberdeen had beaten Rangers to reach the final, and started as
favourites to take the trophy. They had a vintage team which
included Fred Martin in goal, Graham Leggat on the right
wing and Paddy Buckley at centre-forward.

The final attracted tremendous interest and, incredibly, demand out-stripped supply for the 134,000 tickets. The game lived up to expectations, with Celtic emerging as 2-1 winners. A diverted shot from Neil Mochan put them ahead early in the second half, but Buckley quickly equalised, and it fell to Sean Fallon to clinch Celtic's seventeenth Scottish Cup success when he shot past Martin after Fernie had set up the chance with a characteristically skilful run. The Celtic team that day was: Bonnar, Haughney and Meechan; Evans, Stein and Peacock; Higgins, Fernie, Fallon, Tully and Mochan.

Celtic, at this time, seemed to be placing reliance on Ireland as a source of young talent – the only 'new players' described in the handbook published in 1954 being three young Irishmen of whom only Vincent Ryan would make even a modest subsequent impression at Celtic Park. The main claim to fame of another member of the trio, Eamon McMahon, was that he had played for Armagh in the All-Ireland Gaelic Football finals. The Kelly influence, in taking a somewhat starry-eyed view of Ireland as a Celtic breeding-ground, had undoubtedly been at work, but Kelly must also be credited for repeatedly exposing the Celtic management and players to the major footballing influences of the day.

In the summer of 1954 the club undertook a very significant trip to the World Cup finals in Switzerland, for which Scotland had qualified. This was the moment of truth for British football, when it was confirmed that continental superiority was absolute. Scotland were beaten 1-0 by Austria and humiliated 7-0 by Uruguay, who then went on to beat England 4-2 in the quarter-finals. But the great Hungarians beat Uruguay in the semi-final, before going down 3-2 to West Germany in a memorable final. While most of the Celtic party simply enjoyed the holiday, and sympathised with Evans, Fernie and Mochan who were in the Scotland squad, Jock Stein watched and learned – about the amateurish shambles of Scotland's preparations, and about the continental tactics, particularly from the Hungarians, which were revolutionising the game.

The 1954/55 season proved to be an anti-climax, with the League slipping away to Aberdeen who held a three-point lead at the end over Celtic. Even more disappointing was the failure to retain the Scottish Cup. Alloa, Kilmarnock and Hamilton were overcome before Airdrie provided the semi-final opposition. (This was the first 'big game' which your author witnessed, at the tender age of seven, and it was a most distressing experience for me when Bonnar had to pick the ball out of the net within thirty seconds of the start, without a Celtic player having touched the ball!) Celtic eventually secured a draw, and won the replay through two goals from the recently restored John McPhail.

The final against Clyde will be especially remembered by many of that generation who were not among the 106,234 Hampden crowd – for it was the first Scottish Cup final to be televised live by the BBC. The Celtic defence was the same as in the previous year's final, but – at the end of a season marked by the constant re-arranging of the forward line – the attack selected was Collins, Fernie, McPhail, Walsh and Tully. Celtic led at half-time through a Jimmy Walsh goal, but were unable to add to this score, in spite of clear superiority. Then, with only two minutes left, Clyde won a corner on the right and Archie Robertson claimed a famous Hampden goal by scoring 'direct' – the goal-mouth 'swirl' for which the ground was at that time notorious among goalkeepers apparently deceiving Bonnar.

The Celtic forward line was shuffled once again for the replay, with the often inspirational Bobby Collins dropping out, apparently for some disciplinary reason, and Sean Fallon entering the attack. This was the kind of eccentric selection in which Kelly specialised on big occasions – and it was fiercely criticised by the Celtic supporters after Tommy Ring had scored the goal which gave Clyde the Scottish Cup. This defeat can be seen as the dividing line between that brief period of success which brought the Coronation Cup and the double to Celtic Park and the prolonged period of darkness which (apart from one very notable shaft of light) was to hang over Celtic Park for a decade.

The most notable feature of the 1955/56 campaign was the ending of Jock Stein's playing career after a series of ankle injuries. When Jimmy McGrory reported to the annual general meeting of shareholders at the end of the season, he highlighted the injury to Stein in the New Year's Day match at Celtic Park, as 'the turning of the tide against us' in the season. The half-back line of Evans, Stein and Peacock had been one of the great trios in the club's history.

The number of clubs in the top Scottish League increased in this season from sixteen to eighteen, and Celtic achieved a modest points total of forty-one from thirty-four games. The Glasgow Cup was won for the first time since 1948/49 in a 5-3 replay victory over Rangers – at this time a toiling and extremely physical side. But the major disappointment of the season was the second successive defeat in a Scottish Cup final, this time at the hands of Hearts – who featured, at this time, Dave MacKay in midfield and the famous forward trio of Conn, Bauld and Wardhaugh. Bobby Evans had become centre-half and captain, following Stein's departure from the side, and the team he led out on to the Hampden pitch in front of a 133,000 crowd was: Beattie, Meechan and Fallon; Smith, Evans and Peacock; Craig, Haughney, Mochan, Fernie and Tully. In short, Kelly had made another of his odd cup final selections, bringing in young Billy Craig on the right wing for his first cup-tie, and – to the even greater astonishment of the Celtic support – moving Mike Haughney up from his perennial right-back position to inside-forward. (In fairness, it should be pointed out that Collins was unavailable through injury on this occasion.) Hearts coasted to a 3-1 victory, and the frustration of the Celtic supporters over the backroom goings-on reached new heights.

It is worthy of mention that Celtic were not at this time a particularly wealthy organisation. When they went to a building society in 1956 to fund a £90,000 programme of ground improvements, they were turned down for a loan 'due to present government credit measures', and had to sell 4,500 savings certificates to help meet the cost. Nor was Robert Kelly anxious to see the business scale of football grow too large. He warned the 1956 annual general meeting that care must be taken with legislation on matters such as floodlighting and international club football – or 'the big clubs will grow bigger and the middle and small clubs smaller, with the possible weakening of the whole structure'.

# FOURTEEN

## FLEETING GLORY:
## THE WILDERNESS YEARS

THE LEAGUE CUP had been a post-war innovation, based on four-team mini-leagues, with the winner of each qualifying for the quarter-finals. The competition had soon become established as the third major tournament of the Scottish season, at the expense of traditional local trophies such as the Glasgow Cup, but it had not been a happy competition for Celtic who had never, in ten years of trying, reached the final. That omission was remedied during the early stages of the 1956/57 season, in spite of Celtic having been drawn in a tough section with Rangers, Aberdeen and East Fife. Three points from the games against Rangers helped them to qualify, and Dunfermline Athletic and Clyde were then disposed of, taking Celtic through to a Hampden final against Partick Thistle. The two semi-final goals against Clyde were scored by Billy McPhail – some recompense for the 1955 Scottish Cup final disappointment against his old club. After a poor goal-less final against Thistle on the last Saturday in October, Celtic beat them in the replay and thus held the League Cup for the first time, thanks to three goals within a six-minute spell early in the second half. Two came from Billy McPhail and the other from Bobby Collins.

But the rest of the season was an anti-climax for Celtic, with only thirty-eight points collected from thirty-four games in the League and a semi-final replay defeat from Kilmarnock in the Scottish Cup, after Rangers had been vanquished at an earlier stage. It was Celtic's first Scottish Cup victory at Ibrox since 1908, and was achieved through goals from John Higgins and Neil Mochan. The newspapers, always on the lookout for portents, pointed out that Celtic had gone on to win the cup final against St Mirren by 5-1 in that earlier season, but there was to be no repeat performance.

The European Cup had come into existence in 1955/56, due largely to the persistent efforts of the French sports newspaper *L'Equipe*, as part of the movement to build bridges in Europe in the post-war era. Failure on the domestic front would henceforth carry the price of exclusion from the increasingly glamorous prospect of competing with the Europeans – a frustration which the Celtic supporters would have to endure for some time to come.

But, though the process was neither systematic nor always apparent, the seeds of future glory were already being sown behind the scenes at Celtic Park. Robert Kelly, a great admirer of Jock Stein's influence on his fellow players and his growing interest in the tactical side of the game, had offered him a job as coach to the Celtic youngsters. The annual general meeting of shareholders on September 6, 1957 was dominated by excitement at the promise which this initiative held. Jimmy McGrory reported that the past season's highlight had been 'the policy on youth, with Jock Stein taking young boys from school and juvenile teams under his wing'. He was certain that some of them would one day play for Scotland. Kelly waxed eloquent upon the same theme, according to the minutes of the meeting:

*'The misfortune to Jock Stein has in a certain way been good*

*fortune for us. Jock Stein is the ideal person to take on these boys and create a training school which could easily be the nucleus of our teams of the future. There has been a great crop of young Catholic boys from the schools and we wish to bridge the gap between leaving school and junior football, still retaining our live interest during this uncertain period. McNeill and Crerand are outstanding examples of this scheme.'* [Both had been signed on the same day.]

Billy McNeill went to Celtic as a seventeen-year-old part-timer, from Our Lady's High School in Motherwell. There were three promising centre-halves in Catholic schools football at that time, and he believes that it was the personal intervention of Stein which pointed Celtic in his particular direction. In Stein's early days, explained McNeill, there was no great emphasis on tactics or ball-play in the junior side, any more than there was with the first team.

*'It was more that he took an interest. He was prepared to sit down and talk to us and, maybe because I was a centre-half, he was particularly interested in my progress. Suddenly, the whole thing became much more than just reading your name up on the list in the dressing room. John Clark, Jim Conway and I were particularly lucky because, like him, we lived in Lanarkshire and we used to get his company home, listening and talking. The first steak I had in my life was when Jock Stein took the young lads down to Seamill Hydro for a weekend, and let us horse around and enjoy ourselves. He always tried to open up people's imaginations. Celtic at that time used to have lunch every day in Ferrari's Restaurant. Experienced players like Neilly Mochan, Sean Fallon and Bertie Peacock were great for us. They did nothing but talk about football.'*

The same AGM minutes reflect the fact that a less progressive school of thought was also present, with its own views as to the reasons for Celtic's shortcomings of recent seasons. One shareholder asked, did the chairman not think it would be better to have more Catholics in the team – 9, 10, 11? But Kelly vigorously reasserted the founding fathers' doctrine on that matter. It had always been the club's policy to field 'the best possible team regardless of denomination', the chairman declared. Non-Catholics, he added, had throughout the club's history played their hearts out for Celtic, and the same policy would continue. 'With the new school of youngsters, Catholic youth will undoubtedly show up very strongly and have every opportunity to show its worth. The principle is, however, the same as always.' The meeting concurred in his remarks. A few weeks later, Celtic celebrated one of their most famous victories in the never-to-be-forgotten League Cup final of Saturday October 19, 1957. The talking-point of the season so far had been the partnership established by Sammy Wilson, picked up on a free transfer from St Mirren, and Billy McPhail. Once again Clyde were the semi-final victims, and the first ever Celtic-Rangers League Cup final was then in prospect. The teams which lined up in front of 90,185 spectators at Hampden were:

*Celtic:* Beattie, Donnelly, Fallon; Fernie, Evans, Peacock; Tully, Collins, McPhail, Wilson, Mochan.

*Rangers:* Niven, Shearer, Caldow; McColl, Valentine, Davis; Scott, Simpson, Murray, Baird, Hubbard.

Valentine was a centre-half signed a few months earlier from Queen's Park, and the informal tactical decision arrived at by the Celtic players before the game was that they should 'play through the middle'. Never has a tactic been more fully vindicated. Celtic streaked to an astonishing 7-1 victory, and to this day that result is commemorated in the graffiti of Glasgow. For Celtic supporters who had grown accustomed to disappointments, and particularly to the all-too-regular failure of green-and-white guiles in the face of the more physical Ibrox approach, the match rekindled in a single afternoon all the pride and delight of earlier years. In his report of the match, the distinguished Glasgow Herald sports writer Cyril Horne – who was generally sympathetic to the Celtic point of view – opened on this point.

*'Eleven players of Celtic Football Club did more in 90 minutes at Hampden Park on Saturday for the good of the game than officialdom, in whose hands the destiny of the game lies, has done in years and years. For with a display of such grandeur as has rarely graced the great, vast ground they proved conclusively the value of concentration on discipline and on the arts and crafts of the game to the exclusion of the so-called power play which has indeed been a disfiguring weakness in the sport but which has frequently been accredited through the awarding of international honours to the 'strong' men.*

*'So devastating an effect had Fernie, the forward turned wing-half, on Rangers who before the rout of Saturday were still considered as difficult opposition as could be found in the length and breadth of the football land, that the Scottish international selectors must surely now be considering whether they should destroy forthwith the impression that certain players are indispensable for future internationals, and build their sides round this wonderful footballer who achieves his purpose without the merest suggestion of relying on physique and who suffers the crude, unfair attempts of opponents to stop him without a thought of retaliation.*

*'Though Rangers Football Club may not immediately be in a mood to agree, they cannot surely in the near future but decide to change their policy on the field. I am not one who is going to charge their players of Saturday with the ultimate responsibility for the club's humiliation, badly as most of them performed. The culprits are those who have, encouraged by results at the expense of method, not discouraged the he-man type of game that has become typical of the side in recent years.'*

Not since 'a slightly corpulent John McPhail' had played havoc with his opponents in the Coronation Cup had Celtic played football of such quality, opined Horne, and '...how the younger, slimmer Billy McPhail has joined Fernie, Tully and company in the bewildering of Rangers by the same admirable methods. Valentine, not long ago a commanding figure on this same ground, was a forlorn, bewitched centre-half on Saturday, repeatedly beaten in the air and on the ground in a variety of ways, and the disintegration of Rangers' defence undoubtedly stemmed from McPhail's mastery.'

Another major factor in Celtic's dominance lay in Mochan's superiority over Shearer, the Rangers right-back. Wilson and Mochan had achieved a modest 2-0 scoreline at half-time. McPhail headed a third, before Simpson made it 3-1. But before the end, McPhail completed his hat-trick, Mochan scored again and Fernie finished the rout with a last-minute penalty to make it 7-1. 'Never have I seen Rangers so outclassed in half-back play; Fernie, Evans and Peacock were, each in his own distinguished way, tremendous players in everything but brawn and bulk', wrote Horne. The Celtic support's joy was unconfined, and the following week's board meeting minuted recognition of 'the wonderful 7-1 victory over Rangers in the League Cup final, a record score for the final of a major competition. A very happy evening was spent at Ferrari's Restaurant after the match.'

Serious injuries to Fernie and McPhail in a League game against Partick Thistle a few days before Christmas 1957 imposed a severe handicap on Celtic's League title pursuit, which had until then seemed promising. McPhail never fully recovered, and this was a particular disappointment since Wilson, with whom he had formed such a devastating partnership, faded away once it was broken. There were also injuries to Tully and Collins and it became increasingly apparent that several distinguished Celtic careers were now drawing to a close, while the youngsters were not yet ready to take over. The memory of that 7-1 result would keep the Celtic supporters buoyant for a while, but a distant second place in the League, which was won by Hearts, and a disappointing third-round exit in the Scottish Cup to Clyde, who went on to win the competition, had turned the season into another anti-climax. This marked the start of a grim five-year spell.

The relationship between directors and manager at this time was summed up at a board meeting when, after the team had been chosen as usual for a game with Rangers, 'the secretary intimated that a band was necessary at half-time according to our agreement with the magistrates of Glasgow. Mr McGrory was to take up this matter.'

There is another well-vouched-for story which testifies to Kelly's control over affairs. The Celtic first-team bus was on its way to a game against Airdrie when the chairman spotted the reserve goalkeeper, Willie Goldie, standing at a bus-stop. He ordered the driver to pull in and, when Goldie revealed that he was on his way to watch the game, he was taken on board. Kelly enthused over the spirit of the player, who was prepared to make his own way to Airdrie in order to see Celtic play, and by the time the bus reached Broomfield, Goldie was in the team.

In August 1958, the directors were shocked to receive a transfer request from Bobby Collins, 'for domestic reasons'. When he remained adamant that he wanted to leave, he was sold to Everton for £23,550. This was a major loss to Celtic, who would desperately lack the steadying influence of a shrewd, Collins-style inside-forward during the next few transitional seasons. Sean Fallon, whose playing days had ended with a pre-season injury, was added to the coaching staff and there was press speculation that he had leap-frogged over Jock Stein in the line of succession. The directors agreed that Stein 'should make a statement to the press intimating that he himself had asked the directors that Fallon be employed as coach under his scheme. The statement was to settle beyond all doubt who was in charge of the coaching scheme at Celtic Park.'

The break-up of the experienced team continued, however, with the transfer of Willie Fernie to Middlesbrough in December and the retirement of Charlie Tully the following spring. (Tully returned to Ireland, where he managed Bangor, and he died in 1971.) Pat Crerard described Tully as 'the George Best of the fifties'. The memory and legend of Charles Patrick Tully are to this day handed down by Celtic supporters, and nowhere more so than in his native Belfast.

Bobby Evans had missed four months of the season due to a back injury. All of this meant that the youngsters whom Stein had been coaching were drafted into the first team out of urgent necessity. Frank Haffey would soon become the regular goalkeeper in place of Dick Beattie, whose habit of losing inexplicable goals had become unacceptable. The seventeen-year-old Billy McNeill, signed from Blantyre Victoria, made his first-team debut on August 23, 1958, in a League Cup tie against Clyde at Celtic Park. Initially, the instantly impressive McNeill was deputising for Evans at centre-half, and later in the season he also played in the right-back and right-half positions.

Crerand, Auld, Conway, Divers and Colrain were other names with which the Celtic supporters now became familiar.

The 1958/59 season yielded no honours. Celtic went out of the League Cup and Scottish Cup at the semi-final stage to Partick Thistle and St Mirren (who went on to win the trophy) respectively.

The sale of Collins and Fernie did have one beneficial side-effect. Desmond White reported to the board early in 1959 that 'if there was any intention of establishing floodlighting at Celtic Park within the next five years, the present accounting period was the obvious time to embark on this venture', because of the very large profit to which the sale of the two players had contributed. It was agreed to proceed with a scheme costing £33,000. Celtic were regularly in profit during this unproductive period, but they were not noted as high payers in the football world. First-team players were on around £16 per week, and the lure of higher salaries certainly contributed to the determination of Collins and Fernie to export their considerable skills to England.

Jock Stein's first recorded appearance at a board meeting was in November 1958 when he successfully pleaded for a wage increase on behalf of some of his young players, including Bertie Auld and Pat Crerand. He also took the opportunity to obtain a £1-per-week increase for himself! The following May, the board agreed to increase Jimmy McGrory's annual salary to £1,500 plus £250 for each competition won, Stein's to £1,000 and Fallon's to £780. The directors noted with satisfaction that Celtic was the first club in Scotland to establish a provident fund for the players 'in excess of the scheme at present in operation in England under the auspices of the English League'.

At the 1959 annual general meeting, Bob Kelly declared that the club was 'in a more promising position' than at any time in the thirty years he had been connected with it. They had 'reverted to the original conception of the club' by rearing their own players and this policy, declared Kelly, would 'achieve results, if not immediately, in the reasonable future'. Large amounts of money had been ploughed into ground improvements, and the investment in floodlights would soon pay off.

The competitive side of the season which followed provided little immediate encouragement for the support. Celtic failed to qualify from a weak section for the League Cup quarter-finals. Their League form yielded thirty-three points from thirty-four games – only the fifth time in their history that they had failed to average a point a game. Hearts won both of these competitions, while in the Scottish Cup, Celtic went down 4-1 in a semi-final replay to Rangers, who then won the trophy. During that Scottish Cup run, Celtic came within six minutes of the most embarrassing result in their history. Against Elgin City at Boroughbriggs Park, they were a goal behind until John Divers and Eric Smith salvaged their dignity at the last minute.

It was a dreadful season for Celtic, but perhaps the worst news of all was that Jock Stein was to depart, to take over the managership of Dunfermline Athletic. There is no evidence to suggest that Celtic 'farmed him out', as has sometimes been suggested, to gain managerial experience. 'It might have been in the minds of the directors that if I made the grade I should be asked back, but if this was the case I knew nothing about it', Stein later wrote in the *Celtic View*.

On Sunday, March 13, 1960, Stein broke the news of an approach for his services from Dunfermline to Bob Kelly, Desmond White and Jimmy McGrory at Celtic Park. He was immediately offered an increase of £250 per year if he would stay, but Stein insisted that this was an opportunity which he should accept. He then asked for permission to leave Celtic Park immediately so that he could assume command of Dunfermline's struggle against relegation, and this request was reluctantly granted. The following Saturday at East End Park, Dunfermline played their first game under Stein's managership, beating Celtic 3-2 after taking the lead only ten seconds into the match. It was a fitting start to the greatest of all Scottish managerial careers, and Dunfermline duly avoided relegation. If he could do this for Dunfermline, wondered the Celtic supporters, what could he have done for us? Twelve years later, in the course of a BBC television interview, Stein said that he had talked over his position at Celtic Park with Kelly, who 'thought that I had gone as far as I could expect to go with a club like Celtic. I was a non-Catholic and maybe they felt that I wouldn't achieve the job as manager, but I moved out to try and prove that I could be a manager.'

Before the end of the season, Celtic were looking positively incident-prone when they became involved in an unseemly quarrel with the long-serving, much-praised Bobby Evans. During the course of the season, the Celtic board had agreed to the player's request for a new house. They had bought him one in Dumbreck, 'and made a special arrangement with him concerning his house should he finish his career with Celtic'. The minutes of Kelly's report to the annual general meeting stated:

*'It was in consequence with some astonishment that we heard from the manager that he wished a transfer, as we had all hoped that this great servant of the club would finish his days with Celtic. We agreed to let him go but feel assured in our own minds that he could not get a better deal anywhere than with Celtic. It was also with great regret and astonishment that we found he had consented to sign his name to articles which appeared in the* Daily Express, *stating among other things that he had virtually been cheated by the club...'*

Evans went to Chelsea, where he lasted only a season, and Celtic eventually won £500 damages plus costs from the *Daily Express*, but the whole affair did no good for the club's public image at a time when the supporters were already accusing them of parsimony and small-time thinking.

Bertie Peacock was next to retire, home to Ireland, and there were no new signings for 1960/61 as Kelly persevered with the youth policy. Celtic went straight out of the League Cup, having been drawn in the same qualifying section as Rangers. They lost 5-1 to Rangers at Celtic Park in the League, promptly followed by defeats from Third Lanark and Airdrie. There was a note of desperation – although no mistaking the source of decision-making power – at the first board meeting of October 1960 when 'Mr Kelly considered that it was advisable to secure the services of W. Fernie from Middlesbrough for our match with St Mirren. The manager was instructed to contact Middlesbrough immediately and arrange a transfer, a figure in the region of £10,000 having been previously agreed.' The deed was done, and things picked up for a few weeks, though Fernie's second stint at Celtic Park did not last long.

After losing the New Year fixture to Rangers, the directors engaged in serious contemplation of the club's position. In a long overdue realisation that the players' training was inadequate, Bob Rooney was recruited by Kelly from Cambuslang Rangers and gradually, with Fallon, introduced ball-play into the routines. The directors repeatedly discussed the scouting system and came up with the remarkable conclusion that 'a card index system should be introduced, which would indicate how good the scouts were and how good the players observed were' – scarcely an adequate response to a critical situation.

By the end of the season, Celtic were once again nowhere in the title race with thirty-nine points from thirty-four games, and the irony of Stein's departure was reinforced when the

Scottish Cup brought Dunfermline Athletic to Hampden for the final. Scottish football was in a state of shock at this time, following the unprecedented 9-3 defeat of the international side at Wembley. It had been Frank Haffey's misfortune to be brought into the side two days before that game and, inevitably, he had borne the brunt of the ridicule for what had transpired. It was not the ideal preparation for a Scottish Cup final, but, notwithstanding Celtic's erratic form, few could take seriously the possibility that they would not overwhelm the unfashionable Fife club, which would surely be intimidated by the vast Hampden audience. On the day, the crowd numbered 113,328. The wily Jim Rodger, writing in the *Daily Record*, was one of the few who thought it worthwhile to warn:

*'I know this game will be no walkover for Celtic. This may be Dunfermline's first time in the final. But they have behind them the inspiration of that solid man, that sometimes underrated man, Jock Stein, who now has his team playing the blend of soccer that wins cups.'*

Dunfermline duly declined to be overawed, and forced a goalless draw. For the replay, Stein made a couple of shrewd tactical switches, goalkeeper Connachan had the game of a lifetime, and the Celtic supporters were once again left to mourn when Haffey dropped the ball with two minutes left, allowing Dickson an easy chance to score.

At the end of the season, centre-forward Conway – an early product of the youth policy – was sold to Norwich for £10,000 and Bertie Auld to Birmingham for £15,000. A few weeks earlier, the Celtic board had decided to fix the first-team wage level for the coming season at the 'greatly increased terms' of £26 per week, but to cut out lunches on match-days and expenses unless there were 'most exceptional circumstances'.

This was an attempt to compete with the lures of England where, much to Bob Kelly's irritation, the maximum wage had been abolished. The Celtic chairman, who was also president of the SFA, deplored the 'extraordinary weakness' of the English League in meeting the players' demands. It would have 'great repercussions in Scottish football', he feared.

In spite of the conspicuous lack of playing success, Celtic were still making money and the directors agreed at the close of this singularly unproductive season that 'from the point of view of publicity, the profit should be cut down to a figure in the region of £10,000' by writing off part of it to depreciation of assets. There was no evidence that the Celtic directors or shareholders were making much out of the club, since the 20 per cent dividend paid annually did not add up to a lot when applied to the relatively small number of shares, while the director's fee of £150 per annum had remained unchanged for twenty-five years and was scarcely exorbitant. The perceived discrepancy between official attendances and packed terraces was part of Celtic folklore. But there was no indication that the club was willing to lurch voluntarily into a bigger financial league – as Rangers seemed prepared to do at that time, by buying established players.

Sean Fallon recalls that Kelly was 'always talking about Sunderland' as an example of how paying big money for players did not guarantee success.

Between 1960 and 1964, Rangers were once again the dominant force in Scottish football, with one of their greatest sides. They won three out of four League titles, the exception being in 1961/62 when the memorable Dundee team of that era registered its solitary triumph. The Scottish Cup went three times in a row to Ibrox, following Dunfermline's success, while only Hearts' triumph in 1962/63 disturbed a Rangers monopoly over the League Cup. The contrast in fortunes was hard for Celtic supporters to take. In the Celtic handbook for the season of 1961/62, Kelly chided the support for criticism of the team. 'We ask that young players on the threshold of their careers be not ruined by ill-advised attacks on them while they are doing their best.' His promise of 'much to delight us' in the future was taking on a tediously unconvincing ring, and in any case the criticism was far more of the management than of the young players.

Over this period Celtic's performances were often entertaining, they obviously had brilliant players in the likes of Crerand and McNeill, and they won considerably more games than they lost, but somehow they could not get their act together to turn all this into success. In retrospect it seems astonishingly obvious that what was required was a change of manager, in style as well as personality.

Early in the 1961/62 season, a slight youngster called Jimmy Johnstone was brought along to Celtic Park by his headmaster. He was signed on a provisional basis and farmed out to Blantyre Celtic. Tommy Gemmell, from Coltness United, and Bobby Lennox, from Ardeer Recreation, were recruited from the junior ranks. The new *Celtic Song*, recorded by Glen Daly, was issued in October 1961 – but it would still be a while before there was much to sing about. Celtic failed to qualify from their League Cup section, secured a modest forty-six points from their thirty-four League games, and lost 3-1 in the Scottish Cup semi-final to St Mirren, a game marred by a pitch invasion from Celtic supporters. John McPhail, by then a journalist with the *Daily Record*, offered some unwelcome advice to the club after this defeat. The young players like Chalmers, Carroll, Byrne and Gallacher had not developed as expected, he said, because of the lack of an experienced player behind them. Celtic bought Price from Falkirk in an effort to remedy that omission, but this was hardly sufficient to rectify the situation.

There was an early highlight to the season of 1962/63 when Real Madrid came to Glasgow for a charity game. The Spanish club had dominated the European Cup during its early years, and all Scotland remembered the Hampden final of 1960 when they had defeated Eintracht Frankfurt 7-3 in a game which further opened the eyes of the football public to the progress that had been made on the continent. Although Celtic lost 3-1 to a side which included Puskas, di Stefano, Santamaria and Gento, the quality of play of the 'Kelly Kids' offered the supporters a glimpse of what was possible. One observer, Malcolm Munro of the *Evening Citizen*, wrote in advance of the game: 'Celtic can play well up to the 18-yard line. After that – bedlam. It's all right a team being inspired by its support. What's wrong with Celts is that they don't get so much inspired as excited.' But the following day he joined in the praise and opined: 'In his form in the last 45 minutes, Pat Crerand must go down in the same book as Puskas and di Stefano.'

At a time when laps of honour were a novelty, the Celtic supporters demanded one from the defeated side – as well as from the victors. Little did they know the unorthodox manner in which the Celtic players had learned of their selection that night. Twenty minutes before kick-off, trainer Rooney had read out the defence and told them to get changed. The forward line could not be revealed, however, as Mr Kelly had not yet arrived at the ground. Ten minutes before the start, the chairman arrived – and the team list was finalised!

Celtic had finally staggered into the Fairs Cities Cup (forerunner of the UEFA Cup) of 1962/63, as reward for coming fourth in the League. They were drawn against Valencia in the first round, lost 4-2 away and then drew 2-2 at Celtic Park. The following week's board meeting was agitated about the way in which the newspapers had 'written down the value of the Valencia team... it was felt that if Rangers had been playing Valencia, the press's comments would have been very different'.

But the supporters were no longer interested in such trivial grouses. Around this time, insurrection in 'The Jungle' was accompanied by moves to challenge the power of the Celtic board, either through takeover or even by forming an alternative club. The man chiefly associated with these moves was a Glasgow councillor, Bailie James F. Reilly. Eventually, they petered out, but this was the first time in the club's history when some serious calculations took place about where shareholding power lay, in preparation for a challenge which might pose a threat to the dominant factions. In that respect, it was a harbinger of what was to follow 30 years later.

# FIFTEEN

## THE RETURN OF STEIN:
## BACK ON THE ROAD TO GREATNESS

A LOW POINT in Celtic's fortunes came on May 15, 1963 when Rangers gave them a terrible beating in the Scottish Cup final replay at Hampden Park. Ralph Brand and Davy Wilson put Rangers two ahead at the interval, and Celtic were in tatters long before Brand scored the third. All the unease, the feeling of foreboding which had suffused the Celtic support in the run-up to the final, was fully vindicated. There had been just one real glimmer of hope at the end of the first match eleven days earlier, when almost 130,000 spectators had witnessed a 1-1 draw. Then, for some obscure reason, in the continuing tradition of eccentric cup final selections, the highly-promising Jimmy Johnstone was dropped for the replay, along with Jim Brogan. The teams which lined up at this sharply contrasting moment in the two clubs' fortunes were:

*Rangers:* *Ritchie. Shearer, Provan; Greig, MacKinno, Baxter; Henderson, MacMillan, Millar, Brand, Wilson.*

*Celtic:* *Haffey, MacKay, Kennedy; McNamee, McNeill, Price; Craig, Murdoch, Divers, Chalmers, Hughes.*

The replay attendance was 120,273, with the huge Celtic contingent attending more in hope than optimism. And, as so often in the recent past, the hopes turned to dust. The 3-0 scoreline was bad enough, but there was also the knowledge that even that was an inadequate reflection of the gulf which had developed between the rival clubs. Rangers had been so far ahead in every department of the game that, a full twenty-five minutes from the end, thousands of Celtic fans were streaming from the stadium. Some of them burned their scarves, while most angrily proclaimed their disaffection with the club and, in particular, its chairman. This humiliation of their side at the hands of the arch-enemy was the final straw after the disappointment and frustration endured by Celtic supporters through most of the preceding decade. By this time things were so bad that even recalling the 7-1 game was something of an embarrassment – a hollow attempt, drawn from the increasingly distant past, at retaliation in the face of taunts from followers of the ascendant Rangers. On the evidence of the cup final replay it was difficult to see much cause for optimism about the future.

In the League, Rangers took the flag with Celtic in fourth place, a distant thirteen points behind. For a campaign which lasted for only thirty-four matches, it was a huge differential. The annual general meeting heard from Bob Kelly that Celtic appeared to be 'one of the few clubs in Scottish football that are showing a definite profit each year.' If the long-suffering supporters had been privy to this sentiment, the mood of insurrection might have been accelerated. But there was no word of cheer in the manager's report.

*'Mr McGrory stated that once again he had to admit great disappointment in not making the grade in winning one of the major trophies. He went over the season's results*

*culminating in the Scottish Cup final replay with Rangers,*
*where the real issue lay not so much in defeat but in the lack*
*of fight of the team.'*

One shareholder sought to apportion the blame for failure on religious grounds, stating that there had been only Catholics in the cup final team. Was it the policy of the club to try to play an all-Catholic team? This was strongly denied by Kelly, who declared that in recent years the Catholic teams had been very successful in schools' football and were almost unchallenged at the top of the leagues. This was why they had secured the services of more young Catholic players than usual. 'We have at the moment one very promising young player who is not a Catholic and he should go far – Tommy Gemmell. We hope he will be joined by others.'

There was no doubt, indeed, that a pool of considerable promise had formed at Celtic Park. But it all seemed far too unplanned, and the breakneck pace of the 'Kelly Kids' cried out for the introduction of experienced heads, which might cost money to purchase. The youth policy had now been offered for several years to the supporters as the guarantee of better things to come. They were running out of patience, and the anger levelled against Robert Kelly intensified. Those who sat in the directors' box at that time recall the stoicism with which he sat through torrents of abuse from the supporters in the enclosure, just in front of the stand. Demonstrations at the entrance to Celtic Park became commonplace, in the wake of fresh disappointments. When Kelly did choose to reply, it was to tell those who were unhappy with his stewardship to stay away from Celtic Park and come back when they had a winning side.

This was intended as a chastisement to the disloyal, but many faithful Celtic supporters began to take Kelly at his word. In those days of even bigger gates than today's, Celtic's

The Marist, Brother Walfrid, was a central figure in Celtic's founding. A statue outside Celtic Park provides a permanent reminder of his seminal role and the club's charitable origins.

Willie Maley, the pivotal figure in Celtic's first 50 years.

The first picture of the Celtic team, wearing the white shirts with green collars and red Celtic cross.

Members of the Tom Maley Celtic Brake Club in the late 19th century, the earliest form of supporters' clubs.

John Thomson was the 'Prince of Goalkeepers' who tragically died at the age of just 22 on 5 September 1931.

Jimmy McGrory, with 468 goals in 445 appearances, is Celtic's record goalscorer.

The 1936 league championship-winning side.

Captain Jimmy McStay and his triumphant team-mates with the 1937 Scottish Cup.

The legendary Jimmy Delaney in action for Celtic in January 1946.

Jock Stein in action for the Hoops in the 1950s.

Celtic's successful Coronation Cup squad of 1953/54, which would go on to lift the double at the end of the season.

Jimmy Johnstone scores a glorious goal at Ibrox in a 2-2 draw which saw Celtic confirmed as Scottish champions in 1967.

The Lisbon Lions throw their arms up in celebration as the whistle goes for full time in the 1967 European Cup final.

Billy McNeill is mobbed by supporters after Celtic's 1967 European Cup triumph.

The Kings of Europe celebrate their momentous success.

Paradise acclaims Jock Stein and his Lisbon Lions as they parade the 'Big Cup'.

Billy McNeill's winner in the 1965 Scottish Cup final
heralded the start of a golden era for Celtic.

Priceless: a winner's medal from
the 1967 European Cup triumph.

Fans' protests in the early 1990s against
the old board running Celtic.

The rebuilding work at Celtic Park in 1994.

Dramatis personae: Jimmy Farrell, Tom Grant, John Keane, Dominic Keane,
Fergus McCann, Kevin Kelly and Brian Dempsey in March 1994.

Fergus McCann, who set Celtic on a new course in 1994, standing in the magnificently rebuilt Celtic Park.

Pierre van Hooijdonk headed the only goal of the game in the 1995 Scottish Cup final against Airdrie.

The Maestro: Paul McStay was an extraordinary talent, who spent his whole career at Celtic Park.

Wim Jansen and Murdo MacLeod
celebrate 'stopping the 10' in 1998.

Martin O'Neill celebrates the 6-2
Demolition Derby in August 2000.

John Hartson celebrates his wonder goal against Liverpool at Anfield in March 2003.

Lubo Moravcik and Henrik Larsson are two of the finest players to have worn the Hoops.

The Bhoys in Seville: Celtic supporters in the Spanish city of for the 2003 UEFA Cup final.

March 2006 was a sad time for the Celtic family as the player voted the Greatest Ever Celt, Jimmy Johnstone, passed away.

Manager Gordon Strachan with Garry Pendrey, Jim Blyth and the late, great Tommy Burns after the 2007 title success.

Long live the King: Henrik Larsson bids farewell to the Celtic support after seven
magnificent years, having scored 242 goals in 315 appearances for the Hoops.

Shunsuke Namakura's sublime free-kick against Manchester United
in 2006, which beat the English side 1-0.

Leap of Faith: Tommy Burns celebrates Celtic's UEFA Champions League play-off win over
Spartak Moscow. The Celtic legend passed away in May 2008 at the age of just 51.

Ronny Deila raises the SPL trophy after victory over Motherwell at Celtic Park in
May 2016. It was his final act as manager having already declared
that he would stand down at the end of the season.

Brendan Rodgers is unveiled as Deila's successor before
being greeted by the supporters at Celtic Park.

Moussa Dembele scores Celtic's third goal in spectacular fashion against
Manchester City in the 2016 Champions League group stage game at Celtic Park.

The players celebrate Scott Sinclair's goal during the 5-1 victory over Rangers
at Ibrox on 28 April 2017, as Celtic marched relentlessly towards the title.

Lisbon Lions (L-R) Jim Craig, Bobby Lennox, John Clark, Bertie Auld and John Hughes are presented with the Loving Cup at the Lord Provost's Awards in April 2017 to celebrate the 50th anniversary of Celtic's 1967 European Cup triumph.

The Invincibles squad pose with the Scottish Cup, the SPL Trophy and the Scottish League Cup at Celtic Park in May 2017.

attractiveness was rapidly on the wane. They played Rangers five times in the following season, and never did better than a single-goal defeat. In League Cup section qualifiers Rangers twice repeated the 3-0 scoreline. Steve Chalmers broke the scoring duck in the first League game at Ibrox. but it still ended in 2-1 defeat. On New Year's Day, Celtic went down 1 -0. In the Scottish Cup quarter-final, goals by Jim Forrest and Willie Henderson just before and after the interval ensured another unproductive season. Celtic finished the League in third place, eight points behind treble-winners Rangers. By mid March of 1964, the week after the Scottish Cup exit, the normally attractive visit of Hibs could draw only 11,000 to Celtic Park, and interest in the remainder of the season was sustained only by the novelty of the first European run.

During the 1963/64 season, there was at least the consolation of this entertaining and unexpected progress in the European Cup-Winners' Cup, even if qualification had been only by dint of the fact that Rangers were engaged in the European Cup. The youthful enthusiasm and undoubted skills of the Celtic team flourished for the first time in the European arena, and they reached the semi-final by beating FC Basel of Switzerland. Dinamo Zagreb of Yugoslavia and – most impressively – Slovan Bratislava of Czechoslovakia, with 1-0 scorelines in Celtic's favour both home and away. Players such as Billy McNeill and Jimmy Johnstone gained precious experience from this run, and important lessons were learned in ultimate defeat.

Celtic achieved a splendid 3-0 victory over MTK of Budapest at Celtic Park on April 15, 1964, with Jimmy Johnstone scoring one and Stevie Chalmers the other two. Anti-climax was, however, to follow, for Celtic went to Budapest two weeks later, suffered from tactical naivety and lost the game 4-0. In considering the disappointing outcome, the Celtic board bemoaned the quality of refereeing and displayed an unusual appreciation of history.

'It was not thought correct that a referee from Austria should have controlled this match. Austro-Hungary used to be one country and as far as they were concerned, it was to all intents and purposes a home referee.'

Celtic had previously played in the short-lived Friendship Cup against Sedan in 1960/61 and against Valencia in the Fairs Cities Cup in 1962/63. The Cup-Winners' Cup run was, however, their first serious foray, and in Bob Kelly's post-Budapest view, it should have been their last. In a pronouncement notably lacking in foresight, Kelly told the Celtic shareholders at the annual general meeting on May 28, 1964:

*'For the future, surely a better competition would be a British Cup for the top eight clubs in English and Scottish Leagues. This, as well as being an excellent competition in itself, would revitalise the Leagues, where every team would be playing for a place in this lucrative competition.'*

The club's financial position remained healthy in spite of the suffering League gates, due to the European success and the previous season's progress to the replayed Scottish Cup final. But Jimmy McGrory could find no consolation when offering his eighteenth report to shareholders as manager of Celtic.

*'Mr McGrory stated that once again he could not find words to express his disappointment at not having won a major trophy. He then dealt with the playing season. With full maturity in the team, he hoped that he would have something positive to report on next meeting.'*

Indeed, the 1964/65 season opened quite promisingly following the failure of an improbable errand aimed at securing the transfer of the great, but ageing, Alfredo di Stefano of

Real Madrid. Jimmy McGrory and John Cushley, the reserve centre-half who had the advantage of being a fluent Spanish speaker, were dispatched to Spain for negotiations but failed to lure the player to Celtic Park. While there was a tinge of desperation about the initiative, it did at least indicate that Celtic were ready to deviate from their long-held policy of patiently waiting for youth to fulfill its potential.

A free-scoring start to the 1964/65 season, including a 3-1 win over Rangers, offered hope that the corner might at last have been turned. But a familiar pattern then began to develop. The League Cup was lost by a single goal to Rangers. On the following Saturday, there was an embarrassing 5-2 defeat at Kilmarnock, and further League defeats from St Johnstone and Dundee quickly followed. Early in December Celtic were ousted from the Fairs Cities Cup by Barcelona. On New Year's Day at Ibrox, there was yet another 1-0 win for Rangers. By this time, even Billy McNeill was on the verge of asking for a move. He recalled:

*'I was coming on for twenty-five and had been at Celtic Park since I was seventeen. Nothing significant had happened throughout that period and nothing significant looked like happening. There were clubs biting my ear, and I was an internationalist. It is an indication of how bad things were that I was getting to the stage where I was ready for shifting.'*

In the Celtic boardroom, too, the pressure for action was growing. A new director, James Farrell, had been co-opted to the board in mid December, ending a lengthy period during which the club was presided over by the triumvirate of Kelly, White and Devlin. He recalls a clear mood of 'something has got to be done', with Desmond White and himself most anxious for change. Celtic had long been caught in a dilemma over the position of manager. Such was the bond between Kelly and McGrory, and indeed the whole club's loyalty to the latter, that the question never arose of him being removed from office at the cost of his dignity. The presence of McGrory in the manager's chair also fitted in well with Kelly's enthusiasm for controlling the club's fortunes. The Celtic supporters recognised the true nature of the relationship by directing their discontent almost exclusively towards Kelly. It had been widely speculated that Sean Fallon, McGrory's assistant who had been responsible for signing the bulk of the 1964/65 team, might eventually succeed him. On the other hand, the name of Jock Stein was never far from the lips of Celtic supporters and Kelly had maintained contact with him since his departure for Dunfermline. The New Year's Day defeat and reports that Wolves were interested in securing Stein's services may have been two more factors that finally prompted Kelly to take the action which was to transform the nature of Celtic as an organisation, as well as the club's fortunes on the field.

The curriculum vitae which determined Kelly's eventual response to mounting crisis had grown ever more formidable. It was fourteen years since Stein had arrived at Celtic Park from Llanelli, and throughout that period he had demonstrated an uncommon capacity for leading others to success on various fronts. Sean Fallon's injuries had given him the opportunity to flourish as captain of a successful Celtic side. The testimony of his contemporaries is that he was already miles ahead of everyone else in his understanding of the game, and in studying how the investment of energy could be tailored to maximum effect, While the rest simply 'went out and played', Stein was immersing himself in the nuances of the game's structure. The whole concept of a youth policy at Celtic Park – the hope to which Kelly had clung – had its origins in Stein's success as a coach following the end of his playing career.

Misgivings persisted about whether, starved of proper recognition at Celtic Park, he should ever have been allowed to depart for Dunfermline, where his success at East End Park had been both immediate and lasting in its effect. Not only had they avoided relegation and won the Scottish Cup, henceforth Dunfermline would regard themselves as a big club. Through Stein's astuteness in the transfer market, they were able to afford a new stand and a ground commensurate with their transformed status. But Stein's days at East End Park were numbered almost from the moment he first touched the Fife club with success. Hibernian were struggling to regain past glories, and saw him as their ideal man. He joined them in 1964 and led them to the short-lived Summer Cup before the new season was properly underway. This modest triumph reinforced Stein's reputation as a man to rival Midas and run him very close.

It was an astonishing fourteen-year record which pointed, with increasing strength, in only one logical direction. The possibility of Jock Stein returning to Celtic began to crop up informally in the private conversations of directors, as well as on the terracings. After the New Year's Day defeat, Celtic drew with Clyde and lost to Dundee United. John Fairgrieve wrote on January 12, 1965 in the *Scottish Daily Mail*: 'They are being left behind by provincial clubs with a fraction of their resources. They are being left so far behind by Rangers that it is no longer a race.' Also on that day, the four Celtic directors held a special board meeting in the North British Hotel. A formula had been found to release Jimmy McGrory from the managership without loss of face. The terse minutes of that meeting summarised the momentous steps which Kelly had, in effect, decided upon:

*'After much discussion, all have agreed our desire to obtain the services of J. Stein as manager. Mr Kelly was to approach Stein with a view to offering him the position. Fallon was to*

*be offered an increased salary with increased status if Stein was*
*secured. McGrory was to continue as public relations officer.'*

Two evenings later, the Celtic board held its normal weekly meeting, with Jimmy McGrory and Sean Fallon in attendance as usual. The minutes record: "The chairman stated that he had interviewed Stein and that he was willing to join the club as manager. He had asked, however, to be allowed to remain for a time with Hibs as they had a chance of winning the League, and that in any case he would require to give reasonable notice. This was agreed to.'

Having heard this news, the directors proceeded to meet with anxious representatives of the Supporters' Association, who might have been in a happier frame of mind had they known of the bombshell that was soon to break on Scottish football. Celtic were remarkably successful in keeping the impending news out of the press, but speculative reports did begin to appear. On January 28 the board held their weekly meeting and 'in view of the leakage of information, it was considered necessary to make a statement to the press. This was to be arranged for Sunday.'

The day before the news of Stein's impending arrival was made public, Celtic ran riot in their home League game against Aberdeen. As if in salute to an era which, for all its disappointments, had spawned the makings of a world-beating side, they trounced Aberdeen 8-0 with John Hughes scoring five, and Lennox, Murdoch and Auld scoring the others. These names hint at a very significant fact which, in the lauding of Stein's memory, should not be forgotten. It is simply that all but one member of the team which was later to win the European Cup, as well as most of the other key members of that pool, had been assembled by the time the managerial transition occurred.

Sean Fallon's role had been vital, particularly in the closing months of McGrory's reign. It was he who persuaded the manager and Kelly that he should travel south to bring Bertie Auld back from Birmingham City for a £11,000 transfer fee and, for the player himself, the deposit on a house in Glasgow. This was the signing that was to add crucial poise and experience to the side. Similarly, Celtic had long suffered from a goalkeeping problem. Sean Fallon heard that Jock Stein was about to transfer the veteran Ronnie Simpson from Hibs to Berwick Rangers as player-manager. He was given permission to contact Stein and sign the keeper for £2,000 and a signing-on fee of £1,000.

Kelly spared a considerable amount of thought for Fallon's position, and was concerned that he might be affronted by the appointment of Stein. It was arranged that the two men should meet to discuss the new situation in Edinburgh, where Hibs were playing Aberdeen in a midweek game. Having agreed that he could work as assistant to Stein, without a trace of hard feelings, Fallon rushed back to the North British Hotel in Glasgow. He had got wind of the fact that Tommy Docherty was there, trying to sign a youngster called David Hay for Manchester United. Fallon arrived in time, and secured that signature too for Celtic. It has been suggested that Kelly toyed with the idea of a joint managership between Stein and Fallon, but this appears improbable. Fallon himself stated that he never heard of any such proposal and that it would have been 'laughable'.

Stein's first game as manager was at Broomfield in a midweek League game against Airdrie. Celtic won 6-0 and Auld contributed five of the goals. The following evening, the new manager was at the weekly board meeting. Possibly for the first time in the club's history, team selection was not an item on the agenda. Henceforth, that would be the manager's prerogative. Though Stein was always happy to chat with directors and confidantes about the team's performance, and possible improvements, the right to select had firmly and finally been taken away from Kelly and his fellow directors.

The League title was already well out of Celtic's reach, and they were eventually to finish eighth, with Kilmarnock taking the title. But just before Stein arrived, Celtic had scraped through to the Scottish Cup semi-final with a 3-2 win over that same Kilmarnock side. Winning the Cup was now Stein's immediate aim, and the supporters were revitalised by the prospect. But during the first game with Motherwell, Celtic twice had to equalise goals from a striker called Joe McBride, who was wearing the claret and amber and assuming the entire workload up front. Bobby Lennox and Bertie Auld salvaged a replay, and the second match was a 3-0 canter with goals from Chalmers, Hughes and Lennox.

Celtic returned to Hampden on April 24 for the final against Dunfermline. The team which, in front of a 108,000 crowd, took the Scottish Cup to Celtic Park for the first time since 1954 was: Fallon, Young and Gemmell; Murdoch, McNeill and Clark; Chalmers. Gallagher, Hughes, Lennox and Auld. Celtic twice fell behind, and twice Auld equalised. Then, in the 81st minute, Billy McNeill rose above the Dunfermline defence to head home a corner from Charlie Gallagher – a goal that continues to live in the memory of all Celtic supporters who witnessed it. There may never be another day like it in Scottish football, for at the same time. Kilmarnock were winning the League title showdown against Hearts, to take the flag on goal average.

But, for once, the cup made bigger news – for Celtic's victory clearly heralded the birth of a new era in Scottish football. The supporters' faith in the manager's potential for greatness was reinforced. So too was the players' faltering belief in themselves. Many years later, Jock Stein reflected: 'It wouldn't have gone as well for Celtic had they not won this game.' Bobby Lennox recalls that the team bus couldn't move for the exultant throng as they left Hampden. 'Later, once they got used to us winning cups, that kind of thing didn't happen.'

There was nothing infallible about even Stein's judgment, however, as the minutes of a board meeting on April 29, 1965 illustrate. After six weeks as manager, and five days after the Scottish Cup success, he presented to the board a list of players he would like to buy including Joe McBride, and another list of those he would consider selling. The latter category included John Hughes, Charlie Gallagher and Jimmy Johnstone. The minutes testify: 'It was agreed after discussion that we should accept Mr Stein's plans for the strengthening of the team.'

Fortunately for the course of football history, subsequent sales policy was restricted to less conspicuous names. Celtic players of that period believe that Stein must, at that point, have been preoccupied with the need to develop teamwork, rather than give licence to individual skills. Ultimately, his greatest achievement would be to combine both – incorporating the extraordinary skills of Johnstone, in particular, into the team framework.

The annual general meeting, held on August 5, 1965, was a very different affair from its recent predecessors. Jock Stein told the small but exultant gathering that he 'would certainly not consider we had returned to past glories until the League was won'. But a more poignant contribution came from the man who had previously occupied the managerial chair and who, a year earlier, had expressed the hope that 'with full maturity in the team', he would have 'something positive to report on next meeting'. Now, he said, he addressed the gathering with considerable emotion. The minutes record that: 'He was delighted with our success last season. Had he himself been the chooser of his successor, it would have been Mr Stein. He wished Mr Stein every success.' Jimmy McGrory continued for many years to give Celtic valuable service as public relations officer, and Jock Stein went out of his way to show respect for his predecessor's experience and status within the Celtic hierarchy.

For some sections of the press, the footballing significance of Stein's appointment had scarcely been given greater prominence than the sensation of a non-Catholic being appointed as manager of Celtic. This was not a factor which had entered into Kelly's calculations. He had come to respect Stein in the aftermath of the Coronation Cup success. 'They were compatible, maybe because they were both Lanarkshire men', Sean Fallon recalled. Their personal relationship was not particularly close, and Stein never deviated from the view that the best place for football club directors was in the background. But there was mutual respect, and a shared love of Celtic provided the basis for a productive working relationship. With one action, Celtic had confirmed the message that had been repeated throughout the decades – that, while proud of its origins and distinctive identity, the club had always eschewed sectarianism in its employment policies. The appointment of Jock Stein, and the great era which now ensued, impressed that message upon all who had ears to hear and eyes to see.

# SIXTEEN

## LISBON MANIA: CHAMPIONS OF EUROPE

JOCK STEIN'S FIRST major signing as Celtic manager was of Joe McBride, on June 5, 1965. Still five days short of his twenty-seventh birthday, McBride was a ten-year veteran of senior football who had given notable service and a steady flow of goals to five clubs – Kilmarnock, Wolves, Luton, Partick Thistle and Motherwell. It was largely on account of McBride's emotional attachment to Celtic that he accepted Stein's offer for his services, since, remarkably enough, there was a higher bid from the upwardly mobile Dunfermline Athletic. The new broom had arrived at Celtic Park, but the purse-strings were still well under control. McBride recalled:

*'Motherwell wanted me to go to East End Park because they would get a bigger transfer fee – £25,000 against Celtic's £22,500. So I told Dunfermline that I wanted a ridiculous amount of money, in the expectation that they would lose interest. But George Farm, their manager, came back and said they could meet the signing-on fee, though I would be on the same wages as everybody else. That gave me the get-out I needed because, of course, I could earn more at Parkhead in wages. The money had little to do with it – I wanted to play*

*for Celtic. But the truth is that I got £1,000 for joining big Jock and I could have had £5,000 from Dunfermline!'*

McBride proved to be a remarkable bargain. Gifted with the great goal-scorer's instinctive grasp of how attacks will take shape and where the ball will be at the end of them, he completed his first Celtic season with forty-three goals – a post-war record for the club.

The *Celtic View*, edited by Jack McGinn, was launched at the start of the 1965/66 season, and immediately there was plenty to write about. It was an exhilarating season, with Celtic in all-out pursuit of four trophies. A glut of early scorelines served notice that, under Stein's management, the club's traditional emphasis on attacking play was to be reinforced with enthusiasm. Victories such as 8-1 at home to Raith Rovers, 7-1 when Aberdeen came to Glasgow, 4-0 away to Dundee United, 6-1 at home to Stirling Albion, 5-2 at home to Hearts and 4-3 away to Falkirk cluttered this opening burst. Suddenly, it was great to be a Celtic supporter. The only fly in the ointment was a 2-1 defeat at Ibrox in the first derby of the season, but even in that game the manner in which Celtic pursued an equaliser during the final thirty minutes was encouraging.

With Hibs crushed 4-0 in the League Cup semi-final replay the first acid test of the season was the League Cup final on October 23, 1965, with Rangers as the opposition in front of a 107,609 crowd. It was Celtic's first League Cup final since the 7-1 game, and the team was: Simpson, Young and Gemmell; Murdoch, McNeill and Clark; Johnstone, Gallagher, McBride, Lennox and Hughes. Two penalty goals by John Hughes put Celtic in the clear before John Greig reduced the margin near the end. The celebrations on the Hampden terracing were cut short, however, when the team's lap of honour was brought to a hasty conclusion by an invasion of the pitch from the Rangers end. It was an ugly incident, and it led to bans or curtailments on laps of honour in Scotland thereafter. The following week's meeting of the Celtic board recorded dissatisfaction with press coverage of the incident, which directed most of its criticism at Celtic, 'for allowing the players on to the field – only Aitken in the *Evening Citizen* had come out strongly on our side'. The Celtic goal-storm was the product of Stein's tactical approach to the game, as Billy McNeill recalls:

> '*It was no accident that Celtic became such an attack-minded team. Jock believed fervently in forward play and that was why he paid so much attention in the early days to signing goal-scorers. His wisdom proved itself in the number of men in our squad who could find the net. Quite apart from the obvious team members like Joe McBride, Bobby Lennox and Stevie Chalmers, people like Bertie Auld and Bobby Murdoch – to say nothing of Tommy Gemmell – were encouraged to move up and do some damage. I remember specifically Jock telling us one day that a great deal of space could be found on the fringe of the penalty area for players moving forward from the back. That sounds old hat now, but twenty-odd years ago it was brand new. Murdoch and Auld and Gemmell were all briefed to head for that area and see what they could pick up. And, of course, the recognised forwards were instructed, when they were faced with a packed defence, to look for the opportunity to cut the ball back to team-mates supporting from midfield and defence.*'

The tactic paid startling dividends. On Christmas Day, Celtic limbered up with an 8-1 win over Morton, and 1966 was welcomed with a 3-1 stroll at Shawfield against Clyde. The traditional New Year's Day fixture had been moved to a little after the high point of alcohol consumption, and took place at Celtic Park on January 3, with the teams neck-and-neck at the top of the League, each having lost just one game. In the first minute David Wilson put Rangers ahead, and that was still the position at half-time. The Celtic support, which had waited so long, would now have found anti-climax hard to bear – but fortunately it was not to be imposed upon them. Five minutes into the second half, Tommy Gemmell carried the ball to the line and cut back for Steve Chalmers to score. It was the start of a rout, with Chalmers completing his hat-trick and Murdoch and Gallagher bringing the score to 5-1. Who could stop Celtic now?

Meanwhile, the European Cup-Winners' Cup run was going well, Dutch and Danish opposition having been easily disposed of. The quarter-final draw brought Dynamo Kiev to Celtic Park on January 12, 1966, and a remarkable 3-0 win was achieved through two goals from Bobby Murdoch and the other from Gemmell. Never had the encouragement of attacking defenders been better rewarded. The return leg was to be in the relatively temperate Tbilisi a week later, because Kiev was in the grip of winter. It was Celtic's first experience of travelling to Eastern Europe, and Desmond White was wont to recall, until his dying day, the complexities which had to be resolved during the time of the Soviet Union.

First, when visas failed to arrive in time, the game was put back by a week. There were all sorts of difficulties in making the Aer Lingus charter flight acceptable to the Soviet authorities – the least they demanded was that it should be routed via Moscow. In the event, it also had to make an emergency stop at Copenhagen. The game was played and, with the aid of another Tommy Gemmell goal, an excellent 1-1 draw secured. But Celtic's travel difficulties continued when they were diverted on the return journey to Stockholm, where they were snowbound, finally returning to Glasgow on the Friday evening. The following day, in the absence of an offer from the Scottish League to postpone their fixture, they lost 3-2 at Tynecastle.

There were, indeed, three successive away defeats – to Aberdeen, Hearts and Stirling Albion. This tiring and nervous spell came dangerously close to losing Celtic that vital League title, since they allowed Rangers to stay in close contention. But the Stirling slip-up on February 26 proved to be the last, and Celtic were undefeated in the League from then until the end of the season. In the course of nine hectic April days, however, Celtic lost two of the trophies they were chasing. They went to Liverpool in the semi-final of the Cup-Winners' Cup, leading by a Bobby Lennox goal from the first leg. Bill Shankly's great side scored twice, but the game ended in bitter controversy when, with two minutes remaining, Lennox appeared to pull back the crucial aggregate goal – only to see it ruled off. He recalled: 'It was a disgraceful decision. Joe McBride jumped with Ron Yeats and got a touch on to me. One of the full-backs was in front of me, and I played it past him before rounding the goalkeeper.' Thus Celtic were denied their first European final, and the disappointment was all the greater because it was to be played at Hampden.

But Billy McNeill has no doubt that the 'bad experiences' of that campaign stood them in good stead for the next one. Four days later, Celtic played out a goal-less Scottish Cup final against Rangers – but the following Wednesday a famous Kai Johanssen goal took that trophy to Ibrox. It says much for the team's nerve that the three final League games against Morton (2-0), Dunfermline at East End Park (2-1) and Motherwell (1-0) were won, to secure by two points the first League title since 1954. The barren years were most definitely over.

The annual shareholders' meeting on August 11, 1966 heard that though the club had enjoyed 'easily record receipts', there had not been record profits because the wages bill was 'out of proportion' and still rising. Jock Stein, in his report, struck a more visionary note. He was still not satisfied with progress, according to the minutes of the meeting. 'The past was now history and tomorrow was the future of the club. We had many aims in view and, certainly, winning a European competition ranked very high.' It was astonishing that, after less than eighteen months at Celtic Park, he could talk in these terms and still be thought a realist. Increasingly, his profound belief that nothing was beyond the reach of this Celtic team was permeating the minds of those who were under his leadership. The club had just undertaken a long, unbeaten tour of North America, and Billy McNeill was convinced that the crucial breakthrough, in terms of self-belief, had taken place during these weeks of friendship, relaxation and further success. He recalled the excursion with natural fondness – and a deep understanding of its significance.

*'It began with a genuine break in Bermuda. That was just the thing to get us rested and re-charged after winning the Championship. Even during our stay there, in a couple of bounce games against locals, you could sense the strength of spirit that was developing. I remember quite clearly being conscious of the way things were taking shape. The confidence – at times it was downright cockiness – oozed out of us, and we really came to believe that we were the best in the business. We played Spurs three times on that trip, and won them all. They had some team at that time, and they got the shock of their lives. We played twelve matches in all, including a tournament in Los Angeles which we won.*

*'Jock was like a breath of fresh air, knowing instinctively what was best for the players, and how to get them to respond as he wanted. It wasn't hard to believe that we were destined for very big things. We had already won three major tournaments since Jock took over. Then in America, everything came together.*

*There was a bubbling enthusiasm about everything we did and an utter conviction that there wasn't another team on the planet as good as us. At the head of it all was Jock, frequently having to give us a hard time when he felt we needed it. There were an awful lot of good men in our company, but I don't recall bumping into any angels. We could play hard off the field, but we worked hard too. That was crucial to our success.'*

The hurricane, having gathered its energy on the other side of the Atlantic, was ready to sweep all before it. The season opened with a crushing 4-1 victory over Manchester United, complete with their stars from England's World Cup success at Wembley, in a challenge match. Inside three August days, St Mirren and Clyde were crushed 8-2 and 6-0 respectively in the League Cup. The six qualifying games yielded twenty-three goals, of which thirteen came from Joe McBride. The League results were just as spectacular. It was November 5 before a single point was dropped, at home to St Mirren. Throughout the whole season, there were to be only two League defeats – both at the hands of Dundee United. The only other competitive defeat that season would be the away leg of the European Cup quarter-final against Vojvodina.

Of fifty-nine games played in the four major tournaments, forty-eight were won and eight drawn. Celtic amassed 184 goals – an average of more than three per game. The rewards for all this were the Scottish League title for the second season running, the Scottish Cup for the second time since Stein's arrival, the Scottish League Cup for the second season running, and the immortality that went with becoming the first British club to win the European Cup.

Celtic's form en route to the League Cup final had been sensational. The free-scoring pattern set in the qualifying section was maintained with a 9-4 aggregate win over Dunfermline in the quarter-finals. Then Murdoch and McBride scored the goals which beat Airdrie in the semi-final. Once again, Rangers provided the final opposition – and Celtic already had the psychological advantages of a comfortable League win over them as well as a 4-0 trouncing in the Glasgow Cup. The side which lined up at Hampden on October 19, 1966 was: Simpson, Gemmell and O'Neill; Murdoch, McNeill and Clark; Johnstone, Lennox, McBride, Auld and Hughes (Chalmers).

It turned out to be one of the more anxious games for the Celtic supporters to watch during the course of that season, since Rangers held the overwhelming territorial advantage. However, it was a measure of Celtic's capacity for winning at that time that they brilliantly took one of the very few chances which fell to them. In the nineteenth minute, Joe McBride headed the ball down, for Lennox to slam it home. Rangers, for all their relentless attacking, had failed to score.

The Scottish Cup that season was, for Celtic, almost like a rehearsal studio, to be used for firming up their act in advance of other more demanding events. Arbroath, Elgin City and Queen's Park were the early round 'extras', before Clyde caught Celtic in a mood of rare uncertainty in the semi-final, which ended in a no-score draw. Early goals by Auld and Lennox turned the replay into a formality, and the final itself was not much more tense. Aberdeen were the opponents, and they were without the presence of manager Eddie Turnbull, who had become unwell just before the team left for Hampden. They then played as if in a daze, and goals from Willie Wallace, three minutes before and four minutes after the interval, made the rest of the task straightforward. Celtic's cup-winning side that day, April 6, 1967, proved to be identical to the one which would, on May 25, contest the European Cup final.

The most surprising fact about the season was that Celtic's extraordinary League record had not pulled them far clear of tenacious Rangers. After thirty-one League games, Celtic had lost only once – 3-2 at Tannadice on Hogmanay. Yet, with three games left, they could still be overtaken. The remaining games were the return fixture with Dundee United, Rangers at Ibrox and Kilmarnock at home. Astonishingly, by the standards of that season, they again lost 3-2 to United. This meant that a point was required at Ibrox on May 6 if a nerve-wracking last day of the domestic season was to be avoided. Two goals from Jimmy Johnstone duly secured a draw. 'It was a great way to win the title', says Bobby Lennox.

There had been one enforced personnel change during the course of the season. On December 2, 1966, Stein told the board that he wanted to buy Willie Wallace of Hearts, 'whom he considered was necessary to his pool of players. It was decided to secure his transfer if possible.' Four days later, 'Wispy' Wallace was acquired for a £30,000 fee. Billy McNeill said:

*'I remember big Jock telling me about his intention of buying Willie Wallace. He said: 'We're going for Wallace because I think he and Joe McBride could become the greatest striking partnership in the history of the Scottish game, maybe even in Europe too.' There was something very powerful about the way he said it, as though there was no point in anyone arguing otherwise. Mind you, when Jock was in that inspired form, there really was no point in taking any course of action other than believing him. It seemed, though, that Willie had only been at Celtic Park ten minutes when Joe had to go through his bad times. I know they did play together later, but that early pairing, when they were both absolutely at the top of their game was lost. We'll never know just how deadly they might have been together but, looking back. I can't help thinking they would have made a terrifying partnership.'*

It was the cruellest of luck that prevented Joe McBride from going any further in that historic season than the League match against Aberdeen on Christmas Eve 1966. By then he had scored thirty-five goals in twenty-six games. The previous Saturday, Wallace, Chalmers and McBride had all featured on the score-sheet, in the course of a 6-2 victory over Partick Thistle. To say that he suffered a knee injury at Pittodrie is a mild understatement. After eleven years of hard wear and tear, the back wall of McBride's kneecap was starting to flake, and the floating pieces of bone led him in agony. In a highly complex operation, the surgeon managed to save the striker's career. But there was no possibility of him reappearing before the end of the season. Wallace became, effectively, the replacement for McBride alongside Stevie Chalmers. McNeill said:

*'Stevie, the so-called quiet man had his own hardness about him, that snapping tenacity which gives opponents no rest whatever. His contribution summed up what we were like then – full of enthusiasm, application and confidence. That's not to mention, of course, a barrowload of skill throughout the team.'*

The European Cup campaign had started at Celtic Park against Swiss champions Zurich on the evening of September 28, with goals from Gemmell and McBride providing a satisfactory 2-0 cushion for the away trip. It was appropriate, perhaps, that the first goal in Celtic's European Cup career – an anxious sixty-four minutes into the game – was scored by the cavaliering Tommy Gemmell, a man who epitomised the attacking flair and excitement which, now more than ever, was the club's hallmark. Stein decided for the return leg that the European convention of defending the lead which had been established on home territory should be ignored. Celtic went on the attack in Switzerland. Gemmell was given full rein, and remarkably, the great full-back scored two more goals, with a third coming from Stevie Chalmers to complete an outstanding result. In the second round, Celtic were drawn against Nantes of France, with the first leg away from home. Goals from McBride, Lennox and Chalmers helped to secure a 3-1 victory in that game, and the same result emerged from the Celtic Park return on December 7 when Johnstone, Chalmers and Lennox were the scorers. Celtic's form in these first two rounds, against quite substantial opposition, was sufficiently impressive to cause Europe to start taking notice, as the European Cup went into winter recess. The chant 'We're on our way to Lisbon' could be heard permeating the chill Parkhead air during those long winter months.

The first leg of the quarter-finals, which did not take place until March 1, was eagerly awaited by the Celtic support. Celtic were drawn against Vojvodina, the Yugoslav champions, and in a most intelligent move, Stein arranged for a friendly match against Dinamo Zagreb early in February. 'This,' he told the directors, 'would give us an indication of the strength of Yugoslav football'. Stein indulged in some tactical experimentation, and Celtic lost to a last-minute goal. But the knowledge acquired may well have been crucial, for Vojvodina, a powerful side from Novi Sad, proved to be formidable foes. Billy McNeill recalled:

*'They were one of the biggest sides we had ever played against, and they turned out to be the most difficult opponents we had to beat in Europe that season. They had power and skill, but we played so very well against them in Novi Sad. A wee mistake by Tommy Gemmell gave them a one-goal lead - and I remember missing a good chance. But by that time, we probably felt that we could give anyone a goal of a start, and beat them at Celtic Park.'*

Euphoric with the season's success, everyone in the 75,000 crowd at the return game shared the assumption that the one-goal deficit would quickly be cancelled out and the Yugoslavs overtaken. But it proved to be an extremely tense occasion. Eventually, in the fifty-eighth minute, the ever-attentive Stevie Chalmers took advantage of a goalkeeping error to score an aggregate equaliser. The sense of relief was enormous, but still it seemed, as the match crept towards its finish, that the pre-arranged play-off in Rotterdam would be required. In a last great assault, Celtic forced a corner on the right. Charlie Gallagher struck the ball perfectly, and Billy McNeill cannoned it home with his head. 'With Charlie,' said McNeill, 'I always felt I had the chance of getting something. He was such a beautiful striker of the ball. If Vojvodina hadn't put the smallest fellow in their team on the line, it might not have gone in.' There has probably never been a more marvellous climax to a game at Celtic Park.

Semi-finalists Dukla Prague had a fair pedigree to bring with them to Glasgow for the first leg on April 12. Their stars included the great Josef Masopust, who had led his country to the 1962 World Cup final – and for whom McNeill had a great deal of respect based on international encounters. Jimmy Johnstone put Celtic ahead, but the Czechs equalised just before half-time. However, Willie Wallace repaid his transfer fee and much more by scoring his first two European goals, to create a 3-1 lead.

For the second leg in Prague on April 25, Stein took the painful decision to forsake temporarily his precious philosophy of attacking football. Celtic set themselves up for a siege. It was not pretty, but it worked and they secured the 0-0 draw which took them through to the final. Lennox said: 'I spent most of that game standing next to Big Tam. We went out to play defensively, but not that defensively! We didn't have any choice.' McNeill recalled Masopust refusing to shake hands at the end, but later coming into the Celtic dressing room to apologise and telling them he had been so upset because he realised that he would now never get the chance to play in a European final. It was an emotional reaction from a great player which the young Celtic team could understand. Stein was almost apologetic about the manner of his team's achievement, and declared that such defensive tactics would never be adopted again. But nobody at home was about to hold it against the big man. Just this once, surely, the end justified the means. As Lisbon mania took hold of Glasgow, Celtic had to wait another week for a play-off to decide who their opponents would be. The answer turned out to be Internazionale of Milan, rather than CSKA of Sofia.

Four days after Prague, Celtic won the Scottish Cup final and within the following week, the League title race was brought to a satisfactory conclusion. For four Celtic players – Simpson, Gemmell, Wallace and Lennox – this astonishing period also included participation in Scotland's memorable 3-2 victory over world champions England at Wembley. By the time the Celtic squad went to Lisbon, they were already assured the status of legends in their own lifetimes. During the build-up to the final, said McNeill, 'we became aware of being important in football'. The Italian media followed them everywhere.

*'I wonder if they contributed to us winning it, just by the way they boosted our self-image. Then there was all the great excitement of people getting to Lisbon. By the time the official party arrived there, the fans had gone a long way towards winning the hearts of the Portuguese. The punters went there full of fun.'*

It was the perfect psychological backdrop against which to play the most momentous game in the club's history. An expeditionary force, around 12,000 in number, had joined in the joyous pilgrimage. McNeill emphasised the carefree Celtic approach. The night before the game, the team went to the home of an expatriate Scot, to watch an England international on television.

> 'Neilly Mochan said we would walk back to the hotel. Neilly's walks were legendary, and this one was no exception. We were climbing fences and clambering over rocks. What a way to prepare for a European Cup final the next day. I don't know what Inter would have made of it, if they could have seen it. But that was how it was – unbelievably relaxed and everyone really enjoying themselves.'

When it came time to take the field in that never-to-be-forgotten Lisbon setting, the teams had to walk from the dressing room and into a long tunnel. As the referee held them back in this dark space before finally entering the arena, Billy McNeill felt the claustrophobia from which he tended to suffer, while Bertie Auld recalled the Inter players alongside them looking like 'Roman gods'. Something was needed to break the tension and it was the irrepressible Auld who provided it. He started to sing *The Celtic Song* and within seconds the whole team had joined in. To the Italians, it was an astonishing spectacle and the psychological advantage had started to move in Celtic's direction. There was more to follow.

Helenio Herrera, manager of Inter Milan, was the inventor of 'catenaccio', the appallingly defensive system that he had instilled into Inter Milan. At the previous day's training, Stein had been irritated by Herrera's breach of the agreement that Celtic should train first in the stadium – the Italians arrived early, trained and then stayed to watch Celtic. It was a matter of no great importance, but Stein was determined not to let his rival away with anything else. As the backroom staffs emerged for the kick-off, Herrera claimed the home side's bench at the stadium, again in breach of the official allocation. Stein, in his inimitable style, approached the disputed bench and said: 'Naw, you'll have to find another place.' That other place was a hundred yards away and Herrera, not used to being dictated to, had to make the lonely walk with dignity impaired. It was a neat little victory over people who set great store by pre-match intimidation. The greatest significance of the Celtic manager's obvious success came from the effect it had on his own players. Jimmy Johnstone saw the entire bench incident and, twenty years later, recalled thinking: 'The Big Man has Herrera in his pocket.'

It was part of Stein's gift that he could undermine the confidence of the enemy through strategies which also helped to reinforce his own men's belief in their own invincibility. The Celtic players that day took the field singing, laughing and generally giving their Italian opponents a unique psychological puzzle with which to contend. In the idyllic Lisbon setting on that historic Thursday, West German referee Kurt Tschenscher presided over the following teams:

**Celtic:** *Simpson, Craig, Gemmell; Murdoch, McNeill, Clark; Johnstone, Wallace, Chalmers, Auld, Lennox.*

**Inter Milan:** *Sarti, Burgnich, Facchetti; Redin, Guarneri, Picchi; Bicicli, Mazzola. Capellini, Corso, Domenghini.*

At home in Scotland, work stopped and school-rooms emptied as the nation watched its television screens. In Lisbon and London Road the great Celtic roar was stilled after just seven minutes when Jim Craig conceded a penalty-kick, which was converted by Sandro Mazzola. Celtic's response was to attack, attack, attack. Gemmell and Auld both shot against the crossbar. Sarti performed goalkeeping miracles. At half-time, said Billy McNeill, they went in still angry about the penalty award. Stein told them to settle down. 'We could have had three or four by half-time, but Sarti kept them in the game. Jock just told us to keep playing like that and it would come.' In the sixty-third minute, Jim Craig squared the ball across the eighteen-yard line to Tommy Gemmell, whose shot past Sarti was perfectly placed.

Now Celtic had all the advantage of the team which has come from behind and is buoyed by the optimism which that brings. A replay, had it been necessary, would have taken place in Lisbon three days later. But there was now an inevitability about the arrival of the winner, just five minutes from the end. Murdoch shot, Chalmers diverted and Sarti could not adjust quickly enough to the change in direction. The remaining seconds ticked away in a frenzy of excitement, before the final whistle sounded and Celtic were champions of Europe. Bill Shankly walked into the Celtic dressing room, stretched out a hand to Stein and uttered the peerless phrase: 'John, you're immortal.' McNeill makes the point:

*'On and off the field, everybody made a contribution, some loudly, others quietly. Many people refer to the Lisbon Lions as the actual eleven who played that day. There were a lot more fine players than that involved in the all-round achievement. Consider players such as Joe McBride, Charlie Gallagher, John Fallon, John Hughes and Willie O'Neill and you will realise that it was a genuine squad effort. I was reminded of it all in May 1987 when we had a reunion at a supporters' function. They were all there, the entire gang, all still the same, all wise-cracking, ribbing each other, generally having the same kind of fun we had enjoyed twenty years earlier. It all came flooding back.'*

Celtic's return to Glasgow, and their procession through the streets of the East End, was an occasion of deep emotion. The club which had grown out of a poor community, and which had contributed so much to its sense of identity and pride, now returned to it with the highest honour in club football. It was not necessary ever to have seen a game of football in order to share fully and justly in the spirit of the celebration for a wonderful achievement.

Before the game, Stein had told Hugh McIlvanney of the *Observer*: 'We don't just want to win this cup. We want to win playing good football, to make neutrals glad we've won it, glad to remember how we did it.' His every wish had been fulfilled.

The legend of the Lisbon Lions has lived on though their numbers have, sadly, been diminished. Bobby Murdoch – the complete footballer – died in 2001 at the age of 56. Ronnie Simpson died in 2004 at the age of 73, and Jimmy Johnstone passed away in 2006 at the age of 61 after a brave battle with Motor Neurone Disease. But they never die who live in the hearts of those they leave behind.

# SEVENTEEN

## A WORLD-CLASS SIDE:
## AND THE ONE THAT GOT AWAY

IT IS A CURIOUS fact that the Lisbon Lions only ever won one European match, and that was the great final itself. Indeed, they were together for only three games in continental combat – the semi-final second leg in Prague, then in Lisbon, and finally for the opening game of their European Cup defence, at Celtic Park on September 20, 1967. It was only by mischance that Celtic were involved at this stage at all. Normally, there were thirty-three teams in the tournament and the previous season's winners were not included in the preliminary round. However, the Albanian champions withdrew – and so Celtic went into the draw with the rest. It gave them one of the toughest available tests, against Dynamo Kiev of the Soviet Union. On September 20, the Celtic supporters looked on in shocked disbelief as their heroes displayed alarming unsteadiness in defence and went two goals down, before Bobby Lennox pulled one back after sixty-two minutes. So the European Cup holders travelled to Ukraine having to do what no other club had done in the history of the tournament – retrieve a tie after losing the first leg.

The improbable seemed to become the impossible when Bobby Murdoch was sent off after fifty-nine minutes – yet, three minutes later, Celtic were in the lead, thanks to the irrepressible Lennox. Heroic as the attempt was, however, there was to be no glory that afternoon. By this time, away goals counted double in the event of an aggregate draw, so Celtic had to pursue a decisive second. Kiev took advantage of Celtic's frenzied attacking efforts and sneaked an equaliser seconds from the end, to progress on a 3-2 aggregate.

Apart from a 1-0 League defeat at Ibrox, Celtic had opened the season in the manner to which the supporters were becoming accustomed, with the team qualifying undefeated from a uniquely difficult League Cup section which also included Rangers, Dundee United and Aberdeen. The 3-1 win over Rangers at Celtic Park in the section decider should, the directors agreed, 'be minuted as one of our best ever results against Rangers' – the team had come from being a goal down to score in the final, exhilarating thirteen minutes through Wallace, Murdoch and Lennox.

Celtic were also looking forward to the so-called 'World Club Championship' play-off with Racing Club of Buenos Aires, the South American champions. With this in mind, a friendly match with Penarol of Uruguay had been arranged for Celtic Park early in September, and the following week's board meeting noted that it had been 'an excellent game with hardly a foul given; a match between a South American and Scottish side that did great credit to all concerned'. In the wake of all this, the European Cup exit came as an abrupt shock, and just two weeks later, Racing Club came to Hampden Park. Yet another dramatic winner from the head of Billy McNeill gave Celtic a slender first-leg lead – but not before the Argentinians had established their intention to pursue a regime of intimidation based on spitting, hacking and foul-mouthing their opponents.

There are those who argue to this day that the Scottish champions should not have travelled to South America for the return match, that if Racing Club wanted the title so badly that they were prepared to behave like thugs, they should have been conceded the tie and peace allowed to reign. With hindsight, that seems reasonable, but it fails to recognise Stein's burning ambition to lead Celtic to another pinnacle – and where would the club have been without Stein's sense of ambition? It must also be remembered that there were no shirkers in that Celtic squad when it came to a skirmish and the players, in general, shared the manager's determination to go all the way. Billy McNeill recalled:

> 'I never doubted that we should go. It was essential. What happened in the stadium came as a complete surprise to us. I remember going to church shortly after we arrived. The people could not have been more friendly, as the Argentinians are. But the football crowd worked itself up into a frenzy, and the reception we got at the game was nothing short of horrific.'

The worst fears were vindicated by an incident just before the kick-off in Buenos Aires when Ronnie Simpson had to be replaced by John Fallon after being felled by a missile from the crowd. Yet the 120,000 hostile home supporters saw Celtic take the lead with a Tommy Gemmell penalty before Racing Club came back to win 2-1. Once again, there was a case for pulling out and calling the semi-official 'World Championship' a tie. Bob Kelly was strongly in favour of this course of action, but Stein successfully lobbied against it. McNeill says: 'I didn't think we should have gone to Montevideo. There was too much talk along the lines of 'Why are we going?' That was not the ideal preparation for players, because it put other worries in our heads.'

But Celtic pressed on to the Uruguayan capital for the play-off, and the Penarol players who had visited Glasgow a few weeks earlier came along to commiserate over the events in

Buenos Aires, and to add their own horror stories about what the Argentinians were capable of. The game soon developed into the demeaning farce which many had feared all along. The provocation to the Celtic players was immense, and the performance of the Paraguayan referee appalling. But part of the problem, as McNeill recognises, was that 'we went out like avenging angels'. The game should never have taken place, and Stein subsequently admitted frankly: 'Mr Kelly was swayed by our arguments and I now have to say that he was correct in the first place.' The club's dismay had almost nothing to do with the 1-0 defeat, as illustrated by the minutes of the board meeting held on November 9, 1967.

*'The club was disappointed with the result of the second match in Montevideo but the directors were far more disappointed with the conduct of some of the players in that match. Three had been sent off – Lennox, Johnstone and Hughes. Certainly, it was difficult to understand why Lennox and Johnstone were ordered off, but two other Celtic players [Gemmell and Auld] were most fortunate in not being ordered off. What worried the club was the breakdown in control and discipline. We had built up an image of a top-class, well-disciplined side. That image was sadly tarnished. The players had had much to contend with, particularly in the Buenos Aires match... nerves had been strained to breaking point. A stance had, however, to be taken to rescue their good name. It was decided to fine the players – the whole team – £250 each.'*

Just prior to the South American trip, the League Cup had been won with a 5-3 victory over Dundee in the final. Now Celtic had to put the Kiev and Montevideo experiences behind them and concentrate on the all-important business of qualifying again for the European Cup.

It was an epic race for the League title. Celtic had already dropped two points to Rangers and one in a home game against St Johnstone. On December 2 they drew at home with Dundee United, and on January 2 they shared four goals with Rangers at Celtic Park. They then won their remaining sixteen League games to finish with sixty-three points from a possible sixty-eight. But Rangers – who had invested heavily in the transfer market in an effort to break Celtic's supremacy – were doing just as well, and approached their last match of the season, at home to Aberdeen, still unbeaten. They had a favourite's chance of completing a League Championship without defeat for the first time that century. Celtic were idle that day, April 27, and were confirmed as champions for the third successive season when Aberdeen won 3-2. Celtic had to play their final game against Dunfermline the following Tuesday but, already a distance ahead on goal difference, they could afford defeat. In the event they won 2-1, coming from behind with goals from Bobby Lennox in the forty-seventh and seventy-second minutes. In the big upset of the domestic season, the club Stein had taken into the 'big league', Dunfermline, had knocked Celtic out of the Scottish Cup by coming to Glasgow and winning 2-0 in January.

Whatever the disappointments suffered by the Celtic fans at the early exits from the European and Scottish Cups, this was not reflected in the size of their support during those fraught matches on the run-in to the Championship. There were full houses at Tannadice, Tynecastle and Pittodrie. In the penultimate game, at home to Morton, a staggering 51,000 turned up. And there was a capacity 30,000 at East End Park for the grand finale to an unprecedented League campaign. Billy McNeill recalls that night in Dunfermline:

*'We knew that the title was already in our hands, and it would have been easy for us to treat the game as a lap of*

*honour. But the supporters were there in their thousands, and it was part of the character of Celtic players then to see to it that the business was done properly. We went behind, and then fought like demons to come back and win. There was little chance of us celebrating a League victory with defeat on the night. Dunfermline went on to win the Cup and deserved it, because they had beaten us on the way.'*

The 1968/69 season opened with a crowd of over 80,000 at Hampden Park for a friendly match with Leeds United. It then followed a similar pattern to most other Celtic seasons of that era. Another treble of Championship, Scottish Cup and League Cup was recorded in the ledger, and in Europe, the team beat St Etienne of France and Red Star Belgrade of Yugoslavia before succumbing to AC Milan in the quarter-final. Having secured an excellent 0-0 draw in Italy, they went down to a single goal at Celtic Park. The original draw for the first round of the European Cup had paired Celtic with Ferencvaros of Hungary, but the competition was redrawn after Celtic had complained that no Western European club should be 'forced to fulfil any football commitment' in any Warsaw Pact country, following the Soviet Union's intervention in Czechoslovakia. In the emotional atmosphere of the period, this initiative attracted considerable support from other Western clubs in the competition. It was decided by UEFA to redraw the European competitions (though the practical difficulties of travelling between east and west at this time were quoted as the official explanation).

While it was very much in tune with international outrage over events in Czechoslovakia, Celtic's initiative raised a much wider question. Should international sporting contact, at club or national level, be conditional upon political judgments about the calibre of the other country's regime? Clearly, if many such adjudications were to occur, international sporting contact would quickly diminish. This was demonstrated when the Eastern European clubs withdrew from that season's European tournaments in protest against the decision to redraw – even though, by that time, UEFA had decided that the zoning should apply for one round only.

During that season, significant changes were taking place. It is a measure of Jock Stein's ambition for Celtic that he was not prepared merely to consolidate domestic supremacy and bask in the glory of Lisbon memories. He had made the European Cup winnable and, as a result, believed that his ambition should not drop below that objective. This persuaded him to start changing personnel, in the search for a combination that would once again be good enough to go to the very top. There are players from that period who remain adamant that Stein began the break-up of the pool much too early. Joe McBride was allowed to join Hibernian, Willie O'Neill left for Carlisle United and Charlie Gallagher was allowed to negotiate his own terms with Dumbarton. Tommy Callaghan was bought from Dunfermline and Harry Hood from Clyde.

The next great wave of talent which was bursting through at Celtic Park was, paradoxically, part of Stein's dilemma. Kenny Dalglish, George Connelly, Lou Macari, Danny McGrain and David Hay were already part of a second string which would surely itself have finished in the top half-dozen of the old First Division. These youngsters were showing the kind of form which would have won them a place in the first team of any other club in the country. If they were to be held back for the sake of prolonging a legend, could they be blamed for growing unsettled enough to seek their fortunes elsewhere? Stein's decision was to effect the introduction of new blood as painlessly as possible, and to allow some of the more experienced players to go their different ways while they still had something left of their playing careers. On another front, the Lisbon memory was honoured with the announcement of a knighthood for chairman Bob Kelly in the 1969 New Year's Honours List.

Celtic won the League by five points from Rangers in 1968/69. The League Cup campaign included a 10-0 scoreline against Hamilton, with five goals apiece coming from Lennox and Chalmers. Because of a fire at Hampden, the final against Hibs was delayed until April 1969, when Celtic beat them 6-2. As a result, the three legs of the treble were tied up within a three-week period. The season was climaxed by goals from McNeill, Lennox, Connelly and Chalmers, which helped to beat Rangers 4-0 in a joyous Scottish Cup final on April 26, when the Celtic team was: Fallon, Craig, Gemmell, Murdoch, McNeill, Brogan (Clark), Connelly, Chalmers, Wallace, Lennox and Auld.

By the time Celtic reached their second European Cup final in 1970, they had tucked away another League title and another League Cup, and had been runners-up to Aberdeen in the Scottish Cup final. Rangers were again one of the teams eliminated in the League Cup qualifying section, but a game between the clubs at Celtic Park on August 20, 1969 yielded a most unusual episode. The referee, Jim Callaghan, booked John Hughes in the first half. Later, a linesman drew the referee's attention to a clash between Hughes and Johnstone of Rangers. Mr Callaghan spoke to Hughes, but took no further action. Rangers complained to the SFA and after an enquiry, Mr Callaghan – a top official of previously unblemished reputation – was suspended for two months. This was surely the only occasion on which a referee has been suspended, in effect, for not sending a player off. It was difficult to imagine that a complaint on similar grounds from any other source would have met with the same outcome. Celtic met St Johnstone, at that time an exciting side under Willie Ormond, in the final at Hampden, and won by a solitary goal scored by Bertie Auld in the second minute.

Goalkeeper Evan Williams, brought back to Scotland from Wolves, defenders Hay and Brogan, and midfielder George Connelly became first-team regulars in the course of this eventful season. Kenny Dalglish's name would also appear with increasing regularity. After collecting just three points from their first four League games, Celtic recovered more normal form and had the title won by twelve points from Rangers by the time they met Aberdeen in the Scottish Cup final on April 11, 1970. All too often it is possible to reach the closing stages of the Scottish Cup without having been drawn against very substantial opposition. But on this occasion, Celtic had to overcome Dunfermline, Dundee United, Rangers and Dundee to earn their Hampden place in April.

It was a game awash with controversy, most of which surrounded the refereeing of Mr R. H. Davidson of Airdrie (who was not highly regarded in Celtic circles), during a crucial ten-minute spell. First he awarded a penalty kick against Bobby Murdoch for a 'hand-ball' offence which appeared wholly beyond the player's control. Lennox appeared to equalise after Clark, the Aberdeen keeper, had dropped the ball. The referee ruled that a foul had been committed by the Celtic player, and then added insult to injury by declining to award the most blatant of penalty kicks when Lennox was spreadeagled inside the box. Aberdeen eventually won 3-1 and left Stein, in his inimitable fashion, loudly discussing the referee's performance in the Hampden foyer in such carefully chosen language that he was able to make his dissatisfaction known without giving the SFA the chance to charge him with illegal remarks.

Throughout the season, Celtic's European Cup charge had been building up. FC Basel of Switzerland provided the opening opposition and, after a 0-0 draw, goals from Hood and Gemmell at Celtic Park took the team through. Drawn against the mighty Benfica of Portugal, Celtic gained one of the best results in their history – a 3-0 home win, with goals from Gemmell (a memorable thirty-five-yard shot in the second minute), Wallace and Hood. But Celtic needed all of this lead for the second leg in Portugal. As half-time approached Benfica scored twice, and after Celtic appeared to have weathered a second-half storm, the equaliser came in injury-time. Extra-time was played, and Celtic did extremely well in such circumstances to hold out. There were no penalty shoot-outs at this time, and Celtic went through when Billy McNeill called correctly on the toss of a coin.

Celtic drew Fiorentina of Italy in the quarter-finals and, in March, secured another outstanding home result – 3-0, through goals from Auld, Carpenetti (og) and Wallace. A skilful containment job was done in Florence, and only one goal conceded. The semi-final draw brought together the champions of Scotland and England – Celtic versus Leeds United. It would have been an ideal final, and the whole build-up to the first meeting, in Leeds on April 1, implied that this was indeed the apex of the competition.

George Connelly had made a sensational impact in his first season as a regular Celtic player. Possessed of astonishing ball skills, he had first become known to the Celtic faithful as the provider of pre-match entertainment. Prior to one European tie against Dynamo Kiev in 1966, Connelly went round every line on the park, keeping the ball in the air. Bob Rooney recalled Connelly as 'the best young player I ever saw at Celtic Park', with a devastating ability to turn defence into attack with a single, incisive pass. Now Connelly was at the centre of Stein's pre-match battle of tactics and nerves with his friend Don Revie, manager of Leeds. Would Stein risk fielding the youngster in a match of such pressure? Revie wrongly concluded that he would not, and planned accordingly. Connelly played, and scored the winning goal after just forty-five seconds of the match. The Leeds players then spent most of the evening trying to contain the magical Jimmy Johnstone. It was one of Stein's finest tactical successes.

Celtic's superiority in what, inevitably, had come to be regarded as the British championship was confirmed in the second leg, when John Hughes was pitted against Jack Charlton in a classic duel. The game was played at Hampden Park, and a European Cup record crowd of 136,505 – not including those who scaled the walls to get in free – saw goals by Hughes and Bobby Murdoch overcome an early score by Billy Bremner to take Celtic into the final. On this occasion, Celtic were permitted a lap of honour.

Much ink and many words have been expended on analysing why Celtic then lost the final to Feyenoord of The Netherlands, who – though they were doubtless blissfully unaware of the fact – lined up in the San Siro Stadium, Milan on May 6, 1970 with Scottish bookmakers offering the ridiculous odds of 6-1 against them. Numerous excuses have been offered for Celtic's anti-climactic performance. Stein suffered criticism for supposedly underestimating the opposition. The players were accused of worrying too much about their commercial interests, which had been neglected completely prior to the Lisbon final. But this implies that financial naivety, once lost, can then be restored when the occasion demands without any further psychological price being paid, and that is surely itself naive. For all the words and retrospective wisdom, too little attention had been paid to the fact that Feyenoord were an extremely good side, who played brilliantly on the night. The defeat came so unexpectedly because the pre-match assumptions, true to Scottish football tradition, had been so irrationally optimistic.

Celtic had been the innocent underdogs in Lisbon, with everything to play for. Had they lost to Inter Milan, the honour accorded to them would still have been great – the first British club in the European Cup final, ambassadors of attacking football, and so on. This role, brilliantly exploited and turned to advantage by Stein, had been crucial to their psychology and ultimate victory. The circumstances of 1970 were very different, and it is idle to imagine that some sort of replica build-up could have been achieved. Jim Craig, who played in Lisbon and observed Milan at close quarters, was surely near to the mark when he said:

*'There is no doubt in my mind that we climbed our mountain against Leeds in the semi-final. We lulled ourselves into thinking that Feyenoord represented the other side of the peak, and that we were now coasting downhill. Of course, that means that we may have been complacent – but it is also human and understandable.'*

Billy McNeill admitted frankly: 'We totally underestimated them. We didn't recognise that Dutch football was on the ascendancy. In beating Leeds home and away, we allowed ourselves to get carried away. Our preparations for the final were not good. Feyenoord were still in competitive action in Holland, while our season had finished. The full team only played one preparatory game, against Stenhousemuir. Half went to Gateshead to play a friendly, the other half went to Fraserburgh.'

He also thinks the club was too preoccupied with arranging open-top buses and other details of the celebrations which were taken for granted. Bobby Lennox says simply: 'It was the low point in our careers and I'll never forget the feeling. Feyenoord were better than us, yet we were within four minutes of getting another game.'

The teams which lined up in front of a 53,000 crowd in the San Siro Stadium, Milan were:

**Celtic:** *Williams, Hay, Gemmell, Murdoch, McNeill, Brogan, Johnstone, Wallace, Hughes, Auld (Connelly), Lennox.*

**Feyenoord:** *Graafland, Romeyn (Haak), Israel, Laseroms, van Duivenbode, Jansen, van Hanegem, Hasil, Wery, Kindvall, Mouljin.*

Celtic took the lead after thirty minutes with a typical Tommy Gemmell thundering shot from a short Murdoch free kick. But most of the Celtic followers realised that the team was not on top of its task and this was confirmed, within two minutes, when Israel equalised. Feyenoord were now filling precisely the role that Celtic had occupied in Lisbon. They had planned carefully and, encouraged by the equalising goal, relentlessly pursued the winner for most of the time remaining. Celtic held out until the end of ninety minutes, and the game moved into extra time. With no penalty shoot-outs in these more civilised times, a replay would have taken place in Milan two days later. The Celtic fans prayed for this opportunity to regroup and fight again. But four minutes from the end Kindvall struck the winning goal. It was a bitter disappointment for everyone whose hopes were vested in Celtic, and the subsequent recriminations were bitter. 'The scoreline flattered us,' says Billy McNeill. 'Other than Evan Williams, who had a superb match, we did not play well at all.'

Immediately afterwards, Celtic went off on the North American tour to which they were committed. It had been planned as a celebration, evocative of past tours in the same territory, but turned into an unhappy and generally unwanted expedition. Jimmy Johnstone did not go on the tour, supposedly because of his fear of flying. Celtic were involved in a tournament with Manchester United, who promptly beat them 2-0, and an Italian club of no obvious distinction called Bari. Jock Stein abruptly departed for home, leaving Sean Fallon in charge of the team, and Desmond White flew out from Scotland to take overall control. It soon became apparent that, in part at least, Stein's return home was to deal with Johnstone, who was about to ask for a transfer on financial grounds. Then Gemmell and Auld were sent home from New York by Sean Fallon for disciplinary reasons. The full-back also asked for a transfer. Both he and Johnstone were told they could go, and although both affairs petered out, they contributed to an unhappy few months at Celtic Park.

By the time twenty-two shareholders gathered for their annual meeting on September 4, 1970, a proper sense of perspective had been restored. Sir Robert Kelly was already unwell and may well have known that this would be his valedictory address. The club, he declared, had never in its long and illustrious history been in a better position either in the playing sense or financially. He continued:

> *'The name and fame of Celtic is now world-wide, and we are recognised as a top team in Europe... All this gives me great personal satisfaction because in achieving these wonderful triumphs, we have confounded the critics of not so many years ago who laughed to scorn any predictions that we could and would reach such levels. I take this opportunity of paying tribute to our great manager, Jock Stein.'*

For his part, Stein soberly assessed the European Cup disappointment. They had beaten Leeds both home and away 'in the greatest club matches ever' and, with Feyenoord now on their way to victory over their South American counterparts, 'being second to the top team in the world is no humiliation.'

# EIGHTEEN

## GLORY GLORY DAYS:
## AND THE END OF AN ERA

CELTIC'S DIFFICULTIES CONTINUED into the new season, and they lost the League Cup to Rangers through a goal by sixteen-year-old Derek Johnstone in the final. After an inconsistent start to the League programme, however, something approaching normality was restored. By now Celtic had won five League titles in a row, and on each occasion Rangers had been runners-up. But in 1970/71, it was cup-holders Aberdeen – with players such as Bobby Clark, Steve Murray, Martin Buchan and Joe Harper – who emerged as the principal challengers. Danny McGrain, who had signed for Celtic in 1967, entered the first team for the opening League game of the season against Morton, and made intermittent appearances thereafter. Kenny Dalglish replaced Jimmy Johnstone during a 3-1 victory at Broomfield on October 17, 1970. During that season, however, he was to make only one full appearance in the League. It was a neck-and-neck struggle, with Aberdeen heading the table for a long period. However, Celtic went to Pittodrie on April 17 leading by a point, and an early goal by Harry Hood earned them a vital draw. The sixth successive League title was tied up with a 2-0 win over Ayr United twelve days later.

For the closing League game of the season, Stein urged the supporters to turn out in force. With a characteristic burst of showmanship, he had decided to lay on a last farewell by the entire Lisbon Lions team. Ronnie Simpson, now retired, led them out before an emotional crowd of 35,000 which witnessed a 6-1 victory over Clyde in the old style, with Evan Williams in goal as the only alteration from the Lisbon side. John Clark's move to Morton now took place, and Bertie Auld – carried from the field on the shoulders of his colleagues – was transferred to Hibs where he saw out his playing days. The double was completed when, after a 1-1 draw, Celtic beat Rangers 2-1 in the replayed Scottish Cup final. The team that night, May 12, 1971, was: Williams, Craig, Brogan, Connelly, McNeill, Hay, Johnstone, Lennox, Macari, Callaghan and Hood. Macari, who had come in for Wallace following the first game, scored the opener and Hood's penalty goal put Celtic two up before an own goal by Jim Craig resulted in a scoreline that was perhaps closer than it should have been.

In Europe, Celtic made their exit at the quarter-final stage. After easy victories over Kokkola of Finland and Waterford of Ireland, they were drawn against Ajax, pride of Amsterdam. Celtic were learning at first-hand one of the outstanding football lessons of the seventies – that Dutch football had become very good indeed. In their home leg, Ajax built up a three-goal lead and Celtic could pull back only one goal, through Jimmy Johnstone, in Glasgow.

Throughout this season, the board of directors did not meet on a regular basis because of Sir Robert Kelly's illness. However, on February 29, 1971, Messrs White, Devlin and Farrell came together in the North British Hotel to confront a potential crisis. It was not long since Manchester United had been desperate to secure Jock Stein's services, and now press reports were suggesting with too much consistency to be ignored that he was thinking of leaving for Leeds United. It was agreed to point out to the manager that he was being paid a very high salary, that 'loyalty to the club should play a very important part' in his thinking, and that 'we were not prepared to enter into an auction'. The minutes of the meeting added: 'The chairman, who was not present, was very much in agreement and very disappointed that he [Stein] should be so tempted.' The Celtic directors heard of his decision to stay at a meeting on March 22 – the same meeting that accepted Sir Robert Kelly's retirement and decided to make him the club's first honorary president since it had been formed into a limited company. Though matters had been smoothed over with Jock Stein, possibly in deference to the chairman's feelings, the question of the manager's future intentions was now firmly on the agenda, and was regularly to recur.

The 1970/71 season had been significant for another, tragic reason. On January 2, 1971, sixty-six spectators died in an accident on Stairway 13 at Ibrox. When Jimmy Johnstone put Celtic ahead late in the game, Rangers supporters started to leave the ground. But when Colin Stein equalised with seconds left, some of those who had departed prematurely tried to return to join in the celebrations. It was thought that the tragedy occurred when they met the tide of people now rushing away at the final whistle, but this has since proved not be the case. The disaster had far-reaching implications for regulations on stadium construction, attendance limits and crowd control. But its immediate effects were to put football rivalries in perspective, to unite Scotland in grief, and the two clubs in mourning. Players and officials of both Celtic and Rangers attended memorial services in the St Andrew's and Glasgow Cathedrals. Celtic contributed £10,000 to the Ibrox Disaster Fund.

The fine new Celtic stand, financed through the Development Fund set up in the 1960s, was officially opened by Jimmy

McGrory on September 1, 1971, and the supporters were treated to a show game against Nacional of Uruguay, the South American champions – an event which went a long way towards exorcising the vile memory of Montevideo. Celtic opened their League programme with a 9-1 win over Clyde and the seventh successive League title was duly taken by ten clear points from Aberdeen in 1971/72, in spite of this being another season of substantial transition.

The League Cup had, however, provided one of the biggest upsets in post-war Scottish football – the kind of upset, indeed, that keeps the game interesting. Having disposed of Rangers in the qualifying section, Celtic progressed easily to the final on October 23, 1971. With Partick Thistle providing the opposition, it was generally assumed that Celtic would win with ease, even with Billy McNeill out through injury. But Thistle attacked from the start, to sensational effect. Within thirty-seven minutes, they were 4-0 up. It was the kind of scoreline which teleprinters had to repeat in words as well as figures in order to avoid accusations of gross error. Celtic could pull back only one goal, through Dalglish, as young Alan Rough in the Thistle goal revelled in this unique occasion.

Evan Williams carried the can for this embarrassment, and Stein immediately signed Denis Connaghan from St Mirren. He then added the scoring power of John 'Dixie' Deans, a striker in the McBride mould bought from Motherwell at a modest price. Steve Chalmers joined John Clark at Cappielow, Tommy Gemmell was transferred to Nottingham Forest, and Willie Wallace and John Hughes departed for Crystal Palace.

The Scottish Cup was retained with a 6-1 final victory over Hibernian on May 6, 1972. The team was: Williams, Craig, Brogan, Murdoch, McNeill, Connelly, Johnstone, Deans, Macari, Dalglish and Callaghan. The scoreline equalled Renton's record win in 1888, and Dixie Deans' hat-trick was the first in a final since Jimmy Quinn in 1904 against Rangers. McNeill had opened the scoring and Lou Macari contributed two late goals.

With the League and cup double tied up, it was a satisfactory season for Celtic on the domestic front. Easily the most exciting aspect was the emergence of Kenny Dalglish, who won instant acclaim by producing the skills which would eventually cause him to be numbered among the greatest players the British game has ever known. Following his handful of appearances in the previous two seasons, Dalglish played fifty first-team matches during 1971/72, including only one as substitute. He scored seventeen league goals, runner-up to Dixie Deans. Perhaps, in retrospect, the most eloquent testimony to Dalglish's sensational impact that season could be seen in the fact that he was in the Scotland team against Holland on December 1, within a few months of becoming an established first-team player.

Dalglish also helped Celtic to their fourth European semi-final within the space of seven magnificent seasons. Before Christmas they had beaten Boldklub Copenhagen of Denmark and Sliema Wanderers of Malta, but, for a team in transition, Ujpest Dozsa of Hungary seemed like a tough nut to crack. Danny McGrain made his European debut in Budapest, and Celtic established an outstanding 2-1 lead. An early own goal was helpful, but it was another splendid tactical performance, with Lennox and Macari pressurising the Hungarian defence and preventing Ujpest from going all-out for home goals. They did manage an equaliser, but five minutes from the end Macari scored the second. Celtic then conceded the opening goal of the home leg, but a Macari equaliser took them through to the semi-final against Inter Milan.

It was back to the San Siro Stadium, with a team which contained an extremely promising mix of the old guard and the first-class talent which had been confirmed since the last visit to that city. Both semi-final legs were tense, cat-and-mouse affairs and neither yielded a single, decisive goal. The issue was to be decided on penalty kicks – an improvement on tossing a coin but still a nerve-wracking way to decide which club should qualify for a place in the European Cup final. Mazzola scored Inter's first – and then the unfortunate Dixie Deans sent his effort over the bar. The Italians took their other four kicks with confident ease, and so they went through. Deans had to be content with his hat-trick against Hibs in the Scottish Cup final, which included a quite outstanding solo goal.

However, Desmond White looked on the bright side when giving his first report as chairman to the annual meeting of shareholders, and concentrated his remarks on the unprecedented 'seven in a row' which broke Celtic's own long-standing record. He asked: 'How many of us remember now that at the time Celtic won the first of the seven, in season 1965/66, the club had won only three in the previous forty years and only one, in 1953/54, since the Second World War?'

The eighth in a row, 1972/73, was a much tougher League title for Celtic and it was touch-and-go for them to lead Rangers by a single point at the end of it. This was achieved thanks to a run-in of seven successive wins, while Rangers – by now under Jock Wallace – dropped a crucial point at Pittodrie in the penultimate game of the season. This left Celtic requiring a draw from their final game against Hibs at Easter Road. In fact they won 3-0. On the credit side, Dalglish had another outstanding season, McGrain became fully established in the team and George Connelly achieved the best form of his career, to be named Footballer of the Year by Scotland's sports writers. But there was bitter disappointment for Stein when Lou Macari found the bait of more money in England irresistible. He was transferred to Manchester United, and this must be seen as something of a watershed. It was the first time since Stein's arrival at Celtic Park that an important player had been released under such circumstances.

Ominously, and much more seriously, Stein was taken to hospital in January 1973 with a suspected heart attack and spent a short time recovering away from Celtic Park. The League title was Celtic's only honour in 1972/73 – they lost the League Cup Final to Hibs, the Scottish Cup semi-final to Rangers and their European Cup hopes to old rivals Ujpest Dozsa of Hungary, on a 4-2 aggregate in the second round.

A handful of the club's home games during the early part of the season had to be played at Hampden Park, due to weaknesses having become apparent in the design of the Celtic Park stand. The club had good reason to be grateful to a supporter, an experienced steel erector, who was the first to draw attention to defects which might otherwise have had serious consequences. It was an issue which involved the club in legal wranglings for several years.

Although season 1973/74 duly yielded a ninth League title, it was marked by other disappointments and not a little cause for disillusionment. At the same time as Celtic had been touching the heights of 1967, something equally remarkable had been happening in the background – a crop of extraordinary talent was growing up at Celtic Park. If it had stayed together it should have ripened fully by the mid 1970s, but by 1973 a very different scenario was emerging. Macari was gone. David Hay was in dispute with the club over money and was suspended after staying away from training, before being transferred to Chelsea. George Connelly was in the process of turning his back on professional football altogether. Meanwhile, the last of the Lisbon Lions were passing their primes. Bobby Murdoch left for Middlesbrough, to be replaced by the valuable midfield signing of Steve Murray from Aberdeen. Jimmy Johnstone languished in the reserves for much of the season. Against this background, it was extraordinary that Celtic should again emerge from the long League programme as champions – though the fifty-three-point total which won them the title, by four points from Hibs, was the lowest of the sequence.

For good measure they also took the Scottish Cup, beating Dundee United 3-0 in the Tannadice club's first final. The Celtic team on May 4, 1974 was: Connaghan, McGrain (Callaghan), Brogan, Murray, McNeill, McCluskey, Johnstone, Hood, Deans, Hay and Dalglish. Goals from Hood, Murray and Deans secured the trophy in an otherwise forgettable final, played in front of a 75,959 crowd. In the League Cup, however, Celtic had lost the final to Dundee, after apparently doing the difficult part of the job by beating Rangers 3-1 in the semi-final. The final will be remembered by more politically-minded supporters as a symbol of Ted Heath's Conservative Government's declining months. It was played in December with a 1.30pm kick-off, because the restrictions on the use of electricity forbade the use of floodlights. A crowd of only 27,974 stood in the snow and, to their general astonishment, saw Celtic go down to a seventy-fifth-minute goal by Gordon Wallace.

In the European Cup of 1973/74, the early draw favoured Celtic. They easily disposed of Finnish opposition, TPS Turku, but then struggled to beat the unheard-of Danish club Vejle BK by a single goal scored in the away leg. There were more signs of strain when Celtic needed extra time in the quarter-final second leg to defeat FC Basel of Switzerland 6-5 on aggregate. This put them through to yet another European Cup semi-final – this time, alas, against Atletico Madrid. The Spanish club's performance at Celtic Park will go down as one of the most disgraceful in European football annals. The aim was intimidation, and Jimmy Johnstone was the chief target for a succession of assaults. By the end of the night, three Spaniards had been sent off and another seven booked.

Atletico Madrid were fined £14,000 by UEFA, and six of their players were banned for the second leg. It was an inadequate punishment, because their coach, Juan Carlos Lorenzo, had planned to do without these individuals in the return anyway. They had been briefed simply to secure a 0-0 draw at Celtic Park by any means, and this they did. The return was a nightmare from the start, with Atletico supporters and the press joining in the intimidation process from the moment the Celtic party set foot in Spain. A Spanish government official was quoted as saying that 'there could very well be a death if somebody is crazy there.' With the team hotel, and the park, bristling with armed troops, it was a possibility not to be taken lightly. With that kind of build-up, it was scarcely surprising that Celtic went down 2-0, although they held out until thirteen minutes from the end. The whole experience disgusted Stein and soured the memory of the great European years.

George Connelly was by now irretrievably lost to Celtic and top-class football. A gifted, ball-playing defender after the manner of Franz Beckenbauer, the quiet Fifer had never greatly cared for the hassle and publicity which accompanied being in the public eye. A few generations earlier, Jimmy Quinn might have drawn the same conclusion – that football really wasn't worth that kind of bother. Connelly responded by occasionally, and then less occasionally, not appearing where he was expected. A team-mate and friend, searching for Connelly's basic instincts, once asked him what, if he had the choice, he would really like to be. 'A long-distance lorry-driver' was the reply. He envied the freedom and the chance to be on his own, away from smothering influences and hangers-on which are part and parcel of being public property. Connelly remained at Celtic Park for a while longer, but his heart wasn't in it. Visits to Connelly's home by Stein, Sean Fallon and Dr Fitzsimons, the long-serving club doctor, were all to no avail.

By the summer of 1974 the career around which Stein had once said he would rebuild Celtic was effectively at an end.

Stein spelled out the truth to the annual meeting of shareholders in September 1974. They had lost Hay by transfer, the promising Brian McLaughlin by injury and Connelly 'through his own decision'. No club could afford such losses, he warned, and building another team which could aspire to the European Cup would 'obviously take some time'. However, they had now equalled the world record, held by CSKA Sofia, of nine successive domestic championships in succession – and 'God willing, we intend to make it a full decade of Celtic supremacy.'

The following season was Celtic's ninth in the European Cup, but they went out in the first round to Olympiakos of Greece. Jock Stein commented succinctly: 'The only consolation is that if we were not good enough for the competition it was better to get out the way quickly and let others who were get on with it.' It was the end, for the time being, of the club's automatic presence in the premier European competition, for whether by divine intervention or for more prosaic reasons, the dream of a tenth successive League title slipped away in the early months of 1975. Celtic finished in third place, eleven points behind Rangers.

There were the Scottish Cup and League Cup as substantial consolations, won in finals against Airdrie and Hibs respectively. But everyone knew that an era had ended. Billy McNeill confirmed it when, at the age of thirty-five, he retired from playing football following the cup final victory over Airdrie and was carried from the field by his team-mates in salute to a wonderful career. He soon realised that his decision to leave not only Celtic but the whole football world had been premature. Jimmy Johnstone went off to play in the United States. Apart from Bobby Lennox, the Lisbon Lions were gone and the glorious 'nine-in-a-row' era was now merely a memory to savour, the stuff of folklore for all who had witnessed it. But for Jock Stein, and all who cared about him, there was something much worse to follow.

In the early hours of the first Sunday in July, Stein was driving a Mercedes car from Manchester Airport back to Glasgow. He had just returned from a holiday in Minorca and there were four other occupants of the car – his wife Jean, fellow-manager Bob Shankly and his wife, and the Glasgow bookmaker Tony Queen. The road was then notorious for its toll of accidents – sometimes caused by drivers wandering on to a dual carriageway heading in the wrong direction. That was precisely what happened on this occasion – a head-on crash occurred at high speed. Stein was eventually to be awarded substantial damages against the other driver, who was fined for reckless driving, but it was a blow for which there could be no appropriate compensation. According to the testimony of those who knew him best, Stein never fully recovered from that terrible accident, in which Tony Queen was also very seriously injured.

Stein was rushed to hospital in Dumfries, scarcely able to breathe – a condition which had not deterred a policeman from administering a breathalyser test as he lay at the roadside. He was operated on and, within a remarkably short space of time, was making light of his misfortune. The wounds, however, were more than superficial. Tony McGuinness, another friend of long standing, said:

> *'He was never back to the man he was, after the crash. Apart from the physical wounds, it took a lot out of him mentally. He never had a proper night's sleep thereafter. I also believe that he came back to Celtic Park far too early, because of his love for the club. From within a very short time after the accident, he was continuing to act in an advisory capacity.'*

Billy McNeill recalled learning of the accident to the man who had become much more to him than a mere manager, on returning from his own holiday. He rushed to the hospital in Dumfries, but identifies it as one of the great regrets of his career that he did not, at that point, cancel his decision to leave the game and return to the club in what was clearly an hour of need.

The directors, meeting on July 17, 1975, appointed Sean Fallon as acting manager, but a disappointing season followed – defeat in the League Cup final by Rangers, an early exit from the Scottish Cup at the hands of Motherwell and a late collapse in the new ten-club Premier League after leading the table until well into the new year. In Europe, Celtic's return to the Cup-Winners' Cup after their nine-year run in the supreme competition ended at the quarter-final stage at the hands of the East German side Sachsenring Zwickau. It was Celtic's first season since 1963/64 without a major honour. On the brighter side, Dalglish and McGrain both had outstanding seasons, and youngsters like Roy Aitken and Tommy Burns were coming through from Celtic Boys' Club which had been founded in 1971 to bring talented youngsters under the Celtic wing. Johannes Edvaldsson, an Icelandic internationalist defender, was brought to Celtic Park and became a personality in the eyes of the supporters. So too did John Doyle, a fast and direct winger signed from Ayr United late in the season to strengthen the title challenge, but to no avail.

As early as November 1975, the Celtic directors had been reappraising the position in the light of Stein's injuries. 'The question of whether we had lost forever that vital spark which made him the man he was, was still a matter of considerable debate,' the board meeting minutes recorded. 'Time alone will tell.' Two months later, events took a curious twist when director Tom Devlin – Celtic's representative on the SFA – reported to his colleagues that Stein had approached that body to indicate that he was interested in the post of Scotland manager. At a meeting between the directors and Jock Stein at the Ambassador Restaurant on February 3, the manager 'intimated that if Celtic wanted him, he would be only too happy to stay with the club'.

The following week, the directors considered the possibility of approaching Pat Crerand to return to Celtic Park in Sean Fallon's role, with Fallon taking charge of scouting, but this was not pursued. Instead, two months later, they settled on the name of David McParland – former player with Partick Thistle and later their manager – as the man who was to assist Stein as he returned to his full duties at Celtic Park. At his own request Stein took charge for the first time since the road accident when Celtic played Manchester United in a benefit match for Jimmy Johnstone and Bobby Lennox at the end of the competitive season.

Stein was not consulted about the appointment of David McParland, and was not particularly enthusiastic about it, feeling that the directors should have stayed within the Celtic family to bring in the man who, inevitably, would be looked upon as his own potential successor. But they worked well together during the 1976/77 season, with Stein watching from the touchline as McParland took charge of the physical training and practice games in which the Celtic manager had revelled for so long. In a masterly move, Pat Stanton was bought from Hibernian. He had served the Edinburgh club for twelve seasons and had all the experience and midfield drive to make the difference to the transitional Celtic side. Another remarkable signing during this season was of Alfie Conn, from Tottenham Hotspur, though his previous club had been Rangers. Joe Craig, an efficient striker, was bought from Partick Thistle. Happy days returned for the time being to Celtic Park, with another League and Scottish Cup double to conclude (as it would soon transpire) Celtic's catalogue of major honours under Stein's management.

After a tense battle for the League title, Celtic finally triumphed when a Joe Craig volley beat Hibs at Easter Road on

April 16, 1977. In the Scottish Cup the early draws favoured Celtic and they disposed of Airdrie, Ayr United and Queen of the South before two Joe Craig goals beat Dundee in the semi-final. The scene was set for a final against Rangers on May 7, and the attendance figure of 54,252 serves as a reminder that this was a period when public interest in Scottish football had gone into some decline. A penalty goal by Andy Lynch gave Celtic victory in an otherwise disappointing final. The team that day was: Latchford, McGrain, Lynch, Stanton, MacDonald, Aitken, Dalglish, Edvaldsson, Craig, Wilson and Conn.

The season of 1977/78 was Jock Stein's last as Celtic manager, and it was not a happy one. Even before it had begun, Kenny Dalglish's enormous talents had been transferred to Liverpool. Celtic went on a close-season tour of Australia, and Dalglish was left at home after expressing extreme reluctance to join the party. By now he was determined to leave Celtic Park to seek further fame and fortune in England. Liverpool were quick to spot his absence from the touring party, and moved in for his signature. Stein never tried so hard to keep a player at Celtic Park, and was still pleading with him to think again minutes before the deal was concluded for a £440,000 transfer fee.

On top of this blow, Pat Stanton suffered a knee injury which effectively ended his career – the beginning of a string of mishaps to key players. Danny McGrain dropped out for what was to prove over a year with an ankle injury. Celtic lost the League Cup final to Rangers, went out of the European Cup in the second round to Innsbruck, departed from the Scottish Cup to non-Premier League Kilmarnock and languished in the League.

On March 2, 1978 the directors held a special 'crisis' meeting with Jock Stein in attendance to discuss the club's lack of success. It was recorded in the minutes:

*'The chairman mentioned that personnel and staff at Celtic*

*Park was largely the same as it had been 12 years earlier. It was appreciated that long and loyal service had been given by some persons, but the welfare of the club should take priority over personal factors. Mr Stein suggested that David McParland should take control of the first team and that he [Stein] should go with the second team with a view to improving the standard of young players coming through.'*

The directors turned down this remarkable idea, as they were not prepared to vest that degree of confidence in McParland. But the decisive step had been taken and Celtic were now looking for a new manager – with Jock Stein's support and assistance. On April 20 the meeting reconvened in the North British Hotel and Stein declared that there was only one man who could fill the manager's position at Celtic Park – Billy McNeill. Furthermore, he warned, there was no time to lose as McNeill might very soon be tempted to England if no move was made.

Billy McNeill's absence from football had been brief. He had planned to break from the game and concentrate on developing business interests, particularly in the hotel and leisure industries. But after only a season, he succumbed to a request from Hugh Birt, a friend of long standing, to become involved with Celtic Boys' Club. He had turned down some good offers during his self-imposed exile, but midway through season 1976/77, Clyde approached him and he took the plunge. Within a few months, ambitious Aberdeen – looking for a replacement for Scotland manager Ally MacLeod – came on the scene. McNeill was very happy during his one full season at Pittodrie and was to retain a respect and affection for that club, but when Jock Stein eventually asked him about the Celtic job, at a football writers' dinner in Glasgow, he knew that there was only one place he really wanted to go: 'My heart didn't let me think.' Celtic would start the 1978/79 campaign with a new manager, who had been reared and matured in the club's traditions – the man who had held aloft the European Cup.

At the same meeting at which it was agreed to pursue Jock Stein's recommendation of McNeill as manager, and to terminate with 'golden handshakes' the appointments of David McParland and Sean Fallon, an apparently handsome offer was made to the outgoing manager. The minutes record:

*'In view of Mr Stein's long and valued service with the club, it was agreed that at the time a new manager was appointed, Mr Stein be offered an executive directorship with the club as recognition and compensation by the club for these services. Mr Stein indicated that he would be very pleased to accept such a directorship which, presuming Mr McNeill accepted the Celtic job, would take effect at the time of the club's next annual general meeting.'*

For whatever reason, it never did. Billy McNeill regrets that he 'did not make it easier' for Jock Stein to stay at Celtic Park by making it unmistakably clear that his advice, far from being resented, would be warmly welcomed and appreciated. Stein may simply have had second thoughts about accepting a 'working directorship' which would have taken him into the commercial side of the business. When, a few months later, he accepted the managership of Leeds United, he said: 'I did not want to stay with Celtic as a director. I felt I had too much to offer football and I wanted a closer involvement.' James Farrell, who in 1988 was the last surviving director from that period, was in no doubt that Stein would have made 'an excellent director' and regretted that misunderstanding confused the initiative.

*'He had always been interested in the commercial side of the club and was very interested in ideas about raising finance. We*

*felt that this was a job he could do very well, and without too*
*much stress – but it was presented in the press as 'selling tickets',*
*which was completely wrong. There was a feeling at that time*
*that Manchester United's lack of success had something to*
*do with Matt Busby staying on at Old Trafford after he had*
*ceased to be manager. Personally, I felt that was a completely*
*false analogy. Jock would have been a genuine father-figure.'*

The sensational news did not break upon Scottish football for another month. On May 25, Celtic made their official move as McNeill was due to head for the United States on Aberdeen business. Three days later, the great Celtic Park transition was announced. Concluding his statement to the press, Desmond White stated: 'Today we go forward with confidence to our centenary ten years away.' An entirely wrong interpretation has been placed on these events, suggesting that Celtic were reacting to the move by Rangers – announced on May 24 – in bringing John Greig back to Ibrox as manager in place of Jock Wallace. The records prove that the Celtic initiative came, coincidentally, to a climax a few days later – but had its roots in the meetings of March 2 and April 20. No action could be taken, however, until Aberdeen's season was at an end.

On August 14, 1978, Liverpool under Bill Shankly and with Kenny Dalglish in their line-up came to Celtic Park to play in Jock Stein's testimonial match – an emotional occasion, with 55,000 in attendance. Liverpool won the game 3-2. The following evening there was a dinner in the City Chambers to salute the great manager, and next day Leeds United's chairman took the opportunity to make overtures to Stein. A week later it was announced that Stein would be moving to Elland Road as manager, and thus ended the most famous of all careers at Celtic Park. Forty-five days later, Stein left Leeds United to become Scotland's team manager in succession to Ally MacLeod.

# NINETEEN

## SUCCESS UNDER MCNEILL: AND A TEMPORARY PARTING

THE APPOINTMENT OF Billy McNeill as manager was massively popular with the Celtic support, but the team which he inherited was in urgent need of transfusion. Recent signings had been erratic, while the outflow of players since the mid-70s had been debilitating. McNeill quickly made it known to the directors that money would have to be spent, perhaps on a scale which Celtic had not been accustomed to in the past, if success was to be recaptured. At the same time, he took a close interest in the redevelopment of the youth policy which had been the club's pride and joy for so long, but which had faltered somewhat during the '70s. Davie Provan, the winger, was bought from Kilmarnock for £120,000 – a record fee between Scottish clubs – and Murdo MacLeod, a strong midfielder, from Dumbarton for £100,000. Bobby Lennox returned from the United States, while Paul Wilson was sold to Motherwell and Joe Craig to Blackburn Rovers. McNeill told the annual general meeting of shareholders on November 3, 1978 that further purchases would probably be necessary.

There was no instant transformation, however, with early League form uncertain and defeat by Rangers in extra-time of the League Cup semi-final. Out of Europe for the first time since the mid-60s, Celtic were ignominiously removed from the short-lived Anglo-Scottish Cup by Burnley. To Celtic's great advantage, however, an extraordinarily severe winter ensued and League fixtures piled up while McNeill got the house in order. By the time normality was restored in March, Danny McGrain was ready to take his place again after an 18-month absence – and in the captain's role. He had returned to the side in a friendly match against Estoril in Portugal, on a valuable January excursion which helped keep the players match-fit.

During the early part of the League season, no club had broken clear of the pack so that Celtic were still in contention along with Dundee United and Rangers, when the League programme recommenced. Brushing aside a Scottish Cup defeat by Aberdeen, they hit a good run of League results until meeting Rangers at Hampden early in May, of this extended season. Rangers won 1-0 to take a one-point advantage with four games remaining. Celtic pressed on more in hope than expectation, and secured victories over Partick Thistle, St Mirren and Hearts before arriving at their last game of the season – against Rangers at Celtic Park on May 21. The position was clear. Victory would give Celtic the title while anything less would leave Rangers, with two games still remaining, firmly in the driving seat.

It turned out to be one of the most memorable Celtic performances of that era. Rangers led 1-0 at half-time and title hopes seemed to have evaporated when Johnny Doyle was sent off for retaliation shortly after the interval. Lennox came on as a substitute, and Celtic threw everything into attack. Midway through the second half, Roy Aitken headed an equaliser and the Celtic Park roar of encouragement reached new heights. Sensationally, George McCluskey put Celtic 2-1 up after 75 minutes. Now they were 15 minutes away from the title. Joy was short-lived, for Rangers promptly equalised. Seven minutes remaining, and the Rangers defence got into a tangle over a cross from McCluskey. Jackson ended up sending the ball past his own keeper, McCloy. Seldom had the outcome of a League title hung so precariously. If Celtic, with ten men, lost a goal at this stage they were finished. If they could hold firm, the title was theirs. They held firm and, indeed, in the final minute Murdo MacLeod nearly took the roof off McCloy's net with a 20-yard drive which put the issue beyond doubt. It was a night of joy unconfined. Billy McNeill's first season as manager had been climaxed with a League title won in the most dramatic of circumstances. 'It was truly a magnificent affair,' the following week's board meeting agreed. 'Our supporters had been dancing on the terracing, reminiscent of the triumph of 1967.' The Celtic team was: Latchford, McGrain, Lynch, Aitken, McAdam, Edvaldsson, Provan, Conroy (Lennox), McCluskey, MacLeod and Doyle. Roy Aitken, hero of the day, describes it as 'far and away the best game I have played in.'

McNeill knew, however, that the whole Celtic Park set-up still needed strengthening. In his second season as manager there was a quarter-final exit from the League Cup, at the hands of ever-improving Aberdeen, but League progress was good and Celtic were clear leaders as 1980 dawned.

The return to the European Cup had been exciting, with the first expedition to Albania – a country about which little was then known by the outside world, and which was not prepared to allow Scottish supporters or journalists in for the game. In spite of these much-publicised features of the trips, the Celtic directors noted that they were 'received with the utmost friendship and courtesy in Tirana' and the team returned home with an acceptable one-goal deficit. Confusion surrounded the Albanian journey to Glasgow for the return leg, as their visas lay unclaimed in Belgrade until they picked them up in the course of the journey to Glasgow. Then they arrived at Heathrow, without having made hotel arrangements in

Glasgow. This unusual build-up contributed to a 47,000 crowd assembling at Celtic Park, to give the unworldly Albanians a genuinely warm welcome, and to cheer a 4-1 victory for the home side. Celtic then qualified for the quarter-finals with an unexpectedly tight 3-2 aggregate win over Dundalk, the Irish champions. The prospect of a tie with Real Madrid in March whetted the winter appetite of team and supporters.

In time for the European Cup tie, McNeill plunged into the transfer market to spend £250,000 on bringing Frank McGarvey from Liverpool. It was a club, and indeed Scottish, record fee. All was still well on the home front, with Celtic eight points ahead in the League, when Real Madrid came to Glasgow on March 5. In front of a 67,000 crowd, goals from McCluskey and Doyle gave Celtic a 2-0 lead. A fortnight later, however, in the frenzied atmosphere of a packed Bernabeu stadium, Celtic lost an early goal and eventually went out 3-2 on aggregate, bitterly disappointed and aggrieved over weak refereeing. The exit from Europe was bad enough, but it also seemed to trigger a loss of form in the League. On April 5, Celtic lost to Aberdeen in a game which ended defender Tom McAdam's career after he had suffered concussion. Then they went twice to Dundee, to lose 3-0 to United and 5-1 to the Dens Park club. From a seemingly impregnable position, Celtic were on their way to throwing away the Premier League title, which Aberdeen eventually snatched by a solitary point. On May 10, however, some amends were made when George McCluskey scored in extra-time to beat Rangers 1-0 in the Scottish Cup final. The team at Hampden that day in front of a 70,303 crowd was: Latchford, Sneddon, McGrain, Aitken, Conroy, MacLeod, Provan, Doyle (Lennox), McCluskey, Burns and McGarvey.

The aftermath of the game provided one of the most disgraceful scenes in recent Scottish football memory, and brought a sentence of great injustice upon Celtic. The joyful Celtic players rushed towards their own supporters at the final whistle, to acknowledge their celebrations. Some Celtic supporters came on to the track, and the area behind the goal. From the other end, however, there came a malev- olently-intended invasion. As the SFA's own report acknowledged: 'There was no question of celebration in the minds of the fans who invaded from the west end of the ground. They had violence in mind . . .' A pitched battle ensued, with mounted police charging around the centre of the pitch. The police, in Celtic's view, bore considerable responsibility for having only a few officers on duty at the Celtic End at the final whistle. A more realistic presence could have prevented the small and good-natured incursion. But the SFA made no differentiation between the clubs in the punishment handed out – fines of £20,000 each.

The 1980/81 season opened with a testimonial match against Manchester United for Danny McGrain, ten years after he had entered the Celtic first-team. He may well have ended up at Celtic Park only because a Rangers scout who watched him when he was making a youthful name with Queen's Park Victoria XI assumed (wrongly) that Daniel Fergus McGrain could not possibly be of Protestant stock! During the intervening period, he had come to epitomise the Celtic traditions of boundless energy, considerable skill, determination and loyalty, overcoming his diabetic condition and very serious injuries in the process. By common consent, McGrain was one of the world's best full-backs and he would end up as the most-capped player in Celtic's first century. He had been from the same vintage as Hay, Connelly, Dalglish and Macari but was now the only Celtic Park 'survivor' of that formidable group, proud of the fact that he never asked for a transfer throughout his long career at Celtic Park.

Celtic regained the Premier League title in season 1980/81, the second such triumph under McNeill's management, but the season had started indifferently and relations between the manager and board, particularly chairman Desmond White, had begun to deteriorate. McNeill, as a player, had got on well with White. 'He was always very kind to me. Half an hour before a European Cup tie, I could ask for a couple of tickets for friends and he would always oblige. It was a good relationship, and I had a lot of respect for Desmond,' McNeill recalled. But McNeill as a manager was ambitious, sometimes impetuous, and sceptical about White's insistence that Celtic lived on a financial knife-edge. Though the supporters knew nothing about it, matters almost came to a head on November 14, 1980, when a pre-meeting between manager and directors took place, immediately before the shareholders' annual general meeting. The business was to 'discuss the gap that had developed between Mr McNeill and the chairman' and the manager was offered the opportunity to resign. He declined. Five days later, Celtic went out of the League Cup to Dundee United.

By January 1981, Desmond White was seeking economies in the running of the club on items such as 'youth trips, Seamill Hydro, scouting and managerial expenses to England, Ireland etc., and petrol consumption'. The club was now a £1million per year business, and White feared that there could be a substantial loss on the season, partly because of an early and undistinguished exit from the European Cup-Winners' Cup to Romanian opponents. The directors agreed that 'these issues fell on relatively deaf management ears and in our opinion [there was] an unrealistic approach to the seriousness of the problem'. By May, Celtic had won the League title, by seven points from Aberdeen, but had gone out of both the Scottish Cup and League Cup at the semi-final stage to Dundee United. Success had become such a familiar trapping of Celtic Park that a season in which the League title was won was not necessarily regarded as a satisfactory one.

Desmond White complained bitterly at a board meeting that wages had doubled since McNeill's arrival, while gates were going down because of the economic recession in the country. The secretary of the Supporters' Association, George Delaney, was called in for a dressing down. He had written in the Celtic View that McNeill must have the directors' full support in buying players and had complained about a rise in the price of season tickets. 'Mr Delaney observed that the supporters thought that Celtic FC had lots of money. The chairman pointed out that possibly the supporters thought that, but that he, Mr Delaney, should know better, as he had information at times not available to the supporters.' In the event, the annual general meeting held in September 1981 heard that the club had broken even.

There was clearly a gulf between the McNeill approach, and the fiscal caution which Desmond White personified. McNeill tried to re-build a bridge when he told the annual meeting in September 1981 that he had been one of the Kelly Kids and he would like to see now a group of White Kids. The Celtic Boys' Club was playing an increasingly important part in that process, and season 1980/81 had seen the emergence of Charlie Nicholas as an enormous creative and goal-scoring talent – 'the most exciting player I have ever worked with,' said McNeill – while Pat Bonner, from County Donegal, had been confirmed as a first-class goalkeeper after Peter Latchford was injured, and Mark Reid emerged as a valuable home-reared defender. But by this time, the differences between manager and chairman had been exacerbated by matters unrelated to money. McNeill had run into a series of disciplinary problems, both for indiscreet comments about referees, and over a too-public altercation with a journalist for which the club fined him £500. Looking back on this period, McNeill admitted that he was trying to be the club's greatest supporter as well as its manager. The austere Desmond White found such incidents unacceptable, and tensions mounted.

In spite of this background, season 1981/82 produced Celtic's 33rd League Championship success and the third in four campaigns under McNeill. They led from the start and ended up two points ahead of Aberdeen. Though both Frank McGarvey and Charlie Nicholas sustained leg-breaks in the course of this season, a relatively settled side had developed under McNeill, with Bonner, Reid and MacLeod ever-present throughout. McGrain, Aitken, McAdam, Sullivan, Burns and McCluskey were not far behind. It was a very good blend of youth and experience and a teenager with a famous Celtic surname attracted instant rave notices – Paul McStay made his first-team debut against Queen of the South in a Scottish Cup tie on January 23, 1982, and was soon playing with the midfield guile of a veteran. Once again, however, the cup competitions proved unrewarding. Celtic went out of the European Cup in the first round to Juventus, going down 2-0 in Italy after Murdo MacLeod had given them a slender first-leg lead. In the League Cup, they failed to qualify from their section for the quarter-finals and in the Scottish Cup, there was a fourth-round defeat by Aberdeen.

The last day of the League season was reached with Celtic needing to avoid defeat by St Mirren in order to be sure of retaining the title. The situation was that, if Celtic lost 1-0, a five goal victory for Aberdeen over Rangers at Pittodrie would be enough to give them the title. By half-time, there were no goals at Celtic Park while Aberdeen were 4-0 up. It was not until the 63rd minute that George McCluskey scored the goal which relieved the tension, and Celtic finished as 3-0 winners. At the end of the game, the Celtic support tempered the joy of the occasion by chanting the name of Johnny Doyle, the popular winger who had been killed by an electrical accident in his home early in the season.

Having led Celtic to three Premier League titles and one Scottish Cup success during his four seasons as manager, Billy McNeill's tenure should have been extremely secure. In fact, however, relationships were still very difficult behind the Celtic Park facade. The following season opened with the directors taking umbrage over reported comments by the manager, in Holland for a warm-up tournament, about the need to buy two defenders and the board's alleged unwillingness to part with the necessary money. It was agreed to call McNeill before a board meeting in order that he might learn of the directors' displeasure. According to the minute of the meeting held on August 26, 1982, the directors told the manager that they did not want a repeat of such publicity. He responded that he was not responsible for the headlines that appeared. 'The directors unanimously interpreted such outpourings to the press as an obvious attempt to bring pressure on them to spend.'

In season 1982/83, Celtic raced to a League Cup triumph, goals from Nicholas and MacLeod helping them to a 2-1 victory over Rangers in the Hampden final of December 4. By then, however, they were again out of the European Cup in spite of having secured one of their best European results in years – a 4-3 aggregate victory over Ajax, Johan Cruyff and all, in the first round after being held to a 2-2 draw at Celtic Park. George McCluskey scored the winning goal in Amsterdam – another reminder of just how significant a player he was during a period when he tended to be overshadowed by other more publicised figures. Celtic then faced Real Sociedad of Spain with some confidence, but two late goals in the away leg left them with an uphill struggle at Celtic Park. Celtic's commitment to attack led to the loss of a goal midway through the first-half and, though they won the leg 2-1, they were out of Europe in anti-climactic circumstances.

The battle for the Premier League title was a particularly

exciting one, with Dundee United, Aberdeen and Celtic racing neck-and-neck from start to finish.

There was the first New Year's Day victory at Ibrox in 62 years to enthuse over – 2-1 with goals from McStay and Nicholas – but Celtic were dropping too many points against moderate opposition. Their hopes of a third title in a row were eventually destroyed inside three April days – a 3-2 home defeat from Dundee United and a Mark McGhee goal which beat them at Pittodrie took the initiative away from Celtic. On the last day of the season, they were dependent on United slipping up in a Dens Park derby. It did not happen and, although Celtic finished with a memorable 4-2 win over Rangers at Ibrox after being 2-0 down, United's 2-1 victory gave them their first ever title by a point.

In mid-April, Celtic had lost the Scottish Cup semi-final to Aberdeen by a single goal. Charlie Nicholas was missing from the side and this fuelled rumours that his days at Celtic Park were drawing rapidly to a close. Behind the scenes, Billy McNeill was involved in a vigorous rearguard action to keep him, and a remarkable package was put together. Nicholas was offered £400 per week, a £20,000 signing-on fee, a £20,000 interest-free loan and £10,000 to be paid into a pension fund, to yield him £170,000 at the age of 35. The lure of London was too strong, however, and Nicholas signed for Arsenal on June 9, 1983. For Billy McNeill, it was a bitter blow. 'I told Charlie as a manager and as a friend that it wasn't the right thing for him to do at that time,' he recalled.

The month of June 1983 really was an extraordinary one at Celtic Park, as revealed by the minutes of Board meetings. While McNeill was on holiday, a telephone call to Celtic Park informed the club that Sunderland were willing to sell striker Ally McCoist for £210,000. The significance of the call was not appreciated, and no action was taken. 'There appeared to be a lack of proper negotiations on our part,' the directors concluded. McCoist signed for Rangers instead, with devastating effect. When Nicholas finally opted for Highbury, Billy McNeill promptly signed Brian McClair from Motherwell for £70,000, and re-signed Murdo MacLeod and Mark Reid, both of whom had been looking for improved terms. A Rangers bid for MacLeod had been in the offing. Towards the end of the month, reports appeared about the fact that Manchester City had been showing an interest in obtaining McNeill's own services, at a salary of around £40,000. The Sunday Mail of June 27 carried a story which speculated about the manager's dissatisfaction over his level of remuneration, but which contained only one direct quote. 'I find it disappointing that I've never been offered a contract by my present employers,' McNeill was quoted as saying. The back-page story might have been a rather naive attempt to force Celtic's hand, but it had quite the opposite effect. All the tensions which had developed between manager and chairman during the previous three years now exploded.

At 1pm the following day, the Celtic directors – apart from Jack McGinn, who was on holiday – met in the Ambassador Restaurant to determine their response to the Sunday Mail interview. The meeting then moved to Desmond White's office in Bath Street and McNeill was summoned to be present. An uncompromising message was spelt out to him. No Celtic manager in the past had felt the need of a contract, and they were not prepared to negotiate one with McNeill. Neither were the directors prepared to discuss wages with him. McNeill recalled: 'That Monday, when I went up to meet the board of directors, I could not believe what was happening.' A public negotiating gambit had backfired. His position as Celtic manager was now impossible, and three days later he joined Manchester City. Desmond White's justification of the club's response was minuted thus: 'No man is greater than Celtic and had we acceded to Mr McNeill's demands there would have been, in our opinion, no living with the manager.'

The affair gave rise to fierce debate in the press and wherever Celtic supporters met, with McNeill gaining general support in the court of public opinion. In the long-run, his departure may have been in the manager's own best interests. He would return to Celtic Park four years later, with a wider range of experience and a more relaxed temperamental approach. 'But at the time,' he recalled a few years later, 'I was very bitter. That bitterness lasted for about a year. I found it difficult to understand what had happened and I still think there were outside influences at work, driving the wedge between myself and the chairman.' He also recognises, however, that the faults in letting relationships drift towards the final breakdown were not all on one side. Public reaction to the affair dismayed Desmond White. He remained convinced that the club had treated McNeill fairly, and that the application of bargaining pressure through the media was something that could not be tolerated. For him, it was really as simple as that. In the author's last conversation with him, White reflected on his many years of good relations with McNeill and puzzled over where it had all gone wrong. Two strong wills had met, and the outcome was to neither's satisfaction.

On July 4, 1983, David Hay was appointed as Celtic manager with Frank Connor – a former Celtic reserve goalkeeper, who had returned to the club as a reserve coach – as his assistant. John Clark, who had expected to be offered the managerial position on McNeill's departure, left with a golden handshake. Hay was well enough regarded by the Celtic support, but his managerial pedigree was modest. He had been with Motherwell for just one season and had led them to promotion, but had then decided to move to another job in the United States, before the Celtic offer came along. George McCluskey was the next admired face to leave Celtic Park – he was sold to Leeds for £140,000 in mid-July. In the early days of season 1983/84, Hay signed Jim Melrose – a former Partick Thistle favourite – from Coventry and full-back Brian Whittaker from Thistle. Jimmy Johnstone returned to Celtic Park as a part-time coach. In November, the very promising Stirling Albion forward, John Colquhoun, moved to Celtic Park.

But the season turned out to be a disappointment, with Celtic finishing as runners-up in each of the three major domestic tournaments. Aberdeen had become the leading lights of Scottish football and won the League with seven points to spare. In the Scottish Cup final, Alex Ferguson's formidable side completed the double by beating Celtic 2-1 in extra-time, after Roy Aitken had been sent off early in the game. A remarkable League Cup final had been lost 3-2 to Rangers in extra-time. Celtic came back from 2-0 down to equalise with an 89th-minute penalty, but McCoist completed his hat-trick during the additional period. In the UEFA Cup, Celtic beat Aarhus of Denmark and, more memorably, Sporting Lisbon thanks to a 5-0 second-leg win in Glasgow, before losing 2-1 at home to Brian Clough's Nottingham Forest after a goal-less first leg. The fact that no honours were won in Hay's first season did nothing to remove the doubts of the supporters, though thirty-one goals from Brian McClair confirmed the wisdom of McNeill's last signing, and Paul McStay's consistent brilliance prompted reports that Inter Milan were prepared to pay £2million for him.

At the end of the season, Whittaker was sold to Hearts and Hay signed a forward, Alan McInally, from Ayr United. He also made approaches for David Narey of Dundee United, Neale Cooper of Aberdeen and even Joe Jordan of Verona, but none of these came to anything. The supporters were restive, particularly when Celtic went out of the League Cup at the hands of Dundee United, but there was general approval when Hay succeeded in signing Maurice Johnston, a lethal striker who had gone south from Partick Thistle to Watford little more than a year earlier. The fee of £400,000 was a Scottish record. Aberdeen were clearly the best side in Scotland at this time, and they again won the Premier League by seven clear points from Celtic. However, Hay's first success as Celtic manager came on May 18, 1985, when the team came from behind to win the 100th Scottish Cup final in a breathtaking confrontation with Dundee United at Hampden Park. Most who were there still cannot fathom how Celtic managed to come back from the dead.

United were a goal ahead and suffering no threat when Davie Provan, just 14 minutes from the end, sent a perfect free-kick inside the left-hand post of goalkeeper Hamish McAlpine to equalise. Eight minutes later, Frank McGarvey headed home a cross from Roy Aitken for the winner. Given Celtic's uncanny penchant for success on special occasions, victory was perhaps pre-ordained. Celtic supporters did not, however, interpret this isolated success as evidence of renaissance. Indeed, the season had been marked by an episode which was to blight Hay's brief career as Celtic manager and lead, effectively, to two seasons of unhappy failure in European competition – the yardstick by which the supporters measured the quality of each Celtic side, season by season.

As fiascos go, Celtic's Cup-Winners' Cup confrontations with Rapid Vienna in the winter of 1984 were collectors' items. Celtic had beaten Ghent in the first round, but then ran in to a rough-house in Vienna. The Austrians won 3-1, but it was the manner of accomplishment which outraged the Celtic party. A savagely high tackle by Kienast, Rapid's resident delinquent, put Frank McGarvey out of the game. Yet only Alan McInally was sent off, for his first foul of the game. The Austrian team's behaviour was inflamed by the touchline promptings of their Yugoslav coach, Otto Baric, a man who had immersed himself in the waters of controversy at other times and in other places. Two weeks later in Glasgow, Celtic turned on an inspired performance and goals from McClair and MacLeod had equalised the tie on aggregate by half-time. Then Tommy Burns scored a third goal in the 68th minute, and all hell broke loose.

Burns had won the chase for a 50/50 ball with goalkeeper Ehn, prompting outrageous Austrian protests. Very soon afterwards, the brutal Kienast floored Burns with the referee unsighted, but was sent off on the testimony of a linesman. It seemed impossible that the referee could order him off without awarding a penalty, but he did. The referee's tolerance of Rapid's protests undoubtedly helped to lead to serious trouble. With 14 minutes remaining. Celtic were awarded a penalty and the game was stopped for 10 minutes as players and officials argued and gesticulated near to The Jungle touchline. Eventually, missiles were thrown and Weinhofer, the Rapid substitute, collapsed holding his head. Television pictures seemed to confirm that he had not been struck, and an ambulance-man at the scene swore that there was no sign of injury. But the ruse was to succeed. Peter Grant missed the penalty, Celtic won on aggregate – and Weinhofer left the ground with his head swathed in bandages.

The news of a protest to UEFA by the Austrians surprised nobody, but confidence in Glasgow was high, and proved justified when the European authorities found in Celtic's favour on every count except one. The Scots were fined £4,000 and Rapid £5,000, while Kienast was suspended for four matches and manager Baric banned from the touchline for three European matches because of his behaviour. But, because the UEFA Committee vote had been split – information to which none of the parties should have been privy in any case – the Austrians were encouraged to appeal.

Nobody could believe it when the appeal – heard by only three members of a 21-strong committee with some claiming they knew nothing of the meeting – was upheld. Despite the fact that Rapid officials (including their doctor) changed their testimony three times, the match was ordered to be replayed at least 100 miles from Celtic Park and, to complete the perverse way in which the business was handled, the original fine imposed on Rapid was doubled.

The play-off took place at Old Trafford, home of Manchester United, in front of 51,500 and the football – with Celtic sadly out of form and Pacult scoring the only goal – was the least notable element of the match. For the first time in their distinguished European history, Celtic had officially lost both legs of a tie. More seriously, two spectators, in separate incidents, committed assaults on two Austrian players in circumstances which made the local police look shamefully neglectful.

The first man was allowed to climb a fence and run fifty yards before knocking goalkeeper Feurer to the ground in his own goal. The second was actually in custody – being held by the arms at the touchline near the players' tunnel – when he was allowed to swing his leg and kick goalscorer Pacult as he left the field at the end. That meant another worrying afternoon in Zurich, as UEFA deliberated this latest incident. But Celtic's and their fans' generally impressive record over the years prevented the dreaded ban. The club was fined £17,000 and ordered to play their next home European match behind closed doors. It was rather a malodorous sequence of events which left many Celtic men uneasy about the way the directors and management of the club had handled the entire affair, most notably their unseemly haste to agree to the play-off. Most of those who had been at Celtic Park for the second match had argued that the club should make a dignified withdrawal in protest, rather than effectively admit guilt to an offence which appeared not to have been committed.

The season ended on a high note with the Scottish Cup victory over Dundee United. But, as Hay searched for a title-winning side, he sold John Colquhoun to Hearts – a serious misjudgement as it transpired – Mark Reid to Charlton and Frank McGarvey to St Mirren. The UEFA injustice had its impact on the following season, also. Celtic were drawn in the Cup-Winners' Cup against Atletico Madrid and a Maurice Johnston goal secured a good 1-1 draw in Spain. The return leg on October 2 had to be played behind closed doors, as part of the Old Trafford punishment, and Celtic flopped in the unreal atmosphere of a virtually empty stadium. A first half goal put Atletico in a strong position and when Celtic went 3-1 down on aggregate after 71 minutes, the writing was on the wall. Roy Aitken pulled back one goal but there was no prospect of Celtic winning an aggregate lead. It was, without doubt, one of the most miserable afternoons spent at Celtic Park in many a long year, and the harshest retribution of all for the club's minimal responsibility for the Rapid Vienna mess. Celtic went out of the League Cup early, losing to Hibs in a penalty shoot-out in the quarter-final after a 4-4 draw. The Edinburgh club also triumphed in the Scottish Cup quarter-final tie, a last-minute goal giving them a 4-3 win over Celtic.

These undistinguished reverses heightened the sense of unease which had prevailed among the Celtic support since McNeill's sudden departure. A few good youngsters – notably defender Derek Whyte – were breaking through into the first team. But, in spite of the presence of high-quality players like Burns, McClair, McStay and Johnston, the feeling persisted that Celtic were well short of having a top-class side.

David Hay's laid-back approach sometimes appeared to be carried to excess, and he was left in sole command when he parted company with assistant manager Frank Connor in February 1986. Hay was a pleasant and thoughtful man, who preferred to treat players as adults and felt ill at ease with Connor's rough diamond approach. However, he did not always communicate effectively and his reliance on the players' own common sense was sometimes ill-rewarded. The impression developed of a club which lacked direction and discipline. Quite unexpectedly, however, Celtic won the Premier League title on the last day of season 1985/86 – as effective a way as any of heading off criticism in the short-term.

After a poor start to the season, Hearts hit a great streak of form and were on top by the turn of the year. Celtic took only 22 points from their first 18 games but the cut-throat nature of the competition meant that they were still well in touch. However, Hearts continued to go well until they started to drop nervous points in the last few games of the season, while Celtic put in a strong finish. The last day was reached on May 3, 1986, with Celtic needing to win handsomely against St Mirren at Love Street – and then depend on Hearts losing to Dundee at Dens Park. That was precisely what happened. Two goals from Brian McClair, two from Johnston and one from Paul McStay put Celtic 5-0 up after 54 minutes. It was a performance with which no team in the country could have lived. With Celtic's part of the job done in style, attention on the Love Street terraces turned almost exclusively to the transistor radios. To the grief of the Hearts supporters, their team conceded two goals inside the final seven minutes. It was Celtic's title – and the terracing celebrations were of Lisbon vintage. Even in these extraordinary circumstances, David Hay found it difficult to be demonstrative.

# TWENTY

## THE RETURN OF CESAR: AND THE CENTENARY CELEBRATIONS

THE SENSATIONAL LAST-GASP triumph over Hearts brought only brief relief for Davie Hay since the dynamics of Scottish football had been transformed and Celtic were unsure of how to adapt. It was Rangers who made the decisive move by recruiting Graeme Souness as manager and engaging in a policy of spending as much money as was required to guarantee success. In an entirely new development, big-name English players like Chris Woods, Terry Butcher and Graham Roberts found their way to Ibrox. Scottish football was plunged into a ferment of excitement by these developments, and much of the speculation inevitably concentrated on how Celtic would react to them. When the new-look Rangers promptly won the first available competition of 1986/87, the League Cup, the impression began to form of an invincible force in Scottish football – with the power of money certain to sweep aside everything that stood in its way.

It took some time for this pattern to assert itself in the race for the Premier League. Celtic went sixteen games without defeat to build up a clear lead by December. But then everything started to go wrong while, at the same time, Rangers hit an even longer run of consistency. The Celtic support watched with an increasing sense of foreboding as a ten-point lead was whittled away. In the Scottish Cup, Celtic survived an epic three-game third round against Aberdeen, but then exited to Hearts. Just as worrying as the loss of form on the field was the steady build-up of problems off it. With the contracts of key players due to expire at the end of the season, there was non-stop speculation about the club's ability to hang on to the players in question – particularly Maurice Johnston, Murdo MacLeod and Brian McClair. As Johnston's form shaded off and disciplinary problems involving the player increased, it became increasingly apparent that McClair was the more important man to Celtic's long-term thinking, and that Hay's ability to persuade him that his future lay at Celtic Park would be a litmus test of his standing.

The inexorable progress towards surrendering the Premier League title came to a head in the second last game of the season, when Celtic lost at home to Falkirk, by 2-1, a result that summed up the unhappiness which had descended upon the club. The final League game of the season was at Tynecastle, and Celtic lost 1-0. It was Danny McGrain's final appearance as a Celtic player and Ian Paul of the *Glasgow Herald* summed up the great career thus:

> *'The Celtic man really is quite remarkable when you consider the traumas he has overcome during a senior career that began as Celtic were winning the European Cup in 1967. As well as learning to live with, and indeed conquer, the drawbacks of diabetes, he came back from a horrible skull injury to become one of the finest full-backs this country has produced. Yet there he was on Saturday, still urging himself on, still trying always to use the ball sensibly.'*

Celtic's proneness to accident at this time was further exemplified when the intimation to McGrain that he was to be given a free transfer was made in an offhand sort of way, which the Celtic directors immediately recognised as a 'botch-up' which should be redeemed as quickly as possible. In the end, McGrain moved to Hamilton Academicals where his coaching experience proved of immediate value. (He later returned to Celtic in a backroom role and more recently has become has become a valued member of Celtic's first-team coaching squad under Neil Lennon).

Two months before the end of the season, the Celtic directors were beginning to see the writing on the wall for Davie Hay as the prospects for a season without honours, on the eve of the club's centenary celebrations, grew all too real. The first inkling from the minutes of the board meetings came on March 19, 1987, when James Farrell 'reported that he had received information that Billy McNeill would be interested in leaving Aston Villa and returning to Celtic'. For some of Farrell's colleagues, the previous acrimonious parting with McNeill was of too recent memory and the matter was not pursued at this stage. But, by late April, with the League title all but gone, a consensus had developed that changes would have to be made. In addition to the players whose names were increasingly being linked with other clubs, the contracts of Bonner and McStay were about to expire. There was, at this point, little to suggest that any player of stature could be persuaded to remain at Celtic Park.

On May 8, events had been given impetus by the sacking of Billy McNeill as manager of Aston Villa, to whom he had moved ten months earlier from Manchester City. It was a moment of near-despair for McNeill. He was forty-six years of age and living in Cheshire and this was, he recalls, the low-point in his career. He contemplated the possibility of a move to the Middle East, and by May 15 he was engaged in discussions with Airdrie about the possibility of him taking over at Broomfield. Neither of these options greatly appealed to a man who had scaled the heights of professional football. Meanwhile, Davie Hay was going about his team-building plans and, on May 20, he at last plunged into the transfer market to sign Mick McCarthy, the Irish internationalist centre-half, from Manchester City for £450,000. But events were now moving quickly behind the scenes, though the Celtic board was still discussing whether their move for a successor to Hay should be directed at McNeill or at Lou Macari, by now manager of Swindon Town. By the time a special board meeting was held on May 26, in the Bath Street office, it was unanimous that McNeill should be the target.

The following day, Jack McGinn and McNeill – who was in Glasgow for a Lisbon Lions' reunion – met in the unsalubrious setting of a Clydebank car park. The terms on which the deal should be done were more or less sorted out. The scene then shifted that evening to the home of McNeill's old friend, Mike Jackson, where the full Celtic board was present to approve what had been agreed and to welcome back one of the most popular figures in the club's history. The following morning, Jack McGinn offered Davie Hay the opportunity to resign, which he turned down. So he was sacked. A press conference was convened for Celtic Park at 5pm and, with true drama, Billy McNeill was announced as the new Celtic manager. Though the country was in the midst of a General Election campaign, politics were swept off the front pages by the sensational news. McNeill enthused:

*'To say I'm happy doesn't begin to describe how I feel. I'm as excited as I was thirty years ago when I first joined the club as a player. To me, they are the best. This is my club, and I can say that after being with two major English teams. Believe me, they do not compare with this club. I hope I have matured in the four years I have been away. I certainly*

*believe that I have learned a lot as a manager. This is the third time I have joined Celtic and none of the magic has worn off.'*

The sense of excitement was shared by the Celtic support who could now see some prospect of a challenge to Rangers developing in the season ahead. But nobody underestimated the scale of the problems which included the fact that a significant proportion of Celtic's most valuable players were still determined to look to pastures new. Murdo MacLeod, Maurice Johnston and Brian McClair – who had scored 122 goals in his four seasons with Celtic – would all depart. During the summer, McNeill busied himself in the transfer market, bringing Andy Walker from Motherwell for £350,000, full-back Chris Morris from Sheffield Wednesday for £125,000, and – a particularly shrewd move – the vastly experienced Billy Stark from Aberdeen for a mere £75,000. As the players re-assembled for training, McNeill made clear that a tighter disciplinary regime would operate at Celtic Park than in recent times, though it soon became apparent that this would be based on mutual respect between manager and players. Roy Aitken, whose own contract was quickly renewed by McNeill although it still had two years to run, says: 'Straight away, there was more of a settled atmosphere. Whereas through much of the previous season, there had been all this talk about transfers, now everyone knew that they were going to be at Celtic Park for the next few years.'

The team which McNeill built was in the real Celtic tradition, to which the manager was so much attached. 'Chris Morris, Anton Rogan and Derek Whyte are all natural forward-going players,' said Aitken in 1988, looking back on the season. 'We are the only team in Scotland that plays with three men up, to maintain the free-flowing style.' But before all the pieces fell into place, there were to be two more major excursions into the transfer market. Celtic did not make a great start to their centenary season. On August 1, the new-look side lost 5-1 to Arsenal in a challenge match at Celtic Park. Then 42,000 turned out to witness a testimonial game for Tommy Burns, against Kenny Dalglish's Liverpool, which Celtic lost by a single goal. This event provided the opportunity for Danny McGrain and Davie Provan to salute the Celtic support. It was an important act of reconciliation with the veteran full-back, who had missed the chance to say a proper farewell at the end of the season because of the way in which his free transfer had been handled. No less warm was the reception for Provan, whose career had been cut short by the onset of a viral illness, which robbed him of energy and made it impossible for him to contemplate playing professional football again. He was to stay on the staff, to assist with the coaching of young players.

Celtic won the first League meeting of the season with Rangers 1-0, thanks to a Stark goal and this was psychologically important, given the hype which continued to surround the Ibrox club. But during September there were serious set-backs which made it clear that there would be no instant miracle for McNeill. In the League Cup, Celtic went out in the quarter-final to Aberdeen and, even more disappointingly, the UEFA Cup campaign was extremely brief. Goals by Walker and Whyte helped Celtic to a 2-1 first-leg lead over Borussia Dortmund but, in West Germany, they could hold out for only 64 minutes against a side which included Murdo MacLeod – and ended up losing 2-0. This left them free, as the euphemism goes, to concentrate on the League, but it was apparent to McNeill that the attack needed strengthening – and he knew exactly the players whom he wanted to bring to Celtic Park. Big money was involved, but the Celtic board was now of a mind to spend. Indeed, the extraordinary thing was that they could almost balance the books in the season's transfer dealings because of the outflow of players which had occurred shortly after McNeill's arrival. This was in spite of the fact that the club felt 'robbed' by the tribunal finding that Manchester United should pay only £850,000 for McClair who, in the developing age of vast transfer fees, might reasonably have been regarded as worth twice that amount.

In October, McNeill and Jack McGinn travelled south to tie up the transfer of Frank McAvennie from West Ham for £750,000. The player's form had declined slightly after an outstanding first season in London, following his transfer from St Mirren. McNeill had, however, a great respect for the player and believed that his sharpness as a striker could be restored. Meanwhile, McNeill was continuing to show interest in Joe Miller, the young Aberdeen winger, who was also attracting the attention of Liverpool and Manchester United. By November, Aberdeen – resigned to losing the player – decided to settle for a firm bid, rather than await a tribunal finding on what Miller was worth. This worked to McNeill's advantage, and he quickly secured McGinn's agreement for a £650,000 offer. Part of the attraction for the manager of both McAvennie and Miller was that they were both 'Celtic men' by instinct and upbringing. They were both fulfilling the ambitions of youth by signing for the club, and that was the kind of guaranteed commitment which McNeill was seeking. His faith was justified and, as Roy Aitken noted, 'the reason that things went so well for us was that all of the new signings fitted in straight away'.

By early October, Celtic had fallen into third place in the League table, behind Aberdeen and Hearts. But from that point onwards, success was to be virtually uninterrupted. The second meeting of the season with Rangers, at Ibrox, turned out to be an extraordinary affair which earned an unwelcome place in the annals of Scottish football because it led to four players ending up in the criminal courts. The game flared up when Rangers goalkeeper Woods and McAvennie clashed inside the penalty area. There was nothing very violent about the incident, but Butcher and Roberts both rushed into the fray. Woods, McAvennie and Butcher were all sent off while Roberts – who was extremely fortunate to escape the referee's attention – went into goal for Rangers. The rest of the game was played out in a tense atmosphere, and Rangers came from 2-0 down to force a draw. Astonishingly, the Procurator Fiscal's office in Glasgow initiated breach of the peace charges against the four players after the game had been shown on television. The affair dragged on throughout the season before McAvennie was eventually found not guilty, Woods and Butcher were fined. and the charge against Roberts was found 'not proven'. It was an incursion by the law into football which was welcomed by very few.

As 1987 drew to a close, Billy McNeill delighted the Celtic support by tying up long-term contracts with Aitken, Paul McStay and Peter Grant. By this time, the restlessness had disappeared from Celtic Park, to be replaced by a keen sense of purpose. The League points kept piling up while Celtic's rivals showed signs of uncertainty.

A 2-1 defeat by Dundee United on October 24, 1987 would be the last piece of bad news for Celtic supporters during the centenary season. By November 28, when they beat Hibs 1-0 at Easter Road, Celtic were on top of the Premier League and that is where they stayed. A 42,000 crowd turned out at Celtic Park two days later to pay tribute to Davie Provan, who played for just eight minutes of his own testimonial match against Nottingham Forest. Celtic lost 3-1, but there was a nostalgic interlude when Kenny Dalglish – by now manager of Liverpool – came on as substitute for Paul McStay. On the Saturday, it was back to serious League business with Frank McAvennie, proving to be a golden buy, scoring all four goals against Morton at Cappielow. When Celtic won the January 2 fixture against Rangers, through two more McAvennie goals, the prospects for the League title began to look very good indeed. There was a series of close results and uncertain performances, but the important fact was that Celtic continued to accumulate the points while their rivals slipped up.

The decisive game in the campaign, televised live on a Sunday afternoon, fell on March 20 against Rangers at Ibrox. Celtic rose magnificently to the occasion in an electric atmosphere. Paul McStay put them ahead with a memorable goal, which Jan Bartram quickly equalised for Rangers. Instead of holding out for the draw which would have sufficed, Celtic kept going forward and a marvellous corner from Tommy Burns, headed on by Rogan, was chested home by Walker to put Celtic virtually beyond reach in the title race. Roy Aitken said: 'We went into that game with everyone assuming that we would play for a draw. But we knew that if we could come out of it with a win, we would open up a six-point lead at the top of the table. The tactics that day were outstanding and for us to come back and score again after losing the equaliser really said something about the character of the team.'

Celtic went thirty-one games without defeat before on April 16, Hearts beat them 2-1 at Tynecastle to postpone the tying up of the League title. This had the beneficial effect, however, of allowing a capacity Celtic Park crowd to be present the following Saturday when a 3-0 victory over Dundee ensured that Celtic would be champions of the Scottish League in their centenary season – an achievement which had seemed improbable in the extreme, twelve months previously. There were great scenes of green and white celebration as the crowd sang 'Happy Birthday' to Celtic. For Billy McNeill – whose status as 'Cesar' was reinforced among the fans – it was a particularly poignant occasion. It was the 13th Scottish League title he had been involved in – nine as a player and four as a manager and, to lead Celtic to this achievement, he had emerged from the abyss of unemployment. There was special praise too for his assistant, Tommy Craig, who had arrived at Celtic Park a few months before McNeill's return. The two men had agreed to work together on an experimental basis, but Craig – a pleasant personality with a first-class football mind – had soon become the ideal partner in an irrepressible management team.

Meanwhile, the Scottish Cup campaign had been going smoothly following an uncomfortably close shave with lowly Stranraer back in January. Celtic won at home only by an early McAvennie goal and survived a missed penalty, to avoid the indignity of a replay. A Billy Stark goal then beat Hibernian in a replay, after a goal-less draw at Celtic Park. A capacity crowd at Firhill saw goals from Walker, Burns and Stark account for Partick Thistle. Thus Celtic qualified for the semi-finals and a Hampden meeting with Hearts, which produced one of the most remarkable finishes which the national stadium has witnessed. With just three minutes remaining, Celtic trailed by a single goal. The late assault which had been restored as one of the Celtic hallmarks was in full swing – and produced two goals, from Mark McGhee and Andy Walker, to carry the team into the final. Billy McNeill attributed this stunning victory to 'appetite, dedication and pride – that's why we win games late'.

The scene was then set for the final on Saturday, May 14. It was, in every sense, a glorious day. But Celtic's confidence about achieving the club's 11th League and Cup double in the centenary season was dented when Kevin Gallacher put Dundee United ahead early in the second half. For a time, Celtic seemed to be having difficulty in mounting the fight-back which everyone expected. With twenty minutes remaining, McGhee and Stark came on as substitutes and the flow of play was transformed – proof of a masterly tactical move by McNeill. With fifteen minutes remaining, Rogan made progress down the left and crossed for McAvennie to head past Thomson. The minutes ticked away and extra time seemed likely – in itself a welcome enough relief for the Celtic support. But there was now a built-in inevitability to the course of events. With almost the last attack of the game, McAvennie saw an opening in the Dundee United defence and shot through it into the Hampden net. The final whistle blew and a work of footballing fiction could not have produced a more astonishing climax to the game, the season and the century with honour.

# TWENTY-ONE

## WHO OWNS CELTIC?
## SHAREHOLDINGS AND PERSONALITIES
## THROUGH THE YEARS

AT THE TIME of Celtic's centenary, the question of the club's ownership did not seem in doubt, but this is one respect in which the past 30 years has changed everything. At that time, the hold of the two dominant families – the Kellys and the Whites – along with their allies, seemed absolute, but it was to last for only a few more years before irresistible circumstances forced change. In order to understand how that revolution occurred, it is necessary to recall how the previous structure had evolved.

Celtic were incorporated as a private limited company in 1897 with a nominal share capital of £5,000, in 5,000 shares of £1 each. There were, at that time, 201 members of the club and each was allocated a £1 share. In recognition of his outstanding services, John Glass was awarded an additional 100 fully paid-up shares, so that 301 were initially distributed. The remaining 4,699 were sold to members for ten shillings each, according to ability to purchase. A further share issue of 5,000 £1 shares was created in the following year, to raise capital for the club. Once again these were sold for ten shillings, so that there were then 301 fully-paid and 9,699 half-paid shares in circulation.

Inevitably, the great majority of share-buyers were the businessmen of Glasgow's East End. The men who emerged from these early issues as the largest shareholders in Celtic were to be the initiators of lines of succession which survived for more than a century. This was true of James Grant, an Irish publican and engineer who had made his fortune mining diatomite in the Antrim hills and who had acquired 801 shares – almost one-twelfth of the total – by 1898. James Kelly, the player turned publican, held 450 shares by the same time. The Glass shares would soon act as a foundation for the White interest in the club, while the Shaughnessy shares served to retain the Celtic connection within the law firm which continued to carry that name. The full list of significant Celtic shareholders in 1897 and 1898, with addresses, occupations and shareholdings in each year is shown in the table below.

There were at that time many shareholders who held only one or two shares in the club. Many of these were retained within families for sentimental reasons but became significant once the movement for change began. Hitherto dealings in these small shareholdings had scarcely been a significant factor within the club's affairs, though there is evidence that Willie Maley – who had not been one of the original large shareholders – did build up a substantial holding by the 1930s through small acquisitions, his position as club secretary putting him in a strong position to do this. In general, however, the pattern was of the big shareholdings acting as magnets to further significant blocks of shares, reinforcing the pattern of control by a few families.

### Breakdown of Celtic shareholdings, 1897/98

| Name | 1897 | 1898 | Occupation | Address |
| --- | --- | --- | --- | --- |
| John Allison | 100 | 200 | Masseur | 40 Hyde St, Manchester |
| James Cairns | - | 400 | - | 14 South Portland St |
| John Campbell | - | 100 | - | 379 Saracen St |

| Name | | | Occupation | Address |
|---|---|---|---|---|
| John Colgan | 100 | 200 | Cattle dealer | 48 Whitehill St |
| Thomas Colgan | 150 | 300 | Publican | 16 Whitehill St |
| James Cronin | - | 100 | - | Bridge St, Alexandria |
| Bernard Crossan | 100 | 100 | Grocer | 12 Graeme St |
| Michael Docherty | 100 | 100 | Comm. agent | 161 Stockwell St |
| David Doyle | - | 100 | - | Bellshill |
| Michael Dunbar | 150 | 300 | Publican | 429 Gallowgate |
| Thomas Dunbar | 100 | 250 | Salesman | 429 Gallowgate |
| William Flynn | 200 | 400 | Comm. agent | 125 Hospital St |
| John Glass | 100 | 401 | Manager | 597 Gallowgate |
| Patrick Glass | 200 | 401 | Builder | Fairholm Villa, Shawlands |
| James Grant | 400 | 801 | Publican | 49 St Vincent St |
| James Kelly | 200 | 450 | Publican | Stonefield, Blantyre |
| Terence Lynch | 100 | 100 | Brewer | Crownpoint |
| Alex McCann | - | 100 | - | Bellshill |
| David McKillop | - | 100 | - | Kilmarnock |
| James McKillop | 100 | 200 | Egg merchant | 45 Apsley Pl |
| John McKillop | 200 | 400 | Publican | West Nile St |
| William McKillop | 200 | 400 | Restaurateur | West Nile St |
| John H. McLaughlin | 150 | 300 | Publican | Hamilton |
| David McLoskey | 200 | 400 | Traveller | Antrim Terr., Belfast |
| Thomas Moore | - | 100 | - | 97 Quarry St, Hamilton |
| Thomas Nelson | 100 | 200 | Cattle dealer | Bellgrove |
| John O'Hara | 100 | 300 | Publican | 351 Gallowgate |
| Peter Paterson | - | 100 | - | High St |
| John Rafferty | 100 | 201 | Fish salesman | Fish market |
| Joseph Shaughnessy | 300 | 651 | Lawyer | 83 Bath St |
| Peter Souness | - | 100 | - | Motherwell |
| John Warnock | 100 | 201 | Publican | 568 Springburn Rd |

This process had been assisted at various points in the club's history by amendments to its constitution. Article 18 of the first Articles of Association in 1897 stated: 'The Executors or Administrators of the deceased shall be the only persons recognised by the Company as having any title to his share.'

There was no control over whom the shareholding could subsequently be transferred to, but to this was added Article 18A by a special resolution at the annual general meeting of 1933. This decreed that the executor of a deceased shareholder's estate must notify the club within six months of whom the shares were to be transferred to. The nominated person would then 'require to be approved of by the directors, and failing a tender of such transfer within the said period, the directors shall have the right to purchase the holding of the deceased member either on their own behalf or on behalf of any other shareholder of the Company'. This tightened the directors' grip over whom shares could be transferred to, and effectively eliminated the prospect of any unwelcome 'outsider' acquiring a significant stake in Celtic. In 1947 the time limit for transfers was reduced to three months.

The list of directors with shareholdings in 1901 was as follows: J.H. McLaughlin 300; John Glass 301; John O'Hara 390; John McKillop 460; James Grant 801; Michael Dunbar 372; James Kelly 560.

The O'Hara lineage was first to go when John O'Hara, the club's first secretary at its inception, died in 1904 and most of the family shareholding went to John Glass. His place on the board was taken by a Belfast man, Thomas Colgan, described as a publican but with varied business interests in Glasgow, who would soon marry into the Grant family. He and his brother John – a well-known cattle dealer in Belfast – had been shareholders from the outset.

John Glass died in 1906. By curious coincidence, Celtic's founding president passed away within a few days of the Irish hero of whom he had been a close associate and who had laid the centre turf at the new Celtic Park. The connection was recognised in the *Glasgow Star and Examiner*'s headline: 'The Deaths of Michael Davitt and John Glass'. Of Glass, the obituarist wrote that the Home Rule movement had lost 'one of its oldest, most loyal and generous members', while 'in sporting circles, he was a central and admired figure', never missing a Celtic meeting since the club's inception. John H. McLaughlin went further and described Glass as 'the founder and originator of the club'. It was at this point that Thomas White entered the scheme of things.

White was Glass's protege, both in Irish political circles and in relation to Celtic. The Home Government Branch of the Irish National League had taken over the *Glasgow Star and Examiner* in 1903, and White, who had briefly been chairman of the Branch, became a director – thus embarking on a publishing connection that was to be life-long. Yet when he became a director of Celtic in 1906, after inheriting Glass's 401 shares, he was only twenty-two years of age and already a qualified lawyer. Of Irish origins, his family was already well-established in Glasgow and his widowed mother owned a scrap-metal business in Dennistoun. The young Tom White would organise the affairs of the business each morning, before heading off to his law classes at Glasgow University and his wider public activities.

Another of the club's founders, Joseph Shaughnessy, also died in 1906. He had been a bailie in Rutherglen and legal adviser to Celtic from the start. He was also, the obituary noted, 'constantly consulted by the leaders of the trade unions in Scotland'. His son, John, subsequently succeeded him on the board.

In 1909, another strong link with the earliest days was broken through the death of John H. McLaughlin, only in his forties. For someone who apparently knew nothing of football in 1888, he had made a remarkable contribution not only to Celtic but to the development of football in Scotland, having championed the cause of open professionalism and the creation of a Scottish League. His shareholding was broken up, and no member of that family subsequently held office within Celtic.

The most active acquirer of shares in the pre-First World War period was James Kelly, who had become chairman in 1909. A man of extensive business interests – including the cinema in its pioneer days – he appears to have bought out William Flynn, a commission agent, who had been another of the early large shareholders. Tom White, who succeeded Kelly as chairman, was also building up his interest from several sources. The deaths of John McKillop and James Grant, both founding directors, in 1914 left only James Kelly and Michael Dunbar of the original board.

In 1920 there was another issue of shares, raising the nominal share-capital value of the club from £10,000 to £25,000, although only 10,000 of the new £1 shares were taken up. All of these were fully paid, and distributed almost exclusively among existing shareholders on a pro rata basis. Remarkably, this continued to represent the entire shareholding capital base of the company until after its centenary year when the issues of ownership and shareholding raised their heads in a very different context.

The powerful McKillop shareholding was recognised in 1921 when John McKillop, an insurance agent, was elected to the board on the death of Michael Dunbar. Otherwise, the directorships remained unchanged during the 1920s and there were no major shifts in the balance of power. The death of James Kelly in 1931 led to his son Robert being made a director in his place, and to a division of the large Kelly shareholding among at least six members of the family. It seems very likely that the amendment to the constitution, to require directors' approval of share transfers, was prompted at this time by the steady rise in Willie Maley's share interest.

By 1932 he owned 228 shares and acted as trustee for a further 212. Maley's position as secretary put him in the front line for information about potential share transfers – a situation of which he took advantage, and which contributed to a deteriorating relationship between himself and Tom White. The requirement to transfer shares within six months or else risk having them pass to directors or their nominees seems to have prompted James Grant's executor – Thomas Colgan, who had been sitting on the former director's shareholding for twenty years – to transfer a large part of it to Thomas Devlin, a trawler owner from Leith, in 1933.

The next significant development was the retirement of Tom Colgan to Toomebridge in 1940, (John McKillop retired from the board the following year but there was no replacement for either, the opportunity being taken to cut the number of directors to three – Tom White, Robert Kelly and John Shaughnessy.) The 'Toomebridge connection' is complex but important. In 1906 Tom Colgan had married a daughter of James Grant, whose family roots were in Toomebridge. However, Mrs Colgan died on the birth of their daughter, Mary, a short time later. From a young age, Mary lived at Toome House, Toomebridge, with her aunt and uncle, Neil and Felicia Grant, both of whom were unmarried. From the 1920s to the 1950s, Mary and her aunt Felicia would make occasional expeditions to Glasgow for major Celtic occasions although, according to surviving relatives, the ladies' interest in the sport was distinctly limited. Mary's cousin, Brian Grant, recalled joining in these expeditions, which took the Toomebridge party to the Bank Restaurant before and after the game, on to the team bus and even into the dressing rooms. When Tom Colgan retired both from business in Glasgow and as a Celtic director in 1940 he took up residence in Toome House with his daughter and the Grants. He died in 1946 and the Colgan shares were left to Mary who thus became – when the transfer was completed in 1949 – the holder of 1,103 fully-paid and 50 part-paid shares, making her the 'third force' in Celtic behind only the Kellys and Whites.

Tom White died in 1947 at the age of sixty-three, never having fully recovered from an attack of pneumonia which had been brought about by his bravely rescuing a bather from the sea. In later life he had concentrated upon his law practice and his Celtic interest, although his political activities had not entirely subsided. He had been a very close friend and associate of John Wheatley, the first Labour Minister of Health whose other crucial contribution to British politics had been to argue successfully for the compatibility of socialism with Catholicism at a time when the Church hierarchy was resistant to that concept. Wheatley was a partner in the printing firm of Hoxon and Walsh, which was involved in the Labour movement and church work, as well as publishing the Glasgow Eastern Standard. Shortly after the First World War the firm found itself in difficulty and Wheatley sought Tom White's advice. The Celtic chairman joined the business and remained involved until the time of his death. A fluent and witty orator, he was very much in the tradition of the Celtic pioneers as a man with many dimensions to his character.

Desmond White became a director on the death of his father, while Tom Devlin Jnr also joined the board in 1949. Following Col. Shaughnessy's death in 1953, after 41 years as a director, the Kelly-White-Devlin triumvirate sustained itself without additions until 1963. Meanwhile the Toomebridge connection had moved on a few stages – with the ultimate effect of concentrating a huge Celtic shareholding in the hands of one elderly Irishwoman. Sean Fallon recalled, from a team tour of Ireland during the early 1950s, being told by Robert Kelly that the two ladies, Felicia Grant and Mary Colgan, had expressed a desire to meet the 'three Irish boys' in the team – Peacock, Tully and Fallon. The chairman then took them to visit Toome House. A local hotel which the Grant family owned was also a regular stopping-place for Celtic parties over many years.

In 1956 Mary Colgan died, shortly after returning from a trip to the United States with Felicia. The Colgan shareholding was divided between her aunt and uncle. Then the substantial McCloskey shareholding in Belfast also passed to the Grants. As a result of all this, when Neil Grant died in the early 1960s, his sister Felicia found herself the owner of 1,705 fully-paid and 1,752 half-paid Celtic shares – the biggest ownership block, accounting for more than one-sixth of the total shares issued. The fact that Robert Kelly, whose own family holding was of a similar size, maintained a very close personal relationship with the Toomebridge shareholders, and held their proxies, ensured that his power base within the club was unchallengeable throughout the period of his chairmanship. These are the facts behind the legend of the 'old lady in Ireland' who, according to the vague awareness of a generation of Celtic supporters, held the ultimate say in the club's fortunes.

The first 'new name' on the board for more than thirty years was added in 1964, when James Farrell – a partner in the Shaughnessy law firm – was invited to become a director, and was given clearance to acquire 534 former Shaughnessy shares which were at that time held in trust. He had just been instrumental in bringing to fruition the Celtic Development Fund, which would later attract large amounts of money into the club's coffers for the specific purpose of financing ground improvements. The board remained four-strong throughout the next memorable decade in the club's history.

Robert Kelly was knighted in 1969 in the wake of the European Cup triumph, and stepped down from the chairmanship a few months before his death in 1971 to make way for Desmond White. Sir Robert was the club's first president when he died. The Archbishop of Glasgow, the Most Reverend James Donald Scanlan, said at his funeral:

> 'His finest quality was his unshakeable determination, exemplified by his father before him, to maintain the highest standards in the face of adverse criticism and niggling opposition ... He and his fellow directors had never forgotten that the Celtic Football Club was founded in the cause of charity.'

This was indeed true, and it is perhaps an appropriate point at which to comment upon Celtic's respect for the charitable aspect of the club's tradition. Over the years, Celtic have contributed very large amounts to charitable causes – both by playing games on behalf of specific funds and, more generally, by quietly giving donations in response to routine appeals and, occasionally, major disaster funds. Sean Fallon, who attended board meetings over many years, recalled that 'there was never a meeting which didn't end with agreement to give donations here and there'. It is a commitment which is well-maintained up to the present day and while nobody claims that Celtic's prime reason for existing is to raise money for charity – an unworldly expectation – there cannot be any football club in Britain or beyond which can claim anywhere near their record as givers to causes outside football.

In 1973 Felicia Grant died in St John's Nursing Home, Belfast – and so a substantial part of the Grant/Colgan shareholding returned to a member of the family in Scotland. She left half of her shareholding – 852 fully-paid and 877 part-paid shares – to her nephew James Grant, a seafarer with his home in Stepps, Lanarkshire. The son of her brother, Tommy Joe, a colourful character who had departed for Canada many years previously, James Grant was the chief engineer on board a vessel berthed in Leningrad when news reached him that he had inherited a large Celtic shareholding – though it was far short of the 5,000 shares reported at the time. The suggestion that he had overnight become the largest Celtic shareholder made good copy, but it was well wide of the mark. The less spectacular truth was that shares had been accruing steadily over the post-war years to the directors and their families, and by the mid 1970s the White, Kelly and Devlin shareholdings each substantially outweighed Mr Grant's remarkable inheritance. The remaining Grant shares were scattered amongst ten other relatives of Miss Felicia Grant, in County Antrim, Ontario and Michigan. All of this was to become of much greater significance once the struggle for power began.

In 1982 two new directors were appointed – Desmond White's son, Christopher, and Jack McGinn, the club's commercial manager who had gone to the Celtic board in the early 1960s with the idea of creating a newspaper called the Celtic View. Having received official blessing for the then novel idea of a club newspaper, he edited it from 1965 to 1979 when he was appointed commercial manager. The integrity and competence of service which he provided to the club were recognised through an invitation to join the board. McGinn had held no shares in the club prior to becoming a director. This was a real break with the Celtic tradition of keeping directorships within a very close circle, based on the 'lines of inheritance'. Subsequently, Tom Grant – son of James Grant who had inherited the 'Irish' shares – was also co-opted, thus renewing the Grant presence in the Celtic boardroom after a break of almost seventy years.

Desmond White died in 1985 after fourteen years as chairman. Again, he had lived a varied life, which allowed him to place football in a wider social context. As his *Celtic View* obituary observed:

*'In an age when too many mediocrities see football as a well-*

*publicised avenue to self-aggrandisement, Desmond White was the absolute contrast – a well-rounded human being whose prime interest happened to lie in football. Where else would one find the chairman of a football club who read avidly of science and astronomy in his leisure time; who could speak of having found his deepest sense of contact with the infinite at the tops of mountains; who had the perspective on life and human behaviour which can only come from such diversity of interests?'*

White had exercised positive influence on a whole range of matters crucial to Scottish football, during a period when its future was by no means secure. He had a good claim to being regarded as the architect of the Premier League; he had put Celtic in the forefront of a campaign to save Hampden Park as Scotland's national stadium; he was an influential member of the MacElhone Committee which advanced ideas for countering crowd trouble at Scottish football grounds that were subsequently embraced in the Criminal Justice (Scotland) Act. During the last years of his life he sustained a highly effective campaign for rating parity between Scottish properties and those in the rest of the UK. His prime concern was for football grounds, but the ramifications went far wider. The last game which he saw before his death, while on holiday in Greece, was the one in which Celtic won the 100th Scottish Cup final.

On Desmond White's death, the mantle of chairman passed to Tom Devlin who had served quietly as a director for thirty-six years. It was an appointment which crowned his Celtic connection but proved to be regrettably brief, as he died just over a year later. His wife Betty, who had her own strong connections with the club and was no great admirer of the Whites and Kellys, would become an influential ally of those who were seeking change. On Tom Devlin's death, the directors turned to Jack McGinn – already a full-time worker for the club whom they saw as the man best able to fulfill a modern chairman's role at Celtic Park. It was an appointment that McGinn had neither sought nor expected, and it was a remarkable tribute that the major shareholders on the board should have united in deciding to place their trust in him, rather than divide over the dynastic right to succeed.

Prior to the appointment of Tom Devlin, which was in recognition of extremely long service, two Kellys and two Whites had shared the chairmanship of Celtic from 1909 to 1985. Now Jack McGinn took over, after less than four years as a director and with no family pedigree in the Celtic hierarchy. It was an appointment indicative of a new era in football. He was under no illusions about the fickleness of public opinion and the near-inevitability of it being directed at some stage against the men who are believed to hold the purse-strings and the ultimate power in a football club. At the time of Celtic's centenary, McGinn said:

> 'I was there as a youngster when the supporters were shouting at Tom White, not long after the war. Then I heard Bob Kelly taking some terrible abuse in the early sixties from the crowd in front of the directors' box. Desmond White got it because, after all the great success, the club hit problems in the late seventies. Even Tom Devlin had to take some stick during his short time in office.'

It would not take long after the centenary season, in all its glory, had been completed for McGinn's realistic expectation that the Celtic board would come under fire to be vindicated– though this time the demand for change would lead to outcomes which had not previously been contemplated.

The story of how Celtic's ownership structure changed radically in 1994 lay ahead, as did the critical period when Fergus McCann would have effective control of the club and open it up to mass shareholding by supporters. At the same time, he brought in the Irish businessman Dermot Desmond as a substantial investor. At the time of McCann's departure in 1999, Desmond became the largest shareholder in Celtic and his involvement has underpinned the club's subsequent financial stability and success – an overwhelmingly positive force in the view of all who have worked most closely with him. That judgment is shared from afar by Fergus McCann who says simply: "The club is well run and in good hands," while welcoming the fact that there are several other substantial minority shareholders involved.

Celtic plc was reconstituted in 1994 and has a diverse shareholder base including supporters in many parts of the world. The company has three classes of shares listed on the AIM market of the London Stock Exchange and one of McCann's most notable legacies is that, as at August 2017, there were 28,630 ordinary shareholders with a stake in the ownership of Celtic. Apart from anything else, this guarantees well-attended and lively Annual General Meetings. Dermot Desmond's interest in the company included around 35 per cent of the ordinary shares. The next three biggest holders of ordinary shares were Bank of New York (Nominees) Ltd (a nominee company used by a number of shareholders to hold shares in Celtic) with 18.3 per cent; Christopher Trainer with 10.5 per cent and Mark Keane with 6.3 per cent. It is a balance that works well and combines powerful financial underpinning with a unique diversity of shareholder involvement. Peter Lawwell describes Desmond's role as crucial to the club's success, not only through repeated investments at critical points but also as a passionate upholder of the Celtic ethos. Just as the Kellys and White saw themselves, above all, as trustees of the club's history and traditions, so too do the people who have, in the course of the past 30 years, built the current, very solid structure.

# TWENTY-TWO

## THE BATTLE FOR CONTROL: CELTIC SAVED AT THE FINAL HOUR

THE EUPHORIA OF the centenary season had proved to be only a temporary remission from the realities pressing in on Celtic. The world was changing around them and neither the structure nor the vision of the club was equipped to deal with it. Most immediately, the threat came from the transformation of Rangers which had begun with the appointment of Graeme Souness as manager in 1986 and entered a new phase in November 1988 when David Murray acquired control of the club with an unambiguous commitment to buying success, both at home and in Europe.

By the time the two clubs met in the early skirmishes of season 1988/89, Celtic were facing no fewer than five England internationalists in the opposing line-up and lost 5-1 at Ibrox. The stakes in Scottish football had been raised beyond recognition. Not unreasonably, the Celtic supporters wanted to know how their own club was going to respond. They began to question, with ever-increasing intensity, whether the ownership and financial basis on which the club was founded could adapt to meet the challenges set by a transformed football environment. Not only was success demanded on the field but the Hillsborough Disaster on April 15, 1989 had led to the

Taylor Report, accepted by the Government in 1990, which set a time-limit of 1994 for the creation of all-seater stadia.

Millions of words, including several books, have been written about the off-field events that eventually led to the transformation of Celtic into a public company with Fergus McCann as the club's perceived saviour. In general terms, there were three strands of activity which led in that direction. There was the dissatisfaction of supporters, expressed through groups like 'Save Our Celts' and 'Celts for Change', which in the final phase led to a boycott of games. There was the highly practical campaign of share accumulation which eventually challenged the balance of control – an outcome which, in 1988, was believed to be impossible. Ultimately, however, the decisive factor would prove to be cold financial reality. Celtic simply ran out of money and by the beginning of March 1994 the Bank of Scotland was within hours of calling in its debts.

How had the great Celtic Football Club reached this sorry pass? The scale and nature of the problem were described succinctly by the Glasgow lawyer Len Murray, a prominent figure in the machinations to bring about change, when he spoke at the epic Extraordinary General Meeting on November 26, 1993. His contribution was described in their book *Rebels in Paradise* by David Low and Francis Shennan which provides a detailed account, albeit from a particular perspective, of the whole battle for control.

*'In 1987 Celtic had an overdraft of £15,000. In 1992 the figure was £5million. To go from £15,000 to £5million in a period of five years, you might think, took some doing but it does not stop at that. In 1987, the club had no accumulated losses. Indeed there were accumulated profits of £169,000. The reason for that was the old guard, the last of whom was the late Tom Devlin whose widow is with us, had a different*

*approach because they attempted to balance the books'... The club had lost more in the one year ending 1992 than in all the 103 previous years of its history put together – £3.2million... Rangers had a net asset value – that is the value of all its assets minus all its liabilities – of £34.8million. Celtic had an asset value of £571,000 – a mere one-sixtieth of the club they had once outshone. Even Partick Thistle... had a net asset value of £2.2million, four times the value of Celtic... The club, which still had only 20,000 £1 shares – now had liabilities of £7.2million... Personally, I have never come across a company that has survived when its liabilities are 360 times its share capital.'*

As if all that wasn't bad enough, the question of how Celtic were going to meet the key recommendation of the Taylor Report was looming ever larger. The board anguished over the options for years and finally endorsed moving to Cambuslang, a fraught scheme which was unveiled in April 1992. Neither the plausibility nor desirability of this project commended itself to the Celtic support who were, overwhelmingly, in favour of upgrading the existing stadium. On this front too, Rangers were far ahead in addressing the issue and Ibrox was already well-advanced in the process of being converted to an all-seater stadium which would accommodate 50,000. It would not be until Fergus McCann's arrival that the straightforward option of doing the same thing with Celtic Park would finally dispel the prospect of moving away from the club's established home. Even if it was the better solution, such an ambition required money and acumen which Celtic simply did not possess.

The dramatis personae in the struggle for control was many and varied. As in all good dramas, loyalties shifted and plots abounded. But in general, the issue was about whether the traditional 'ruling families' – the Whites and the Kellys –

should continue to maintain control over the club's fortunes or if a different structure should be embraced which would bring in new leadership and desperately needed capital. The board tried in various ways to address the latter issues while retaining their own controlling interest which they regarded as a form of trusteeship they did not wish to surrender. Few of these initiatives were blessed with either gratitude or success while some of the appointments made by the old regime as it sought to shore up its position merely poured fuel on the fire. However, it would be perverse to assume that none of the actions taken by the board, or individual directors, in this period were driven by a loyalty to the club's traditions or indeed that they did not protect Celtic from outcomes that would have been extremely uncertain in their consequences.

As Len Murray pointed out, Tom Devlin had been the last of the old guard (and his widow, Betty Devlin, herself of strong Celtic lineage, became a valuable supporter of the movement for change). The board had undergone generational change with the Kelly mantle passing to Kevin Kelly, nephew of Sir Robert, who joined in 1971. Desmond White's son, Chris, became a director in 1982 and company secretary on the death of his father three years later. Tom Grant had taken up the family interest which had, for so long, been exercised by proxy granted from Toome House. Jimmy Farrell, through the Shaughnessy connection, was now the longest-serving board member but without any great power base while Jack McGinn always recognised that his tenure as chairman depended on the goodwill of 'the families'. In any event, he was increasingly involved in the affairs of the Scottish Football Association of which he became Treasurer in 1989 and later President.

As matters worsened both on and off the park, the board had made its first move to bring in new expertise. Their choice by May 1990 was Brian Dempsey, a property developer and prominent Celtic fan who had already been giving them commercial support. Chris White, distrustful of Dempsey's motives, was unenthusiastic and the compromise was that Michael Kelly, a notably successful Lord Provost of Glasgow and now a public relations consultant, would also be co-opted, thereby bolstering the Kelly-White axis. It did not take long for a fall-out to occur. Brian Dempsey was removed from the board just five months after his appointment and promptly became a leading figure in the movement for change. This bitter estrangement resulted from the fact that, on joining the board, Dempsey had advanced plans for a new stadium as part of a development at Robroyston, five miles from Celtic Park.

When Dempsey and Kelly joined the board in May 1990, Celtic's preferred option was still to redevelop Celtic Park, largely funded by the inclusion of office accommodation. Indeed, draft plans had been enthused over by the board only weeks earlier. Chris White told a board meeting on April 26 that the cost was estimated at between £30-50million and that 'such a development would be at least twice as big as any investment made by Rangers and (the board) required expert guidance in considering such a momentous decision'. It was in this context that it was agreed to recruit Dempsey. By June 25, however, White was fighting a rearguard action against endorsement of an entirely different project at Robroyston. According to the Board minute he urged delay on these grounds:

*'The club is committing itself to a minority interest in a partnership with another developer and also committing itself to an application for planning permission to build a stadium on the Robroyston site. It was considered prudent to think deeply about this development and possible alternatives before taking irreversible decisions.'*

Meeting on July 3, 'the directors discussed their own preferences regarding existing stadia. The Italian stadia incorporating running tracks were considered to be lacking in atmosphere and the Parc des Princes in Paris was considered by most to be an ideal arena for football'. The fanciful tone of that discussion suggested that the Robroyston plan had gained support from most of the directors. On July 26, Dempsey sought to seal the deal. The minute records: 'Mr Dempsey gave the Directors copies of the proposed development agreement and Joint Venture agreement; all in connection with a proposed development of 535 acres of land at Robroyston.'

Chris White remained totally opposed: 'Mr White pointed out that giving approval to this development meant committing the club to moving from its own home of one hundred years to a site out of the city. This was not a decision that should be taken without a great deal of consideration and reflection. He reiterated his long-held feeling against a move away from the existing stadium, especially a move as far as Robroyston. Mr Dempsey said that he did not have the same sentimental attachment to the existing stadium (which was) not capable of being developed properly on the site as it stands.'

It was a seminal moment in the club's history and the Board minutes confirm how close Celtic came to embracing the Robroyston option. In that respect, Chris White's stance was the essential prerequisite for the redevelopment of Celtic Park which was to follow with such dramatic effect a few years later. In the short-term, however, the distrust between White and Dempsey had become terminal. On September 13, the Board held a special meeting in the Albany Hotel to consider eight stadium options, including Robroyston and the existing site, and agreed to delay a decision for two more months. The annual general meeting was due to be held on October 26. At a board meeting three days before, the depth of the distrust between White, supported by

Michael Kelly, and Dempsey was confirmed when White and Dempsey disagreed over information relating to the ownership of areas of land at Robroyston.

Three days later, the Board met at Celtic Park immediately prior to the Annual General Meeting when White and Michael Kelly informed Dempsey that they would be recommending to shareholders that they should not endorse his co-option to the Board. Celtic AGMs were still small, formal affairs and there were 34 shareholders present or represented by proxies that evening. It was most unusual for a vote to be called at all, far less on the basis of shareholding strength. When Dempsey's co-option came up for approval, he won the vote on a show of hands with four board members – McGinn, Kevin Kelly, Farrell and Grant – supporting him. When the poll was called, however, Dempsey lost by 733 votes to 472 with 20 abstentions. Robroyston was dead in the water but the movement for change had found a leader. How many within it would, with hindsight, have had any enthusiasm for a move to Robroyston is more doubtful.

Increasingly, the backroom dramas at Celtic Park were played out in the media as well as in the boardroom with debilitating effect. The term 'downward spiral' might have been coined to describe the process. Managers and players were trying to get on with the job of producing a winning team but were acutely aware of the chaos that was developing around them. It was a dreadful period in the history of the club but matters were about to take a turn for the worse. By mid-1990, Jack McGinn had informed the board of his intention to step down as chairman – he did not actually do so until October of the following year – and advocated the appointment of a Chief Executive. Head-hunters were engaged and an impressive field of candidates assembled. The choice of Terry Cassidy, a former newspaper executive with a taste for both conflict and publicity, was to prove an almost unmitigated disaster at a time when the club desperately needed stability, leadership and business acumen.

His early months in the post included an acrimonious dispute with the club's shirt sponsor which left them with no revenue from that source. Much worse, a memo which he had written about how to dispose of Billy McNeill's services as manager found its way into a tabloid newspaper, causing massive offence not only to an iconic Celtic figure but also to the entire support. Celtic Park was soon awash with highly-paid executives with no known affinity to the club other than their connections to Cassidy, while the debts mounted and success on the park remained elusive. In one celebrated episode, Cassidy's son – who had found a billet as retail manager – ordered replica kit shorts in equal numbers to the tops whereas the normal proportion of sales was in the ratio of 15 to one. Years later, thousands of pairs of shorts remained unsold. There were few dull moments when Terry Cassidy was around but the club was in severe danger of becoming a music hall joke.

Encouraged by these developments, the movement for change was advancing on all fronts. Forensic efforts instigated by David Low, a specialist in corporate takeovers, were being made to identify and track down even the smallest shareholders in the club. This process started early in 1991 when Low became aware through other business involvements that a member of the Kelly family living in California had indicated that he wished to sell his Celtic shares. For decades, any shares coming on the market had been bought by 'the families' for a nominal price. Under the articles and associations of Celtic Football Club Ltd, the board had the right to block the transfer of shares to anyone of whom they did not approve. Michael Kelly maintains that this practice was consistent with the concept of 'trusteeship' by ensuring that the shares had 'no monetary value' and were not traded commercially. However, as soon became clear, the arrangement depended on consent and was vulnerable to a concerted attack which involved establishing a monetary value for shares.

This approach was triggered when Low learned that the Californian shareholder had been offered £3 per share. Low had them independently valued at almost £60 each – 20 times what the Celtic board was prepared to offer. Eventually, they were bought by John Keane for £160 each, giving him his first foothold in ownership of the club, initially as an ally of Dempsey. Keane, a native of County Mayo, had built a successful business in Scotland, and was to become a significant figure in the ultimate rescuing of the club from the threat of financial oblivion.

By October 1991, the Californian episode had led to an alliance between Dempsey and Low. The strategy was to obtain support from small shareholders and any allies who could be detached from acquiescence in the role of 'the families'. Even if the Celtic board refused to register share transfers to people of whom they did not approve, the existing shareholders could grant their proxies to the 'rebels', which the board could not block. Low recalls:

> *'The weapons in the war would be shareholder lists, proxy agreements, company law, contracts, meetings and money. The army would be shareholders and supporters, people who had been forgotten or ignored, punters whose views were not taken seriously enough. The campaign would take two years… The last EGM, which the board narrowly won, followed two years and one month afterwards in November 1993. That was the board's fatal victory. That was when the defences began crumbling until they finally toppled fourteen weeks later.'*

Unknown to most of those who were lining up to oppose 'the families', Fergus McCann had entered the scene from afar early in 1989. He was a lifelong Celtic supporter who had built a successful golf tourism business in Canada, to which he emigrated in 1963. His credentials as a Celtic man were beyond dispute since it was well remembered in his home community of Kilsyth that, before emigrating, he had been the treasurer and bus convener of the Croy Celtic Supporters' Club. Fergus's father had been the rector of St Modan's High School, the Catholic secondary for Stirlingshire which Fergus attended. Purely as a supporter, he had maintained a close interest in the club throughout his time in Canada. (When the author met Fergus in Boston to interview him for this book, he was touched to note that Fergus's copy of the original *A Century With Honour*, had been a Christmas gift from his mother in 1988). Here indeed was a successful man with a visible Celtic connection who believed that he might be able to assist the club in its increasingly difficult circumstances. Probably the biggest mistake the old Celtic board made was not to take McCann more seriously when he first approached them. McCann recalls:

*'I never had a plan initially to get into a takeover situation. There were a couple of ways in which I thought I could help. My initial intention was to support a competent board with some capital and marketing activity. There was none of either. But what I found when I first met them was a board that was basically out of its depth and didn't really understand what I was talking about. Ignorance bred fear and fear bred scepticism. The main emotion I found myself dealing with was fear of change, of something bad happening. That was throughout the families.'*

On April 27, 1989, when the Board still consisted of only McGinn, White, Kevin Kelly, Farrell and Grant, the following was minuted: 'Proposals put forward by Fergus McCann to provide finance for various capital expenditures linked with equity purchase by Fergus McCann and giving him a very high-profile position within the Club was unanimously rejected by the Directors.' On August 3, the minute recorded: 'Mr McCann's latest proposals were discussed and it was hoped that this was a final discussion on this subject. Latest proposals were rejected by the Directors.'

His early contacts with the Celtic board changed McCann's view of what was required and also his own potential role. Further meetings and correspondence only served to increase McCann's level of frustration and determination to pursue his interest in taking a decisive role in the club's affairs. He still believes that 'if it wasn't for the influence of Michael Kelly, something might have been worked out'. For his part, Kelly says that from the time he first met McCann early in 1991, he had no doubt that 'he wanted to come in with full control' which the Celtic board was not prepared to concede.

By mid-1991, a few months after Dempsey's ejection from the board, McCann decided that an alliance with him was the best way to advance their shared interest in change. 'We became a group at that time. I believed that I needed to work with Brian Dempsey because he was the director who had been removed by the families. He had also established a connection with the supporters.' Indeed, since his removal, Dempsey had become the star turn at supporters' events aimed at forcing the pace of change including the founding meeting of 'Save Our Celts' which was held in Shettleston Town Hall in February 1991. The Lisbon Lion, Jim Craig, was another much-applauded speaker while both Farrell and Grant took their places on the platform, bringing tensions within the board into the open. One of the founders of 'Save Our Celts', Willie Wilson, later said: 'We arrived a bit too soon for the support to embrace such radical change,' but, along with the growing influence of irreverent fanzines, they had sown the seeds of organised dissent among the club's supporter base.

McCann came with his own plans for refinancing the club and was not supportive of the share-buying tactic. The relationship between himself and Dempsey was never comfortable. David Low recalls of the group he was dealing with: 'There were various agendas and relationships were very tetchy, particularly those involving Fergus who was determined that none of the money he was willing to put in would be used to pay off the people whom he saw as responsible for creating the situation in the first place. It all fell apart several times during the two years.'

The stadium issue was continuing to prove both difficult and divisive for the Celtic board. By late 1990, a company called Superstadia had appeared on the scene offering plans for a development at Cambuslang. This venture envisaged a new stadium being part of a much larger complex with Celtic as minority partners. One of the many difficulties was that the site was believed to be heavily contaminated from its former industrial use. There was also a very large pylon in the middle of it. The financial credentials of Superstadia were dubious and the plans came under intensive media scrutiny. Cassidy was a strong advocate of the Cambuslang project and the board, facing increasing financial pressures, began to look at it as a lifeline – which required a considerable suspension of disbelief. McCann said:

*'Before I got in, Robroyston was off the agenda and it was clear that Cambuslang would not fly. It was all to be done with other people's money. I had never doubted that the answer was to redevelop Celtic Park into a 60,000 seater stadium. Long before I got in there, I measured the distance from the cemetery to the touchline – 42 yards – in order to*

*work out how the stand to replace The Jungle could be built
and how many it would hold.'*

McCann's steadfast support for the redevelopment of Celtic
Park was a major factor in winning him the approval of
supporters – and also acted as a direct challenge to the board's
reliance on the Cambuslang plan which was to drag on, in
increasingly surreal circumstances, until the ultimate nemesis
in early 1994. At the end of October 1991, Jack McGinn stood
down as chairman to be replaced by Kevin Kelly. McGinn –
devoid of personal ambition and reluctant to engage in the
bitter battle which had now been signaled – continued to
represent Celtic on the SFA. As Fergus McCann acknowledges:
'Jack only ever thought of the good of the club'. By then,
however, financial storm-clouds were beginning to loom. At
the time of Kevin Kelly's succession, the Bank of Scotland told
Celtic that they would need to recapitalise through a share
issue. The urgency of this imperative was spelt out after the
Celtic board met their legal advisers at McGrigor Donald, a
leading Glasgow law firm, following the Bank's warning. Kevin
Sweeney, one of the partners specialising in corporate finance,
gave them his response to the Bank of Scotland's intervention
in uncompromising terms:

*'On examination of the balance sheet we were immediately
and predictably struck by the low level of capital base
from which the company operates. Our second reaction
was that the balance sheet was completely underpinned
by the Development Fund reserve and in the absence of
which would show a considerable deficit .... We consider it
imperative that the issued share capital be increased at the
earliest opportunity. The position is serious enough for the
directors to contemplate future possibilities which up to now*

*have been unthinkable like the demise of the company or its
acquisition by someone with access to huge funds.'*

So, as 1992 dawned, the Celtic board were in no doubt about
the seriousness of their fiscal position though they did not yet
fully appreciate the organised nature of the opposition. This
soon became apparent when Jim Doherty, a member of the
Grant family who was working closely with Low and Dempsey,
gave a television interview. The operation to buy control of
shares – fronted by Dempsey, organised by Low and financed
by John Keane – had been bearing fruit. With support from
Farrell and Grant, they believed they could command 30 per
cent of the voting strength among existing shareholders. The
'rebels' were demanding seats for Low, Doherty and Dempsey
on the board as well as the removal of Michael Kelly and
White. Otherwise they would requisition an Extraordinary
General Meeting. It was a full-scale takeover bid.

An acrimonious board meeting was held on February 21,
1992 at which Kevin Kelly reported on a meeting with Low
and Doherty. He did not believe that they had the money to
back up their demands. The board was divided on whether
to formally meet Low and Doherty to discuss their demands
with Farrell and Grant wishing to do so. The Board's response
was itself to call an Emergency General Meeting with a view to
removing Farrell and Grant, who were now seen as an enemy
within. At the same meeting, they agreed to co-opt David
Smith, a well-established business figure who was expected
to strengthen the board's commercial acumen. The EGM fell
on the eve of a Celtic v Rangers Scottish Cup semi-final –
symptomatic of how the off-field battle had by now impinged
on the priority of winning football matches.

Shortly before the EGM, the 'rebel' plans suffered a set-
back when Tom Grant switched sides by entering a voting pact

with the Kellys and Chris White, so that four of the six Celtic directors were now part of a legal agreement to vote as a block. However, the EGM went ahead in order to remove Farrell and co-opt Smith. After an emotional plea for his own survival, in which he defined 'the real issue' as 'whether the White/Kelly axis is to be allowed to control Celtic', Farrell remained as a director on a poll vote of 745 to 681. If the Celtic board had any doubts previously about the effectiveness of Low's campaign of share and proxy accumulation, this vote dispelled it. While there was undoubtedly personal sympathy for Farrell which went beyond the 'rebels', the outcome provided hard evidence that the position of the 'families' was under threat as never before.

The 'rebels' would never get beyond 40 per cent control over shares in the club. Low, in retrospect, says that this was almost irrelevant – the polarisation between the two sides was now so complete as to make the situation 'unsustainable'. Increasingly, the question was not of whether change would occur but when – and on what terms for the outgoing board. The lack of success on the field of play, the acrimony felt by a large proportion of the support towards the board and – increasingly – the pressure coming from the Bank of Scotland to reduce the club's overdraft were all pointing towards the same conclusion. However, in fairness to the Board's stance at that time, the rebuff given to the Low-Doherty-Dempsey axis had good justification and – as it turned out, though it was certainly not part of their thinking at that time – left the door open to the eventual arrival of Fergus McCann. Michael Kelly claimed:

*'A group of people got together and planned the downfall of the club so they could buy it on the cheap. I didn't trust these people and I fought them tooth and nail for which I make no apology. I would exclude Fergus McCann from all of that.'*

Indeed, the extent to which McCann had been treated as outsider, regarded with suspicion by the Board, appeared to be receding according to be a minute of their meeting on May 5, 1992:

*'The Deputy Chairman reported on his meeting with Fergus McCann which had been inconclusive and unproductive. Dr Kelly had been disappointed that Fergus McCann had now stated that he would not now be pursuing his fund-raising. Dr Kelly had attempted to contact Fergus McCann the previous night without success. He understood Mr McCann just wanted to go away.'*

This proved to be a quite serious misreading of McCann's intentions. Terry Cassidy had continued to prove a deeply divisive figure. Shortly after taking over as manager, in June 1991, Liam Brady had told a Board meeting of his 'dissatisfaction with some of the actions of the Chief Executive' and went on to list a series of interferences and media comments. At the Board meeting on February 21, 1992, Jack McGinn referred to Cassidy as 'a man in our midst creating unhappiness at the Club' and accused him of 'pushing aside the Board'. Yet Cassidy's most high-profile hour was yet to come. In April 1992, in the face of much evidence and many warnings, Celtic went ahead with the announcement of Cambuslang as its preferred stadium option after Cassidy had spoken publicly on the subject without authority. Even then, it was astonishing that the Board should commit itself in this way. Less than two months earlier, according to a Board minute of February 13, 1992, there had been a meeting with Superstadia: 'At that meeting, the Celtic directors expressed their disappointment that Superstadia were not further advanced in their discussions with the Bank (while) the site seemed to have contaminated areas.'

In spite of these well-founded concerns, the high-profile public announcement went ahead via the *Celtic View* just five weeks later. The fantastical plans for a £100million complex were announced under the headline 'Paradise Found' while a particularly smug photograph of Cassidy accompanied the claim: 'The World's Best Stadium for the World's Best Fans'. It did not take media or supporters long to appreciate that there was minimal substance to this ballyhoo, particularly on the question of where the money was going to come from. Terry Cassidy was finally dismissed as Chief Executive in October 1992 and David Smith, who had been made vice-chairman, became increasingly prominent in the club's affairs. At the annual general meeting, held just before Christmas, he revealed under intense questioning that the Bank of Scotland was in the process of taking security over Celtic Park to underwrite the debt.

The campaign of share accumulation had pretty much hit a dead end and while the 'noises off ' continued incessantly, the biggest pressures on the board were coming from the Bank of Scotland and also the vociferous hostility of many supporters. The bank debt was steadily mounting and the money spent on players, in an effort to support Liam Brady's managership, took them increasingly close to the £5million overdraft limit. Meanwhile the Cambuslang project was still being pursued though progress was slow and the Taylor deadline was closing in. Outline planning consent was granted in May 1993 but that did not mean a lot. The hopes vested in the Brady period era by the supporters brought some respite but when these turned to dust, the clamour for change became even louder and, in September 1993, found a voice through the formation of 'Celts for Change' which operated under the slogan 'Back the Team; Sack the Board'. Fergus McCann's well-orchestrated campaign, with the offer of enough money to eliminate the club's debt and invest in the future, was increasingly seen as the club's best option.

It was clear that there was going to be a showdown and it was eventually set for November 26, 1993 in the form of an Extraordinary General Meeting. By that time, McCann had made his proposal. He would put in £8.5million plus £2million in soft loans. Four named others would put in £1million each. The fans would be invited to subscribe £5.4million. In all, it was billed as a £20million package. The annual accounts showed that, on June 30, 1993, the debt to the Bank stood at £4.7million and rising. With the EGM approaching, the 'rebels' needed a united front. In reality, however, there were deeply conflicting objectives and ambitions among them and removal of the existing board was the only unifying theme. In particular, Gerald Weisfeld – who had sold the *What Every Woman Wants* chain of stores – had his own plans for a takeover and had bought most of Dempsey's shares. It was a time of many meetings as the board sought a peace deal and the 'rebels' papered over their own divisions. When the EGM finally took place, a large and noisy crowd had assembled outside Celtic Park. Jack McGinn referred to 'the horrible tone of language' and the 'disgusting behaviour of some of them'. They did not represent the Celtic supporters he knew. Right was not all on one side.

The meeting became the platform for Fergus McCann to set out his stall and also to face close questioning. The voting pact involving the Kellys, White, Grant and Smith was, he said, 'designed only to protect their own position and is not in favour of the club, nor does is truly reflect truly what directors' responsibilities should be'. He was looking for 50 per cent control with his shares 'locked in' for a five-year period before being offered to all the shareholders who then existed 'so that all the shares would continue to be held by Celtic people'. James Farrell told the meeting of the warning from McGrigor Donald almost two years earlier about the urgent need to expand the shareholding base, yet nothing had been done about it. He described McCann's scheme as 'an unparalleled offer in the history of soccer in Britain and from a man and a group of people whom I know to be Celtic supporters and not lepers'. It was a fiery, eloquent meeting which ended with the votes of the 100 shareholders present splitting down the middle, and on a poll vote well short of the two-thirds majority needed for the pro-McCann resolution to succeed.

While the board had won the battle, the war was continuing to go badly. McCann's package represented, perhaps for the first time, a credible alternative to the status quo and the vast majority of supporters rallied behind it. Michael Kelly recalls his surprise at the lack of support for the concept of a 'club held in trust', which he was trying to argue for, as opposed to a Public Limited Company. It was, he maintains, purely the success of Rangers which drove that mood. In truth, it was also the inescapable fact that the old financial model was incapable of sustaining the required investment and also that most supporters had been persuaded that the board were not so much trustees as owners who were not prepared to lose their control.

On Friday, February 25, 1994, as pressure mounted, the Celtic board gave one last throw of the dice – their own hastily-assembled plans for a Celtic PLC. In a press release, David Smith announced 'a comprehensive and visionary package of radical measures designed to take the club into a glittering new future in the 21st century'. This involved the fateful and, as it soon transpired, untrue claim that 'cornerstone funding of £20million has now been committed' to the Cambuslang development. The capital structure was to be 'totally recast', raising up to £6million which would 'reduce borrowing and strengthen the team'. The club would 'go public' later in the year with a Stock Market listing and a Board 'drawn from the ranks of those used to conducting the affairs of a public company' while some existing directors would 'become members of a Club Board whose primary role will be to ensure that the traditions, spirits and traditions of the Club are safeguarded'. It was all far too late in the day, offered reluctantly against the background of impending disaster and failing the crucial test of credibility in the eyes of supporters particularly when the supposed providers of the 'cornerstone' – a merchant bank called Gefinor based in Geneva confirmed that the deal was far from done and depended on Celtic raising £30million.

The same afternoon, a board meeting was held at Celtic Park with Dr Roland Mitchell, Bank of Scotland general manager in Glasgow, in attendance. According to the minute, Mitchell described the proposals in the press release as 'very exciting and eminently sensible. He is supportive of the project; however in the difficult six-week period ahead, the Bank would be looking for further comfort in view of the anticipated rising overdraft'. In fact, the Bank was now working to its own agenda, a fact of which the board was well aware. The minute also recorded: 'Dr Mitchell did not make reference to a faxed letter which he had received that morning from Mr Fergus McCann offering to take over the debt of Celtic Football Club'.

As far as the Bank of Scotland was concerned, that was a more attractive offer than the 'existing and eminently sensible' proposals which the Board had pulled out of the hat. The board meeting continued acrimoniously after Mitchell departed from it. Retrospective endorsement was required for the press release and six directors agreed to it. James Farrell dissented 'because he believed that Fergus McCann's proposals, as outlined at the earlier Extraordinary General Meeting, were a better route for the Club'.

The Weisfeld group was by now active in the field on its own account and they too had made their approaches to the Bank. While McCann remained resistant to buying the shares of existing directors, the Weisfeld group – which also included the

Glasgow businessman Willie Haughey – was prepared to do so in order to gain control. Indeed, they were confident almost to the last minute that they had achieved that result. But this was prior to the final act in the drama which was precipitated on March 3, 1994 in a letter from Mitchell to Kevin Kelly. This followed a meeting that day involving Mitchell and four board members – Kelly, McGinn, Grant and Farrell who were joined by Dominic Keane, a banker and then ally of McCann. Seeing the writing on the wall and the only alternative to be the Weisfeld-led group, the four had broken ranks to support the McCann package. This was the meeting at which, in effect, the Bank of Scotland decided to back the McCann plan – and to bring Celtic down if the full Board declined to acquiesce in it. Mitchell wrote:

*'I am delighted that we seem to have identified an acceptable way forward and that, therefore, the immediate and dire peril facing the Club can be averted. I have to say that some of the disclosures made by Mr Keane on behalf of those Board members present about the operation of Celtic's affairs at Board level in the recent past were staggering.'*

He went on to list the points of agreement which included asking David Smith to resign. Critically, Mitchell continued:

*'The Bank has agreed to continue to honour cheques drawn on the Celtic account on the following conditions: (a) By 12 noon tomorrow a cash collateralised or otherwise acceptably supported Guarantee for the sum of £1million is put in place to support the Bank's overdraft; (b) This Guarantee will be superseded by a £5million cash collateralised Guarantee which will be made available once Mr Fergus McCann has reached the UK and has had a chance to apprise himself of the situation, latest the middle of next week.'*

Kevin Kelly called John Keane at his home that night. Although Keane had entered the fray as an associate of Dempsey, he was now firmly behind McCann – who continues to pay tribute to him as 'one man who always delivered exactly what he said he would'. Kelly explained the situation – the club needed the guarantee of £1million the following morning in order to avoid administration. John Keane (whose honourable role in these events was recognised in 2013 when he was invited to unfurl the league flag) said: 'Administration was unthinkable. It would have been a slur on the name of the Club'. Keane's bank manager was on the steps of the Bank of Scotland the next morning to pledge the money. Meanwhile, McCann was arranging for the £1million to be wired from New York. Neither transaction was guaranteed to be completed in time to meet the noon deadline. Eventually, McCann's money did arrive and the paperwork was completed at the Bank of Scotland with eight minutes to spare. Meanwhile, at Celtic Park, the board was meeting for the last time in the form that had survived for over a century.

The seven of them had convened at 10 o'clock that morning. Michael Kelly, who had been excluded along with David Smith and Chris White from the meeting with Mitchell, voiced his strong objections to what had been done. He was 'appalled' by Dominic Keane's presence at the meeting where 'critical decisions were taken'. He described the conduct of his four colleagues as 'precipitate and wrong'. The chairman, Kevin Kelly, responded by calling on the three directors who were outside the new pact to 'resign as directors of all Celtic companies'. In mid-afternoon, the meeting adjourned while the action moved elsewhere in the city. When it reconvened at 10.25pm, it was to consider 'the purchase and sale agreement which had been prepared during the course of the day'. After 15 minutes, White, Smith and Michael Kelly left the meeting which then agreed to co-opt Fergus McCann and Dominic Keane to the board, the latter as company secretary. At 10.50pm, the meeting concluded and the crowds which had gathered outside received confirmation of the day's tumultuous events.

It soon became apparent that Brian Dempsey's proclamation – 'The rebels have won!' – required some qualification. Fergus McCann had certainly won and so had those supporters who believed that change was necessary in order to save the club. But before long it would become clear that McCann had his own very firm views on how the club and the business should be run – and that there was little place in this scheme of things for others who had been prominent in the events of the previous three years.

# TWENTY-THREE

## THE LEAN YEARS:
## THE LONG ROAD BACK TO SILVERWARE

THE CLIMAX TO the centenary season was always going to be a hard act to follow but nobody yet realised the length or depth of the challenges ahead. There was not much transfer movement in the summer of 1988, but later the club did secure Tommy Coyne from Dundee. The season began with a friendly to celebrate the centenary. Real Madrid, Inter Milan and Manchester United were touted as potential opponents but the game which emerged was against Cruzerio of Brazil, resulting in a 4-2 Celtic victory. The league flag was unfurled against Hearts, and Frank McAvennie scored the only goal of the game. A 5-1 defeat at Ibrox – the worst result in the fixture since 1960 – was quickly followed by a quarter-final League Cup exit to Dundee United. There was also early European disappointment. Against Honved of Hungary, the away leg was lost 1-0, but Celtic won the return 4-0. In the second round, Celtic lost 1-0 on aggregate to West German champions Werder Bremen.

In the New Year derby, without Paul McStay and, for much of the game, McAvennie, Celtic succumbed to a 4-1 defeat at Ibrox. It was the start of a poor run which eventually took them into third place in the League. The board had also come into dispute with McAvennie, a prolific goalscorer, who wished to return to London. Eventually Celtic yielded to his transfer requests, selling him back to West Ham United for £1.2million, believing that they had found a replacement in former striker Maurice Johnston. This, however, turned into an embarrassing fiasco when Johnston signed instead for Rangers.

On April 15, 1989, tragedy struck Liverpool Football Club as 96 people died during the FA Cup semi-final versus Nottingham Forest at Hillsborough. Fifteen days later Celtic hosted a benefit match against Liverpool to help raise money for the affected families. As *You'll Never Walk Alone* echoed around the stadium, the emotion was too much for many of the 57,437 fans. One Liverpool fan noted that 'It must have taken us ten minutes to get on to the terrace. Most of the Celtic supporters kept hugging us and saying that they felt for us'. A 4-0 loss was irrelevant and £500,000 was raised.

The disappointments of the season were cast aside when Celtic secured the Scottish Cup for the second season in a row, thereby denying Rangers a treble. In front of a 72,069 crowd, the 13th Scottish Cup final between the clubs was decided by a 41st-minute Joe Miller goal. He pounced upon Gary Stevens' error to score and Celtic won the Scottish Cup for the twenty-ninth time. However, it also proved to be the last trophy won under Billy McNeill and, indeed, for six long years.

The Maurice Johnston saga dominated the summer as Billy McNeill sought to strengthen his squad. He looked to Italy and brought Paul Elliott from Pisa, a commanding defender whom he had known from his spell at Aston Villa. The Polish pair, Wdowczyk and Dziekanowski, were recruited, along with Mike Galloway from Hearts and John Hewitt from Aberdeen while Mark McGhee returned to Newcastle and Mick McCarthy left for Lyon. McNeill was trying to catch up with Rangers but the 1989/90 season turned out to be a trophyless disappointment. Even its two most memorable dramas ended in anti-climax. The first was the European Cup-Winners' Cup home leg against Partizan Belgrade. Celtic went into the game with a 2-1 deficit but turned things round to lead 5-3 on the night and 6-5 on aggregate through four goals from Dariusz Dziekanowski and one from Andy Walker. With two minutes to go, Celtic Park was silenced when their opponents took advantage of poor defending to score and thus go through on away goals. In the absence of competitive European football, a friendly was arranged with Ajax on December 6, 1989 and Celtic won 1-0 in what was Tommy Burns' last game before he moved to Kilmarnock.

Celtic finished a dismal fifth in the league and the last hope was the Scottish Cup. A Tommy Coyne goal gave them victory over Rangers and hopes rose. They needed a replay to defeat Dunfermline in the quarter-final and then disposed of Clydebank in the semi-final, but the team's form was not good as the final against Aberdeen approached. At the end of extra time, there had been no goals so the outcome hinged upon penalties which Celtic lost 9-8. For only the second time since 1962, they were facing a season without European competition.

Billy McNeill's position was now being called into question. The Board minutes show that he repeatedly tabled requests, without much success, for two organisational reforms – the provision of modern training facilities and the restructuring of Celtic Boys' Club as a proper youth development wing of the club. The financial position was worsening rapidly and the divisions within the club were increasingly public. Nonetheless, in the summer of 1990, McNeill was allowed to invest in the recruitment of John Collins from Hibernian who became Celtic's first million-pound player. Charlie Nicholas was brought back from Aberdeen while defender Martin Hayes joined from Arsenal for £650,000. Hayes turned out to be an extremely poor investment, wasting money the club could ill-afford. With Roy Aitken departing for Newcastle United and Billy Stark to Kilmarnock, Paul McStay became the club captain.

It was to be another disappointing season. The League Cup final was lost to Rangers, 2-1 after extra-time, and a dreadful run of League results left Celtic in mid-table. The minutes of the Board meeting held on December 13, 1990 included the terse comment: 'Kevin Kelly expressed his concern at continuing poor performances on the field of play. The Club had won eight matches out of the last 32'. The newly-appointed Chief Executive, Terry Cassidy, was now in place and was soon seeking to orchestrate McNeill's removal. Celtic finished third in the league, thereby qualifying for the new UEFA Cup, but the last straw was probably when they lost 4-2 to Motherwell in the replayed Scottish Cup semi-final. McNeill said afterwards that he had 'never felt so down' after a game.

The board meeting of May 9, 1991 was informed that 'Dr Kelly had sent a memorandum to the directors stating that he believed it was time to end the manager's employment … each of the other directors affirmed that they believed the manager should go'. Two weeks later, the decision to dismiss was implemented – though typically of the era, the waters of public opinion had by then been muddied by the leaking of a document written by Cassidy in which he laid out a strategy for removing McNeill. In a battle for supporters' sympathy between Billy McNeill and Terry Cassidy, irrespective of results, there was only going to be one winner. The removal of Billy McNeill as Celtic manager for the second time, though perhaps inevitable, thus ended up as another public relations disaster.

The final choice of his replacement was between two Irish internationalists, neither of whom had any managerial experience. After tortuous debate, the board finally opted for Liam Brady over Frank Stapleton. Brady's Irish credentials made him a popular choice with the supporters but he had no idea of the backroom mayhem that was developing or the financial constraints he would be under – scarcely the ideal backdrop to a first managerial appointment.

Season 1991/92 was another let-down in spite of an influx of players – goalkeeper Gordon Marshall from Falkirk, Gary Gillespie from Liverpool, Tony Cascarino from Aston Villa. Later in the season, Tony Mowbray was signed from Middlesbrough and Tom Boyd joined Celtic from Chelsea in exchange for Cascarino. Probably the biggest embarrassment of the season was a 5-2 aggregate drubbing at the hands of unglamorous Neuchatel Xamax of Switzerland in the second round of the UEFA Cup. It was a result that haunted Brady throughout his brief tenure but was an all-too-accurate reflection of where Celtic now stood in Europe. One of the season's few consolations was a 2-0 win at Ibrox – the first win there in four years – but ten days later at Hampden, Celtic were knocked out of the Scottish Cup and the league campaign resulted in a third-place finish.

One of the unfortunate victims of this period was Paul McStay, a great player with an impeccable Celtic pedigree, who was doomed to spend the latter part of his career in unsuccessful Celtic teams. It seemed that he had had enough when, after losing to Hibs 2-1 in the last game of the season, he threw his shirt into the crowd in what appeared to be a farewell gesture. The board minutes of April 10, 1992 recorded:

*'Mr Smith and Mr Grant had spoken to Paul McStay in order to give him some reassurance regarding the Board's unity, stadium development and the Board's support for the manager in his efforts to strengthen the team. These comments were well-received by Paul but he will take as long as possible to make up his mind regarding his future.'*

It spoke volumes for McStay's loyalty to the club he had joined as a 16-year-old in 1981 that he was still at Celtic Park when season 1992/93 began and indeed until his retirement five years later. However, there was to be no early improvement in Celtic's fortunes. Rangers won the treble while Celtic finished third in the league and didn't reach either the League Cup or Scottish Cup final. They exited from the UEFA Cup in the second round, losing both legs to Borussia Dortmund – though at least they had beaten Cologne to get there.

An indifferent start to season 1993/94 which included a League Cup defeat by Rangers, soon meant the end of Liam Brady's brief reign. After a series of poor results, culminating in a 2-1 defeat by St Johnstone, Brady offered his resignation on the bus back from Perth. In most opinions, he never really stood a chance because of the disharmony and financial stringencies which now dominated the club's affairs. However, the negative consequences of discord worked in both directions – it helped to doom Brady's prospects but his failure, in turn, was critical in sealing the fate of the board. As far as onfield success was concerned, his appointment had been virtually the last throw of the dice on which they placed great hope. Frank Connor, the former goalkeeper who had been on the backroom staff, held the reins until a new manager could be appointed. This turned out to be Lou Macari. He, too, arrived with the goodwill of the support because of his Celtic pedigree but his stay would be even briefer than Brady's.

All the drama for the remainder of the season took place away from the field of play. By the end of the season, Celtic were under the control of Fergus McCann, the old board had gone, and a new era beckoned. However inspirational all of that may have been to the long-suffering supporters, there was still evidence required that Celtic could recover where it mattered most – in their standing as a football club of achievement and high repute. Lou Macari's insouciant management style was never likely to be acceptable to McCann. The former player had kept his family home near Stoke-on-Trent in spite of undertakings to move to Scotland. To McCann, this alone merited dismissal which was duly confirmed at a board meeting June 14, 1994. Macari continued to pursue legal remedies against the club for several years thereafter, finally losing at the Court of Appeal in 1999 when the judge, Lord Rodger of Earlsferry, commented:

*'Perhaps predictably, Mr McCann's approach was wholly different from the one followed by the previous board of directors. In particular, the old board had adopted a somewhat laissez-faire attitude to management, exemplified by their perception that the manager must be allowed a free hand and left on his own to get on with the job.'*

It was a dispute which epitomised the much harder-edged commercial approach which now dominated Celtic Park – hardly surprising given the fate of the previous regime and the huge financial risk that McCann had taken. He recalls that his own preference at that time would have been to appoint a continental coach to replace Macari but he was prevailed upon to offer the job to Tommy Burns who was certainly the fans' choice for the role. He had cut his managerial teeth with Kilmarnock and had succeeded in keeping them in the Premier League. McCann's impatience with the finer points of football protocol were in evidence when he approached Burns without seeking Kilmarnock's approval. Celtic were fined £100,000 and eventually ordered to pay £200,000 in compensation – the start of an extremely fractious relationship between McCann and the Scottish Football Association.

McCann's immediate priority was the rebuilding of Celtic Park, the alternative idea of a move to Cambuslang having been consigned to the ashes of history. This forced a move for the season to Hampden Park, though McCann's view that the SFA could have been more flexible if they had so chosen was subsequently exonerated. The redundant pitch at Celtic Park was sold at £5 a sod, raising £15,000 for charity. New regulations meant that, for the first time, the Hoops would have numbers on their backs. The new era was dawning and an early victory at Ibrox, through goals from Collins and McStay, raised hopes that success might come sooner rather than later under Burns. Celtic's league form was erratic. They lost the League Cup final on penalties to Raith Rovers, but silverware finally returned to Celtic Park in the form of the Scottish Cup through a tense 1-0 victory over Airdrie in the final, secured by a Pierre van Hooijdonk goal after just nine minutes. The Celtic team that day was: Bonner, Vata, Boyd, McNally, McKinlay, McLaughlin, Grant, McStay, Collins, Donnelly (O'Donnell) and van Hooijdonk (Falconer).

It was scarcely a great final and the Celtic supporters who formed the great majority of the 36,915 attendance reacted as much from relief as joy. It was a cup full of firsts – the first since 1989, the first under the new regime, the first under Tommy Burns' management and Paul McStay's captaincy. Just as importantly, in the League encounters with Rangers that season, Celtic had won two, lost one and drawn one. Parity was perhaps in sight but the run of successive League titles for Rangers was still edging upwards.

Celtic returned to their home ground for the following season with the new North Stand complete, the opening ceremony performed by comedian and Celtic fan Billy Connolly. It would turn out trophyless again but the winds of change seemed to be blowing in the right direction. Players like Jackie McNamara from Dunfermline, Morten Wieghorst from Dundee and Jorge Cadete from Sporting Lisbon joined the ranks during the course of the season. The outcomes in each competition were all the more disappointing because they were head-to-heads with Rangers who inflicted a 1-0 defeat in the League Cup and later won the Scottish Cup semi-final 2-1, while in the League, the margin between the clubs was four points – close by recent standards. In the Cup-Winners' Cup, Celtic were drawn against Dinamo Batumi of Georgia which was, quite literally, a war zone. Simon Donnelly was quoted as saying that he could hear shelling in the background as he went to sleep. Having survived that test, Celtic drew Paris Saint-Germain and held them to 1-0 in France. The return leg, however, saw a classic performance from PSG who won 3-0 and received a standing ovation from the Celtic support. They went on to win the competition.

The season was notable for an episode involving the SFA which further supported McCann's scepticism towards the organisation and particularly the power wielded by Chief Executive James Farry, who had repeatedly refused to register the signing of Jorge Cadete from Sporting Lisbon. Farry, whom McCann now recalls simply as 'a bureaucrat', misinterpreted the rules and faced down all arguments with the effect that Cadete's registration was confirmed too late for him to take part in the Scottish Cup semi-final against Rangers. McCann pursued the claim for compensation and full exposure of what had occurred until eventually, at a tribunal almost three years later, the truth was finally confirmed. Farry was dismissed by the SFA two weeks later with a £200,000 pay-off while Celtic were awarded £10,000 compensation.

Much was now happening on all fronts at Celtic Park in terms of investment, player recruitment and professionalism in the club's affairs. Celtic were coming close – but time was pressing in. Rangers had now won eight successive titles and Celtic's great record of nine-in-a-row under Jock Stein was within their sights. Burns wanted an attacking side in the Celtic tradition and was imaginative in putting towards a cosmopolitan squad. The following season promised much but proved to be both unproductive and chaotic – a condition to which the 'three amigos' made a fair contribution. Pierre van Hooijdonk and Jorge Cadete were joined in the summer of 1996 at Celtic Park by Paolo Di Canio. The excitable Italian with great talent as a striker and an unerring capacity for controversy cost Celtic £750,000. The three were not together for long and all were, in their own ways, both brilliant and difficult. Di Canio's skills endeared him to the Celtic support but his erratic behaviour eventually tried their patience. It was McCann who coined the 'three amigos' tag in response to what he saw as their unreasonable demands and unstable behaviour. At the end of his first season, in which he made thirty-seven appearances and scored fifteen goals, Di Canio was voted Player of the Year by the Scottish Professional Footballers' Association. After the break, he declined to return from Italy, spuriously claiming a breach of contract. Celtic eventually sold him to Sheffield Wednesday for £4.3million.

By the end of 1996, the board – by now composed of business heavyweights – had pretty much decided that Tommy Burns had to go, though they reluctantly agreed to retain him for the remainder of the season. McCann – with whom there had been a complete breakdown of relations – grudgingly agreed that 'unpleasant though it may be for him, he was willing to proceed as usual, support the manager and also bring in additional players'.

Worsening form saw the prospect of winning the league slip away in the early months of 1997. The clincher was a bitterly contested game at Celtic Park on March 16, 1997 which Rangers won 1-0. Goals from Mackay and Di Canio gave Celtic a 2-0 win over Rangers in the Scottish Cup quarter-final. But then in the semi-final replay, Falkirk beat Celtic 1-0, finally prompting the dismissal of Burns. At a special meeting in London on April 15, the board agreed on McCann's suggestion not just to seek a replacement but also 'to follow the Arsenal model' by splitting the posts of General Manger and Head Coach. Both quests were pursued with vigour in the weeks that followed.

The nine-in-a-row record had been equalled and Celtic had to find the man who would, against all odds, provide the leadership necessary to prevent it being beaten. McCann personally led this search and this time it went global. With advice from Andy Roxburgh, the former Scotland manager now occupying a major role with UEFA, he drew up an international short-list of suitable candidates. It was hard work and on July 10, 1997, the board heard 'a very detailed account of the identification and elimination of the candidates, culminating in only one of the short-listed candidates being ultimately available'. Enter Wim Jansen, a key member of the Feyenoord team that had beaten Celtic in the 1970 European Cup final, now coaching in Japan, with Murdo MacLeod as his assistant. Enter also Jock Brown, a high-profile Glasgow lawyer and part-time football commentator, in the new role of General Manager in charge of transfer negotiations and other matters of football administration.

Paul McStay had retired through injury at the end of the season and Celtic brought in a clutch of new players – Darren Jackson from Hibernian, the defender Stephane Mahe from Rennes, Dutch winger Regi Blinker who was part of a 'trade' with Sheffield Wednesday which saw Di Canio leaving. Although Jock Brown was heavily criticised for his role in that piece of business, it went on to serve Celtic's interests well – the club got rid of the troublesome Di Canio at a handsome profit and reunited Wim Jansen with his former Feyenoord protégé. Craig Burley, a Scottish internationalist who had spent seven years at Chelsea, was also recruited along with goalkeeper Jonathan Gould from Bradford City. There was one more recruit who was to prove of historic importance – Henrik Larsson. Again, the connection was through Jansen and Feyenoord where Larsson had been playing for four seasons. He wanted to leave but first had to win a contract dispute with the club who then sold him to Celtic for £650,000 – possibly the best money the club ever spent.

This enhanced squad had the task of stopping Rangers, now at the top of their spending orgy and desperate for the record run of titles. An inauspicious 2-1 defeat by Hibs in the opening league game, with substitute Larsson's mis-placed pass creating the opening for the winner, scarcely lifted the spirits. A home defeat at the hands of Dunfermline put Celtic at the bottom of the league. Things looked up with a 2-0 victory over St Johnstone, prompted by a memorable Gould save, followed up by goals from Larsson and Jackson. If this result had gone wrong, as it might well have done, history might have been different with Jansen's position not entirely secure. A defeat at Ibrox was a set-back and Richard Gough, on scoring the only goal of the game, held up two hands to indicate the number 10. He was being premature. A few weeks later the clubs met again at Celtic Park and the game was in its dying moments when Alan Stubbs headed an equaliser for Celtic. It was another crucial moment in the season.

There started to be cautious optimism about the fateful season's prospects when Celtic developed a good run in the League Cup which concluded with a stirring 3-0 victory over Dundee United in the final at Ibrox on November 30, with goals from Marc Rieper, Larsson and Burley. But the real breakthrough in terms of self-belief came with the New Year fixture which Celtic won 2-0 with goals from Burley and – memorably – a 25-yard shot from Paul Lambert who had joined the club two months earlier. Lambert, at the age of twenty-eight, already had a truly extraordinary career behind him, never mind what was still to come. He won his first Scottish Cup winner's medal with St Mirren at seventeen before transferring, after eight years in Paisley, to Motherwell who qualified for the UEFA Cup by finishing second in season 1994/95. This brought them up against Borussia Dortmund who were sufficiently impressed to sign Lambert. In his only complete season in Germany, he became the first Scottish player to win a European Cup medal with a non-UK team in the first season of the revamped UEFA Champions League. His performances against Manchester United in the semi-final and Juventus in the final were outstanding and his status among the Dortmund fans heroic. But he had not settled in Germany and wanted home – an outcome secured by Wim Jansen and Jock Brown who negotiated a £1.9million transfer deal.

Jansen had completed the strengthening of his side with the recruitment of Rieper to solidify the defence and Lambert to add midfield guile. The scene was now set for the hard grind towards the final day of the season with the balance of advantage switching back and forth between Celtic and Rangers while Hearts also put in a strong challenge. The issue became Celtic's to decide when, in their second last game of the season, Rangers lost at home to Kilmarnock – referee Bobby Tait, never highly-regarded at Celtic Park, was presiding over his last game and seemed to add on an inordinately long period of additional time with the score at 0-0. However, it was Kilmarnock, rather than Rangers, who took advantage. Celtic now needed three points from two games to guarantee the title. The first of these was at Dunfermline but only a 1-1 draw was achieved. Brian Quinn recalls the journey back to Glasgow as 'funereal'. This meant it all came down to a home game on the last day of the season against St Johnstone while

Rangers were playing at Tannadice. On a day as tense as any in the oldest supporter's memory, Henrik Larsson scored with a shot from outside the penalty area after two minutes and the celebrations finally began when the enigmatic Norwegian striker, Harald Brattbakk, latched on to a cross from Jackie McNamara to sweep home the necessary finish. Brattbakk had proved erratic in his goal-scoring efforts since being signed from the Norwegian club Rosenborg in December 1997. But with one goal, he wrote himself into Celtic mythology for ever. The Celtic team that day was: Gould, Boyd, Annoni, McNamara, Rieper, Stubbs, Larsson (Blinker), Burley, Donnelly, Lambert (Wieghorst), O'Donnell (Brattbakk).

The supporters were delirious. While the emphasis was on having 'stopped ten in a row', there was also the more positive fact that this was Celtic's first Scottish League title since the centenary season of 1987/88. Small children had turned into young men and women while waiting for this great day. The name of Wim Jansen would forever be associated with it – but behind the scenes, it was already clear that Jansen's stay at Celtic Park would be briefer than originally intended. The partnership with Jock Brown was, at best, uneasy. Jansen and his deputy, Murdo MacLeod, believed that Brown too often moved into their territory of team management. Jansen, MacLeod and David Hay, who had returned as assistant general manager, formed a knowledgeable and close-knit team but Hay resigned in November because of the tensions which existed. Brown, for his part, reported to the board as early as December 1997 that 'Wim Jansen had no interest at all in any broader aspect of the club's affairs' outside of the first-team squad. Jansen had particularly irritated McCann that month by refusing to go to watch Brattbakk play for Rosenborg while insisting on signing him, as McCann recalled.

*'We even put on a plane for him. We paid £7,000 for the plane but he wouldn't go. You shouldn't spend £2million on a player from looking at a video. They all look good on videos. He threatened to walk out if we didn't sign Brattbakk so we had to sign him. It was hard dealing with Wim Jansen.'*

Equally, Jansen found it hard dealing with McCann and Brown. He had decided before the end of the season that irrespective of the outcome, he would not be returning. He said: 'As a coach, you stand or fall by your own ideas and not with the ideas of other people. If there are two ways of thinking, there is a big problem for the club'. Jansen ended that problem in his own way, leaving behind a shocked and saddened group of players. Paul Lambert said simply: 'He was a terrific manager'.

Brown, on the other hand, retains an honourable place in McCann's recollections and he largely blames 'jealousy of his former colleagues' in the Scottish media for the steady flow of bad press which Brown received. 'He was there and they weren't. He was delivering as a general manager'. At a board meeting on October 23, 1998, Fergus McCann 'expressed his support of Mr Brown in these difficult times and it was acknowledged that his abilities were very valuable to the company. He assured Mr Brown that the public aspect would not overrule the Board's perspective'. More cautiously, Dermot Desmond 'emphasised the need to address how the company/club communicated with the media as it was apparent the present approach resulted in criticism'.

Less than two weeks later, on November 5, the board met again at Celtic Park and 'after lengthy discussion and much consideration, resolved to terminate the contract of employment of Jock Brown'. It was all change once again at Celtic Park.

# TWENTY-FOUR

## THE McCANN ERA:
## REBUILDING ON AND OFF THE PARK

FERGUS McCANN'S FIVE years in charge of Celtic was rich in paradoxes. He was the man who put his money where his mouth was as Celtic supporters had pleaded for over the years. Yet for much of his time at Celtic Park, he was subjected to cruel derision for not having done enough. Under his direct influence, the club appointed a manager who stopped 'ten in a row'. Yet when the manager left after a season, having arrived to a chorus of supporter-skepticism and media ridicule, it was McCann who was blamed and barracked.

Such was the frenzy of the period that all sense of perspective was in danger of being lost. Celtic had been saved from the brink of bankruptcy but that brought no guarantee of instant success. The immediate priority was to build a magnificent stadium which was duly delivered, on time and on budget at Celtic's historic East End home with talk of moving to the outer reaches of Glasgow a mere bad memory. But building a stadium and a successful team at the same time was more difficult. McCann was entitled to some benefits of doubt from the supporters even if no such concession could be expected from the unrelentingly hostile Scottish media.

He says now: 'I had no idea the level of publicity I would have to deal with. As a supporter, it is all about the players and the manager. That is the way it is in this country. Nobody knows who owns the New York Mets – who cares? The owners of a club are just seen as owners. The level of publicity they have to deal with is tiny compared to what goes on in Glasgow.' McCann recalls one journalist, who he believes to have been hired by a spurned adversary, 'digging for dirt' in every corner of his life, past and present, in order to write a hostile book about him. He has often thought about writing his own but believes that it would re-open too many old wounds for no good reason.

The conduct of the Bank of Scotland, even after he had taken over the club, continues to rankle. McCann believes that they, along with David Smith, tried to push the sale of the club in the direction of Gerald Weisfeld and to 'get rid of me'. When McCann confounded them by coming up with the money, there was still no easing of the pressure:

*'I put a deposit of £11million into the Bank of Scotland to show that the money was there. They could see that this was for real – that this guy had the money. I had taken them completely off the hook – they were never going to collect that £5.2million they were owed otherwise. Ten months later, after the bank had been fully paid off, Charles Barnett, who was interim financial director, went to the Bank of Scotland to learn what they could offer in loan finance. Their proposal was £2.5million fully secured, little more than an insult. Later on, we went down the road to Manchester and obtained £10million from the Co-op Bank unsecured. What I resented enormously was trying to do a business deal in Scotland and being treated in that way.'*

By the end of 1994, all of the old board had gone and McCann was both chairman and chief executive. He was dependent on a small group of close advisers whose praises he continues to sing – finance director Eric Riley, accountant Charles Barnett, commercial director David Kells and public relations manager Peter McLean. His first priority was to initiate the stadium improvements, thereby putting beyond doubt the question of where Celtic's future lay. In the summer of 1994, The Jungle as well as the East and West Terracings were demolished. The plans were finalised in December and they were for the marvellous 60,000 stadium that we know today. This was McCann's greatest legacy to the club – the vision to realise that it would soon be possible to fill a 60,000-seater stadium which would become one of the great footballing stages of Europe. He explained the basis of that confidence:

*'I felt that not so long before, there were very big crowds at big games. The whole season ticket concept was something foreign to the club but it was the key to delivering big gates. It was a progressive decision to match reconstruction to the growth in season ticket sales. A lot of it was to do with the right kind of marketing.'*

McCann knew the season ticket principle from ice hockey in Canada – 'if you didn't have a season ticket you didn't get in' – and had been shocked to discover Celtic's dismissive attitude towards season ticket holders of whom, when he arrived, there were only 7,000. By the time he left, there were 53,000 and revenue from the advance purchase of season tickets had become the cornerstone of Celtic's financial model.

Celtic Park reopened with a friendly against Newcastle United on August 5, 1995. Bang on schedule Celtic were back in their own home in time for the start of the new season. The newly-completed structure had a capacity of 26,970 while the main stand held 7,850. Phase two was completed in August

1996 with the opening of the 13,006 capacity East Stand. This was the only point in the process when McCann became nervous about the scale of the undertaking and there was a great deal of heart-searching at a board away-day in August 1997 about whether to proceed for the time being with completion of the West Stand – or Jock Stein Stand as it became.

By then there were 41,000 season ticket holders and McCann's strategy had been to build in line with the growth of that market. Ultimately, the decision to go ahead was taken after a paper from the commercial director, David Kells, warned that 'development of the West Stand is key to maximising revenue' by creating facilities which would allow the club to realise its potential support but also 'to develop a meaningful function business'. The board's subsequent decision to err on the side of boldness was soon rewarded. By the time Celtic played Liverpool on August 8, 1998, the project was complete. The Jock Stein Stand brought the capacity to 60,832. At that time it was the biggest club stadium in Britain and had cost £40million to build – a substantial sum and a protracted project. But surely, in retrospect, it was the only one that was ever worth considering for the future home of Celtic. Years had been wasted, much bitterness engendered and millions of pounds squandered on pursuing what almost nobody wanted – a move away from Celtic Park. In this respect as in many others, McCann delivered exactly what he had promised.

His second great triumph was the share issue which was required to complete the funding jigsaw on which his takeover was based and which would underpin his stadium plans. Once again, no time was wasted. The offer to buy shares in Celtic plc was launched on December 21, 1994 – scarcely the most propitious time to be seeking hard cash from thousands of people while the team was not at that point covering itself in glory. The key to its success lay in McCann's strongest business asset, his marketing skills. He presented himself not as a financial saviour but as a fellow-supporter:

*'I went to my first game with my father in 1954 when I was 13-years-old. And in the nine years that followed, before I went to Canada, there were many disappointments. In fact, I never saw a Scottish League Championship won by Celtic until I returned on a visit in 1988. Not all the memories were great. One game that stays in my mind was a league match at Kilmarnock on a rainy Wednesday evening in March of 1963. Before a sparse crowd, Celtic lost by six goals to nil. Yes, 6-0, a result that is unthinkable today. The mood in the Croy CSC bus returning home that night was sombre. But I remember the talk about a young Celtic player who had appeared in the team for the first time. He was a 5'4" tall, 18-year-old redhead named Jimmy Johnstone. He looked the part with lots of talent but the view was that he did not have size or strength to make the grade. How wrong we were. Just think what was accomplished in the decade that followed…'*

This was marketing genius – pitched directly at the hearts and minds of Celtic supporters. The message was unmistakable – out of despair could come hope and revival if only they would help to make it happen. McCann recalled:

*'It was a really tense time waiting to see if that money would be raised. We had a target of £5.4million from the fans. It was very slow at first and there was a deadline of February 24. We could have pulled it in January – we had just lost a League Cup final to Raith Rovers. But we decided to go ahead and believed that people would look at the longer term. The offer was due to close at 10 o'clock on a Saturday morning. We started to get a heavy response on the Thursday.*

*I was in my office on the Friday night. It was pouring rain and I looked out of my office. People were queuing to get in – they had not put it in the mail, they turned up in person. At that moment, I felt a huge responsibility to these people. We eventually got £10million – 10,000 at an average of £1,000 each. That's quite a lot of people. It still is the only really successful issue to fans for real money. That was the key part of that whole share issue.'*

Having established a functioning Public Limited Company, McCann now wanted a board of directors who would carry weight in financial circles. The decision had been taken in December 1994 to create two boards – one for the plc and another, retaining the Celtic Football and Athletic Club title, which would deal mainly with supporters' issues. None of those who had been involved in the campaign to remove the old board were retained for long on the plc board which functioned for a time, with only McCann and Riley as directors and Kevin Sweeney (who later becames a director) as Company Secretary. McCann set about a recruitment process which entailed checking out likely-sounding names on the boards of FTSE 100 companies as well as personal contacts and recommendations. Over the space of the next two years, he recruited three heavyweights – Dermot Desmond, Sir Patrick Sheehy and Brian Quinn. The structure which emerged made complete business sense but inevitably created some resentments which, in turn, helped stoke the negative publicity which McCann continued to suffer from in spite of the advances that were being made.

The first major recruit to McCann's plc board was Dermot Desmond who also at the time of the share issue became a significant shareholder in the club. Dermot Desmond was by then an extremely successful figure in the Irish business community. In 1981, he had founded his own firm which grew to be the biggest independent stockbroker in Ireland. He was the visionary behind the creation of an Irish Financial Services Centre in Dublin. And crucially, he had a strong pre-existing interest in football and Celtic. Desmond recalled:

*'I grew up playing soccer and following soccer. I was selling programmes at Drumcondra from ten or eleven years of age. Naturally, with the Irish connection, I always followed Celtic and took an interest in their progress. So when somebody said to me in Dublin at the beginning of 1995 that Celtic were raising money, I was interested. I looked at the numbers and they were trying to raise £4million (from a core investor). I thought it needed £8million. I met Fergus for lunch at the Dorchester in London and he agreed with that and I agreed with his philosophy of what he was trying to do which is really the same as now. We were not going to get into debt. We were not going to live in a perennial land of hope that we would do well in Europe or sell a player or win a trophy. It had to be a sustainable model and not depend on any of these short-term factors. I agreed to put £4million in and underwrite another £4million.'*

It was the start of a long and hugely beneficial relationship with the club. Sir Patrick Sheehy, on the other hand, had little interest in football before becoming a director but, by common consent, brought an invaluable level of expertise in financial planning, corporate policy and risk management to the board. McCann recalls: 'I cold-called him. He just liked the idea and we were very fortunate to get him. He could deal with the City people. He knew how to handle that stuff very well'. Sir Pat Sheehy – formerly chief executive of British American Tobacco and mainly associated in the public mind with a report on police pay – joined on the same day, March 1, 1996, as Brian Quinn. A lifelong Celtic supporter who grew up in Govan, Quinn was first asked by McCann to join the board the previous year but could not do so until he retired from his senior position in the Bank of England. McCann says: 'I was very pleased about obtaining such prominent, wise and accomplished people for the Celtic plc board – not only for the credibility which they added to the organisation but for the advice and input on major strategy issues we had to deal with'. However, as Quinn recalls, the Board which McCann assembled was not always acquiescent:

*'There was a bit of both autocrat and builder of consensus in Fergus's style as chairman. He wanted his new board to succeed and had ambitions to get a listing on the Stock Exchange at some point, which he did. So he was hoping to build a harmonious board and at meetings frequently took pains to seek and follow advice. However, it is important to remember that Fergus combined the positions of Chairman, CEO and majority shareholder – a combination that bestows enormous power in one individual; particularly one who had a very clear aim of earning a significant profit on his investment in a short period of time. Fergus was a man in a hurry and he became increasingly reluctant to do anything that might weaken his freedom of action. From the beginning, but particularly as time passed, it became common for us to learn about such matters as the signing of new players from media reports, which was embarrassing at the least.'*

McCann says that there were 'very few occasions of disagreement' and defends the distinction he made between 'issues of personnel and policy'. However, his fellow-directors' concerns were brought to a head at a board meeting held in Preston prior to a UEFA Cup match and Quinn says that though communications improved, 'relations were never quite so positive subsequently'. But he adds: 'Fergus was a determined, strong-minded and sometimes stubborn individual, not overloaded with charm or finesse. But he had great vision and energy and drove the business of the company forward as Chairman'.

One of McCann's first moves after taking over in 1994 had been to bring in Peter McLean as the head of public relations and the club's official spokesman charged with getting the club's message across in the face of considerable media hostility and also to stem the leaks from within which had long been debilitating. As one observer noted: 'At Celtic Park, a secret is something you tell people one at a time'. McLean met with limited success in plugging the leaks or improving relations with sections of the media who appeared irreconcilably opposed to the idea that things might actually be getting better at Celtic Park, though the response to the share issue suggested that the supporters, if not the press, had received the positive messages. He was also deputed by McCann to undertake a more fundamental review of the club's images and objectives. When McLean applied for the job, he recalls, he had put together 'an overall proposal that looked at the ethos and history of the club and how activities reflected this – or did not – at the time'. Integral to this approach was the revival of a more structured approach to Celtic's charitable objectives and also a more pro-active rejection of bigotry in all its forms. McLean is in no doubt about the scale of McCann's contribution:

*'Fergus McCann is the most principled person I have ever met and had the pleasure to work with. It is obvious the progress he made for the club – the vision, the structure and methods, the stadium. What I think is sometimes overlooked is that he was always prepared to address issues that were at the very*

*core of the club's identity. Fergus really liked the ideas I put forward as they matched his own vision for the club and we worked on a number of initiatives which hopefully helped to reawaken and emphasise why Celtic is a special institution in so many people's lives. These included the original Social Mission Statement that had the input of many Celtic fans and was published in draft form with thousands of Celtic supporters offering their thoughts from around the world. I vividly remember one letter came from Tasmania! All the letters were handed unopened to the people behind 'Not the View', the Celtic fanzine which had not been seen as friendly to the club by the former board, so the views could be assessed independently. David Watt and, I think, Gerry Dunbar reviewed the letters and a massive 92 per cent of fans said that the Mission Statement reflected how they saw the club. It then became an important document for the management, players, staff and fans of Celtic to live up to – rightly proud of a joint Scottish and Irish identity, a club open to all and opposed to bigotry in all its forms.'*

Brian Quinn said: 'By inviting supporters to become shareholders, Fergus gave them the feeling that they owned Celtic in a tangible way, but his other masterstroke was to resurrect the charitable connection which had withered away over the years, without ever being entirely lost. The supporters loved that aspect of the club's self-definition as something differentiating Celtic from others in a very positive way'. The charitable giving and support for fund-raising was formalised through the establishment of the Celtic Charity Fund while other deep-rooted issues in Scottish society were challenged in a unique way through the creation of the Bhoys Against Bigotry initiative. Peter McLean says: 'The project had a massive impact and I think Celtic still benefit from that today. The atmosphere in the stadium changed for the better and it also enabled the club to act not only against any Celtic supporter behaving in a bigoted way, but also opposition fans. This was supported by the police. It created a sea change in Scottish society and was eventually given a European Commission award'.

While all of this activity was being generated behind the scenes, it was, as ever, the performance of the team on the field of play that primarily interested the supporters, though the great majority of them also bought into the longer-term vision for the club that was in the process of development. Nobody had a bigger vested interest in securing success than Fergus McCann – both as a supporter and as the major shareholder. Throughout his time at Celtic Park, McCann never wavered from his stated intention of departing after five years in control. The minute of a board meeting on April 11, 1997 recorded: 'Mr McCann stated it was still his intention to leave the club in the summer of 1999'. By the following July succession planning was already underway with Sir Patrick Sheehy urging 'at least a two-month overlap period for the Chief Executive with Mr McCann' at the time of his departure. At the same meeting, a committee was established under Sir Pat, and also including Quinn and McCann himself, to start looking for a successor in that aspect of the role. Given the thought and effort that went into planning for the post-McCann era, it seems surprising that the outcomes were to prove so short-lived.

The level of abuse hurled at McCann via the Scottish media during his tenure was extraordinary, even by the standards of those who penned it. Their constant cry was for Celtic to spend more money, regardless of whether they had it or not – a route that would later be confirmed as the road to ruin for another club which was constantly held up as a shining example to the Celtic board. For example, James Traynor, then of the *Daily Record*, celebrated one of Celtic's shrewdest signings for decades with the observation: 'If McCann really were a supporter, someone out of the same mould as the thousands of foot soldiers who bought into the dream almost five years ago, he would be able to lift his eyes from his ledgers and see the damage his refusal to break his pay structure is causing… If anything, the signing of Lubomir Moravcik at a cut price has merely caused them further embarrassment'. Inevitably, there were sections of the support who were prepared to endorse this reckless advice while McCann made little attempt to conceal his contempt for the 'speculate to accumulate' school of football economics. Brian Quinn says:

*'Fergus transformed Celtic from a family-owned, poorly managed football club into a modern company with the necessary introduction of financial discipline and professional management. He saw Celtic as a quite different kind of enterprise, run according to market principles and generating a return on investment, of which he would be the main beneficiary. By seeking and adopting a Stock Exchange listing, he also committed the club to certain standards of conduct – including fitness and propriety of its directors as well as providing accountability to its stakeholders – and all without losing the unique identity of the club. Quite a feat.'*

It is probably true that the contribution of Fergus McCann to the history of Celtic Football Club was only fully appreciated after his departure which duly provided another opportunity for supporters and investors to buy shares in the club – and was also the cue for a further protracted round of media sniping. The sale of his entire holding was a resounding success and McCann left Glasgow with a handsome profit for which he is entirely unapologetic.

*'I had promised to go after five years and basically I was a hostage to that commitment. I didn't know five years in*

*advance how it was going to turn out – I could just as easily have lost everything I put in. I paid the bill and I got the problems. Fortunately, it turned out well not just for me but for the supporters and for everyone who invested in the club.'*

During these five years in Glasgow, Fergus McCann also married and became the father of three children. When the appointed time arrived, the family left for Boston where much of his time is now devoted to running his own charitable trust. He retains four Investor Club seats in the North Stand as a gesture of continuing support for the club but has only used them on a couple of occasions. He takes wry pride in the fact that there are two supporters' clubs named after him – 'one in Camberley and one in Brazil'. Rarely has there been a more extraordinary or idiosyncratic intervention in the fate of a major sporting institution but the principal epitaph to Fergus McCann's time at Celtic Park must surely be: 'He delivered what he promised'. There are many Fergus McCann stories but the one I like best came from a Glasgow taxi driver who used to pick him up quite regularly. Fergus would invariably instruct: 'No small-talk, driver, and don't deviate from the route'. That is a fair metaphor for his own time in charge of Celtic.

Each time we revel in a great European night at Celtic Park, we should spare a thought for the bottom line of what life would have been like without Fergus. Instead of experiencing the joys of Paradise, we could have been in Robroyston, Cambuslang – or worse.

# TWENTY-FIVE

## REVOLVING DOOR:
## CELTIC'S MANAGERIAL MERRY-GO-ROUND

THE DEPARTURE OF Wim Jansen after only one season was interpreted by a number of fans as another unarguable reason to revile Fergus McCann and Jock Brown. That single campaign under the Dutch coach had, after all, yielded Celtic's first championship in a decade, denied Rangers the dreaded 10-in-a-row, secured the Scottish League Cup and generally raised hopes that Celtic had finally emerged into a dazzling new era of recovery and prosperity. As managing director and general manager respectively, McCann and Brown were widely portrayed as destructive influences, immovable in their determination to adhere to financial prudence, even at the risk of creating friction between themselves and employees who had for a variety of reasons established themselves as heroic figures in the eyes of supporters.

There is little doubt that a generally hostile press, often orchestrated by people with ill-will towards the regime, had contributed substantially to the frequent vilification and belittling of McCann and Brown. This combination of Jansen's decision to quit and anti-McCann propaganda culminated in the infamous and absurd booing by some supporters when he unfurled the 1997/98 league championship flag at Celtic Park.

It was also in this atmosphere of distrust that Dr Jozef Venglos was appointed successor to Jansen, precipitating further unrest among supporters who had anticipated a marquee signing as the new manager. The less enlightened of the club's followers appeared to be unimpressed by the curriculum vitae of a man who had a doctorate in physical education, an outstanding pedigree as a club and international coach, and a global reputation as one of football's luminaries, regularly delegated by FIFA to lecture to academies throughout the world.

Some quarters of the media were equally tactless in their reception of the urbane, intelligent Slovak, favouring headlines such as 'Doctor Who?' Since the composers of those insults could not possibly be ignorant of Venglos's credentials, such disparagement simply confirmed their determination to perpetuate an image of Celtic as a by-word for ineptitude, and this, despite four years of mounting evidence of McCann's success in bringing the club from near-obsolescence to a successful and economically sound condition. Behind the scenes, Venglos's appointment had resulted from the usual uncertainties of the process. Indeed, on the eve of the 1998 World Cup finals, Jock Brown had advised the Board that someone quite different was lined up for the job – Egil Olsen who would 'sign a contract with the club after Norway's opening match with Morocco but there was to be no announcement until 48 hours after the end of his involvement in the World Cup'. However, that prospect soon passed as did the suggestion that the French coach, Gerard Houllier, might be an option. However, the swirling speculation did nothing to make the job easier when Venglos was finally unveiled as the new manager.

No amount of scepticism could undermine the new manager's well-cultivated manners and easy accessibility. The fact that he was not from the normal run of football managers – a credential which greatly commended him to Fergus

McCann – was confirmed by an incident that occurred early in his tenure, during a press conference with print journalists. Kilmarnock had drawn Sigma Olomouc, a club from Venglos's native Slovakia, in the UEFA Cup and the reporters thought it would be an idea to get some information on them, to assist with their match previews. 'What do you know of Olomouc, Doctor Jo?' he was asked. 'Ah, yes,' he replied. 'It is the ancient seat of the kings of Moravia.'

Venglos's one season in charge turned out to be barren in terms of trophies, but vastly significant by other measures. If Wim Jansen's parting gift to Celtic was the peerless Larsson, Venglos' would prove to be almost a match. He would be Lubomir Moravcik and, by the time he left four years later, it was entirely feasible to argue that, had he been in his mid-twenties rather than thirty-three when signed from Duisburg in Germany, the little Slovakian midfielder would have been elevated to the same heights of esteem as the great Swede.

Brown had asked Venglos if he could recommend anyone from his wide experience and the manager immediately nominated Moravcik, but added that he had not seen him for a year and the player was now thirty-three. Venglos assured the general manager that Moravcik, by then a legend in his own country and glorified by the French after eight years between St Etienne and Bastia, was an extraordinary talent but the problem could be whether or not he still had 'the legs' to play regularly in a physically demanding league. The two men travelled to see him play in an international against a Portugal side that was emerging as one of the strongest in Europe. Slovakia were beaten 3-0 at home, but Moravcik's performance was marked by exceptional skills with both feet and seemingly endless stamina. Brown and Venglos agreed that they had to bring him to Glasgow.

The general manager was even more gratified to discover, on his mission to Germany to open talks, that Moravcik, for some reason, was not in the Duisburg coach's favour. He would be very happy to join Celtic and be re-united with his old national team coach, Dr Venglos. In addition, Brown was able to sign Moravcik for considerably less than even the paltry £300,000 reported by the newspapers. Despite the midfielder's history and reputation, confirmed by seventy caps, his arrival prompted a reception as indifferent as the one accorded to Venglos himself. One tabloid distinguished itself with a headline that may never be usurped as the most ill-informed in the history of Scottish sports journalism: 'Celtic Sign Dud Czech'.

It was one more example of the attitude of many in the media towards Celtic's resurgence as a club and a business. Just an hour before Moravcik made his first full start for the club, against Dundee, news of Jock Brown's departure became public. Moravcik gave an exhilarating exhibition of his talents in that match, serving notice that he and Larsson (a hat-trick scorer in a 6-1 victory) would form a great partnership. If the Dundee performance was uplifting, the one which followed two weeks later was breathtaking. This was the second derby match of the season and, despite having secured a scoreless draw in the first at Ibrox, Celtic approached this one in the knowledge that defeat would leave them thirteen points in arrears.

Moravcik began to remove that prospect as early as the 12th minute, when he scored the first of his two goals. Before the match was two-thirds complete, he had his double and Larsson matched him, with Mark Burchill making the final score 5-1. That Celtic should contrive to share the honours in the derby series, remaining unbeaten at Ibrox with two draws – winning one and losing the other at home – and still lose the championship by six points was testimony to their general inconsistency and a tendency towards surprising set-backs. This would be confirmed by their fall to Airdrie at the first hurdle of the League Cup, while they would lose an uninspiring Scottish Cup final to Rangers.

By the time the Moravcik and Larsson-inspired side embarked on an unbeaten run between the start of 1999 and the end of April, irreparable damage had been done. An away defeat to St Johnstone on April 24 virtually terminated their interest in the title. More ominously, the statistics meant that Rangers could confirm themselves as champions at Celtic Park a week later, in the last derby match of the season. A bad night was not confined to the 3-0 reversal on the field, but involved the felling of referee Hugh Dallas by a coin thrown from the crowd. It was an event that prompted the football authorities to try to ensure that the two clubs would never again meet in a potential championship decider.

Venglos's departure at the end of the season would be no shock, as it had been understood from the outset that he would be essentially an interim manager. By now sixty-three, he had less taxing assignments ahead of him. But, while not contributing to the trophy cabinet, he also demonstrated his eye for value by acquiring the tall, powerful Swede, Johan Mjallby, and the gifted, if volatile Mark Viduka. Mjallby would become a valuable contributor in defence, while Viduka, the Australian son of Croatian parents, proved a frequent and exciting goalscorer. Viduka's move to Celtic was formalised only after a series of events that left Fergus McCann, the meticulous man of business, dumbfounded in frustration. Having announced they had signed the player in December 1998, Celtic became entangled in a highly public wrangle about the terms of his transfer from Dinamo Croatia (as Dinamo Zagreb were temporarily renamed). It was not until February, 1999 that Viduka began his career with Celtic. This chaotic start, however, would prove to be a portent, as the striker went on to demonstrate a temperament capable of driving managers to distraction. In the case of his next manager at Celtic, Viduka's easily-stoked fire would be a significant factor in driving him out of the job.

That Fergus McCann and Jozef Venglos should take their leave of Celtic almost simultaneously in the summer of 1999 seemed appropriate. Both men had set personal deadlines for the severance of their connection with the club and their times had come. At sixty-three, Venglos recognised his own time in top-level football was at a dignified end and would effectively retire for three years before making a brief re-appearance (for one season) as coach of JEF United Ichihara in Japan. However, the twin departures left three vacancies – chairman, chief executive and manager. The board's head-hunting process came up with Frank O'Callaghan as chairman followed by Allan MacDonald as Chief Executive, a contrast in styles to say the least. O'Callaghan's background as chairman of a major hotel group scarcely prepared him for the rough, tumble and intensive scrutiny of the football world. Thoroughly well-intentioned, he saw it as his role to support the Chief Executive. The problem with this was that Allan MacDonald was a forceful character, used to getting his own way, and tending to see challenges, particularly from the board, as obstructions to be faced down. However, the non-executive directors were of a standing not to be trifled with and a recipe for internal conflict was soon created.

Before he left, McCann's last legacy had been to sign Henrik Larsson on a new contract. For the third year in succession, however, Celtic were managerless in the close season, and there was widespread apprehension among the supporters about who might come next. There had been initial scepticism towards both Jansen and Venglos, not to mention the acquisition by them of players they had scarcely heard of in Larsson and Moravcik. That had changed dramatically and even the most cynical might now concede that there was much to be said in favour of managers with a wider European vision and contacts book, but there was still a strong desire for the next manager to be a more familiar figure with a connection to the club. This ambition was to be at least semi-fulfilled by the flurry of activity which ensued and flowed directly from the appointment of MacDonald.

Universally acclaimed as one of the greatest players to have worn the green and white Hoops, Kenny Dalglish had also distinguished himself in the red of Liverpool and as a manager at Anfield, where he won three league championships, two FA Cups and one League Cup. There had also been high achievement at Blackburn Rovers, where he would, improbably, win another league title. Dalglish's career, however, was marked by both triumph and tragedy. He was a player in 1985, when Liverpool's European Cup final against Juventus was overshadowed by the deaths of 39 Italian supporters at the Heysel Stadium in Brussels. And, having succeeded Joe Fagan as manager after Heysel, he was in charge in 1989, when 96 Liverpool fans were killed in the crush at Hillsborough Stadium in Sheffield during the FA Cup semi-final with Nottingham Forest. In 1997, Dalglish had made a brief and not particularly successful return to management with Newcastle United.

MacDonald had idolised Dalglish as a player and wanted the former manager to take charge of the team at Celtic Park. (The author recalls a conversation five years earlier when MacDonald was still managing director of BAE Jetstream at Prestwick in which he declared his ambition to be Celtic chief executive and then to bring in Dalglish as manager). When the time came however, Dalglish stated his preference for a role that would not exert the pressures of everyday involvement as first-team coach and agreed to become director of football. His would be a triumphant return to the East End of Glasgow, although there were murmurs of surprise when it was announced that his choice as manager would be his former Liverpool team-mate, John Barnes. Brian Quinn recalled:

*'The backdrop to these appointments was the frequent changes*

*in managers in the preceding years. Fergus was quick on the trigger and we had Macari, Burns, Jansen and Venglos in a very short time. The Board was looking for some degree of stability in the position. Allan MacDonald was new and made much of his friendship with Kenny Dalglish and it seemed certain the appointment would go down well with the fans. He (Dalglish) did not want to return as full-time manager and was enthusiastic about John Barnes in the role, despite having no previous experience. Frank O'Callaghan was pretty keen which some of the non-executive directors put down to his memories of Kenny as a player. Strongly urged by Allan MacDonald, the Board decided to appoint the Dalglish-Barnes team and Frank organised a dinner at which we all met. I remember that I sat beside John Barnes at the table. He was articulate and had definite ideas about how he proposed to set out the team. As I remarked to my colleagues afterwards, he is intelligent and knows his football, but can he make them play?'*

The Jamaica-born Barnes had been an outstanding contributor to the Liverpool cause and boasted almost 80 England caps, but Celtic and Rangers have never been places for rookie managers, no matter how distinguished the playing careers. No such doubts would prevent the more feverish elements in the media acclaiming Dalglish and Barnes as 'the dream team' who would restore Celtic's fortunes. Dalglish heightened anticipation by declaring that Barnes would show himself to be the most brilliant young manager in the game. Expectations were reinforced when Stiliyan Petrov was bought from CSKA Sofia for £2.8million and the £5.75m paid for the Israeli, Eyal Berkovic, made him the most expensive player in Scotland at that time. When the Brazilian defender, Raphael Scheidt, was recruited on a near-£5m fee, however, nobody except the purchasers knew that he had been signed purely on the strength of video evidence of his abilities. That would prove a costly misjudgment.

When the team opened the championship campaign with a crushing 5-0 defeat of Aberdeen, it prompted the kind of hyperbolic reaction from the press that succeeds only in tempting providence. One report even claimed that 'any doubts they (the supporters) may have harboured over the coaching inexperience of Barnes will have disappeared'. The momentum would break in only the third outing, however, with a 2-1 defeat by Dundee United. It was the first set-back but would not be anywhere close to the last. It was in Europe that the worst damage was sustained and it was not confined to the home-and-away defeats by Olympique Lyonnais – both 1-0 – that eliminated Celtic from the UEFA Cup as early as the second round. After only thirteen minutes of the match in France, Larsson fell awkwardly in a challenge from Serge Blanc and sustained a compound fracture of the leg. The appalling injury kept him out of action for the rest of the season – he returned as a sub in the final league game against Dundee United – and there was concern for a time that it could end his career.

Larsson would recover so comprehensively that he would become the greatest and most celebrated Celtic (and Sweden) player of the age, but Barnes would enjoy no such fortune. A season that would end in ignominy had begun with spectacular promise. Seven of the opening eight matches were won and Larsson and Viduka had scored fifteen goals between them (seven and eight respectively), culminating in a 7-0 victory over Aberdeen. Larsson would be injured just five days later and the winning run was abruptly halted by defeat at home to Motherwell.

That was a fixture from which the reward for victory would have been a leap to the top of the league. Instead, Celtic were still in second place when they approached the first derby meeting of the season at Ibrox. Celtic led 2-1 thanks to a double from Eyal Berkovic. However, the team's capitulation in the second half, ending in a 4-2 defeat, would prove to be an indicator of what lay ahead. Despite some faltering by Rangers, Celtic under Barnes could not be relied upon to take advantage. They approached the next match with Rangers at Celtic Park on a run of four straight victories, but managed only an uninspiring 1-1 draw, once again having led, this time through Viduka.

The impression was growing that there was something seriously amiss with the character and commitment of the team as a series of poor results followed. In four successive league games, they went ahead before conceding goals which led to draws or defeats. A 3-2 defeat at home to Hearts, after going 2-0 up, took Barnes to the edge of the credibility precipice. The fatal blow was delivered three days later, when Inverness Caledonian Thistle, then of the First Division picked up the biggest prize of their short history, a 3-1 victory at Celtic Park in the third round of the Scottish Cup. Barnes resigned, along with assistant coaches Eric Black and Terry McDermott, the following day. It emerged that Viduka had refused to appear for the second half after a dressing-room showdown – damning confirmation that Barnes and his staff had lost the confidence of the players. Brian Quinn said of Barnes:

*'He got off to a strong start so the speed and completeness of his failure to sustain the early success was something of a shock. Put in his place by Mark Viduka, who was supported surprisingly by Lubo Moravcik, he simply collapsed and informed Allan MacDonald he was resigning forthwith. Nice man that he was, he did not have the strength of personality needed to deal with difficult characters such as Viduka.'*

Barnes had been ridiculed in the media over his frequent use of largely unfathomable jargon and his adherence to 'innovative' tactical systems which few, if any, understood. The impression that this incomprehension extended to the players as well fans compounded the criticism. The media had also latched on to the fact that MacDonald had been the instigator of Dalglish's, and thereby Barnes' appointment for reasons that had hardly been based on objective analysis. It was a potent mixture as the results went awry.

Barnes's short tenure at Celtic Park had been an unhappy experience, and his departure would be followed by those of Dalglish and MacDonald within a few months. Dalglish reluctantly agreed to fill the managerial vacancy for the rest of the season, but would turn out to be almost as controversial as his friend and predecessor. There was a strong hint of taking revenge on reporters when he decided to hold his weekly press conference in a well-known 'Celtic-minded' pub in the Gallowgate. Dalglish insisted with tongue firmly in cheek that it was part of a new policy of 'transparency' – that ordinary fans deserved to see how the manager went about his work.

By the time of the last derby meeting of the season Celtic, dispirited, aimless and apathetic, lost 4-0 at Ibrox. *The Sun*, seizing the opportunity to inflict retaliation, reported that 'Dalglish staged his press conference in a bar on Friday and turned out a pub team yesterday'. By then, it was hard to remember that Celtic had actually won a trophy under Dalglish, the Scottish League Cup. Celtic faced Kilmarnock in the semi-final just eight days after the Inverness fiasco and won 1-0 through a Lubo Moravcik goal.

The final would be against Aberdeen, who had clearly become Celtic's favourite opponents. Before that Hampden Park rendezvous, they had recorded three league victories over the Pittodrie side by an aggregate score of 18-0. They would complete their league assignments with later with a 5-1 win over the Dons. The League Cup final was a little less spectacular, but goals from Vidar Riseth and Tommy Johnson gave Celtic an uncomplicated 2-0 victory.

After the last humbling at the hands of Rangers, the season ebbed towards a merciful end and included a defeat by Hearts and draws with Dundee, Hibernian, Motherwell and St Johnstone. The league campaign concluded with the Barnes/Dalglish team twenty-one points behind Rangers. But the general sourness that had permeated the club through a largely miserable season persisted to the end. Dalglish's contract was terminated under protest and following some legal wrangling he accepted a financial settlement and left the club. Allan MacDonald was due to begin contract renewal talks as his agreement would expire at the end of the year, but he announced in September that he would be quitting his post and leaving football.

MacDonald's departure seemed symbolic of the last farewell of the Barnes/Dalglish era, a time that, for many supporters, had recalled the cheerless years immediately before the accession of Fergus McCann. But, while the first half of the millennium year, 2000, will be remembered with a grimace by the Celtic support, it was indeed to prove a year of two halves, and will also be remembered as the beginning of the age of redemption to be triggered by the arrival of Martin O'Neill.

# TWENTY-SIX

## THE ROAD TO SEVILLE: MARTIN O'NEILL RESTORES CELTIC AT HOME AND ABROAD

ON FERGUS McCANN'S departure, Dermot Desmond had bought a significant proportion of his shares and thus became the largest Celtic shareholder. Desmond had always been respectful of McCann's position and had been a strong source of support to him. However, he had also learned lessons from the way in which certain key matters were handled – not least, the over-regular appointment of new managers. This time, he was not prepared to rely on the judgment of others without being convinced in his own mind that Celtic had the right man for the job. Dermot Desmond recalled:

*'The appointment of a new manager was what really created the crisis with Allan MacDonald. He wanted Guus Hiddink who was then with Real Betis – he was lined up and a deal was agreed. I was not going to take on a manager unless I met him, looked in his eyes and liked what I saw. I hired a plane and Brian Quinn and Pat Sheehy came down with me. We met Hiddink and had a long conversation but I didn't like Hiddink. Brian and Pat agreed with me but Allan MacDonald didn't, particularly when I said that I would go and look for a new manager. So then I got Alex*

*Ferguson to contact Martin O'Neill and Martin's response was: 'What took you so long to ask me?' I had dinner with him and I was absolutely convinced he was the right person. Brian Quinn and Pat Sheehy felt the same way – that he was a different calibre of person.'*

Brian Quinn became chairman in succession to Frank O'Callaghan just as Martin O'Neill arrived. He was wary of taking the job for three main reasons:

*'I know myself and suspected that I would be consumed by the job and my other work would suffer. I also lived near London and could not always be available at short notice to deal with unexpected problems. Finally, I did not relish working with Allan MacDonald. I was not wrong about any of these concerns. The club was soundly-based financially and the board had some first-class directors. Eric Riley was a rock. Above all, it was important to begin to win football competitions on a fairly regular basis. Martin had persuaded Dermot to increase his financial backing for the club. In a way, this support was tacit rather than explicit but none the less real for that. We began to buy – and pay – a series of players who lifted the club to a different level.'*

Martin O'Neill arrived at Celtic Park on June 1, 2000, with his trusted assistants John Robertson and Steve Walford, but unaccompanied by the unease that had haunted supporters whenever the managerial chair required filling since Billy McNeill vacated it in 1991. O'Neill was not only a well-known Celtic sympathiser, but his record with middle-to-lower order teams in England, from Grantham Town through Wycombe Wanderers and Norwich City to Leicester City, had established his reputation for improbable achievement. He had captured two League Cups with Leicester and made them a force to be reckoned with in the Premiership. There was also his impressive playing career, served mainly with the astonishingly successful Nottingham Forest team of Brian Clough, at whose feet he had learned much, crowned with a European Cup winner's medal in 1980.

If Celtic supporters were already happy with the O'Neill appointment, their anticipation was heightened by reports of his first day at work, spent mainly in the company of the media. Veteran journalists were immediately in awe of O'Neill's credibility, eloquence and charisma. Glenn Gibbons of The Guardian described it as 'an introduction to the most strikingly impressive and authoritative personality to have arrived at Celtic since Jock Stein. Even the most sceptical were convinced that day that they had just encountered a figure worthy of the challenge to Dick Advocaat and Rangers.'

Those impressions could not have been more thrillingly vindicated. Before the season was four weeks old, Celtic had won their first five league matches including a stunning 6-2 victory over Rangers. That first derby match of the season not only featured an exhilarating team performance, but confirmed the arrival of another heroic figure to set beside Henrik Larsson and Lubomir Moravcik – Chris Sutton. The tall striker had already scored three times in the opening four matches, but when he drilled the ball into the Rangers net just fifty-one seconds after the kick-off on August 27, 2000, and made it 6-2 by completing his double in the 90th minute, Celtic supporters were persuaded that another true star had arrived.

Sutton had endeared himself to the club's followers with his very first utterance. Asked about his ambitions at Celtic, he replied: 'Well, the first thing we have to do is put Rangers in their place.' He had been a gigantic figure at Blackburn Rovers, forming the famous 'SAS' strike partnership with Alan

Shearer that secured the English league title in 1995. After Blackburn were relegated four years later, Sutton made a big-money move to Chelsea where he had a miserable season. By paying £6million to bring him to Glasgow, O'Neill rekindled the striker's enthusiasm and form. There was a similar backdrop to the equally inspired recruitment of Alan Thompson – an idol at Bolton Wanderers before moving to Aston Villa, where things had not worked out.

O'Neill's first signing had been the Belgium central defender Joos Valgaeren. In acquiring Valgaeren from the Dutch club, Roda JC after watching him in action for Belgium at the European Championships of 2000, O'Neill confessed to having broken one of his own laws. 'I've always made it a strict rule not to buy a player on the strength of his work over a couple of weeks with his national team,' he said. 'I would always prefer to assess him coping with the everyday demands of a club environment. But Joos was very impressive playing for Belgium in a tough group, so I've made an exception.'

Within months, the signings would also include Didier Agathe from Hibernian and Neil Lennon who joined from Leicester City where he had previously enjoyed a close relationship with O'Neill. This was to prove a critical signing for Celtic which extended far beyond Lennon's 214 appearances as a player and latterly as captain. A native of Lurgan in the north of Ireland, he was already a vastly experienced midfielder, having spent five seasons with Crewe Alexandra after being freed as a youth by Manchester City, then another five at Leicester. Neil Lennon recalled a long Celtic love affair:

*'I grew up on the stories of the Lisbon Lions in the mid to late seventies. Our Boys' Club played out of the Lurgan Celtic Supporters' Club and although we never got the chance to see Celtic, we knew these almost mythical figures from the men*

*talking about them – Mr Stein, Jinky, Big Billy. Then later,*
*the likes of Paul McStay, who was a wonderful player, played*
*a big part in my desire to play football.*

*'In 1986 or so, John Kelman, the chief scout at the time,*
*phoned my father and said they would like to take me for a*
*trial to Celtic. I was bouncing off the walls at that time but*
*it never materialised. As my career progressed, I was always*
*looking at how Celtic were doing. The nineties was a dry*
*period for the club but the style of football they played, with*
*Tommy Burns at the helm, was very pleasing on the eye. I*
*always wanted to play there – it was a bit like Yosser Hughes*
*in "Boys from the Black Stuff". I would watch Celtic playing*
*and say: 'I could do that'.*

*'When Martin went from Leicester, there was only one*
*place I wanted to go. I was very high-profile at the time and*
*there was interest from other clubs. I remember having a chat*
*with him about the Celtic job and I told him he had to go for*
*it and he asked if I would go with him. I had signed a new*
*contract and it took three or four months for me to get there. At*
*that time, Leicester were second or third in the Premier League*
*but it didn't change my outlook. I wanted to join Celtic.'*

With such exceptional talents as Larsson, Moravcik and Paul
Lambert already at the club, O'Neill had created a potent
blend. The opening unbeaten run would stretch to sixteen
league games, comprising fourteen victories and two draws but
was abruptly ended by Rangers at Ibrox on the last weekend of
November. The 5-1 defeat at Ibrox was an unexpected shock
for a Celtic support that had travelled in great expectation
– not least because O'Neill's side went into the fray with a
fifteen-point lead. There was little to choose between the teams
as Rangers led 1-0 at half-time and Larsson equalised early in
the second half, before Rangers ran riot.

It was, however, the last joyful experience they took from the meetings that season. In the remaining league matches, Celtic won 1-0 at home and 3-0 away, and they eliminated Rangers in the semi-final of the League Cup, winning 3-1. That trophy was secured by a 3-0 defeat of Kilmarnock in the final.

By the time Celtic bulldozed Alex McLeish's Hibernian, also 3-0, in the final of the Scottish Cup (a double from the peerless Larsson and the other from McNamara), the league championship had been won by fifteen points and O'Neill had captured the club's first domestic treble since Jock Stein in 1969 and only Celtic's third in the fifty-five years since the inauguration of the League Cup in 1946. It was a season that could not have been imagined 12 months earlier. The Scottish Cup-winning side was: Douglas, Mjallby, Vega, Valgaeren, Agathe, Lennon, Lambert (Boyd), Moravcik (McNamara), Thompson (Johnson), Larsson, Sutton.

O'Neill's second Scottish Premier League title was, if anything, won even more impressively than the first. The team climbed to the top of the league after only three matches and remained there for the remainder of the campaign. The manager, whose innate restlessness kept him alert to possibilities, had taken advantage of Rangers' decision not to sign John Hartson by adding him to the Celtic squad in August, soon after the start of the domestic programme. After a quiet start as he achieved full fitness, Hartson announced his arrival with a spectacular hat-trick in a 5-1 victory over Dundee United that was also a portent of the successful five seasons he would spend at Celtic Park, racking up more than 100 goals. Celtic were in the midst of an unbeaten run that stretched to eighteen games of which only one was drawn. During this period, from July 29 to December 15, 2001, they conceded only seven goals – and never more than one in any match. The run included two victories over Rangers, the first by 2-0 at Ibrox and then 2-1 at home. All of this left the champions thirteen points ahead before the unbeaten run ended on December 22, with a 2-0 reversal against Aberdeen at Pittodrie.

Even these breathtaking exploits, however, were subordinate to the excitements of the campaign in Europe. O'Neill had instantly demonstrated his talent for inspiring players with his pre-match addresses and deploying them astutely to maximise their individual capabilities during the visit to the Amsterdam ArenA to face Ajax in the final qualifier for the UEFA Champions League group stage. Celtic, in control from the outset, left with a remarkable 3-1 victory, thanks to goals from Bobby Petta, Didier Agathe and Chris Sutton. The return in Glasgow was lost 1-0, but the aggregate win took Celtic into a group to savour, alongside Juventus, Porto and Rosenborg. The opening match in Turin brought the kind of fluctuating fortunes, and ultimate cruelty, that would ripple through the entire, six-match series. Having fallen two goals behind to a double from the French striker, David Trezeguet, Celtic's resilience brought a colossal effort to restore parity, with Stiliyan Petrov and Henrik Larsson – the latter in the 86th minute – producing the goals that seemed certain to earn a merited point.

Instead, there was only bitterness to take from the Stadio delle Alpi when the German referee, Helmut Krug, awarded Juventus a penalty in the last minute after the substitute, Nicola Amoruso, had gone down in a challenge from Joos Valgaeren. There was widespread agreement that no foul had been committed and the Italian had been guilty of duping the ill-positioned referee. It was a moment that seemed to presage the disappointment of failing to reach the knockout stage despite winning all three home matches and taking nine points, a total that would normally have been enough. Events in Turin ultimately cost Celtic their due place.

But the fervour which surrounded the 1-0 victories over Porto (Larsson) and Rosenborg (Thompson) and, of course, the 'revenge' 4-3 win over Juventus on an impossibly theatrical night, confirmed Celtic Park as one of the most exhilarating and demanding venues in Europe, a reputation that has continued to grow in the years since. Finishing third in the UEFA Champions League group brought Celtic the consolation of being 'parachuted' into the third round of the UEFA Cup, but they could hardly have drawn more difficult opponents than Valencia of Spain. Another near miss, losing on a penalty shoot-out after a 1-0 away defeat and a 1-0 home win, ended a momentous few months in the continental theatre.

At home, the defeat by Aberdeen in December turned out to be the first and last of the championship. Astonishingly, O'Neill's dominant champions completed the remaining nineteen games unscathed, including two 1-1 draws with Rangers and won the title with an unprecedented 103 points. The total broke down into thirty-three victories, four draws and that solitary defeat. This kind of form made the failure to defend the two other trophies won the previous season all the more surprising. Celtic were beaten in both competitions by Rangers, by now under the management of Alex McLeish, a 2-1 loss in extra-time in the semi-final of the League Cup and a 3-2 defeat in the Scottish Cup final.

Martin O'Neill's third season at Celtic Park proved to be among the most paradoxical in the club's history. It was reasonable to argue that a campaign which concluded without a single trophy had been as memorably thrilling as the manager's first, when he landed the domestic treble. The bewildering eccentricities of 2002/03 included overall victory in the four-match series of league collisions with Rangers – two wins, one draw, one defeat – but the loss, by one goal, of the championship itself. There was also elimination at the quarter-final stage of the Scottish Cup at the hands of Inverness Caledonian Thistle, a result made the more shocking by the match that had preceded it. Finally, there was the defeat by Rangers in a League Cup final. Yet for a generation, it will be remembered simply as the season of Seville.

The European adventures had started inauspiciously, with an aggregate defeat from FC Basel of Switzerland in the final qualifying round of the UEFA Champions League. Having secured a 3-1 lead from the home leg, Celtic lost 2-0 in the return and dropped into the UEFA Cup which turned out to be a blessing, albeit heavily disguised at the time. The journey to Seville began routinely with a 10-1 aggregate victory over Lithuanian side, FK Suduva. But next up were Blackburn Rovers in a meeting that became quite heated after a first game in Glasgow in which Celtic played moderately and won 1-0. Graeme Souness, the former Rangers manager now in charge of Blackburn, told his own players that they had been 'men against boys' and this found its way into the newspapers. It was the kind of motivational tool O'Neill could wield like a virtuoso. By the visit to Blackburn, the Celtic players were so well-conditioned they controlled the match from the start, ensuring a comfortable victory with goals from Henrik Larsson and Chris Sutton.

The Spaniards of Celta Vigo were next, a 1-0 win at home (Larsson) and a 2-1 defeat away (Hartson) ensuring progress on the away goals rule. VfB Stuttgart of Germany in the fourth round looked daunting, but Celtic followed their 3-1 home win by racing into a 2-0 lead in the return, eventually losing 3-2 to a late goal, but enjoying an aggregate 5-4 triumph. Predictions that their run was at an end were thick on the ground after drawing Liverpool and an off-form Celtic could only manage a 1-1 draw at home. But O'Neill's reputation as a motivator soared when Alan Thompson and John Hartson brought the conspicuously superior Scottish champions a 2-0 victory at Anfield and Larsson revealed the significance of the manager's role. The laconic Swede was conciseness itself, referring to O'Neill's pre-match address to the players simply as 'the most impressive I've ever heard.'

Larsson himself would open the door to the final with the only goal of the match against Boavista in Oporto, the first leg of the semi-final having been drawn 1-1. The goal came late and O'Neill later reflected on how close they had come to anti-climax: 'I couldn't believe, as we went into the last 10 minutes behind on away goals, we were about to go out to the least impressive team we'd met'. Boavista's city neighbours, Porto, in the charge of the then little-known Jose Mourinho, were the opponents in the final in Seville.

The event saw a reputed 80,000 Celtic fans invade the historic city, without a hint of trouble – probably the biggest collective party ever enjoyed by Celtic supporters and reputed at that time to be the biggest travelling support in the game's history. On the evening of May 21, 2003, some 35,000 of them headed for the final showdown while tens of thousands more crowded the squares and bars of Seville. It was Celtic's first European final since 1970 and the venue could not have been better. Christopher Davies in the *Daily Telegraph* summed up the scene:

*'The atmosphere inside the Estadio Olimpico as the game started was as good as it gets – noise without nastiness, passion without punch-ups. It was also an Andalucian Celtic Park as the majority of spectators were clad in green and white, albeit with painfully pink skin... After a first half where tempers rather than technique were the talking point, the second half burst into life with Celtic showing the spirit that had taken them this far by twice coming from behind. Man for man, the Portuguese champions may have been superior but Celtic's drive, passion and never-say-die attitude with outstanding individuals such as Henrik Larsson and Didier Agathe made them a match for Jose Mourinho's side.'*

For Celtic, it was to be a night of sustained hope, intense pride and ultimate disappointment. Despite a colossal individual performance from Henrik Larsson which won him the Man of the Match award, capped by his two memorable goals, Celtic went down 3-2 in extra-time to a side which, the following season, would win the UEFA Champions League. Porto specialised in gamesmanship and O'Neill said afterwards that Mourinho's team 'spent most of the time cheating on us'. On the stroke of half-time, Celtic suffered a blow when Derlei followed up a parried save by Douglas from Deco to put Porto ahead. Within two minutes of the re-start, Larsson headed home a fabulous goal from Didier Agathe's cross but Celtic could only hold parity for seven minutes before Deco sent Alenichev through to score from 12 yards. It was again Celtic's turn to hit back and Larsson squared the match three minutes later from Alan Thompson's corner. More than half an hour was then played out in an atmosphere of caution with both sides desperate to avoid the fatal mistake. But extra-time was to prove Celtic's undoing. The sending-off of Bobo Balde for a second yellow card only five minutes into the added half hour helped tip the balance and with eight minutes remaining, defensive confusion allowed Derlei to score. Dermot Desmond reflected: 'It was a night of joy and disappointment with a great atmosphere and great support. People will wait a long time to take such a journey again.' For Neil Lennon, there are mixed memories:

*'I don't have too many recollections of the game. I know we didn't play as well as we could have done in the first-half and we were a goal down. At half-time, Martin was saying 'Come on, you know you're better than this,' and we'd probably shown Porto a bit too much respect. In the second half we were much better, and I felt as the game went on and we got it back to 2-2 that there was only one team going to win it, and that would*

*have been us. There was nothing between the teams, when you consider what Porto went on to do the following year. I felt it showed what a really good team we had and I felt that if we had made the last 16 of the Champions League the following year who knows where we could have ended up.*

*'We were distraught after the game. We were all at that point in our careers where you're thinking would you get to another European final. Obviously Henrik went on to win the Champions League with Barcelona, but for that group you're thinking that could be it. There were great memories and it was a great achievement. And the support we had that night was incredible. There was a new generation who had never seen Celtic in a European final before, and then there was the older generation who had seen the Lions in 1967 and '70. And to see different generations coming together for that one night was very special.'*

It had been an extraordinary joyride, and while it was happening, there were domestic slips. In one astonishing week in March, Celtic lost the League Cup final to Rangers, beat Liverpool at Anfield and were evicted from the Scottish Cup at Inverness. Having gone 2-0 down to Rangers, they were brought back into it by Larsson. As Celtic dominated the second half, Hartson scored a goal which, TV replays confirmed, was erroneously disallowed for offside on the advice of a linesman. Then, with Sutton having been carried off with a broken wrist and Neil Lennon sent off, Hartson missed a penalty in the dying minutes, squandering the chance to take the match into extra-time. Although O'Neill rested some players for the visit to Inverness, the team was strong enough, but a flat performance brought a 1-0 defeat.

In the league, some improbable set-backs had left Celtic eight points and eight goals behind Rangers as they approached the last derby match of the season. It was a mere three days after the

UEFA Cup semi-final victory over Boavista and the supporters arrived at Ibrox for a party, carrying beach balls and dressed like cartoon Spaniards. Onfield, the team was emphatically superior to Rangers in a 2-1 victory that had seemed unlikely. Celtic would go on to win their next four matches, while Rangers dropped two points at Dundee. On the last day, therefore, the great rivals were level on points and goal difference, but Rangers had scored more. While Celtic were winning 4-0 at Kilmarnock, Rangers beat Dunfermline 6-1 at Ibrox – with a 90th minute penalty kick – and took the title by a goal. The strangest thing of all about the season was the widespread notion that Celtic were the best team in the country, despite Rangers having lifted the treble.

Celtic regained their title the following season. Neil Lennon later reflected that, in the seven years he spent as a player at the club, the 2003/04 team was the strongest. One glance at their list of achievements would make the former captain's assessment entirely understandable. In the process of winning the championship by seventeen points, Celtic established a British record of twenty-five successive league victories; the unbeaten run, including draws, stretched to thirty-two. During the season, they also won all five of their matches with Rangers, four in the championship and one in the Scottish Cup, with an aggregate of 8-1. Neil Lennon said:

*'All of us peaked. We had seen great years before but that season was fantastic – 25 SPL wins in a row and some great performances in Europe. If we had got through to the last 16 in Lyon, you just never know – we were playing so well that season. Though we were all in our early thirties, we were playing our best football then.'*

In Europe, they contested a group that included two of the continent's most powerful sides at the time, Olympique Lyonnais of France and Bayern Munich of Germany. But for one of their worst European performance under Martin O'Neill, against Anderlecht, and a defensive error in the away match to Bayern, they would have won the group, instead of finishing third. Dropped into the UEFA Cup, they reached the quarter-finals, eliminating Barcelona on the way. Their reward for dismissing the Catalan giants was a pairing in the last eight with another daunting Spanish side, Villarreal. A 1-1 draw at Celtic Park and a 2-0 defeat in Spain testified to Villarreal as an emerging force.

The win over Rangers in the Scottish Cup paved the way for a 3-1 victory over Dunfermline Athletic in the final, which would turn out to be Henrik Larsson's farewell appearance. He delivered two of the three goals as a parting gift with Petrov getting the other, as Celtic came from behind to triumph. The Celtic team that day was Marshall, Agathe, McNamara, Varga, Balde, Lennon, Petrov, Pearson (Wallace), Thompson, Larsson, Sutton. No player in modern times has gained such affection and respect from Celtic supporters as the graceful, gifted Swede whose name is indelibly linked with Jansen and O'Neill managerships and particularly the season of Seville. He left incredible memories behind and his occasional returns to the stadium, usually for charitable events, have given the Celtic support opportunities to confirm that his name will live long in the club's memories and legends.

Hibernian ended the challenge for the League Cup at the quarter-final stage, but, as a season of atonement for the barrenness of the previous year, 2003/04 gave the support abundant reasons to be cheerful.

Before what would prove to be his last season, O'Neill had introduced the eighteen-year-old winger, Aiden McGeady, to the first team in the last month of season 2003/04 and he had briefly restored the highly promising Liam Miller, a young Irish midfielder whose Celtic career had begun in 2000 at the age of nineteen, but whose subsequent three years had been sabotaged by injuries. Miller made such an impact that he was lured to Manchester United – to O'Neill's deep disappointment – after only 43 appearances (including 19 starts) in a Celtic jersey.

Martin O'Neill's first three years at Celtic Park had been a huge and exhilarating success, but it had not come cheaply and tensions about the balance between the desirable and the affordable had been an ongoing source of boardroom tension. As early as January 10, 2002, the Chief Executive, Ian McLeod – who had succeeded Allan MacDonald – suggested that 'a different focus on player trading and acquisition, such as concentrating on Bosman ruling players for whom no transfer fee would be required, might be adopted'. It was certainly not O'Neill's habit or intention to be so constrained although his methods did not necessarily depend on high spending. Brian Quinn recalled:

> *'One of Martin's great strengths was the ability to get the best out of players. His words counted because he had been a successful player himself, a European Cup winner and part of a team that had won the English First Division. He had the uncanny knack of choosing to sign players who were no better than moderate, who provided just what was needed at the time but who, when they left Celtic, sank without trace – Ramon Vega, Stanislav Varga, Bobo Balde and others. Financially, this helped to pay for the expensive signings – although they were not exactly cheap – and at least in this respect maintained some sense of budgetary discipline. But the real value was that these players performed above themselves and made an important contribution to the team's success. Martin was a real team leader.'*

The concerns about mounting losses continued throughout the Seville season. The board minute of October 17, 2002 delivered a terse warning: 'If no action was taken to address the forecast shortfall, the Company would breach covenants on borrowing limits which it was not prepared to do'. The previous month, a loss of £15.6million for the financial year was projected and while the UEFA Cup run ameliorated that outcome, it did not change the underlying reality that – even as a title-winning Scottish side doing exceptionally well in Europe – Celtic were living far beyond their means.

Peter Lawwell, an accountant by profession, joined the club in September 2003 following Ian McLeod's return to his successful career in retailing. Whereas his predecessors had sometimes suffered from doubts about where their footballing loyalties lay, Lawwell was a lifelong supporter who had previously served a short stint at the club in the early 1990s. Subsequently, he cut out a high-flying career with major Scottish companies. When the Celtic post again became vacant, Lawwell was employed as Commercial Director with Clydeport whose chief executive, Tom Allison, had been a Celtic director since 2001. Allison had no doubt that Lawwell was the man for the job and, having recommended him, stepped back from the selection process. Fortunately, the rest of the board agreed with his assessment. Dermot Desmond describes him as an 'exceptional chief executive' who has since turned down approaches from Arsenal and other leading clubs because of his deep commitment to Celtic. His determination to run Celtic according to a sound business model has at times attracted criticism, but the more that became known about events elsewhere in Glasgow, the higher the level of vindication. Peter Lawwell explained:

*'When I arrived, there were serious issues around the finances of the club. The shareholders had supported Martin's regime. Before Martin, Celtic were in the wilderness and had lost credibility in Europe. All of that was transformed under him*

*but it came at a price. Between 2000 and 2005 there were accumulated losses of £50million which ultimately were funded by the shareholders and by increasing debt. There was a realisation that the debt had to be reduced to a manageable level. Celtic had to live within its means. The policy of cash break-even, self-sustaining but with the re-investment of all income into the team, the club and the brand was established.'*

Martin O'Neill had not taken kindly to the changed financial environment, particularly as the team he had assembled was now in quite urgent need of refreshment. Going into season 2004/05, it was, generally speaking, the tried and tested who would be entrusted with the task of maintaining Celtic's pre-eminence at home and progress in Europe – but with one notable exception. The incomparable Larsson, now approaching thirty-three and after seven years in the Hoops, left the club and signed a one-year deal with Barcelona. The new parameters for spending would be reflected in O'Neill securing the Brazilian midfielder, Juninho, on a free transfer from Middlesbrough, and the Senegal striker, Henri Camara, on loan from Wolverhampton Wanderers. Juninho's Celtic career could not have started more encouragingly, as he made his debut in the 1-0 defeat of Rangers in the first derby match. However, like Camara, he soon proved disappointing and was only an occasional selection thereafter. Camara was sent back to Wolves during the transfer window in January and O'Neill brought the talented Wales forward, Craig Bellamy, on loan on the last day of the month to fortify the push towards retaining the league title. Reinforcements were necessary because of an inconsistency in the team, who proved to be alarmingly vulnerable at home.

After the desperate disappointment of 2003, history would repeat itself, with Celtic again losing the title on the last day to their age-old rivals. This time, however, it was even worse as they held a two-point lead and required victory over Motherwell at Fir Park to ensure retention of the championship. Their objective was in sight just two minutes from the end as they led 1-0, but the premature celebrations were silenced by a double in the dying stages from Scott McDonald – a self-confessed Celtic fan, the Australian striker would sign for the club two years later – and, with Rangers beating Hibs 1-0 in Edinburgh, the league was snatched away in the most painful of circumstances. The real damage, however, had been sustained in the unconvincing home form which saw them lose four matches at Celtic Park, compared with only two away.

The suspicion that some of Celtic's resilience had left along with Larsson began to form as early as November, when the League Cup quarter-final against Rangers was lost in extra-time after O'Neill's side had led until late in the 90 minutes on a goal from John Hartson. But they had recovered enough of their steel to eliminate Rangers at the first hurdle in the Scottish Cup, with a 2-1 victory secured by goals from Sutton and Hartson. The ultimate reward for that performance would be the final at Hampden a week after the loss of the league title, when a goal from Alan Thompson brought Martin O'Neill a trophy in what would soon be revealed to have been his last match as manager. The Celtic team which beat Dundee United through an Alan Thompson goal on May 28, 2005 was Douglas, Agathe, Balde, Varga, McNamara, Petrov, Lennon, Thompson (McGeady), Sutton, Bellamy, Hartson (Valgaeren).

Martin O'Neill's era may have passed at Celtic Park and ultimately it was not matters of football which determined the timing of his departure but the fact that his wife, Geraldine, was battling a serious illness. For Celtic supporters, it was the end of an extraordinary era, by turns richly rewarding and agonisingly frustrating, characterised by an intriguingly effective manager and a set of exceptionally gifted players.

# TWENTY-SEVEN

## SUCCESS UNDER STRACHAN:
## THREE-IN-A-ROW AND
## EUROPEAN PROGRESS

THE CELTIC BOARD'S need to produce a coup from their search for a new manager in 2005 was heightened by the status of the man who had vacated the position. Martin O'Neill's achievements in the preceding five years had transformed not only outcomes but expectations. Not least, O'Neill's prolific trophy-gathering at home and exhilarating adventures in Europe had reaffirmed the collective preference for hiring a manager with an identifiable spiritual connection with the club – which essentially meant Celtic or Irish.

The man unveiled as his successor on June 1, 2005 did not fit either of these credentials. Gordon Strachan was the Edinburgh-born, Hibernian-supporting midfielder who had been an exceptional young talent with Dundee, flourished at Aberdeen and confirmed his status with five years at Manchester United, followed by six at Leeds United where he captained the team to the Second Division title and, at the age of thirty-five, the championship itself. Now forty-eight, Strachan had enjoyed mixed fortunes as a manager with Coventry City and Southampton though the common thread was over-achievement with relatively limited resources. This time, there were none of the uncertainties that had attended previous managerial changes. Dermot Desmond explained:

*'I knew for some time about Martin leaving. He had told me about Geraldine's illness and he was going to give time to look after her so I knew at least six months before he left. You are continuously looking at potential managers because you never know when you are going to be looking for someone new. It was apparent that Gordon had the passion and the knowledge and the skill-set. Martin's were going to be big boots to fill and we needed someone who could handle that. Gordon did a great job. He was very easy to work with – uncomplicated, humorous, got on with it.'*

Brian Quinn said that the Board had considered a number of potential names once it was realised that O'Neill would be leaving.

*'Gordon Strachan was out of a job at the time, having announced that he needed a break from managing, so he was an obvious candidate. Nonetheless, we decided to look at other names including Tony Mowbray who was doing very well at Hibs. However, it was felt that it was something of a risk to go with someone so early in his career. Around this time, Dermot intervened to say that that he had met Gordon Strachan, had sounded him out about coming to Celtic and had received a generally positive response, so the two tracks converged simultaneously.'*

Celtic lost the league title at Motherwell on May 21, 2005 – 'that terrible match' as Dermot Desmond described it, speaking for all who suffered the same sense of desolation. 'The next day, there was a meeting at my house in London with Martin and Gordon.

Martin gave his views. In spite of the circumstances, he went through it all very professionally and that was how the transition took place.' Between that meeting and the announcement of Strachan's appointment, O'Neill presided over his last game – the Scottish Cup final victory over Dundee United.

Despite a history of high achievement and the evidence that here was the kind of steely, single-minded figure ready-made for the trials that await any Celtic manager, Strachan would arrive at Celtic Park to a welcome from the support that could most kindly be described as 'reserved' though, in truth, his only deficiency in some eyes was his lack of Celtic pedigree. It was then Strachan's misfortune that his debut as manager came slightly sooner than he would have preferred with unfortunate consequences.

Not for the first or last time, Celtic suffered from the woeful Scottish co-efficient which, irrespective of the club's own performance history in Europe, determines the stage at which competitions are entered. This meant that Celtic were in the draw for the third qualifying round, against opposition from either Kazakhstan or Slovakia. After the first-leg, it looked likely to be a journey to the furthest point on the European football map. But Artmedia Bratislava snatched a late aggregate winner and so, for his first game as manager, Gordon Strachan led his team to the Slovakian capital. Due to the exceptionally high turnover of players that close season, it was very much a team still in the making with several of those who took the field on July 27, 2005 having come together only within the preceding few days. That was exactly how it looked as Celtic slumped to their worst ever defeat in Europe, a surreal 5-0 procession towards David Marshall's goal, made even worse by a broken cheek-bone for Chris Sutton. It was a stunning blow for the new manager to have to pick himself up from so soon. After in game in Bratislava, Dermot Desmond went into the dressing room to speak to the manager and the team who were in shock. Strachan knew that he would be castigated by the press, but Desmond told him that his first review would be after the last game of the season so he was to do what he did best and get on with the job.

Three days later, in the opening league match at Motherwell, Strachan's team squandered a 3-1 half-time advantage to trail 4-3, before a last-minute goal from Craig Beattie secured the draw. Anger over the Artmedia result was reduced from boiling point when the second leg in Glasgow brought a 4-0 victory, but being out of Europe was still a major disappointment. With the transition towards a more cost-conscious approach now embedded, the new signings had included the Japanese midfielder, Shunsuke Nakamura, the Polish goalkeeper, Artur Boruc and his countryman, Maciej Zurawski. A week after the Motherwell debacle, Nakamura served notice that he would be a treasure with a brilliant debut against Dundee United. Goals from John Hartson and Craig Beattie brought a comfortable victory. The new Celtic formula was beginning to kick in – great signings could be achieved at relatively modest cost if the world-wide scouting system delivered the goods. Nakamura was an outstanding example. Peter Lawwell said:

'We paid two million euros for Nakamura who was with Reggina in Italy at the time. The recommendation came through an Italian agent. Gordon had a look at him and also spoke to Andy Roxburgh for an opinion. It was a great signing and a pointer to how we had to go. By the time Gordon came in, there was an acceptance that we were not able to purchase and pay English Premier League players. That was now unaffordable because the explosion in media values for the EPL had created levels of transfer fees and wage inflation that put these players out of our reach. So we had to look for the same quality of players in different markets as we set about *rebuilding the squad. It was still a good budget by Scottish standards but the important principle had been established that there was a budget for the manager to work within.'*

Artur Boruc was another inspired signing within this new regime, initially on loan from Legia Warsaw. Since the second match against Artmedia, Boruc had displaced Marshall and would never relinquish that first-choice status throughout his five years and 162 appearances. Encouraging signs of recovery from the Artmedia debacle were dimmed in the first derby meeting of the season. Celtic not only lost 3-1, but Alan Thompson was sent off after twenty-three minutes, while the vehement protests of the captain, Neil Lennon, to referee Stuart Dougal after the final whistle brought him the equivalent of a red card. In response to this exacting test of their resilience, Strachan's players responded by winning twelve of their next thirteen games, including successive victories over Rangers. The only blemish in the run came from a 1-1 draw at home to Hearts, who had made themselves serious contenders for the title.

It would not be until two games later, with the 4-2 victory over Dundee United at Tannadice, that Celtic would go top. By the time they met Rangers in the league during that period – the third of the season – Celtic's victory took them three points clear. That comfortable 3-0 win had been preceded just ten days before by a 2-0 triumph that would eliminate their rivals from the League Cup and allow Strachan to go on and land his first trophy with the club in the 3-0 success against Dunfermline in the March 2006 final. Even so, the celebrations were noticeably short of personal acclaim for the manager, who would have realised by then that nothing less than the league title would eradicate the lingering memory of Artmedia.

The league form continued to be uncertain but Rangers were having a poor season and eventually finished third. Hearts provided the main opposition and Celtic gradually drew clear but their form was erratic as demonstrated in the first days of 2006. On New Year's Day, Celtic travelled to Tynecastle to confront Hearts, by then their closest challengers. Almost characteristically in that season, they would fall 2-0 behind before hitting their stride. Strachan summoned Stephen Pearson from the bench and he changed the flow, scoring within five minutes. From a Nakamura free-kick, Stephen McManus headed the equaliser. As the game moved into added time, Nakamura repeated the routine and McManus bundled the ball over the line for a theatrical 3-2 victory. The ecstasy that greeted that extraordinary climax would be matched by dismay just seven days later.

Few potentially one-sided matches can have enjoyed the build-up that preceded Celtic's Scottish Cup third-round tie with Clyde of the First Division. Strachan had signed the former Manchester United and Ireland captain Roy Keane, as well as the captain of China, the defender Du Wei. Each made his debut in what was regarded as a gentle introduction to the hurly-burly of the Scottish game. On a bumpy pitch in Cumbernauld, the 2-1 defeat was wholly deserved. The unfortunate Du Wei was replaced at half-time and never appeared again. Keane's stay was brief, the veteran midfielder announcing his retirement in early June. He did, however, capture his last honour in the League Cup final victory and contributed to the run-in to the championship, which Celtic won from Hearts by seventeen points.

Having spent his first season convincing the majority of fans that he knew how to win trophies, Gordon Strachan began the second with an overhaul of the playing squad that made it unambiguously his own team. Before, and in the course of the campaign, he recruited twelve players and released ten, including the sale of Stiliyan Petrov to Aston Villa. The departures also included John Hartson, Charlie Mulgrew, Stan Varga, Didier Agathe, Ross Wallace, Dion Dublin, Mo Camara, Stephen Pearson and, in mid-season, Shaun Maloney. The close-season imports were Gary Caldwell, Derek Riordan, Kenny Miller, Evander Sno, Jiri Jarosik, Lee Naylor, Jan Vennegoor of Hesselink – a £3million addition from PSV Eindhoven – and Thomas Gravesen. They would be joined by Steven Pressley, Paul Hartley and Mark Brown during the January transfer window.

With Rangers struggling from the outset of new manager Paul le Guen's tenure, Celtic enjoyed an unusually comfortable run to the turn of the year, including a 2-0 victory in the first derby match of the season. By the end of December, they had built an extraordinary seventeen-point lead over their rivals, who lay third, behind Aberdeen. During this period, the excitement was monopolised by Celtic's adventures in the UEFA Champions League. Having qualified automatically for the group stage, they were drawn alongside Manchester United, Benfica and FC Copenhagen.

Opening with a visit to Old Trafford might have seemed daunting, but Strachan's players acquitted themselves with great credit, losing 3-2 after leading in the first half when United's equaliser had come from a very dubious penalty award. A 1-0 home win over the Danes was followed by one of Celtic's most impressive performances in the UEFA Champions League, a 3-0 triumph over Benfica. They would lose the return in Lisbon by the same score after Gary Caldwell had set the tone with an early own goal, but the supreme moment arrived when Manchester United travelled to Glasgow. United, unsurprisingly, had much of the possession in the match, but did not often translate that into a genuine threat.

When Celtic were awarded a free-kick some thirty-five yards out in the eighty-first minute, Nakamura executed a breathtaking conversion, the ball seemingly still accelerating as it crossed the line high to the left of goalkeeper Edwin van der Sar. Astonishingly, the high points of the match had still to unfold. When United were once again the beneficiaries of a penalty decision as Shaun Maloney was said to have handled. Gary Neville, the United right-back, told Neil Lennon as Louis Saha prepared to take the kick, 'I think he'll miss'. The striker would indeed be foiled by Artur Boruc's diving save. It would be some time after the final whistle before it was realised that a combination of results meant that Celtic had qualified with a match to spare, thanks to winning their head-to-head with United on away goals. In the last 16 for the first time, they were paired with AC Milan and, after a goal-less first leg at Celtic Park, performed with great credit to secure the same scoreline in Italy, only to fall to an extra-time goal from the Brazilian, Kaka. It was a measure of Celtic's achievements in the tournament that Milan should go on to win it by beating Liverpool in the final in Athens.

The European experience seemed to inspire the team at home, as they started 2007 with seven straight victories and clinched the championship with four matches to spare. But even though the personnel had changed markedly, there was still a tendency to stumble in unlikely circumstances; they were ousted from the League Cup on penalties by Falkirk. By way of compensation, the run to the Scottish Cup final included victory at Inverness in which Celtic came from behind with two goals in the last two minutes. The league and cup double was completed with a nervous 1-0 defeat of Dunfermline on May 26, 2007. The team that day was: Boruc, Perrier-Doumbe, McManus, Pressley, Naylor, Nakamura, Lennon (Caldwell), Hartley, McGeady (Beattie), Miller, Vennegoor of Hesselink. The goal was scored by the Cameroon defender Jean-Joel Perrier-Doumbe with six minutes remaining in one of a handful of appearances he made for the club.

On the approach to the attempt at a third successive title in 2007/08, Celtic paid £4.5million to Hibernian for Scott Brown, a record fee between two Scottish clubs, which was to prove a great investment for more than a decade to come. They also signed Massimo Donati from Milan and Scott McDonald from Motherwell. Neil Lennon went to Nottingham Forest on a free transfer and £5m was recouped through the sale of Kenny Miller to Derby as well as David Marshall and Craig Beattie, to Norwich and West Brom respectively. The title defence began with a bland scoreless draw at home to Kilmarnock, but, in the course of winning their next five matches, the team would rack up twenty-two goals. Rangers were now under the guidance of Walter Smith and it would be the closing weeks of the season before the championship would really crackle.

Off the park, Brian Quinn's seven years of chairmanship came to an end when he retired at the annual general meeting in November 2007. Almost uniquely for a football club chairman, his formal departure was marked by a standing ovation from the near-1,000 shareholders present. At the end of his tenure, though not necessarily at all points during it, the supporters appreciated not only the dignity with which he had led the club's affairs but also the necessity of the prudent financial regime that he had presided over which left Celtic as not only the reigning champions of Scotland, standing restored in Europe, but also as a virtually debt-free club. Brian Quinn said:

*'By the time I left in 2007, I regarded the rebuilding of the Celtic board as probably my most important accomplishment. I do not think it is appreciated how difficult it is to chair a company whose previous majority shareholder, chairman and CEO had been combined in one person for a period of five years. It was vital to find three people who shared a common*

*view of how the world works and who can work together. When I became chairman, after a two-year interregnum, there was much work to be done to build on the fundamental changes that Fergus had introduced. In my view – and this took me some time to realise – this could only be delivered with the support of a high-quality board of directors and in particular that of Dermot. He, Peter and I shared the view that Celtic must reflect the highest standards in all it does and that is the basis on which we proceeded and worked together. It gives me a lot of pleasure now to hear Celtic invariably referred to at UEFA as one of Europe's leading clubs.'*

In the meantime Celtic were again pre-occupied by another UEFA Champions League campaign in the closing months of 2007. Having qualified for the group stages by dint of a memorable penalty shoot-out save by Boruc against Spartak Moscow at Celtic Park after two 1-1 draws, Strachan's side drew AC Milan, Benfica and Shakhtar Donetsk. Once again, three home victories gained passage into the last 16, putting another gold star on Strachan's credentials. There was concern at the end of the match against Milan when a supporter ran on to the field and patted the Milan goalkeeper, Dida, on the cheek. The Brazilian made to chase him and then collapsed on the turf holding his face. It might have been very serious for Celtic but in the immediate aftermath Carlo Ancelotti, the Italian coach, gave a demonstration of his class. Asked if his club would take the Dida incident further, Ancelotti said, 'No, no, it had nothing to do with the football, and the better team won the match. The incident with the goalkeeper was nothing.'

The season was marked by tragedy when Phil O'Donnell, the former Celtic midfielder, collapsed just before he was to be substituted by Motherwell in their match against Dundee United on December 29. He was pronounced dead at Wishaw

General Hospital, the cause later found to be heart failure. A popular player, O'Donnell's death was widely mourned and, at the request of his family, Celtic's matches against Rangers and Motherwell, due within a few days, were postponed. This would bring a backlog that would have a significant influence on the closing stages of the championship.

Before then, Celtic again exhibited their fallibility in cup competitions when they lost 1-0 to Aberdeen in the Scottish Cup quarter-final. Five months earlier, they had exited to Hearts at the same stage of the League Cup. Those turn-of-the-year postponements meant they would play Rangers three times in a month and when Celtic lost the first, at Ibrox, by a single goal, they fell six points behind with a match more played. A week later, they lost to Motherwell and their prospects of retaining the title seemed to have receded.

By the time of the second Rangers meeting, on April 16, the deficit was down to one point, but the Ibrox side had two matches in hand. The game was exceptionally dramatic. Nakamura's opener for Celtic was cancelled out before Carlos Cuellar handled on the goal-line and was sent off. An injured Allan McGregor saved Scott McDonald's penalty, seemingly clinching the draw that might also secure the championship. But Jan Vennegoor of Hesselink delivered the winner in the third minute of injury-time. Celtic's 3-2 victory in the final derby collision was the fourth of seven successive wins to the end of the campaign. Rangers, meanwhile, had dropped points and by the last day, the clubs were level on points, but, on goal difference, Celtic had an advantage of four.

That climactic night, May 22, 2008, was preceded by another sad episode in the Celtic history. Tommy Burns died of skin cancer one week before, his funeral at St Mary's, Abercromby Street, Calton, taking place just two days before Celtic were due to play at Dundee United and Rangers were at Aberdeen. Gordon

Strachan's moving tribute to Burns included the testimony that 'being Tommy's mate was the best thing of all about coming to Celtic.' Rangers manager Walter Smith and assistant Ally McCoist, who had been Tommy's colleagues as Scotland coaches, were pallbearers at the funeral, an indicator of their friendship with and affection for the Celtic man. Large crowds lined the streets of the East End as the cortege passed in tribute to a highly-respected figure as player, manager and coach. A plaque by the entrance of Celtic Park now salutes his service to the club.

On a nervous and emotional night at Tannadice, Celtic beat United 1-0 through a second-half goal from Venegoor of Hesselink after the stands had erupted to the news that Rangers were losing at Pittodrie. Gordon Strachan had, therefore, achieved a straight three league titles in a row and taken the club to the last 16 in Europe on two occasions, with a Scottish Cup and League Cup thrown in, during his first three seasons at Celtic Park – an extraordinary record of success as all rational supporters fully recognised. Not only that, but Strachan had embraced the doctrine of relative austerity which required the books to more or less balance.

Strachan's fourth season at Celtic Park was to be his last. Despite the capture of the League Cup with a 2-0 victory over Rangers in the final, it turned out to be a somewhat anti-climactic season. Possibly Strachan's own enthusiasm had been eroded by the refusal of either media or a minority of supporters to accord him the recognition he merited. The European misadventures typified the season. Drawing Manchester United, Villarreal, and Aalborg in their UEFA Champions League group, they failed even to beat the Danes, a scoreless draw at home followed by a 2-1 defeat away. A loss away to the Spaniards, a 3-0 reversal at Old Trafford and a 1-1 draw with United in Glasgow meant that the only victory, in the last match at home to Villarreal, was meaningless.

Having brought in future cult heroes Paddy McCourt and Georgios Samaras, as well as the stylish Marc Crosas from Barcelona, Celtic began the defence of their title with a 1-0 home win over St Mirren after Tommy Burns' wife, Rosemary, had raised the league flag. However an early home defeat in the first derby match – Kenny Miller, by now with Rangers, scoring twice – was a set-back but by the time the teams met again at Ibrox at the end of December Celtic held a four-point lead. Celtic's prospects were further enhanced when a stunning Scott MacDonald second-half goal secured the point. But confidence in a fourth successive title proved to be premature. The board was well aware of the need to strengthen the defence in the January transfer window but a series of efforts to achieve this came to nothing and a heavy price would be paid. This erratic season soon went into decline and a St Mirren team that Celtic had crushed 7-0 in the league on February 28 eliminated them from the Scottish Cup with a 1-0 win just seven days later. The League Cup success in March would be a brief respite from the overall blandness though Celtic somehow contrived to go into the final derby match with a one-point lead due to Rangers' own inconsistencies during the period. Celtic lost 1-0 at Ibrox and while, in theory, the league went to the last day, there was no sense of expectation and Celtic could only draw with Hearts. Gordon Strachan resigned the following day, terminating a distinguished four-year stay at Celtic Park which would create both mutual respect and a lasting affinity with the club. Peter Lawwell said:

> 'Gordon came in at a difficult time for the club when we had to recalibrate the way we operated financially. He took over from Martin O'Neill who was outstandingly successful and popular. He inherited Martin's squad, some of whom

*were coming to the end of their time here and included very strong characters. He had an awful start against Artmedia, so it was a tough task. He was a delight to work with. He understood the limitations of being Celtic manager at that time and just got on with it, winning three titles in a row and taking us into two last-16s in the Champions League. History will show he was a great Celtic manager. You don't really understand the intensity and pressures of being Celtic manager unless you are in the job and Gordon had to put up with a lot of criticism in spite of what he was delivering. But he handled it all with great style and dignity.*

*'Over that period we realised that we had to do a lot more to support the new strategy. We set about raising money for a state-of-the-art training facility at Lennoxtown, through another share issue underwritten by Dermot. We also set aside money to invest in technical facilities – recruitment, sports science, performance analysis and the Academy. If you cannot afford to buy Champions League players then you have to create Champions League players. We invested not only in the bricks and mortar but in the people, processes and technologies of a top-class European football club. We hired John Park as head of scouting, Chris McCart as head of the Youth Academy and a number of other key appointees.'*

Before the end of the season, Strachan simply felt that his time at Celtic Park had run its course and family ties were pulling him back to the south of England. The team he had built was on the verge of breaking up and, always a man with a balanced outlook and a life away from football, he was ready to take a break. Once again in the summer of 2009, the search was on for a manager. John Reid, who had succeeded Brian Quinn as chairman, explained:

*'The search for a manager settled on three names – Owen Coyle, Roberto Martinez and Tony Mowbray. Extensive discussions took place with all three but ultimately the first two would not move. Tony Mowbray seemed to fit the bill. He was part of the Celtic family – a former player and captain who was credited with the introduction of the iconic 'Huddle'. He was hugely respected as a man by the Celtic support because of the character he had shown during his playing days and through the period of his wife Bernadette's illness, which sadly proved terminal. He brought his own management team with him and there was a wholesale change of playing staff, backed by the Board. Why it didn't work out is, as ever, a matter for speculation. He arrived pretty late in the close season due partly to the protracted discussions with the various candidates. He always seemed tentative and insecure. His family never moved to Glasgow. The players he brought in didn't deliver for him and his commitment to an open style of football made his team vulnerable in the rough and tumble of the Scottish game.'*

Mowbray's stint as manager of Celtic for less than one season was distinguished mainly by its disappointments. His failure epitomised the essential truth of football – that nobody can predict with certainty how a manager or a player will fare at a particular club. It all started well enough with five victories and a draw in his opening six matches. But the first crack would appear in the seventh, the first of the season's showdowns with Rangers at Ibrox. The home side were 2-0 ahead after only 16 minutes and, although Aiden McGeady pulled one back, defeat ensued and an apparent lack of spirit in the team concerned the fans even more. Already eliminated from the League Cup by Hearts in the quarter-final ten days earlier, they would go on to ever more unconvincing performances. The view among supporters was that the team lacked strength of character and it was felt that the manager's sympathetic personality was failing to motivate the players. By the end of March, Celtic lagged ten points behind Rangers and meetings between the two clubs had reflected that gap. The last straw, however, was an embarrassing 4-0 midweek defeat by St Mirren. Mowbray was sacked the next day and is unlikely to have drawn much solace from the fact that caretaker manager Neil Lennon won all eight of the remaining league matches – including a 2-1 defeat of Rangers.

# TWENTY-EIGHT

## NEIL LENNON AND THE CLUB
## THAT 'MEANS A WORLD'

NEIL LENNON HAD long been earmarked as a possible Celtic manager but events drove his evolution into that role more quickly than had been anticipated. After leaving Celtic as a player in 2007, he went briefly to Nottingham Forest and then Wycombe Wanderers but Celtic engaged him as first-team coach in 2008, undoubtedly with an eye to his future potential. Dermot Desmond said:

> 'We brought Neil back to really reinforce his Celtic connection and help to deflect some of the attention away from Gordon. We felt he had the intelligence and the passion to become a good manager. When Tony Mowbray didn't work out, we asked Neil to step in and we felt then that he confirmed his capabilities. Like all young managers, he would need to learn his way. Nobody becomes a great manager on the day.'

There was some talk about putting in a mentor to support him but no practical candidate for this role emerged and the idea was overtaken by events. Lennon thus became Celtic's youngest manager on June 9, 2010 at the age of thirty-eight with Johan Mjallby as his deputy, along with Garry Parker and Alan

Thompson as his assistants. He came with the reputation of being a player who attracted unusually strong and contrasting emotions from supporters and detractors. The need to address this head-on by demonstrating respect for the player had been recognised by Martin O'Neill when, at the end of a game at Ibrox in November 2004, during which Lennon suffered a particularly high level of abuse from the home support, the manager put his arm around the captain and took him towards the Celtic supporters in a shared salute. At the time, O'Neill explained: 'Neil Lennon, for whatever reason, suffers dogs' abuse at every single away ground and particularly here, obviously. He is well thought of by the Celtic fans for what he has done for us... It was to show that Neil Lennon is very popular with our fans and I don't want anyone to forget that.'

Neither the adulation nor the hostility had greatly diminished when, almost five years later, Lennon was confirmed as manager – a dimension that added to the complexity of the challenges he would face. The close season saw the now familiar high turnover in the first team squad when the most notable outgoing was Aiden McGeady for a then club record of £10.8million to Spartak Moscow. The gifted McGeady had been a product of Celtic's Youth Academy and this one outcome alone more than justified the commercial, as well as footballing, rationale for maintaining such a system at the highest level. Boruc, McManus and Fortune were among the other departures and later in the season Marc Crosas, who had been much appreciated by the supporters also left for the Russian club Volga – though no former player remains a keener supporter via social media.

Lennon also signed several players who were to be key members of his squad for several seasons to come. Defender Charlie Mulgrew returned from Aberdeen, his contract having expired. Joe Ledley joined from Cardiff City and Scunthorpe United striker, Gary Hooper, arrived in Glasgow with a £2million price tag. A connection through Israel had been developed and the first arrival from this source was the Maccabi Haifa midfielder Beram Kayal. The internationalism of the Celtic scouting system now knew no boundaries and left-back Emilio Izaguirre joined from the Honduran side Motagua while, nearer to home, the free-scoring Irish striker Anthony Stokes was recruited from Hibernian. With Boruc gone, Celtic needed a goalkeeper and the target was Fraser Forster who came, initially on loan, from Newcastle United. What all of this pointed to was the extraordinarily extensive and sophisticated system of player identification and tracking that had been developed under John Park.

Lennon's first European campaign as manager started early and did not last long. Celtic were still suffering from what was in danger of becoming a self-perpetuating reputation for away defeats in Europe and the pattern was resumed when Braga of Portugal scored three without reply in the third round of UEFA Champions League qualifying. A 2-1 home victory still determined a drop down to the UEFA Cup where a 2-0 home win was followed by 4-0 slump in Holland so that Celtic were out of Europe before the end of August. The league form was variable, one highlight being an SPL record 9-0 victory over Aberdeen at Celtic Park. An early 3-1 defeat by Rangers was compensated for by a 2-0 victory in the New Year fixture, a game in which Georgios Samaras really began to win over the Celtic fans with two goals – the second a penalty after his own spectacular run into the area ended in him being brought down. Kris Commons joined from Derby County during the January transfer window and Celtic went on a winning run which included the elimination of Rangers from the Scottish Cup in a replayed tie.

That game, however, brought its own off-field drama which was to have extensive repercussions. Two Rangers players were sent off and there was a heated exchange between Neil Lennon and the Rangers manager, Ally McCoist, at the end of the game. The two Rangers players received only fines in spite of the referee having been manhandled. McCoist was also fined but Lennon was given a four-game ban from the dugout, a decision which Paul McBride QC, who represented him, described as having made 'a laughing stock' of the SFA. It also strengthened the belief that Celtic were not getting a fair crack of the whip from either referees or the football authorities – scarcely a new complaint.

These concerns were reinforced by an episode at Tannadice on October 17 2010 when Celtic were awarded a penalty but the referee, Dougie McDonald, then rescinded his decision – blaming, inaccurately as it turned out, the advice of a linesman who then resigned as an official. The fall-out from this incident and other criticism levelled at the refereeing fraternity led them to engage in an unprecedented strike on the last weekend of November. The SPL brought in foreign referees and Celtic's game was handled by officials from Luxembourg. Celtic's case for integrity and transparency was forcefully argued by John Reid, whose political background had bequeathed a willingness to take on difficult issues which had often been swept under the carpet in the past. As media pressure grew, McDonald retired from refereeing and the influential referees' supervisor, Hugh Dallas, left soon afterwards. The SFA later agreed to reforms aimed at achieving higher refereeing standards and greater independence in the assessment process.

More sinister events were to follow. In April 2011, two 'viable' parcel bombs sent to Lennon's home address were intercepted as part of a wider campaign against prominent Celtic-supporting figures. The culprits were subsequently apprehended and jailed but the immediate effect was to create another diversion of a thoroughly unpleasant nature.

The month of May was full of drama. Celtic beat Dundee United 4-1 but then went down 3-2 at Inverness to hand the title initiative back to Rangers. Two victories over Kilmarnock and Hearts renewed the pressure but the midweek fixture at Tynecastle was notable for another shocking incident when a Hearts fan attempted to assault Lennon on the touch-line, an incident captured by the TV cameras. Extraordinarily, an Edinburgh jury subsequently found the charge against the man 'not proven'. The title race went to the last day of the season but Rangers needed only to win at Kilmarnock, which they duly did while Celtic beat Motherwell 4-0 on a day of almost perverse celebration and demonstration of support for Lennon who made his position clear at the end of the game. He was not going to be driven out of Scottish football or indeed society. 'This isn't the end, this is just the beginning,' he told the supporters to acclaim. Just to confirm the point, Celtic rounded off a tumultuous season by winning the Scottish Cup with goals from Ki Sung Yueng, Mulgrew and an own-goal against Motherwell. The team that day was: Forster, M. Wilson, Majstorovic, Loovens, Izaguirre, Commons (Forrest), Brown, Ki, Mulgrew, Samaras (Stokes), Hooper (McCourt).

In preparation for season 2011/12, Celtic made another of their shrewdest buys when they paid £900,000 to the Belgian club Beerschott for the powerful Kenyan midfielder Victor Wanyama, while Mo Bangura was acquired from the Swedish club AIK. Defenders Kelvin Wilson from Nottingham Forest and Adam Matthews from Cardiff City were also recruited while Shaun Maloney departed for Wigan Athletic. Celtic were soon involved in a bizarre controversy when they survived into the Europa League group stages because the Swiss side FC Sion were disqualified for fielding ineligible players after beating Celtic 3-1 on aggregate. Celtic inherited a place in Sion's group which also included Atletico Madrid, Udinese and

Rennes. Celtic's away performances continued to undermine potential progress though in the last game of the series, a draw in Udinese was the portent of better things to come, though Celtic did not go through.

Domestically, the season was one of the most extraordinary in the annals of Scottish football. For many years, and with the exception only of the Martin O'Neill period, Celtic had been acutely aware of being outgunned in financial firepower by Rangers. Indeed the Rangers owner, David Murray, had made the notorious boast that 'for every five pounds Celtic spend, we will spend ten'. This had become a fact of life which had to be contended with, though it was never quite clear where the ten pounds was coming from. The whole question of Rangers' finances, their borrowings and relationship with the tax authorities started to unravel following the banking crisis of 2008 which led to the takeover of the Bank of Scotland by Lloyds and an entirely different approach to lending and borrowing.

It is not the role of this book to describe in detail the remarkable events which transpired at Ibrox in this period. Suffice to say that Rangers, under pressure from both the Bank and from Her Majesty's Revenue and Customs, first went into administration on February 14, 2012 and then liquidation when no deal could be made with the creditors on June 14, 2012. The immediate impact of administration was to cost them a ten-point penalty in accordance with the SFA rules but the ramifications went much further than that. Following liquidation, the assets of the former company were sold to a new entity called Sevco Scotland Ltd which sought and obtained a transfer of Rangers' SFA membership. The club thus became eligible to play in the lowest tier of the Scottish Football League and on July 31 changed its name to The Rangers Football Club Ltd. For several seasons to come there would be no top-flight Scottish league games in which they were involved.

Celtic maintained a dignified silence throughout the period of these events, allowing the proper authorities, both inside and outside football, to pursue their responsibilities. When pressed to talk about the affairs of Rangers, Chief Executive Peter Lawwell replied succinctly: 'I don't want to talk about other clubs. We are not defined by other clubs. We have our own brand, our own values and our own traditions'. Asked if he 'pined' for the Rangers fixture, he replied: 'You miss the pros and not the cons so it balances itself out, but you definitely wouldn't swap it for the Champions League.'

At the point of Rangers entering administration, Celtic were already four points ahead in the league race, having at one stage been fifteen points behind. A winning run of seventeen games turned the positions around, with Celtic going top of the league against Rangers in December after winning the derby at Celtic Park 1-0 thanks to a Joe Ledley goal. The title could have been secured at Ibrox on March 25 but this turned into a 3-2 defeat and another unpleasant event with Cha and Wanyama sent off while Neil Lennon was also red-carded for his protests against the referee's performance. Celtic eventually got across the line at Rugby Park with a 6-0 victory over Kilmarnock for Lennon's first title. It had been a ragged season overshadowed by off-field events, refereeing controversies and disciplinary incidents. Celtic lost the chance of a league and cup double when they went down 2-1 to Hearts in the Scottish Cup semi-final, another game riddled with refereeing inconsistencies with Lennon's protests again leading to a touchline ban. It was clear by this stage that, whatever the injustices that may have been suffered, a disciplined response was essential.

The best news of the 2012 close season was that the transfer of Fraser Forster, hitherto on loan from Newcastle United, had been secured for £2million. In the absence of Rangers, Celtic started the campaign as clear favourites for another title. The first game at home to Aberdeen was won 1-0 after the league flag was unfurled by one of the true legends of Celtic history, the Iron Man from Sligo, Sean Fallon, by then 90-years-old. Sean sadly passed away on January 18, 2013. Celtic's league form was erratic with much of the focus for both players and supporters on the European campaign. Two rounds of qualifying were required and Celtic had the toughest available draws at these stages – first against HJK Helsinki of Finland, who were already halfway through their season. Celtic won the home leg by the perilous margin of 2-1 through goals from Hooper and Mulgrew. Apprehension about a trip to Finland as early as August 8 to play on an artificial pitch proved groundless with goals from Ledley and Samaras relieving the tension. The next tough draw was against Henrik Larsson's old club, Helsingborgs, with the first leg in Sweden. Celtic took an early lead through Commons and then had Forster to thank for great saves which protected the advantage until Samaras completed a 2-0 win. At Celtic Park, Hooper and Wanyama completed the task and Celtic had navigated a tough route into the group stages where they were drawn against Barcelona, Benfica and Spartak Moscow.

However, the group stages demonstrated not only the quality of players who had been assembled but also the rapidly developing maturity of Neil Lennon's coaching expertise. The way in which he set out his team against each opponent became increasingly impressive as unpredicted points started to accumulate. A goal-less draw at home to Benfica was no more than adequate. The next game was sensational – an away victory in Moscow. Celtic took the lead early after great work from Wanyama, a superb cross from Lustig and an efficient finish by Hooper. Spartak replied with two goals before Celtic equalised through a deflected shot from Forrest. Then in the dying seconds, Izaguirre crossed for Samaras, at his very best, to head into the net. This meant three European away wins in a row, including a first group-stage victory. The jinx had been well and truly overcome.

The best was yet to come. At the Nou Camp, Celtic came agonisingly close to taking a point from a game that they contested superbly at a tactical level. They took a first-half lead from a Samaras header but conceded an equaliser close to half-time. Forster was outstanding in the second-half and a great result was beckoning when, with over ninety-three minutes played, Jordi Alba ghosted behind the Celtic defence to score. In the week of the club's 125th anniversary, Barcelona came to Celtic Park. Their officials joined in the celebratory service held in St Mary's Church, the parish where Celtic were born, the night before the game, reinforcing the bond of mutual respect between the two clubs – each of which laid claim to being 'more than just a club'. It was one of the greatest nights at Celtic Park. Once again, Barcelona had the majority of the play but Celtic were brilliantly organised to counter them. After 21 minutes, Mulgrew took a corner from which Wanyama scored. Time after time, Barcelona tried to thread their way through the resolute Celtic defence and failed. Then, in the 83rd minute, Celtic Park went into sheer delirium. A long kick from Fraser Forster was missed by Xavi and latched on to by Tony Watt who was just off the bench. With extraordinary calm, he dispatched the ball past the onrushing Victor Valdes. A youngster who had cost £100,000 from Airdrie had put Celtic 2-0 up against Barcelona. Lionel Messi scored a late goal and the last minutes were agonising in their intensity, but, to coincide with this landmark in the history of the club, Celtic held on to win 2-1.

There was temporary anti-climax when Celtic lost 2-1 to Benfica in Lisbon so that Neil Lennon's side needed to better the Portuguese side's result in the last round of games on December 5, 2012. On a freezing night at Celtic Park, the tension was unbearable as the home side took the lead against Spartak through Hooper in the 21st minute before the Russians equalised on 38 minutes. At the Camp Nou, Benfica were holding Barcelona to a goal-less draw. If it had stayed like that, Benfica would go through. With ten minutes remaining, Celtic were awarded a penalty when Samaras was brought down and Kris Commons stepped up – wrongly believing that Barcelona had taken the lead. In truth, a place in the last 16 depended on his effort. Commons lashed the ball into the net, and Celtic had not only qualified but had amassed 10 points for the first time in the group stages. It was a massive personal triumph for Neil Lennon as a coach as well as for his team. He said:

*'The players have performed a miracle. Nobody gave us a prayer in this group but we qualified and deservedly so. This means the world to me.'*

Disappointingly, the miracle could not be sustained. Celtic were drawn next against Juventus. Efe Ambrose, who had returned only that day from the Africa Cup of Nations where he had helped Nigeria win the tournament, made a couple of critical errors and Celtic lost 3-0 at Celtic Park. On a lashing wet night in Turin, the Celtic fans conjured up a classic display of support in the face of adversity and were given a standing ovation by the Juve fans, but the team lost 2-0 and a great adventure was over. At home, the opposition had gradually fallen away in spite of Celtic's mixed form and the title was won by sixteen points from Motherwell. In the Scottish Cup, an Anthony Stokes header in extra-time gave Celtic a 4-3 victory in a hard-fought and thrilling semi-final against Dundee United. The opponents in the final were Hibernian who failed to rise to the occasion and lost 3-0 to two first-half goals from Hooper and a late one from Ledley. Celtic had secured the double and the

Celtic team that day was: Forster, Izaguirre, Wilson, Mulgrew, Lustig, Brown (Ambrose), Commons (Samaras), Ledley, Forrest (McCourt), Stokes, Hooper.

In the close season, Celtic sold Victor Wanyama to Southampton for £12million and Gary Hooper to Norwich for £5.2million while Kelvin Wilson returned south to Nottingham Forest. For the supporters, it was disappointing to lose such key players, particularly with early UEFA Champions League ties beckoning. But this was now the established model to which Celtic must adhere, realising the value of players while they were within contract and then re-investing in the next group of players. The cycle depends on fresh young talent coming up through the clubs's Youth Academy or being bought at modest cost in the transfer market. Dermot Desmond defines the wider philosophy within which this approach is set:

> *'Our objective is to apply intellectual capital above financial capital. If we do everything to a uniform standard of excellence – our training facilities, our scouting, our sports science, our marketing, our brand development – then we can compete successfully at all levels. For everybody involved, it is a passion. We have a responsibility to ensure that what we do is in the best short, medium and long-term interests of the club.'*

The new recruits in the summer of 2013 included Virgil van Dijk from FC Groningen who immediately formed an impressive partnership with Efe Ambrose in the centre of defence, Amido Balde, a tall striker from Vitoria Guamaraes and the Finnish internationalist Teemu Pukki. Celtic were in even earlier action for the 2013/14 UEFA Champions League, again due to the capricious impact of the Scottish co-efficient which was repeatedly dragged down by the failure of other clubs to advance past the earliest stages in Europe. The heady nights of Barcelona and Spartak Moscow seemed but distant memories as Celtic navigated a course past Irish side, Cliftonville (5-0 aggregate), the problematic Elfsborg of Sweden (a solitary home goal) and then Shakhter Karagandy of Kazakhstan, who were bidding to become the first club from their country to qualify for the group stages of a European competition.

The game was transferred from the club's home ground in a small mining town to the national stadium in the capital, Astanya. A capacity crowd, which included the country's President, gave Shakhter tremendous encouragement and they responded with a 2-0 victory, a goal coming in each half, which left Celtic's hopes of qualification hanging by a thread. The Kazakhs came to Glasgow in a mood of great confidence but on yet another memorable European evening, it was Celtic who went through. Kris Commons scored on the stroke of half-time, Samaras brought things level three minutes into the second half and then, just as it looked as if the game was heading for a tense period of extra-time, James Forrest struck in added time, driving home a Stokes pass for a truly golden goal. It was fitting that a player reared within Celtic's Youth Academy had delivered the great prize of cutting-edge European football to the club and its supporters for another season.

Uniquely, the draw for the group stages brought together four former winners of the highest honour in European club football – Ajax, Barcelona, Celtic and AC Milan. Neil Lennon reflected:

*'First, it is a privilege. Sometimes you have to take a wee moment to yourself and realise what you are doing – the magnitude of the job, the pride in what you are doing. You want to put out a team that gives the supporters pride. I think that is very, very important. This club craves to compete at the highest level and I know that Champions League football means everything to everyone involved at the club.'*

Unfortunately, while the achievement in once again qualifying was substantial, the group stages proved to be an anti-climax. The draw could hardly have been tougher with Celtic pitted against AC Milan, Ajax and Barcelona. A 2-1 home win against Ajax secured the only three points although the margins of error were fine. In the opening encounter at the San Siro Stadium, Celtic held their own for more than 80 minutes before conceding two goals. Then, at home to Barcelona, a solitary goal by Cesc Fabregas in the 76th minute separated the teams. Hopes were raised when goals from Forrest and Kayal secured the 2-1 home win over Ajax but the return game ended in a disappointing single goal defeat. With qualification beyond them, Celtic slumped to a 3-0 home defeat to AC Milan before a 6-1 drubbing at the Nou Camp emphasised the distance still to be travelled to reach the highest echelons of European competition.

The domestic season brought mixed fortunes. Early exits from the League Cup and Scottish Cup, at the hands of Morton and Aberdeen respectively, were offset by a strong league performance that saw the title won by a margin of 29 points. In the January transfer window, Lennon made two important signings, Leigh Griffiths from Hibs and the midfielder Stefan Johansen from Strømsgodset in his native Norway, while Joe Ledley was transferred to Crystal Palace. The mighty goalkeeper, Fraser Forster, broke the club record set by Charlie Shaw in 1921-22 of ten clean sheets in a row and his run eventually ended after 1256 minutes of football when Celtic sustained their first league defeat of the season against Aberdeen in late February. When Celtic clinched the title with a 5-1 win at Firhill, it was the earliest conclusion to a League campaign since season 1928-29.

Neil Lennon's four seasons as manager had been successful by any reasonable standard. They had embraced three successive league titles and two Scottish Cup wins. He had twice led Celtic into the group stages of the Champions League and once into the last 16. Several of the players he signed proved to be of outstanding value to the club. In other respects, however, it had been a challenging time for a manager who, within the Scottish goldfish bowl, attracted devotion and hostility in equal measure and whose passion for the game and the club he loved regularly brought him into conflict with over-eager authority. At the end of the season, Neil decided that it was time for a break from these pressures and stood down as manager, noting that the club was in 'a very strong position' and wishing it well for the future. Neil Lennon would remain a highly regarded figure within the Celtic family which he had served so well as player, captain and manager.

# TWENTY-NINE

## THE 'RONNY ROAR'
## AND TWO MORE TITLES

WITH NEIL LENNON'S departure, the club faced the search for a new manager with little time to spare before the next European campaign began. The options were limited and, with the transfer market spiraling upwards on the back of vastly increased television fees to English Premiership clubs, the imperative of developing talent from within the club became even stronger. This brought into consideration the name of Ronny Deila, then manager of the Norwegian club Strømsgodset which had just won its first league title in 43 years, with an attacking brand of football and a strong emphasis on physical fitness. Deila, whom Celtic had first encountered during the Stefan Johansen transfer negotiations, was attracting respect as a coach well beyond Norway and had visited clubs like Manchester City and Barcelona to study their methods. His name had been linked with several clubs before Celtic's interest arose.

Peter Lawwell explains:

*'Ronny had become a successful manager in Norway by developing young players and creating a team which, on paper, should not have had any chance of winning the*

*Norwegian league. Our contacts at Manchester City had raised his name as an outstanding developer of young players, whom they were tracking. We interviewed him, initially as a potential number two, and were very impressed. Having gone through other options, we decided to back our own judgment and bring him in as number one. In an environment where transfer fees were escalating so rapidly, we needed to shift the emphasis even more strongly towards bringing through our own players and Ronny fitted that model. We also felt that we had a little time with Rangers still out of the league.'*

Celtic were aware of the potential loss of their outstanding goalkeeper, Fraser Forster, who wanted to return to an English Premiership club and strengthen his claims to an England international role. With uncanny timing, a solution of great lasting value presented itself in the shape of Craig Gordon. A Scottish internationalist with Hearts, Gordon had transferred to Sunderland in 2007 for £9 million – at that time the largest fee ever paid for a goalkeeper by a British club. However, his time there was plagued with injuries which regularly limited his availability. In May 2012, Sunderland did not renew his contract. Gordon was then without a club for two years while undertaking cutting-edge medical treatment in an effort to regain full fitness. He considered a coaching role and drawing a line under his playing career, but Celtic's goalkeeping coach, Steve Woods, had maintained close contact and persuaded him to start training at Celtic Park, initially as a potential understudy to Forster. In July 2014, Gordon signed for Celtic and made his debut in a pre-season game against Dresden, creating an immediate impression. As confidence grew in his fitness, he became the natural successor to Forster who, after taking part in the early European rounds, was transferred to Southampton on August 8 for £10 million.

The start of the 2014-15 season brought not only a new manager, who was joined by John Collins as his deputy, but also a temporary home. With Celtic Park due to be used for the opening ceremony of the Commonwealth Games, early fixtures were transferred to Murrayfield Stadium in Edinburgh. While the lasting benefits to the club were enormous, since the Commonwealth Games role triggered a transformation of the environment around Celtic Park, the immediate effects of the disruption were less easy to measure in footballing terms. The campaign started well enough with a 5-0 aggregate win over KR Reykjavik of Iceland. However, the next tie exposed defensive vulnerabilities in Deila's preferred style of attacking play. Celtic were drawn against Legia Warsaw and suffered a 4-1 thrashing in Poland before going down by two goals at Murrayfield. At this point, an alert UEFA official noticed that Legia had an ineligible player on the substitutes' bench, who had come on for the last few minutes in Edinburgh. Celtic played absolutely no part in the process that followed which resulted in the club being awarded a 3-0 'victory' and hence progress to the play-off stage on the away goals rule. There was no enthusiasm within Celtic for progressing in this way but it certainly opened up a golden opportunity when the draw produced Maribor of Slovenia as opponents in the play-off round. The first leg ended in a 1-1 away draw, apparently setting the scene for entry into the group stages. However, on a dismal night at Celtic Park, an inept performance culminated in a goal for Maribor in the 75th minute and Celtic had squandered the unexpected opportunity thrown up by the Legia Warsaw affair.

Though the Europa League place was no more than Celtic deserved, the group stages did at least provide some early encouragement. Home wins against Dinamo Zagreb and Astra Girgiu of Romania, plus two away draws, were enough to see Celtic through to the last 32 where Inter Milan provided the opposition. Extending a European run into the New Year is always an aspiration of the supporters and there was a full Celtic Park for the visit of Inter Milan on February 19. They were rewarded with a pulsating game in which Celtic recovered from the loss of two early goals before needing a spectacular stoppage time equaliser from John Guidetti to level the tie at 3-3. In the return, a week later at the San Siro stadium, Celtic played most of the game with ten men due to Virgil Van Dyjk being sent off for two yellow cards. Nonetheless, the defence held out until the 88th minute before a single goal ended Celtic's interest in the competition. This moderate European run had progressed in parallel with an uncertain League record and growing doubts among the support about Ronny Deila's strategy. However, he became proactive in meeting supporters' groups, explaining what he was trying to do at Celtic Park and generally buying himself some time in which to turn his plans into a more convincing style and consistency on the park. As his confidence grew and results became more reliable, Ronny's air-punches to supporters after the home games were reciprocated with the 'Ronny Roar'. For a time, it looked as if Celtic's bold experiment in bringing in a young, relatively inexperienced and personally well-liked coach just might succeed.

Jason Denayer, a young Belgian internationalist, had come in on loan from Manchester City in August to form a strong centre-back pairing with Van Dijk. Flanked with great consistency by Lustig and Izaguirre, they settled into a formidable back four. Johansen found top form which would win him Scottish Player of the Year honours. In all, Celtic appeared close to building a fine, settled side with several outstanding performers. The key moment in the SPL campaign came on November 9, when Celtic went to the top through a 2-1 victory over Aberdeen at Pittodrie in front of a capacity crowd. Having gone behind in the first half to an Adam Rooney goal, Celtic quickly equalised through Johansen. With eight minutes left, Scott Brown was sent off for a second yellow card but just as it seemed the advantage had swung towards the home side, Virgil Van Dijk scored from a Johansen corner to bring relief to the Celtic support and set the club on what was, thereafter, a more assured progress towards the league title which was eventually won by 17 points from Aberdeen.

In the League Cup, victories over Hearts and Partick Thistle led Celtic to a semi-final tie against Rangers, by now in the Championship having, post-liquidation, not been accepted back into the SPFL. When the teams lined up at Hampden on February 1, it was the first time they had met in almost three years and the old rivalries were undimmed. On the park, however, the gulf which separated the sides was apparent and the 2-0 margin, secured through first-half goals from Griffiths and Commons, scarcely did justice to it. This opened the way for a final against Dundee United which was again won comfortably by a 2-0 margin with goals from Commons and Forrest to give Ronny Deila his first Scottish trophy.

This success encouraged speculation that Deila might, for all the early doubts, be leading Celtic towards a treble in his first season as manager. The Scottish Cup had brought away victories over Hearts and Dundee. Then Leigh Griffiths kept Celtic in the competition at Tannadice with an equaliser against Dundee United, before Celtic won the replay 4-0. The weeks running up to Celtic's semi-final with Inverness Caledonian Thistle on April 19 were full of treble speculation and everything seemed to be on course when Virgil van Dijk secured an early lead. Then, however, things started to go wrong with one of the most controversial pieces of refereeing in the recent annals of Scottish football. A Leigh Griffiths shot was heading for the net when an Inverness defender clearly stopped it with his hand. The awarding of a penalty and sending-off seemed inevitable but to the astonishment of everyone in Hampden, referee Steven McLean waved play on. This incident changed the pattern of the game and it was Celtic who were reduced to ten men ten minutes into the second half when Craig Gordon was sent off for bringing down an opponent inside the box. Celtic's ten men held on until three minutes from the end of extra time when David Raven's winner gave the Highland team its place in the final. There was a real feeling that the hand-ball incident had changed not only the course of the game but also the destination of the Scottish Cup and hence the rare chance of a treble, which would have done no harm to Ronny Deila's standing as a Celtic manager. As it was, his first season in charge had been, on balance, reasonably satisfactory – two out of three domestic trophies and an honourable exit form Europe, albeit after a disastrous start. There were grounds for optimism about the season to follow.

However, that sentiment was soon heavily qualified by results. As was now inevitable, Celtic faced three Champions League qualifying rounds to reach the group stages, facing tough tasks before the domestic season had even begun. Stjarnan of Iceland were overcome on a 6-1 aggregate. The first game at Celtic Park was notable for the scoring debut of Derdryck Boyata in the centre of defence, replacing Denayer whose loan spell had ended. There was then an arduous assignment against Qarabag of Azerbeijan. Another headed goal from Boyata in the 82nd minute at Celtic Park created an uncomfortably narrow advantage to carry to Baku, leaving no illusions about the resourcefulness of the opposition. On a tense evening in the Tofiq Bahramov Stadium, Celtic played with great fortitude to secure a no-scoring draw and hence entry into the play-off round, where they were drawn against Malmö of Sweden. Once again, the prospects for Group Stage qualification, with all its implications both for supporter interest and club resources, looked good but, once again, they ended in anti-climax. After ten minutes of the first leg at Celtic Park, goals from Griffiths and Bitton sent the crowd into raptures of anticipation. Early in the second half, Malmö pulled one back but Griffiths quickly scored again. A 3-1 lead to take to Sweden might have sufficed but with the last kick of stoppage time, Malmö scored again and the advantage – both tactical and psychological – moved in their favour. Something approaching fatalism set in and a week later, on a thoroughly miserable night in Malmö, Celtic went down 2-0. It might have been different if a perfectly good goal by Nir Bitton just before half time had been allowed to stand by the Serbian referee but the general opinion was that excuses would not suffice – on this form, Celtic were well short of the European elite status to which they aspired.

The departure of the majestic Virgil Van Dijk had been anticipated once Celtic were out the Champions League and he signed for Southampton, bringing the club a £13 million fee. With Denayer also gone and several of the previous season's star performers – notably Stefan Johansen – failing to rise to the same heights, there was a distinct feeling of unease around the club and among the supporters. Neither, this time, did the Europa League bring any consolation. Two draws – Ajax away and Fenerbahçe at home – were followed by three straight defeats, two of them at the hands of a Norwegian club, Molde, who finished top of the group. Celtic were effectively out of Europe by October and failed to win a game in their section. Neither did the domestic season provide much inspiration. While Celtic's progress to a fifth consecutive SPL title was never in doubt, hopes of anything more memorable ended when Ross County knocked them out of the League Cup at the semi-final stage. By this time, discontent with the style of play and lack of excitement at Celtic Park was having a marked impact on attendances and the 'Ronny Roar' was a thing of the past. The players, who had been generally supportive of Deila in his first season, were unconvinced by changes to the backroom team and apparent loss of direction, particularly on fitness-related issues which had been among the manager's proclaimed strong suits when he arrived.

On April 17, Celtic faced Rangers, still a Championship side, in the Scottish Cup semi-final at Hampden. Rangers went ahead through Miller and Erik Sviatchenko, the Danish defender, signed from FC Midtjylland in the January transfer window, equalised. In spite of intense pressure, Celtic could not find a winner and the game went into extra time. McKay again put Rangers ahead before Tom Rogic brought the game level once more and Leigh Griffiths came agonisingly close to clinching it in the final minute. The penalty shoot-out proved the undoing of Celtic with three misses from the first seven efforts which were enough to put Rangers through to the final. However, the real damage had been done long before then with a Celtic team which – in this of all sporting theatres – did not look fit enough or good enough to satisfy expectations or justify the investments that had been made.

Peter Lawwell said:

*'In the first season, everyone was delighted with Ronny's progress and he was very unfortunate not to win the treble. Then he was unlucky to lose Van Dijk and Denayer. After Malmö, he was under immediate pressure and he really felt it. We were winning in the league but not in the style that the supporters expected and then the Rangers semi-final was a turning point. We realised, and Ronny realised, that it wasn't going to happen. The appropriate way to proceed was for him to take his team to a second championship and leave Celtic*

*on the best of terms. That is the way it worked.'*

For his part, Ronny Deila retains a great respect for the club and takes pride both in his league titles and the players he signed – including Craig Gordon and Stuart Armstrong – as well as those he brought through from the youth set-up, notably Kieran Tierney and Callum McGregor. Two years after the Inverness cup semi-final, he was asked if he would still be Celtic manager if his team had won that treble. He replied: 'Yes, I think so.' Such are the thin lines of football. There were, however, aspects of his time in Glasgow that he does not miss: 'The worst of it was that every time you went out your door, people knew who you were and you could not get peace anywhere.' That is definitely not the Norwegian style and ultimately it helped convince Ronny that it was the right time to part, while maintaining a lasting respect and affection for the club, which was widely reciprocated.

# THIRTY

## BRENDAN RODGERS, 'THE INVINCIBLES' – AND REMEMBERING LISBON

THE CELTIC BOARD had taken a calculated risk with the appointment of Ronny Deila, a young and relatively inexperienced coach with a growing reputation who might have been the man to lead a significant cultural change and bring through young talent. Some of that had worked and some had not. After two seasons of disappointment in Europe and the inevitability of a stronger domestic challenge, it was essential to de-risk the next managerial appointment, insofar as that is ever possible in football. Several experienced figures were available but one name stood out. Once lines of communication to Brendan Rodgers were opened up, shortly after the Scottish Cup semi-final, a consensus quickly developed that he offered the best possible option and was truly capable of raising the game at Celtic Park. A preliminary discussion with Peter Lawwell established that Brendan was interested and the broad terms on which he was prepared to take the job. Events moved quickly.

This was followed by an interview which involved Dermot Desmond, the principal shareholder. Dermot recalls:

*'We had a shortlist when Peter and I interviewed Brendan*

*but it became very clear that he was the obvious person for the job – on account of his experience with Liverpool, Swansea, Reading, Chelsea but also because of his background. He understood the whole Celtic culture. He wanted to create a footballing experience in the Celtic tradition, playing attacking football. He didn't want to buy teams; he would make teams. At the end of the interview, both Peter and I knew this was the man for us; we'd got to put our best foot forward to get him, and that's what we did. He would bring value to the club by making us competitive at a different level – which he has undoubtedly done'.*

The news that Brendan was to become Celtic manager was confirmed on May 20 2016. Peter Lawwell spoke for all at Celtic Park when he said: 'We wanted to bring one of the biggest and best names to the Club to match our own aspirations and those of our supporters. We believe that, in appointing Brendan, we have done that.' The positive response from the supporters was overwhelming. Three days later, he gave his first media conference at Celtic Park and appeared on the pitch before 13,000 supporters who had turned out on a summer's evening. Many of his family, from Carnlough in County Antrim, were with him. As would become his hallmark, Brendan struck exactly the right note in his words to supporters: 'My first game was in 1984, a friendly between Celtic and Finn Harps. From that, I've been in the Celtic family. I understand the values of this club, the expectations and the pressures here because it's not just about winning; it's about winning with style and identity.'

It was a first encounter that instantly solidified the bond between manager, club and supporters, as members of one Celtic family.

When he first met the board, Brendan presented a weighty

document entitled 'One Vision, One Club' which defined his philosophy of the game and the objectives which informed it. This was also the 'bible' from which the coaches would operate, throughout the club. Apart from the fundamentals of his approach to how his teams should play and the technical means of implementation, the document embraced the need for players to 'feel the need to defend the club's history and culture'. It all read like a masterclass in a rational, intelligent approach to football and, as the months unfolded, it acted as a reliable reference point to what was happening on the field of play. Every manager comes with his own style and talents but it was clear that in terms of thoroughness, thoughtfulness and consistency of focus, Brendan Rodgers was about to bring something exceptional to Celtic Park – the 'different level' which supporters now anticipated.

The players too were, in the main, immediately enthused. Scott Brown met Brendan in London:

*'He asked me how long I could play at the top level and I said two years. I wasn't as fit as I had been in the previous five or six seasons. He said it was a fresh start for everyone and that is exactly how it worked out. Everyone is in much better shape. The way we play is the way I love playing football – attacking, closing people down, pressing up the park.'*

It was quickly evident that Brendan was prepared to give every player on the books a chance, including those who had moved to the fringes or suffered loss of form in the previous season. If they could conform to his standards and fit in with his plans, they stayed. Others were phased out. This process started at a notably successful training camp in Slovenia where the mutual respect and understanding between players and manager was confirmed. Brendan had brought in Chris Davies, who had worked with him at Swansea and Liverpool, as his assistant. Glen Driscoll, another long-term associate, became head of performance while John Kennedy and Stevie Woods remained within the backroom team.

There could have been no more unlikely venue for Rodgers' first game as manager. The team travelled straight from Slovenia to Gibraltar for the first of the Champions League qualifiers against Lincoln Red Imps. At one end of the pitch sat the Rock of Gibraltar and at the other a runway with passenger jets taking off and landing. In between was an artificial surface of primitive standards. It proved to be the setting for a surprise outcome with Celtic losing to a single goal. A week later, as expected, this was overturned by a 3-0 victory at Celtic Park. The process of change was underway. Of those who took part in the Gibraltar defeat, Ambrose, Ciftci and, subsequently, Janko would not be part of future plans. Rodgers' first signing was Moussa Dembele, a 19 year-old French-born striker, who came in from Fulham in late June. Stefan Johansen did not feature in early games and was soon on his way to Fulham; Kris Commons later went on loan to Hibs. On July 25, Rodgers brought in Kolo Toure, who had played for him at Liverpool and was now 35, to add defensive experience as further European ties loomed. The next qualifying round pitted Celtic against Astana of Kazakhstan – tough opponents and a very long journey.

The first leg was played in the Kazakh capital and Celtic fell behind to a first-half goal. However, an equaliser from Leigh Griffiths with 12 minutes remaining made for an optimistic flight home. In Glasgow, the tie swung towards Celtic as Griffiths scored from the penalty spot on the stroke of half-time. Astana equalized after Craig Gordon attempted a headed clearance. The game seemed to be heading for extra-time when Dembele, who had come on as substitute, was tripped inside the box and, with virtually the last action of the game, stepped up to put Celtic through in dramatic fashion. Amidst the relief, Brendan Rodgers also had a word of caution for the Celtic support who had sometimes shown impatience in this roller-coaster of a game: 'Instead of having that edginess, trust the players, trust our game model and as we saw here, eventually we can get there.' It was advice that was soon seen to be eminently reasonable, as patience became a hallmark of the Celtic style.

The play-off round brought a trip into the relatively unknown when Celtic were drawn against the Israeli champions, Hapoel Beersheba. At Celtic Park, on a night of high drama, the team raced to a three goal half-time lead with Rogic scoring first followed by two from Griffiths. By the hour mark, however, the scoreline was back to 3-2 and 'shades of Malmö' was the thought. Indeed, Leigh Griffiths voiced it afterwards when he said: 'I think last year we would've crumbled . . . I'm sure the boys who were here then were thinking that. But the manager has instilled in us an attitude to keep going and it's made a massive difference.' This time Celtic reasserted themselves with goals from Dembele and Brown to take a 5-2 lead to Israel. Even then, it proved to be a tight squeeze into the group stages. By the 48th minute, Celtic were two down and had also survived a missed penalty. The remainder of the game was an exercise in desperate defending, with a back four of Janko, Lustig, Toure and Tierney. Amidst almost unbearable tension, Celtic held on. According to the *Jerusalem Post*, 'Beersheba's usually stoic coach, Barak Bakhar, had to cut short his post-match interview after failing to control his emotions' while Brendan Rodgers described it as 'my longest 90 minutes as a manager'. Unusually, Celtic did not fly home until the following day so there was time to celebrate and reflect on the first landmark in Brendan's time at Celtic Park – qualification for the Champions League group stages. There had also been confirmation of the lesson, that clearing these hurdles in the months of July and August will always be a fraught challenge.

Meanwhile, the domestic season started well with SPL wins over Hearts, St Johnstone and – by a clear 4-1 margin – Aberdeen. Just in time for the opening game at Tynecastle, and then for the Hapoel Beersheba ties, Celtic signed Scott Sinclair from Aston Villa on a four year contract. This was to prove a hugely influential signing of a fast, elegant and incisive player who would flourish in Scottish football. Sinclair had played under Rodgers at Swansea City and it was a prime example of how the manager's presence at Celtic Park was critical to bringing in high calibre players. Remarkably, Sinclair scored in each of his first six SPL outings. The fourth of these was against Rangers who had entered the top flight of Scottish football but proved to be no match for a rampant Celtic performance which yielded a 5-1 victory at Celtic Park, a game in which Moussa Dembele – signed for less than £300,000 – struck twice and demonstrated his enormous potential as a goal-scorer of the highest order.

With every game, Celtic's confidence and quality of performance developed further. The return of Boyata, Simunovic and Sviatchenko created stability in an area of the team which had been problematic in the early European ties. Patrick Roberts, a highly-skilled young winger who was on loan from Manchester City, began to flourish. Already Celtic's domestic dominance was beyond doubt but September 13 2016 brought a sharp reality check in the larger theatre of Europe. Celtic were drawn in an exceptionally difficult group alongside Barcelona, Manchester City and Borussia Mönchengladbach. Inevitably, it was part of the learning curve rather than offering much in the way of qualification prospects. Matchday one took Celtic to the Nou

Camp where Messi – who scored a hat-trick – Neymar and Suarez combined to devastating effect. Celtic lost 7-0, the club's biggest ever defeat in Europe. This was followed by a brave 3-3 draw with Manchester City on a truly great European night at Celtic Park, with Dembele scoring twice – the second of which, from a position with his back to the goal, will live long in the memory. After the excitement generated by this performance, the next home game proved an anti-climax with Celtic going down 2-0 to their German opponents. A 2-0 defeat by Barcelona at Celtic Park, with Messi scoring both goals, was sandwiched between two respectable away draws against Borussia Mönchengladbach and Manchester City. In the last of these games, Patrick Roberts was named Man of the Match against his parent club. The group stages had yielded only three points but also a vast amount of experience in competing at this level. Brendan Rodgers reflected: 'It was a huge learning experience, especially for the younger players. What we took encouragement from was the degree of improvement over the period of the group stages. An immense effort had gone into qualifying which was enormously important for the club and that also helped to create the platform for what was achieved in the remainder of the season.'

The home defeat to Barcelona formally ended Celtic's chances of progressing but four days later, on November 27, they secured the first trophy of the season with a 3-0 League Cup final victory over Aberdeen at Hampden. Celtic had beaten Motherwell, Alloa and Rangers – through another Dembele goal – on the way to the final. The team was Gordon, Lustig, Simunovic, Sviatchenko, Izaguirre; Brown, Rogic (McGregor); Roberts (Bitton), Armstrong, Forrest (Griffiths), Dembele. A great opening goal from Tom Rogic was followed by a classic James Forrest solo effort to give Celtic a two goal interval lead and Dembele added a third after Forrest, who was named Man of the Match, was brought down. Brendan Rodgers observed:

'It's something tangible to show for our efforts. Everyone has talked about the great start and the great football, but you want something to show for it. This was our first chance and I felt the players were magnificent.'

In the league, steady progress was maintained. By the end of the year, the only points dropped had been in an early draw at Inverness but it was not only the run of results that was thrilling the Celtic support but also the highly entertaining style of play. European commitments meant that Celtic had some catching up to do on fixtures and they played eight times in December, the last of these against Rangers at Ibrox on Hogmanay. Rangers took the lead through Miller in the 12th minute but this proved a false dawn for the home side. After 33 minutes, Dembele struck home from a perfectly-placed Sinclair corner. Midway through the second half, Patrick Roberts came on as substitute for Forrest and made an immediate contribution to what proved to be the winning goal with a perfect pass to Armstrong who squared the ball for Sinclair to finish the move. It was another masterclass in one of Brendan Rodgers' key themes – the need to stay calm after a set-back. For the Celtic support, it was also a great way to see out 2016.

Celtic took their winter break in Dubai, this time without any friendly fixtures; after an arduous six months of non-stop competition, the players needed a real break and rest. By now, two objectives were clear on the horizon – the elusive treble and the unprecedented achievement of going through the season undefeated in all domestic competitions. As the weeks went by, both moved closer to fulfillment. By early March, Celtic had eased through the first three stages in the Cup with wins over Albion Rovers, Inverness Caledonian Thistle and St Mirren. Progress in the league was also uninterrupted, though twice – against Motherwell and St Johnstone – Celtic had to come from behind. They were two goals down at half-time at Fir Park and it needed the kind of late goal in which Tom Rogic had come to specialize in to secure a 4-3 victory. In another thrilling game at McDiarmid Park, a Moussa Dembele hat-trick helped turn things round in what was in the end a 5-2 victory.

March 12 brought the second home league game against Rangers. Stuart Armstrong – one of the season's great success stories – put Celtic ahead after 35 minutes but Celtic failed to turn clear superiority into further goals and Hill snatched an equaliser for Rangers with three minutes remaining. The sixth SPL title in a row was confirmed on April 2 2017 with a devastating 5-0 victory over Hearts at Tynecastle, with Scott Sinclair – soon to be acclaimed as Scotland's Player of the Year by both his peers and the press – scoring a hat-trick.

The Scottish Cup semi-final pitted Celtic against Rangers in what would be their fifth meeting of the season, on April 23. By now the size of the stakes was unmistakable – not just a place in the final but also the massive prospects of a Celtic treble plus an unbeaten domestic season. To add to the Hampden scenario, Rangers had a new manager and also raised hopes after the recent draw at Celtic Park. However, Celtic dominated the game from start to finish. After 11 minutes, Moussa Dembele set up Callum McGregor to slot home a fine goal. Four minutes after half-time, Griffiths – who had substituted for the injured Dembele – was brought down inside the box and Sinclair converted the penalty. Thereafter, the outcome was beyond doubt and Celtic were on their way to the final against Aberdeen on May 27th. The following week, Celtic recorded their biggest ever score at Ibrox to again crush Rangers by the margin of 5-1. In the end, the league was won by 30 clear points with Aberdeen in second place.

Throughout the season, celebrations had been underway to mark the 50th anniversary of the Lisbon Lions becoming the first British club to win the European Cup. The 67th minute of every game was marked by the flashing of cellphone torch-lights and singing to match – *In the Heat of Lisbon* – from the Celtic support. All of the celebrations were due to come to a head in the week running up to the Cup Final. No producer of epics could have conceived of a more dramatic conclusion to an unforgettable, highly symbolic season. Now only one barrier stood in the way of only the fourth treble in the club's history and also an unbeaten, 47-game domestic record. On a wet but glorious day at Hampden, the Celtic team was: Gordon, Lustig, Simunovic, Boyata, Tierney (Rogic); Brown, Armstrong; Roberts (Sviatchenko), McGregor, Sinclair, Griffiths.

Aberdeen were in no mood to pave the way for history-makers, started on the offensive and took the lead after nine minutes through a fine strike from Jonny Hayes. Within two minutes, Celtic equalised with an equally good goal from Stuart Armstrong. The game remained finely balanced and full of incident. Kieran Tierney had to be substituted after falling victim to a flying elbow. Both sides made and missed chances in a Cup Final worthy of the occasion. Tension mounted as it moved into stoppage time. Could the deadlock be broken? Thirty-five yards out, Tom Rogic picked up a pass from Stuart Armstrong. He headed straight towards the penalty area, dragged the ball past two Aberdeen defenders and spotted his opportunity for a right foot shot between goalkeeper Lewis and the near post. Delirium! In the most dramatic possible style, the Celtic team of 2016-17, under Brendan Rodgers, had secured their place in history. They were The Invincibles.

# STATISTICAL APPENDICES

## THIS SECTION CONTAINS STATISTICS UP THE END OF THE 2016/17 SEASON

### HONOURS

SCOTTISH LEAGUE WINNERS (*48 Times*)
1892/93, 1893/94, 1895/96, 1897/98, 1904/05, 1905/06, 1906/07,
1907/08, 1908/09, 1909/10, 1913/14, 1914/15, 1915/16, 1916/17,
1918/19, 1921/22, 1925/26, 1935/36, 1937/38, 1953/54, 1965/66,
1966/67, 1967/68, 1968/69, 1969/70, 1970/71, 1971/72, 1972/73,
1973/74, 1976/77, 1978/79, 1980/81, 1981/82, 1985/86, 1987/88,
1997/98, 2000/01, 2001/02, 2003/04, 2005/06, 2006/07, 2007/08,
2011/12, 2012/13, 2013/14, 2014/15, 2015/16, 2016/17

SCOTTISH CUP WINNERS (*37 Times*)
1892, 1899, 1900, 1904, 1907, 1908, 1911, 1912, 1914, 1923, 1925,
1927, 1931, 1933, 1937, 1951, 1954, 1965, 1967, 1969, 1971, 1972,
1974, 1975, 1977, 1980, 1985, 1988, 1989, 1995, 2001, 2004, 2005,
2007, 2011, 2013, 2017

LEAGUE CUP WINNERS (*16 Times*)
1956/57, 1957/58, 1965/66, 1966/67, 1967/68, 1968/69, 1969/70,
1974/75, 1982/83, 1997/98, 1999/00, 2000/01, 2005/06, 2008/09,
2014/15, 2016/17

EUROPEAN CUP WINNERS 1967

EMPIRE EXHIBITION TROPHY 1938

CORONATION CUP WINNERS 1953

# RECORDS

RECORD ATTENDANCE
92,000 v Rangers, 1938

RECORD VICTORY
11-0 v Dundee, 1895

RECORD DEFEAT
0-8 v Motherwell, 1937

MOST LEAGUE GOALS IN ONE SEASON
50 – Jimmy McGrory, 1935/36

MOST PREMIER/SPFL GOALS IN ONE SEASON
35 – Brian McClair, 1986/87 and Henrik Larsson, 2000/01

# LEAGUE RECORD YEAR BY YEAR

| SEASON | P | W | D | L | F | A | GD | Pts | Pos |
|--------|---|---|---|---|---|---|----|----|-----|
| 1890/91 | 18 | 11 | 3 | 4 | 48 | 21 | 27 | 25 | *3 |
| 1891/92 | 22 | 16 | 3 | 3 | 62 | 21 | 41 | 35 | 2 |
| 1892/93 | 18 | 14 | 1 | 3 | 54 | 25 | 29 | 29 | 1 |
| 1893/94 | 18 | 14 | 1 | 3 | 53 | 32 | 21 | 29 | 1 |
| 1894/95 | 18 | 11 | 4 | 3 | 50 | 29 | 21 | 26 | 2 |
| 1895/96 | 18 | 15 | 0 | 3 | 64 | 25 | 39 | 30 | 1 |
| 1896/97 | 18 | 10 | 4 | 4 | 42 | 18 | 24 | 24 | 4 |
| 1897/98 | 18 | 15 | 3 | 0 | 56 | 13 | 43 | 33 | 1 |
| 1898/99 | 18 | 11 | 2 | 5 | 51 | 33 | 18 | 24 | 3 |
| 1899/00 | 18 | 9 | 7 | 2 | 46 | 27 | 19 | 25 | 2 |
| 1900/01 | 20 | 13 | 3 | 4 | 49 | 28 | 21 | 29 | 2 |
| 1901/02 | 18 | 11 | 4 | 3 | 38 | 28 | 10 | 26 | 2 |
| 1902/03 | 22 | 8 | 10 | 4 | 36 | 30 | 6 | 26 | 5 |
| 1903/04 | 26 | 18 | 2 | 6 | 69 | 28 | 41 | 38 | 3 |
| 1904/05 | 26 | 18 | 5 | 3 | 68 | 31 | 37 | 41 | 1 |
| 1905/06 | 30 | 24 | 1 | 5 | 76 | 19 | 57 | 49 | 1 |
| 1906/07 | 34 | 23 | 9 | 2 | 80 | 30 | 50 | 55 | 1 |
| 1907/08 | 34 | 24 | 7 | 3 | 86 | 27 | 59 | 55 | 1 |
| 1908/09 | 34 | 23 | 5 | 6 | 71 | 24 | 47 | 51 | 1 |
| 1909/10 | 34 | 24 | 6 | 4 | 63 | 22 | 41 | 54 | 1 |
| 1910/11 | 34 | 15 | 11 | 8 | 48 | 18 | 30 | 41 | 5 |
| 1911/12 | 34 | 17 | 11 | 6 | 58 | 33 | 25 | 45 | 2 |
| 1912/13 | 34 | 22 | 5 | 7 | 53 | 28 | 25 | 49 | 2 |
| 1913/14 | 38 | 30 | 5 | 3 | 81 | 14 | 67 | 65 | 1 |
| 1914/15 | 38 | 30 | 5 | 3 | 91 | 25 | 66 | 65 | 1 |
| 1915/16 | 38 | 32 | 3 | 3 | 116 | 23 | 93 | 67 | 1 |
| 1916/17 | 38 | 27 | 10 | 1 | 79 | 17 | 62 | 64 | 1 |
| 1917/18 | 34 | 24 | 7 | 3 | 66 | 26 | 40 | 55 | 2 |
| 1918/19 | 34 | 26 | 6 | 2 | 71 | 22 | 49 | 58 | 1 |
| 1919/20 | 42 | 29 | 10 | 3 | 89 | 31 | 58 | 68 | 2 |

| SEASON | P | W | D | L | F | A | GD | Pts | Pos |
|--------|---|---|---|---|---|---|----|----|-----|
| 1920/21 | 42 | 30 | 6 | 6 | 86 | 35 | 51 | 66 | 2 |
| 1921/22 | 42 | 27 | 13 | 2 | 83 | 20 | 63 | 67 | 1 |
| 1922/23 | 38 | 19 | 8 | 11 | 52 | 39 | 13 | 46 | 3 |
| 1923/24 | 38 | 17 | 12 | 9 | 56 | 33 | 23 | 46 | 3 |
| 1924/25 | 38 | 18 | 8 | 12 | 77 | 44 | 33 | 44 | 4 |
| 1925/26 | 38 | 25 | 8 | 5 | 97 | 40 | 57 | 58 | 1 |
| 1926/27 | 38 | 21 | 7 | 10 | 101 | 55 | 46 | 49 | 3 |
| 1927/28 | 38 | 23 | 9 | 6 | 93 | 39 | 54 | 55 | 2 |
| 1928/29 | 38 | 22 | 7 | 9 | 67 | 44 | 23 | 51 | 2 |
| 1929/30 | 38 | 22 | 5 | 11 | 88 | 46 | 42 | 49 | 4 |
| 1930/31 | 38 | 24 | 10 | 4 | 101 | 34 | 67 | 58 | 2 |
| 1931/32 | 38 | 20 | 8 | 10 | 94 | 50 | 44 | 48 | 3 |
| 1932/33 | 38 | 20 | 8 | 10 | 75 | 44 | 31 | 48 | 4 |
| 1933/34 | 38 | 18 | 11 | 9 | 78 | 53 | 25 | 47 | 3 |
| 1934/35 | 38 | 24 | 4 | 10 | 92 | 45 | 47 | 52 | 2 |
| 1935/36 | 38 | 32 | 2 | 4 | 115 | 33 | 82 | 66 | 1 |
| 1936/37 | 38 | 22 | 8 | 8 | 89 | 58 | 31 | 52 | 3 |
| 1937/38 | 38 | 27 | 7 | 4 | 114 | 42 | 72 | 61 | 1 |
| 1938/39 | 38 | 20 | 8 | 10 | 99 | 53 | 46 | 48 | 2 |
| 1939/40 | 5 | 3 | 0 | 2 | 7 | 7 | 0 | 6 | |
| 1940-46 | No League due to the Second World War | | | | | | | | |
| 1946/47 | 30 | 13 | 6 | 11 | 53 | 55 | -2 | 32 | 7 |
| 1947/48 | 30 | 10 | 5 | 15 | 41 | 56 | -15 | 25 | 12 |
| 1948/49 | 30 | 12 | 7 | 11 | 48 | 40 | 8 | 31 | 6 |
| 1949/50 | 30 | 14 | 7 | 9 | 51 | 50 | 1 | 35 | 5 |
| 1950/51 | 30 | 12 | 5 | 13 | 48 | 46 | 2 | 29 | 7 |
| 1951/52 | 30 | 10 | 8 | 12 | 52 | 55 | -3 | 28 | 9 |
| 1952/53 | 30 | 11 | 7 | 12 | 51 | 54 | -3 | 29 | 8 |
| 1953/54 | 30 | 20 | 3 | 7 | 72 | 29 | 43 | 43 | 1 |
| 1954/55 | 30 | 19 | 8 | 3 | 76 | 37 | 39 | 46 | 2 |
| 1955/56 | 34 | 16 | 9 | 9 | 55 | 39 | 16 | 41 | 5 |
| 1956/57 | 34 | 15 | 8 | 11 | 58 | 43 | 15 | 38 | 5 |

| SEASON | P | W | D | L | F | A | GD | Pts | Pos |
|--------|---|---|---|---|---|---|----|-----|-----|
| 1957/58 | 34 | 19 | 8 | 7 | 84 | 47 | 37 | 46 | 3 |
| 1958/59 | 34 | 14 | 8 | 12 | 70 | 53 | 17 | 36 | 6 |
| 1959/60 | 34 | 12 | 9 | 13 | 73 | 59 | 14 | 33 | 9 |
| 1960/61 | 34 | 15 | 9 | 10 | 64 | 46 | 18 | 39 | 4 |
| 1961/62 | 34 | 19 | 8 | 7 | 81 | 37 | 44 | 46 | 3 |
| 1962/63 | 34 | 19 | 6 | 9 | 76 | 44 | 32 | 44 | 4 |
| 1963/64 | 34 | 19 | 9 | 6 | 89 | 34 | 55 | 47 | 3 |
| 1964/65 | 34 | 16 | 5 | 13 | 76 | 57 | 19 | 37 | 8 |
| 1965/66 | 34 | 27 | 3 | 4 | 106 | 30 | 76 | 57 | 1 |
| 1966/67 | 34 | 26 | 6 | 2 | 111 | 33 | 78 | 58 | 1 |
| 1967/68 | 34 | 30 | 3 | 1 | 106 | 24 | 82 | 63 | 1 |
| 1968/69 | 34 | 23 | 8 | 3 | 89 | 32 | 57 | 54 | 1 |
| 1969/70 | 34 | 27 | 3 | 4 | 96 | 33 | 63 | 57 | 1 |
| 1970/71 | 34 | 25 | 6 | 3 | 89 | 23 | 66 | 56 | 1 |
| 1971/72 | 34 | 28 | 4 | 2 | 96 | 28 | 68 | 60 | 1 |
| 1972/73 | 34 | 26 | 5 | 3 | 93 | 28 | 65 | 57 | 1 |
| 1973/74 | 34 | 23 | 7 | 4 | 82 | 27 | 55 | 53 | 1 |
| 1974/75 | 34 | 20 | 5 | 9 | 81 | 41 | 40 | 45 | 3 |
| 1975/76 | 36 | 21 | 6 | 9 | 71 | 42 | 29 | 48 | 2 |
| 1976/77 | 36 | 23 | 9 | 4 | 79 | 39 | 40 | 55 | 1 |
| 1977/78 | 36 | 15 | 6 | 15 | 63 | 54 | 9 | 36 | 5 |
| 1978/79 | 36 | 21 | 6 | 9 | 61 | 37 | 24 | 48 | 1 |
| 1979/80 | 36 | 18 | 11 | 7 | 61 | 38 | 23 | 47 | 2 |
| 1980/81 | 36 | 26 | 4 | 6 | 84 | 37 | 47 | 56 | 1 |
| 1981/82 | 36 | 24 | 7 | 5 | 79 | 33 | 46 | 55 | 1 |
| 1982/83 | 36 | 25 | 5 | 6 | 90 | 36 | 54 | 55 | 2 |
| 1983/84 | 36 | 21 | 8 | 7 | 80 | 41 | 39 | 50 | 2 |
| 1984/85 | 36 | 22 | 8 | 6 | 77 | 30 | 47 | 52 | 2 |
| 1985/86 | 36 | 20 | 10 | 6 | 67 | 38 | 29 | 50 | 1 |
| 1986/87 | 44 | 27 | 9 | 8 | 90 | 41 | 49 | 63 | 2 |
| 1987/88 | 44 | 31 | 10 | 3 | 79 | 23 | 56 | 72 | 1 |
| 1988/89 | 36 | 21 | 4 | 11 | 66 | 44 | 22 | 46 | 3 |

| SEASON | P | W | D | L | F | A | GD | Pts | Pos |
|--------|---|---|---|---|---|---|----|-----|-----|
| 1989/90 | 36 | 10 | 14 | 12 | 37 | 37 | 0 | 34 | 5 |
| 1990/91 | 36 | 17 | 7 | 12 | 52 | 38 | 14 | 41 | 3 |
| 1991/92 | 44 | 26 | 10 | 8 | 88 | 42 | 46 | 62 | 3 |
| 1992/93 | 44 | 24 | 12 | 8 | 68 | 41 | 27 | 60 | 3 |
| 1993/94 | 44 | 15 | 20 | 9 | 51 | 38 | 13 | 50 | 5 |
| 1994/95 | 36 | 11 | 18 | 7 | 39 | 33 | 6 | 51 | 4 |
| 1995/96 | 36 | 24 | 11 | 1 | 74 | 25 | 49 | 83 | 2 |
| 1996/97 | 36 | 23 | 6 | 7 | 78 | 32 | 46 | 75 | 2 |
| 1997/98 | 36 | 22 | 8 | 6 | 64 | 24 | 40 | 74 | 1 |
| 1998/99 | 36 | 21 | 8 | 7 | 84 | 35 | 49 | 71 | 2 |
| 1999/00 | 36 | 21 | 6 | 9 | 90 | 38 | 52 | 69 | 2 |
| 2000/01 | 38 | 31 | 4 | 3 | 90 | 29 | 61 | 97 | 1 |
| 2001/02 | 38 | 33 | 4 | 1 | 94 | 18 | 76 | 103 | 1 |
| 2002/03 | 38 | 31 | 4 | 3 | 98 | 26 | 72 | 97 | 2 |
| 2003/04 | 38 | 31 | 5 | 2 | 105 | 25 | 80 | 98 | 1 |
| 2004/05 | 38 | 30 | 2 | 6 | 85 | 35 | 50 | 92 | 2 |
| 2005/06 | 38 | 29 | 5 | 4 | 93 | 37 | 56 | 92 | 1 |
| 2006/07 | 38 | 26 | 6 | 6 | 65 | 34 | 31 | 84 | 1 |
| 2007/08 | 38 | 28 | 5 | 5 | 84 | 26 | 58 | 89 | 1 |
| 2008/09 | 38 | 24 | 10 | 4 | 80 | 33 | 47 | 82 | 2 |
| 2009/10 | 38 | 25 | 6 | 7 | 75 | 39 | 36 | 81 | 2 |
| 2010/11 | 38 | 29 | 5 | 4 | 85 | 22 | 63 | 92 | 2 |
| 2011/12 | 38 | 30 | 3 | 5 | 84 | 21 | 63 | 93 | 1 |
| 2012/13 | 38 | 24 | 7 | 7 | 92 | 35 | 57 | 79 | 1 |
| 2013/14 | 38 | 31 | 6 | 1 | 102 | 25 | 77 | 99 | 1 |
| 2014/15 | 38 | 29 | 5 | 4 | 84 | 17 | 67 | 92 | 1 |
| 2015/16 | 38 | 26 | 8 | 4 | 93 | 31 | 62 | 86 | 1 |
| 2016/17 | 38 | 34 | 4 | 0 | 106 | 25 | 81 | 106 | 1 |

*Four points deducted season 1890/91

# EUROPEAN RESULTS YEAR BY YEAR

**Season 1962/63:** Inter-Cities Fairs Cup
*First round, 1st Leg:* Valencia 4-2 Celtic
*2nd Leg:* Celtic 2-2 Valencia

**Season 1963/64:** European Cup-Winners' Cup
*First Round, 1st Leg:* FC Basel 1-5 Celtic
*2nd Leg:* Celtic 5-0 FC Basel
*Second Round, 1st Leg:* Celtic 3-0 Dinamo Zagreb
*2nd Leg:* Dinamo Zagreb 2-1 Celtic
*Quarter-final, 1st Leg:* Celtic 1-0 Slovan Bratislava
*2nd Leg:* Slovan Bratislava 0-1 Celtic
*Semi-final, 1st Leg:* Celtic 3-0 MTK Budapest
*2nd Leg:* MTK Budapest 4-0 Celtic

**Season 1964/65:** Inter-Cities Fairs Cup
*First Round, 1st Leg:* Leixoes 1-1 Celtic
*2nd Leg:* Celtic 3-0 Leixoes
*Second Round, 1st Leg:* Barcelona 3-1 Celtic
*2nd Leg:* Celtic 0-0 Barcelona

**Season 1965/66:** European Cup-Winners' Cup
*First Round, 1st Leg:* Go Ahead Deventer 0-6 Celtic
*2nd Leg:* Celtic 1-0 Go Ahead Deventer
*Second Round, 1st Leg:* Aarhus GF 0-1 Celtic
*2nd Leg:* Celtic 2-0 Aarhus GF
*Quarter-final, 1st Leg:* Celtic 3-0 Dinamo Kiev
*2nd Leg:* Dinamo Kiev 1-1 Celtic
*Semi-final, 1st Leg:* Celtic 1-0 Liverpool
*2nd Leg:* Liverpool 2-0 Celtic

**Season 1966/67:** European Cup
*First Round, 1st Leg:* Celtic 2-0 FC Zurich
*2nd Leg:* FC Zurich 0-3 Celtic
*Second Round, 1st Leg:* FC Nantes 1-3 Celtic
*2nd Leg:* Celtic 3-1 FC Nantes
*Quarter-final, 1st Leg:* Vojvodina Novi Sad 1-0 Celtic
*2nd Leg:* Celtic 2-0 Vojvodina Novi Sad
*Semi-final, 1st Leg:* Celtic 3-1 Dukla Prague
*2nd Leg:* Dukla Prague 0-0 Celtic
*Final:* Celtic 2-1 Inter Milan

**Season 1967/68:** European Cup
*First Round, 1st Leg:* Celtic 1-2 Dinamo Kiev
*2nd Leg:* Dinamo Kiev 1-1 Celtic

**Season 1968/69:** European Cup
*First Round, 1st Leg:* St Etienne 2-0 Celtic
*2nd Leg:* Celtic 4-0 St Etienne
*Second Round, 1st Leg:* Celtic 5-1 Red Star Belgrade
*2nd Leg:* Red Star Belgrade 1-1 Celtic
*Quarter-final, 1st Leg:* AC Milan 0-0 Celtic
*2nd Leg:* Celtic 0-1 AC Milan

**Season 1969/70:** European Cup
*First Round, 1st Leg:* FC Basel 0-0 Celtic
*2nd Leg:* Celtic 2-0 FC Basel
*Second Round, 1st Leg:* Celtic 3-0 Benfica
*2nd Leg:* Benfica 3-0 Celtic (*Celtic won on Toss of Coin*)
*Quarter-final, 1st Leg:* Celtic 3-0 Fiorentina
*2nd Leg:* Fiorentina 1-0 Celtic
*Semi-final, 1st Leg:* Leeds United 0-1 Celtic
*2nd Leg:* Celtic 2-1 Leeds United
*Final:* Celtic 1-2 Feyenoord

**Season 1970/71:** European Cup
*First Round, 1st Leg:* Celtic 9-0 KPV Kokkola
*2nd Leg:* KPV Kokkola 0-5 Celtic
*Second Round, 1st Leg:* Waterford 0-7 Celtic
*2nd Leg:* Celtic 3-2 Waterford
*Quarter-final, 1st Leg:* Ajax 3-0 Celtic
*2nd Leg:* Celtic 1-0 Ajax

**Season 1971/72:** European Cup
*First Round, 1st Leg:* B 1903 Copenhagen 1-2 Celtic
*2nd Leg:* Celtic 3-0 B 1903 Copenhagen
*Second Round, 1st Leg:* Celtic 5-0 Sliema Wanderers
*2nd Leg:* Sliema Wanderers 1-2 Celtic
*Quarter-final, 1st Leg:* Ujpest Dozsa 1-2 Celtic
*2nd Leg:* Celtic 1-1 Ujpest Dozsa
*Semi-final, 1st Leg:* Inter Milan 0-0 Celtic
*2nd Leg:* Celtic 0-0 Inter Milan (*Inter Milan won 5-4 on penalties*)

**Season 1972/73:** European Cup
*First Round 1, 1st Leg:* Celtic 2-1 Rosenborg
*2nd Leg:* Rosenborg 1-3 Celtic
*Second Round, 1st Leg:* Celtic 2-1 Ujpest Dozsa
*2nd Leg:* Ujpest Dozsa 3-0 Celtic

**Season 1973/74:** European Cup
*First Round, 1st Leg:* TPS Turku 1-6 Celtic
*2nd Leg:* Celtic 3-0 TPS Turku

Second Round, 1st Leg: Celtic 0-0 Vejle
2nd Leg: Vejle 0-1 Celtic
Quarter-final, 1st Leg: FC Basel 3-2 Celtic
2nd Leg: Celtic 4-2 FC Basel
Semi-final, 1st Leg: Celtic 0-0 Atletico Madrid
2nd Leg: Atletico Madrid 2-0 Celtic

**Season 1974/75:** European Cup
First Round, 1st Leg: Celtic 1-1 Olympiakos Piraeus
2nd Leg: Olympiakos Piraeus 2-0 Celtic

**Season 1975/76:** European Cup-Winners' Cup
First Round 1, 1st Leg: Valur 0-2 Celtic
2nd Leg: Celtic 7-0 Valur
Second Round, 1st Leg: Boavista 0-0 Celtic
2nd Leg: Celtic 3-1 Boavista
Quarter-final, 1st Leg: Celtic 1-1 Sachsenring Zwickau
2nd Leg: Sachsenring Zwickau 1-0 Celtic

**Season 1976/77:** UEFA Cup
First Round, 1st Leg: Celtic 2-2 Wisla Krakow
2nd Leg: Wisla Krakow 2-0 Celtic

**Season 1977/78:** European Cup
First Round, 1st Leg: Celtic 5-0 Jeunesse d'Esch
2nd Leg: Jeunesse d'Esch 1-6 Celtic
Second Round, 1st Leg: Celtic 2-1 SWW Innsbruck
2nd Leg: SWW Innsbruck 3-0 Celtic

**Season 1979/80:** European Cup
First Round, 1st Leg: Partizan Tirana 1-0 Celtic
2nd Leg: Celtic 4-1 Partizan Tirana
Second Round, 1st Leg: Celtic 3-2 Dundalk
2nd Leg: Dundalk 0-0 Celtic
Quarter-final, 1st Leg: Celtic 2-0 Real Madrid
2nd Leg: Real Madrid 3-0 Celtic

**Season 1980/81:** European Cup-Winners' Cup
Preliminary Round, 1st Leg: Celtic 6-0 Diosgyori Miskolc
2nd Leg: Diosgyori Miskolc 2-1 Celtic
First Round, 1st Leg: Celtic 2-1 Politehnica Timisoara
2nd Leg: Politehnica Timisoara 1-0 Celtic
(*Politehnica Timisoara won on the away goals rule*)

**Season 1981/82:** European Cup
*First Round, 1st Leg:* Celtic 1-0 Juventus
*2nd Leg:* Juventus 2-0 Celtic

**Season 1982/83:** European Cup
*First Round 1, 1st Leg:* Celtic 2-2 Ajax
*2nd Leg:* Ajax 1-2 Celtic
*Second Round, 1st Leg:* Real Sociedad 2-0 Celtic
*2nd Leg:* Celtic 2-1 Real Sociedad

**Season 1983/84:** UEFA Cup
*First Round, 1st Leg:* Celtic 1-0 Aarhus GF
*2nd Leg:* Aarhus GF 1-4 Celtic
*Second Round, 1st Leg:* Sporting Lisbon 2-0 Celtic
*2nd Leg:* Celtic 5-0 Sporting Lisbon
*Third Round, 1st Leg:* Nottingham Forest 0-0 Celtic
*2nd Leg:* Celtic 1-2 Nottingham Forest

**Season 1984/85:** European Cup-Winners' Cup
*First Round, 1st Leg:* KAA Gent 0-1 Celtic
*2nd Leg:* Celtic 3-0 KAA Gent
*Second Round, 1st Leg:* Rapid Vienna 3-1 Celtic
*2nd Leg:* Celtic 3-0 Rapid Vienna (Tie ordered to be replayed)
*2nd Leg:* Celtic 0-1 Rapid Vienna (Played at Old Trafford)

**Season 1985/86:** European Cup-Winners' Cup
*First Round, 1st Leg:* Atletico Madrid 1-1 Celtic
*2nd Leg:* Celtic 1-2 Atletico Madrid

**Season 1986/87:** European Cup
*First Round, 1st Leg:* Shamrock Rovers 0-1 Celtic
*2nd Leg:* Celtic 2-0 Shamrock Rovers
*Second Round, 1st Leg:* Celtic 1-1 Dinamo Kiev
*2nd Leg:* Dinamo Kiev 3-1 Celtic

**Season 1987/88:** UEFA Cup
*First Round, 1st Leg:* Celtic 2-1 Borussia Dortmund
*2nd Leg:* Borussia Dortmund 2-0 Celtic

**Season 1988/89:** European Cup
*First Round, 1st Leg:* Honved 1-0 Celtic
*2nd Leg:* Celtic 4-0 Honved
*Second Round, 1st Leg:* Celtic 0-1 Werder Bremen
*2nd Leg:* Werder Bremen 0-0 Celtic

**Season 1989/90:** European Cup-Winners' Cup
*First Round, 1st Leg:* Partizan Belgrade 2-1 Celtic
*2nd Leg:* Celtic 5-4 Partizan Belgrade
(*Partizan Belgrade won on the away goals rule*)

**Season 1991/92:** UEFA Cup
*First Round, 1st Leg:* Celtic 2-0 Germinal Ekeren
*2nd Leg:* Germinal Ekeren 1-1 Celtic
*Second Round, 1st Leg:* Neuchatal Xamax 5-1 Celtic
*2nd Leg:* Celtic 1-0 Neuchatal Xamax

**Season 1992/93:** UEFA Cup
*First Round, 1st Leg:* FC Cologne 2-0 Celtic
*2nd Leg:* Celtic 3-0 FC Cologne
*Second Round, 1st Leg:* Borussia Dortmund 1-0 Celtic
*2nd Leg:* Celtic 1-2 Borussia Dortmund

**Season 1993/94:** UEFA Cup
*First Round, 1st Leg:* BSC Young Boys 0-0 Celtic
*2nd Leg:* Celtic 1-0 BSC Young Boys
*Second Round, 1st Leg:* Celtic 1-0 Sporting Lisbon
*2nd Leg:* Sporting Lisbon 2-0 Celtic

**Season 1995/96:** European Cup-Winners' Cup
*First Round, 1st Leg:* Dinamo Batumi 2-3 Celtic
*2nd Leg:* Celtic 4-0 Dinamo Batumi
*Second Round, 1st Leg:* Paris St Germain 1-0 Celtic
*2nd Leg:* Celtic 0-3 Paris St Germain

**Season 1996/97:** UEFA Cup
*Qualifying Round, 1st Leg:* FC Kosice 0-0 Celtic
*2nd Leg:* Celtic 1-0 FC Kosice
*First Round, 1st Leg:* Celtic 0-2 Hamburg SV
*2nd Leg:* Hamburg SV 2-0 Celtic

**Season 1997/98:** UEFA Cup
*First Qualifying Round, 1st Leg:* Inter Cabel-Tel 0-3 Celtic
*2nd Leg:* Celtic 5-0 Inter Cabel-Tel
*Second Qualifying Round, 1st Leg:* FC Tirol Innsbruck 2-1 Celtic
*2nd Leg:* Celtic 6-3 FC Tirol Innsbruck
*First Round, 1st Leg:* Celtic 2-2 Liverpool
*2nd Leg:* Liverpool 0-0 Celtic (*Liverpool won on the away goals rule*)

**Season 1998/99:** UEFA Champions League
*First Qualifying Round, 1st Leg:* Celtic 0-0 St Patrick's Athletic
*2nd Leg:* St Patrick's Athletic 0-2 Celtic

*Second Qualifying Round, 1st Leg:* Celtic 1-0 Croatia Zagreb
*2nd Leg:* Croatia Zagreb 3-0 Celtic

UEFA Cup
*First Round, 1st Leg:* Vitoria Guimaraes 1-2 Celtic
*2nd Leg:* Celtic 2-1 Vitoria Guimaraes
*Second Round, 1st Leg:* Celtic 1-1 FC Zurich
*2nd Leg:* FC Zurich 4-2 Celtic

**Season 1999/2000:** UEFA Cup
*Qualifying Round, 1st Leg:* Cwmbran Town 0-6 Celtic
*2nd Leg:* Celtic 4-0 Cwmbran Town
*First Round, 1st Leg:* Celtic 2-0 Hapoel Tel Aviv
*2nd Leg:* Hapoel Tel Aviv 0-1 Celtic
*Second Round, 1st Leg:* Olympique Lyon 1-0 Celtic
*2nd Leg:* Celtic 0-1 Olympique Lyon

**Season 2000/01:** UEFA Cup
*Qualifying Round, 1st Leg:* Jeunesse d'Esch 0-4 Celtic
*2nd Leg:* Celtic 7-0 Jeunesse d'Esch
*First Round, 1st Leg:* Celtic 2-0 HJK Helsinki
*2nd Leg:* HJK Helsinki 2-1 Celtic
*Second Round, 1st Leg:* Bordeaux 1-1 Celtic
*2nd Leg:* Celtic 1-2 Bordeaux

**Season 2001/02:** UEFA Champions League
*Third Qualifying Round, 1st Leg:* Ajax 1-3 Celtic
*2nd Leg:* Celtic 0-1 Ajax
*Group Stage:* Juventus 3-2 Celtic
Celtic 1-0 FC Porto
Celtic 1-0 Rosenborg
FC Porto 3-0 Celtic
Rosenborg 2-0 Celtic
Celtic 4-3 Juventus

UEFA Cup
*Third Round, 1st Leg:* Valencia 1-0 Celtic
*2nd Leg:* Celtic 1-0 Valencia (*Valencia won 5-4 on penalties*)

**Season 2002/03:** UEFA Champions League
*Third Qualifying Round, 1st Leg:* Celtic 3-1 FC Basel
*2nd Leg:* FC Basel 2-0 Celtic (*FC Basel won on the away goals rule*)

UEFA Cup
*First Round, 1st Leg:* Celtic 8-1 FK Suduva
*2nd Leg:* FK Suduva 0-2 Celtic

*Second Round, 1st Leg:* Celtic 1-0 Blackburn Rovers
*2nd Leg:* Blackburn Rovers 0-2 Celtic
*Third Round, 1st Leg:* Celtic 1-0 Celta Vigo
*2nd Leg:* Celta Vigo 2-1 Celtic (*Celtic won the away goals rule*)
*Fourth Round, 1st Leg:* Celtic 3-1 VfB Stuttgart
*2nd Leg:* VfB Stuttgart 3-2 Celtic
*Quarter-final, 1st Leg:* Celtic 1-1 Liverpool
*2nd Leg:* Liverpool 0-2 Celtic
*Semi-final, 1st Leg:* Celtic 1-1 Boavista
*2nd Leg:* Boavista 0-1 Celtic
*Final:* Celtic 2-3 FC Porto

**Season 2003/04:** UEFA Champions League
*Second Qualifying Round: 1st Leg:* FBK Kaunas 0-4 Celtic
*2nd Leg:* Celtic 1-0 FBK Kaunas
*Third Qualifying Round, 1st Leg:* MTK Hungaria 0-4 Celtic
*2nd Leg:* Celtic 1-0 MTK Hungaria
*Group Stage:* Bayern Munich 2-1 Celtic
Celtic 2-0 Olympique Lyon
Anderlecht 1-0 Celtic
Celtic 3-1 Anderlecht
Celtic 0-0 Bayern Munich
Olympique Lyon 3-2 Celtic

UEFA Cup
*Third Round, 1st Leg:* Celtic 3-0 FK Teplice
*2nd Leg:* FK Teplice 1-0 Celtic
*Fourth Round, 1st Leg:* Celtic 1-0 Barcelona
*2nd Leg:* Barcelona 0-0 Celtic
*Quarter-final, 1st Leg:* Celtic 1-1 Villarreal
*2nd Leg:* Villarreal 2-0 Celtic

**Season 2004/05:** UEFA Champions League
*Group Stage:* Celtic 1-3 Barcelona
AC Milan 3-1 Celtic
Shakhtar Donetsk 3-0 Celtic
Celtic 1-0 Shakhtar Donetsk
Barcelona 1-1 Celtic
Celtic 0-0 AC Milan

**Season 2005/06:** UEFA Champions League
*Second Qualifying Round, 1st Leg:* Artmedia Bratislava 5-0 Celtic
*2nd Leg:* Celtic 4-0 Artmedia Bratislava

**Season 2006/07:** UEFA Champions League
Group Stage: Manchester United 3-2 Celtic

Celtic 1-0 FC Copenhagen
Celtic 3-0 Benfica
Benfica 3-0 Celtic
Celtic 1-0 Manchester United
FC Copenhagen 3-1 Celtic
*First Knock-Out Round, 1st Leg:* Celtic 0-0 AC Milan
*2nd Leg:* AC Milan 1-0 Celtic

**Season 2007/08:** UEFA Champions League
*Third Qualifying Round, 1st Leg:* Spartak Moscow 1-1 Celtic
*2nd Leg:* Celtic 1-1 Spartak Moscow (*Celtic won 4-3 on penalties*)
*Group Stage:* Shakhtar Donetsk 2-0 Celtic
Celtic 2-1 AC Milan
Benfica 1-0 Celtic
Celtic 1-0 Benfica
Celtic 2-1 Shakhtar Donetsk
AC Milan 1-0 Celtic
*First Knock-Out Round, 1st Leg:* Celtic 2-3 Barcelona
*2nd Leg:* Barcelona 1-0 Celtic

**Season 2008/09:** UEFA Champions League
*Group Stage:* Celtic 0-0 Aalborg BK
Villarreal 1-0 Celtic
Manchester United 3-0 Celtic
Celtic 1-1 Manchester United
Aalborg BK 2-1 Celtic
Celtic 2-0 Villarreal

**Season 2009/10:** UEFA Champions League
*Third Qualifying Round, 1st Leg:* Celtic 0-1 Dinamo Moscow
*2nd Leg:* Dinamo Moscow 0-2 Celtic
*Fourth Qualifying Round, 1st Leg:* Celtic 0-2 Arsenal
*2nd Leg:* Arsenal 3-1 Celtic

UEFA Europa League
*Group Stage:* Hapoel Tel Aviv 2-1 Celtic
Celtic 1-1 Rapid Vienna
Celtic 0-1 Hamburg SV
Hamburg SV 0-0 Celtic
Celtic 2-0 Hapoel Tel Aviv
Rapid Vienna 3-3 Celtic

**Season 2010/11:** UEFA Champions League
*Third Qualifying Round, 1st Leg:* Braga 3-0 Celtic
*2nd Leg:* Celtic 2-1 Braga

UEFA Europa League
*Play-Off Round, 1st Leg:* Celtic 2-0 FC Utrecht
*2nd Leg:* FC Utrecht 4-0 Celtic

**Season 2011/12:** UEFA Europa League
*Play-Off Round, 1st Leg:* Celtic 0-0 FC Sion
*2nd Leg:* FC Sion 3-1 Celtic (*Sion expelled*)
*Group Stage:* Atletico Madrid 2-0 Celtic
Celtic 1-1 Udinese
Rennes 1-1 Celtic
Celtic 3-1 Rennes
Celtic 0-1 Atletico Madrid
Udinese 1-1 Celtic

**Season 2012/13:** UEFA Champions League
*Play-Off Round, 1st leg:* Celtic 2-1 HJK Helsinki
*2nd Leg:* HJK Helsinki 0-2 Celtic
*Third Qualifying Round, 1st Leg:* Helsingborgs IF 0-2 Celtic
*2nd Leg:* Celtic 2-0 Helsingborgs IF
*Group Stage:* Celtic 0-0 Benfica
Spartak Moscow 2-3 Celtic
Barcelona 2-1 Celtic
Celtic 2-1 Barcelona
Benfica 2-1 Celtic
Celtic 2-1 Spartak Moscow
*First Knock-Out Round, 1st Leg:* Celtic 0-3 Juventus
*2nd Leg:* Juventus 2-0 Celtic

**Season 2013/14:** UEFA Champions League
*Second Qualifying Round, 1st Leg:* Cliftonville 0-3 Celtic
*2nd Leg:* Celtic 2-0 Cliftonville
*Third Qualifying Round, 1st Leg:* Celtic 1-0 Elfsborg
*2nd Leg:* Elfsborg 0-0 Celtic
*Play – off Round, 1st Leg:* Shakhter Karagandy 2-0 Celtic
*2nd Leg:* Celtic 3-0 Shakhter Karagandy
*Group Stage:* A.C. Milan 2-0 Celtic
Celtic 0-1 Barcelona
Celtic 2-1 Ajax
Ajax 1-0 Celtic
Celtic 0-3 A.C. Milan
Barcelona 6-1 Celtic

**Season 2014/15:** UEFA Champions League
*Second Qualifying Round, 1st Leg:* KR Reykjavik 0-1 Celtic
*2nd Leg:* Celtic 4-0 KR Reykjavik

*Third Qualifying Round, 1st Leg:* Legia Warsaw 4-1 Celtic
*2nd Leg:* Celtic AWARDED Legia Warsaw (3-0)
*Play-off Round: 1st Leg:* NK Maribor 1-1 Celtic
*2nd Leg:* Celtic 0-1 NK Maribor


UEFA Europa League
*Group Stage:* Red Bull Salzburg 2-2 Celtic
Celtic 1-0 Dinamo Zagreb
Celtic 2-1 Astra Giurgiu
Astra Giurgiu 1-1 Celtic
Celtic 1-3 Red Bull Salzburg
Dinamo Zagreb 4-3 Celtic
*First Knock-out Round: 1st Leg:* Celtic 3-3 Internazionale
*2nd Leg:* Internazionale 1-0 Celtic


**Season 2015/16:** UEFA Champions League
*Second Qualifying Round, 1st Leg:* Celtic 2-0 Stjarnan
*2nd Leg:* Stjarnan 1-4 Celtic
*Third Qualifying, 1st Leg:* Celtic 1-0 Qarabağ
*2nd Leg:* Qarabağ 0-0 Celtic
*Play-off Round, 1st Leg:* Celtic 3-2 Malmö
*2nd Leg:* Malmö 2-0 Celtic


UEFA Europa League
*Group Stage:* Ajax 2-2 Celtic
Celtic 2-2 Fenerbahçe
Molde 3-1 Celtic
Celtic 1-2 Molde
Celtic 1-2 Ajax
Fenerbahçe 1-1 Celtic


**Season 2016/17:** UEFA Champions League
*Second Qualifying Round, 1st Leg:* Lincoln Red Imps 1-Celtic
*2nd Leg:* Celtic 3-0 Lincoln Red Imps
*Third Qualifying Round, 1st Leg:* Astana 1-1 Celtic
*2nd Leg:* Celtic 2-1 Astana
*Play-off Round, 1st Leg:* Celtic 5-2 Hapoel Beersheba
*2nd Leg:* Hapoel Beersheba 2-0 Celtic
*Group Stage:* Barcelona 7-0 Celtic
Celtic 3-3 Manchester City
Celtic 0-2 Borussia Mönchengladbach
Borussia Mönchengladbach 1-1 Celtic
Celtic 0-2 Barcelona
Manchester City 1-1 Celtic

# EUROPEAN RECORD BY COUNTRY

|  | P | W | D | L | F | A |
|---|---|---|---|---|---|---|
| Albania | 2 | 1 | 0 | 1 | 4 | 2 |
| Austria | 8 | 2 | 2 | 4 | 14 | 17 |
| Azerbaijan | 2 | 1 | 1 | 0 | 1 | 0 |
| Belgium | 6 | 3 | 1 | 2 | 9 | 4 |
| Croatia | 6 | 3 | 0 | 3 | 9 | 9 |
| Czech Republic | 4 | 2 | 1 | 1 | 6 | 2 |
| Denmark | 12 | 7 | 2 | 3 | 16 | 8 |
| England | 20 | 7 | 7 | 6 | 22 | 24 |
| Finland | 8 | 7 | 0 | 1 | 30 | 4 |
| France | 14 | 5 | 2 | 7 | 20 | 18 |
| Georgia | 2 | 2 | 0 | 0 | 7 | 2 |
| Germany | 20 | 3 | 5 | 12 | 14 | 25 |
| Gibraltar | 2 | 1 | 0 | 1 | 3 | 1 |
| Greece | 2 | 0 | 1 | 1 | 1 | 3 |
| Hungary | 12 | 7 | 1 | 4 | 24 | 13 |
| Iceland | 6 | 6 | 0 | 0 | 20 | 1 |
| Israel | 6 | 4 | 0 | 2 | 11 | 6 |
| Italy | 25 | 5 | 8 | 12 | 20 | 33 |
| Kazakhstan | 4 | 2 | 1 | 1 | 6 | 4 |
| Lithuania | 4 | 4 | 0 | 0 | 15 | 1 |
| Luxembourg | 4 | 4 | 0 | 0 | 22 | 1 |
| Malta | 2 | 2 | 0 | 0 | 7 | 1 |
| Netherlands | 15 | 7 | 2 | 6 | 23 | 20 |
| Northern Ireland | 2 | 2 | 0 | 0 | 5 | 0 |
| Norway | 2 | 0 | 0 | 2 | 2 | 5 |
| Poland | 4 | 1 | 1 | 2 | 6 | 8 |
| Portugal | 25 | 12 | 4 | 9 | 32 | 28 |
| Republic of Ireland | 8 | 6 | 2 | 0 | 18 | 4 |
| Romania | 4 | 2 | 1 | 1 | 5 | 4 |
| Russia | 6 | 3 | 2 | 1 | 9 | 6 |
| Slovakia | 6 | 4 | 1 | 1 | 7 | 5 |
| Slovenia | 2 | 0 | 1 | 1 | 1 | 2 |
| Spain | 34 | 7 | 7 | 20 | 26 | 57 |
| Sweden | 6 | 4 | 1 | 1 | 8 | 4 |
| Switzerland | 18 | 11 | 3 | 4 | 38 | 19 |
| Turkey | 2 | 0 | 2 | 0 | 3 | 3 |
| Ukraine | 10 | 3 | 3 | 4 | 11 | 14 |
| Wales | 4 | 4 | 0 | 0 | 18 | 0 |
| Yugoslavia | 6 | 3 | 1 | 2 | 14 | 9 |
| **TOTAL** | 325 | 147 | 63 | 115 | 507 | 367 |

# LIST OF SCOTTISH CUP WINNING TEAMS

### 1892

**Celtic 5-1 Queen's Park (Campbell 2, McMahon 2, og)** Cullen, Reynolds, Doyle, W Maley, Kelly, Gallacher, McCallum, Brady, Dowds, McMahon, Campbell

### 1899

**Celtic 2-0 Rangers (McMahon, Hodge)**

McArthur, Welford, Storrier, Battles, Marshall, King, Hodge, Campbell, Divers, McMahon, Bell

### 1900

**Celtic 4-3 Queen's Park (Divers 2, McMahon, Bell)** McArthur, Storrier, Battles, Russell, Marshall, Orr, Hodge, Campbell, Divers, McMahon, Bell

### 1904

**Celtic 3-2 Rangers (Quinn 3)** Adams, McLeod, Orr, Young, Loney, Hay, Muir, McMenemy, Quinn, Somers, Hamilton

### 1907

**Celtic 3-0 Hearts (Somers 2, Orr)** Adams, McLeod, Orr, Young, McNair, Hay, Bennett, McMenemy, Quinn, Somers, Templeton

### 1908

**Celtic 5-1 St Mirren (Bennett 2, Quinn, Somers, Hamilton)** Adams, McNair, Weir, Young, Loney, Hay, Bennett, McMenemy, Quinn, Somers, Hamilton

### 1911

**Celtic 2-0 Hamilton (Quinn, McAteer)** Adams, McNair, Hay, Young, McAteer, Dodds, McAtee, McMenemy, Quinn, Kivlichan, Hamilton

### 1912

**Celtic 2-0 Clyde (McMenemy, Gallacher)** Mulrooney, McNair, Dodds, Young, Loney, Johnstone, McAtee, Gallacher, Quinn, McMenemy, Brown

### 1914

**Celtic 4-1 Hibernian (McColl 2, Browning 2)** Shaw, McNair, Dodds, Young, Johnstone, McMaster, McAtee, Gallacher, McColl, McMenemy, Browning

### 1923

**Celtic 1-0 Hibernian (Cassidy)** Shaw, McNair, W. McStay, J McStay, Cringan, McFarlane, McAtee, Gallacher, Cassidy, McLean, Connolly

**1925**

**Celtic 2-1 Dundee (Gallacher, McGrory)** Shevlin, W McStay, Hilley, Wilson, J McStay, McFarlane, Connolly, Gallacher, McGrory, A Thomson, McLean

**1927**

**Celtic 3-1 East Fife (McLean, Connolly, Robertson og)** J Thomson, W McStay, Hilley, Wilson, J McStay, McFarlane, Connolly, A Thomson, McInally, John McMenemy, McLean

**1931**

**Celtic 4-2 Motherwell (R Thomson 2, McGrory 2)** J Thomson, Cook, McGonagle, Wilson, J McStay, Geatons, R Thomson, A Thomson, McGrory, Scarff, Napier

**1933**

**Celtic 1-0 Motherwell (McGrory)** Kennaway, Hogg, McGonagle, Wilson, J McStay, Geatons, R Thomson, A Thomson, McGrory, Napier, H O'Donnell

**1937**

**Celtic 2-1 Aberdeen (Crum, Buchan)** Kennaway, Hogg, Morrison, Geatons, Lyon, Paterson, Delaney, Buchan, McGrory, Crum, Murphy

**1951**

**Celtic 1-0 Motherwell (J McPhail)** Hunter, Fallon, Rollo, Evans, Boden, Baillie, Weir, Collins, J McPhail, Peacock, Tully

**1954**

**Celtic 2-1 Aberdeen (Fallon, Young og)** Bonnar, Haughney, Meechan, Evans, Stein, Peacock, Higgins, Fernie, Fallon, Tully, Mochan

**1965**

**Celtic 3-2 Dunfermline Ath (Auld 2, McNeill)** Fallon, Young, Gemmell, Murdoch, McNeill, Clark, Chalmers, Gallagher, Hughes, Lennox, Auld

**1967**

**Celtic 2-0 Aberdeen (Wallace 2)** Simpson, Craig, Gemmell, Murdoch, McNeill, Clark, Johnstone, Wallace, Chalmers, Auld, Lennox

**1969**

**Celtic 4-0 Rangers (McNeill, Lennox, Connelly, Chalmers)** Fallon, Craig, Gemmell, Murdoch, McNeill, Brogan (Clark), Connelly, Chalmers, Wallace, Lennox, Auld

## 1971

**Celtic 2-1 Rangers (Macari, Hood)** Williams, Craig, Brogan, Connelly, McNeill, Hay, Johnstone, Macari, Hood (Wallace), Callaghan, Lennox

## 1972

**Celtic 6-1 Hibernian (Deans 3, Macari 2, McNeill)** Williams, Craig, Brogan, Murdoch, McNeill, Connelly, Johnstone, Deans, Macari, Dalglish, Callaghan

## 1974

**Celtic 3-0 Dundee United (Murray, Hood, Deans)** Connaghan, McGrain (Callaghan), Brogan, Murray, McNeill, P McCluskey, Johnstone, Hood, Deans, Hay, Dalglish

## 1975

**Celtic 3-1 Airdrie (Wilson 2, P McCluskey)** Latchford, McGrain, Lynch, Murray, McNeill, P McCluskey, Hood, Glavin, Dalglish, Lennox, Wilson

## 1977

**Celtic 1-0 Rangers (Lynch)** Latchford, McGrain, Lynch, Stanton, MacDonald, Aitken, Dalglish, Edvaldsson, Craig, Wilson, Conn

## 1980

**Celtic 1-0 Rangers (G McCluskey)** Latchford, Sneddon, McGrain, Aitken, Conroy, MacLeod, Provan, Doyle (Lennox), G McCluskey, Burns, McGarvey

## 1985

**Celtic 2-1 Dundee United (Provan, McGarvey)** Bonner, W McStay, McGrain, Aitken, McAdam, MacLeod, Provan, P McStay (O'Leary), Johnston, Burns (McClair), McGarvey

## 1988

**Celtic 2-1 Dundee United (McAvennie 2)** McKnight, Morris, Rogan, Aitken, McCarthy, Whyte (Stark), Miller, P McStay, McAvennie, Walker (McGhee), Burns

## 1989

**Celtic 1-0 Rangers (Miller)** Bonner, Morris, Rogan, Aitken, McCarthy, Whyte, Grant, P McStay, Miller, Burns, McGhee

## 1995

**Celtic 1-0 Airdrie (van Hooijdonk)** Bonner, Boyd, McKinlay, Vata, McNally, Grant, McLaughlin, P McStay, van Hooijdonk (Falconer), Donnelly (O'Donnell), Collins

## 2001

**Celtic 3-0 Hibernian (McNamara, Larsson 2)** Douglas, Agathe, Mjallby, Vega, Valgaeren, Lambert (Boyd), Lennon, Moravcik (McNamara), Larsson, Sutton, Thompson (Johnson)

## 2004

**Celtic 3-1 Dunfermline Ath (Larsson 2, Petrov)** Marshall, Agathe, Varga, Balde, McNamara, Petrov, Lennon, Thompson, Pearson (Wallace), Larsson, Sutton

## 2005

**Celtic 1-0 Dundee United (Thompson)** Douglas, Agathe, Varga, Balde, McNamara, Petrov, Lennon, Thompson (McGeady), Bellamy, Hartson (Valgaeren), Sutton

## 2007

**Celtic 1-0 Dunfermline Ath (Perrier-Doumbe)** Boruc, Perrier-Doumbe, Pressley, McManus, Naylor, Nakamura, Lennon (Caldwell), Hartley, McGeady, Miller (Beattie), Vennegoor of Hesselink

## 2011

**Celtic 3-0 Motherwell (Ki Sung Yueng, Craigan og, Mulgrew)** Forster, Wilson, Loovens, Majstorovic, Izaguirre, Brown, Ki Sung Yueng, Mulgrew, Commons (Forrest), Samaras (Stokes), Hooper (McCourt)

## 2013

**Celtic 3-0 Hibernian (Hooper 2, Ledley)** Forster, Lustig, Wilson, Mulgrew, Izaguirre, Commons (Samaras), Brown, (Ambrose), Ledley, Forrest (McCourt), Stokes, Hooper

## 2017

**Celtic 2 – 1 Aberdeen (Armstrong, Rogic)** Gordon, Lustig, Šimunović, Boyata, Tierney (Rogic), McGregor, Brown, Armstrong, Roberts (Sviatchenko), Forrest

# LIST OF LEAGUE CUP WINNING TEAMS

### 1956/57
**Celtic 3-0 Partick Thistle (B McPhail 2, Collins)** Beattie, Haughney, Fallon, Evans, Jack, Peacock, Tully, Collins, B McPhail, Fernie, Mochan

### 1957/58
**Celtic 7-1 Rangers (B McPhail 3, Mochan 2, Wilson, Fernie)** Beattie, Donnelly, Fallon, Fernie, Evans, Peacock, Tully, Collins, B McPhail, Wilson, Mochan

### 1965/66
**Celtic 2-1 Rangers (Hughes 2)** Simpson, Young, Gemmell, Murdoch, McNeill, Clark, Johnstone, Gallagher, McBride, Lennox, Hughes

### 1966/67
**Celtic 1-0 Rangers (Lennox)** Simpson, Gemmell, O'Neill, Murdoch, McNeill, Clark, Johnstone, Lennox, McBride, Auld, Hughes (Chalmers)

### 1967/68
**Celtic 5-3 Dundee (Chalmers 2, Hughes, Lennox, Wallace)** Simpson, Craig, Gemmell, Murdoch, McNeill, Clark, Chalmers, Lennox, Wallace, Auld (O'Neill), Hughes

### 1968/69
**Celtic 6-2 Hibernian (Lennox 3, Wallace, Auld, Craig)** Fallon, Craig, Gemmell (Clark), Murdoch, McNeill, Brogan, Johnstone, Wallace, Chalmers, Auld, Lennox

### 1969/70
**Celtic 1-0 St Johnstone (Auld)** Fallon, Craig, Hay, Murdoch, McNeill, Brogan, Callaghan, Hood, Hughes, Chalmers (Johnstone), Auld

### 1974/75
**Celtic 6-3 Hibernian (Deans 3, Wilson, Murray, Johnstone)** Hunter, McGrain, Brogan, Murray, McNeill, P. McCluskey, Johnstone, Dalglish, Deans, Hood, Wilson

### 1982/83
**Celtic 2-1 Rangers (Nicholas, MacLeod)** Bonner, McGrain, Sinclair, Aitken, McAdam, MacLeod, Provan, P McStay (Reid), McGarvey, Burns, Nicholas

### 1997/98
**Celtic 3-0 Dundee United (Rieper, Larsson, Burley)** Gould, Boyd, Mahe,

McNamara (Annoni), Rieper, Stubbs, Larsson, Burley, Thom (Donnelly), Wieghorst, Blinker (Lambert)

## 1999/2000
**Celtic 2-0 Aberdeen (Riseth, Johnson)** Gould, Boyd, Riseth, Mjallby, Mahe, McNamara, Wieghorst, Petrov, Moravcik (Stubbs), Johnson (Berkovic), Viduka

## 2000/01
**Celtic 3-0 Kilmarnock (Larsson 3)** Gould, Healy, Mjallby, Vega, Valgaeren, Lambert, Lennon, Moravcik (Smith), Larsson, Sutton, Petta (Crainey) (Boyd)

## 2005/06
**Celtic 3-0 Dunfermline Ath (Zurawski, Maloney, Dublin)** Boruc, Telfer, Balde, McManus, Wallace, Nakamura, Keane (Dublin), Lennon, Petrov, Maloney, Zurawski

## 2008/09
**Celtic 2-0 Rangers (O'Dea, McGeady)** Boruc, Hinkel, Loovens, McManus, O'Dea (Wilson), Brown, Hartley (Samaras) (Vennegoor of Hesselink), Nakamura, Caldwell, McDonald, McGeady

## 2014/15
**Dundee United 0 -2 Celtic (Commons, Forrest)** Gordon, Ambrose, Denayer, van Dijk, Izaguirre, Brown, Bitton (Henderson), Commons (Forrest), Johansen, Stokes, Griffiths (Guidetti)

## 2016/17
**Aberdeen 0 – 3 Celtic (Rogic, Forrest, Dembele pen)** Gordon, Lustig, Šimunović, Sviatchenko, Izaguirre, Brown, Armstrong, Roberts (Bitton), Rogic (McGregor), Forrest (Griffiths), Dembele

# MILESTONE GOALS

**1,000**
First goal 3-0 (H) league win over Port Glasgow Ath on
Jan 7, 1905 – Hamilton 2, Ward og

**2,000**
Third goal 5-0 (H) league win over Raith Rovers on
Feb 3, 1917 – McColl 2, Gallacher 2, McAtee

**3,000**
Goal 4-1 (A) league defeat to Falkirk on
Apr 6, 1927 – Alec Thomson

**4,000**
First goal 2-1 (A) Scottish Cup win over Third Lanark on
Jan 22, 1938 – Johnny Crum

**5,000**
First goal in 3-2 (H) defeat to St Mirren on
Apr 17, 1957 – Mike Haughney 39 mins (pen)

**6,000**
First goal in 2-0 (A) league win over Dunfermline on
Dec 18, 1965 – Stevie Chalmers 62 mins

**7,000**
Last goal 5-0 (H) Scottish Cup win over Albion Rovers on
Feb 5, 1972 – Bobby Murdoch, 76 mins

**8,000**
First goal 4-1 (H) League Cup win over Hamilton Accies
on Sep 24, 1980 – Charlie Nicholas, 26 mins

**9,000**
First goal 2-2 (A) league draw with Dundee United on
Sep 16, 1989 – Chris Morris 30 mins

**10,000**
First goal in 4-1 (A) Scottish Cup win over Stranraer on
Jan 28, 2001 – Joss Valgaeren 24 mins

**11,000**
Third goal in 3-0 (H) league win over Kilmarnock on
October 31, 2009 – Niall McGinn 78 mins

*LEAGUE GOALS*

**1,000**
First goal 4-1(H) league win over Partick Thistle on
Feb 1, 1908 – McLean 2, McMenemy, Somers

**2,000**
Last goal 3-2 (A) league win over Airdrie on
Apr 30, 1921 – McInally, Gallacher, McLean

3,000
Fourth goal 7-0 (H) league win over Cowdenbeath on
Sep 19, 1933 – McGrory 3, Napier 3 (2 pens), H O'Donnell

4,000
Last goal 6-3 (H) league win over Kilmarnock on
Oct 2, 1954 – Willie Fernie, 71 mins

5,000
Second goal 2-0 (A) league win over Motherwell on
Apr 8, 1967 – Tommy Gemmell, 79 mins (pen)

6,000
Second goal 2-1 (H) league win over Dundee U on
Apr 28, 1979 – Andy Lynch, 68 mins (pen)

7,000
Goal in 1-0 (A) league win over Airdrie
on Jan 23, 1993 – Tommy Coyne, 6 mins

8,000
First goal 2-1 (H) league win over Inverness CT on
Sep 24, 2005 – Craig Beattie, 57 mins

9000
Last goal 5-0 (A) league win over Hearts on
April 2, 2017 – Scott Sinclair (pen), 86 mins

## SCOTTISH CUP GOALS

1,000
First goal 2-0 (N) Scottish Cup semi-final win over
Dundee on Apr 7, 1977 – Joe Craig 79 mins

## LEAGUE CUP GOALS

1,000
First goal 2-0 (H) League Cup third-round win over
Raith Rovers on Sep 25, 2012 – Gary Hooper 12 mins

*Goal Milestones do NOT include:*
Abandoned games,
Title play-off in 1905,
Second World War games,
Curtailed 1939/40 Season,
World Club Championship games,
Drybrough Cup games,-
Anglo-Scottish Cup games,
(H) Rapid Vienna match in 1984